THE MIND ALIVE ENCYCLOPEDIA
THE ANIMAL KINGDOM

To Philip
On your thirteenth birthday
Lots of love,
Mum xxxx

THE MIND ALIVE ENCYCLOPEDIA

THE ANIMAL KINGDOM

Marshall Cavendish London & New York

Edited by Thomas Browne

Published by Marshall Cavendish Books Limited
58 Old Compton Street, London W1V 5PA

© Marshall Cavendish Limited 1968, 1969, 1970, 1977

Printed in Great Britain by Severn Valley Press

ISBN 0 85685 302 X

This material has previously appeared in the
partwork *Mind Alive*.

Pages 2 and 3: The razorbill (*Alca torda*) is a
familiar bird of the north Atlantic coasts.
Razorbills, like most other marine birds, nest in
colonies. They show many adaptations to their
particular way of life, such as the oiled plumage
and thick layer of fat which protect the birds
when swimming at sea for long periods.
Pages 4 and 5: The common prawn (*Crustacea
leander serratus*) lives in shallow inshore
waters. Whereas vertebrates have a bony
internal skeleton, crustaceans have a hard
external covering known as the exoskeleton.
Page 6: Found only in Borneo and Sumatra, the
Orang Utan (*Pongo pygmaeus*) is one of
man's closer relatives. The gradual destruction
of its habitat makes it one of the species most
in danger of extinction today.

Introduction

It is impossible not to be fascinated by the variety of creatures who share our world. There are many single species of insect alone which far outnumber Man in their world-wide distribution. The very existence of Man depends totally on the inter-relationships of other living things and the maintenance of that complex and delicate balance. So it is in our own interest to explore this parallel world – a world where fact often reads like fantasy.

This book aims to give a sound background knowledge of animal biology. At the same time it presents information in a clear and entertaining manner, with the help of over five hundred stunning photographs and diagrams. So learning becomes a pleasure, and a complex subject is opened up to the layman as well as the student. *The Encyclopedia of the Animal Kingdom* describes the division of creatures into invertebrates, fish, reptiles, birds and mammals. It tells the stories of bird migration, the organization of insect communities, how the bee sucks, and how the kangaroo gives birth. It reveals the hidden secrets of the chrysalis and the egg.

Why do certain animals die out while others multiply? Creatures must adapt to survive, but we also have a duty to protect species in danger of extinction. This wide-ranging encyclopedia discusses this question and dozens of others which are of concern to every thinking individual. With its logical format and comprehensive index, it is a valuable addition to any home library.

Contents

Picture Credits

Life at a simple level

Near the bottom of the scale in the animal world stand the protozoans and multicells, simple yet diverse organisms. They are the first stage in the development of true animals.

WHATEVER SIZE a living organism may be, it must carry out all those activities which enable it to continue its existence. Food must be taken in and used for energy production and building the materials of the body, while the waste must be disposed of. To do this animals move about and react to stimuli, seeking food and going from one favourable spot to another. In addition to these activities which affect the individual, the species has to be perpetuated by reproduction. With a complicated body composed of many cells, it may be comparatively simple for special parts of the body to be set aside for carrying out these functions, but what if the animal or plant consists of one cell only?

Protozoa are animals of this sort. Each one is a single cell. Within this cell must be carried out all the physiological functions which are necessary for life – and, indeed, whose presence makes us define the cell as a living thing. This complexity must be on a molecular level, not a cellular one. If we take distribution in many kinds of habitat as evidence of success, then the protozoa are a highly successful group. They are to be found in fresh water and in the sea, living on the surfaces of other animals and inside them. But like all the lower animals, they can exist only where they can be wet, for they have no defence against loss of water from the body. Once in air they face death by dehydration.

Spots of living jelly

Probably the most famous protozoan animal is *Amoeba,* whose fame comes from the popular belief that it is a simple spot of jelly something like the first living things. But this is a misconception. Amoeba is a highly complex animal, although at first sight this is not obvious. It has a body composed of one cell with a single nucleus, just as any living cell has. The cytoplasm in which the nucleus lies is not a simple jelly, it is divided into a clear region, the *ectoplasm,* on the outside and a granular *endoplasm* within. Among the granules of many shapes and sizes are, for example, the *mitochondria,* in which energy is released from sugar in the cell.

Both feeding and movement are connected in this animal. When it moves it thrusts out a *pseudopodium* in the direction in which it will move. This is a finger-like protrusion of the body. Slowly, all the granular endoplasm flows into it, transferring the animal from one place to another. Some kinds of Amoeba seem to have a hind-end which is part of the cell specialized in some unknown way and which follows on in any movement of the whole animal.

A number of theories have been put forward to account for this amoeboid movement. What ever is going on concerns the molecules which make up the substance of the animal. Perhaps, as one theory suggests, the endoplasm contains parallel straight protein molecules. At the 'front' these become folded up, thus drawing the rest of the body forward to them as they contract in length. The completely folded molecules pass back again to the rear, as they form a tube around the folding molecules and the straight ones behind them. On reaching the 'tail', they unfold to move forward in the endoplasm once again. But the flow is not as simple as this, for it has been noticed that the pseudopodia are not in contact with the ground along their length, but are raised

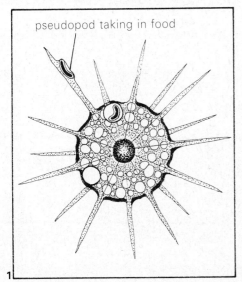

pseudopod taking in food

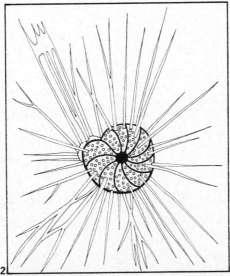

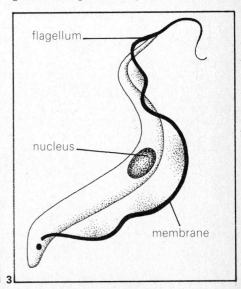

flagellum

nucleus

membrane

1 *Actinophrys sol* is a common Heliozoan, which is a fresh-water protozoan. The radiating pseudopods are used for taking in food, several of them working together when the object is large.
2 *Foraminifers* are common in sea water and have a chalky shell. Deposits of these protozoans have formed the chalk cliffs at Dover and the chalk beds in Mississippi and Georgia.
3 *Trypanosomes* are parasitic in both Man and animals. They are transmitted by the tsetse fly, and cause African sleeping sickness.
4 A top view of a young jellyfish shows the eight lobes containing the sense organs and the central mouth.
5 Radiolarian ooze covers vast areas on the floors of tropical seas. The individual organisms are clear when magnified.

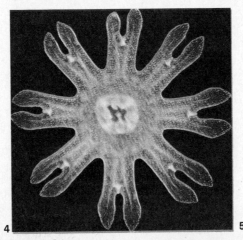

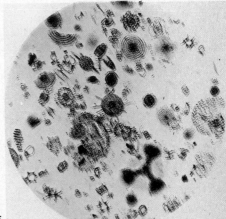

on strut-like projections. There is still much to be learned about this apparently simple behaviour.

When it is feeding, Amoeba thrusts out its body around a diatom or some other food particle, forming a hollow like the intucked finger of a glove. This closes over, engulfing the diatom in a spherical vacuole, the food vacuole in which it is digested by enzymes poured into it by the surrounding cytoplasm.

The pseudopodia of its relatives the *Heliozoa,* found in fresh water, are long and thin. They are supported by firm rods. These animals move by rolling along on these spiky pseudopodia. When the lower ones retract they start the movement in a particular direction which is continued as, successively, neighbouring ones on the same side shorten.

Simple yet complex

The *Radiolaria* and *Foraminifera* have skeletons, either of calcium carbonate (in Foraminifera) or silica (in Radiolaria). Outside the skeletons the cytoplasm forms a mass of finely branched pseudopodia on which food is captured. The dead skeletons rain down through the water to form radiolarian and foraminiferous oozes which are characteristic deposits on the sea bed in certain parts of the world. All these animals belong to the Sarcodina.

If Amoeba is deceptively simple in appearance, many of the ciliate protozoa look as complex as they are. Their complexity increases as we view them with the higher and higher magnifications which are possible with the electron microscope. Most of them move rapidly about by means of their *cilia* which are tiny whip-like threads. Within each is a characteristic arrangement of fibres found wherever there are cilia in the animal world. A pair of fibrils run up the centre and nine pairs are arranged around the outer part of the cilium. These must be the cause of the cilium's movement, though they are so small that there is so far little knowledge about how they produce their typical pattern of movement, but it is possible that some process not unlike that in human muscle is causing them to move.

The cilia which cover the body are grouped in pairs in some species (*Paramecium aurelia*) or singly in others *(P. bursaria),* in small pits of a lattice-work formed in the outer layer of the cell. On the ridges of the lattice are *trichocysts,* flask-shaped objects which can discharge a fine thread which allows the animal to anchor itself as it feeds. These may also have a defensive function.

These common ciliates, the species of *Paramecium,* will be found along with many others in almost any pond. The body of the animal is slipper-shaped, with a deep trough on one side which forms a gullet. This is lined with cilia arranged rather differently from those which cover the body. The cilia in the gullet beat so that food, usually bacteria and the like, are moved down it to the small area at the end where these food particles are absorbed in the body to form food vacuoles.

The structural complexity of Para-mecium, paralleled in many other ciliates,

is a good example of the possibilities that are available for making a variety of structures even at a molecular level. Cilia, trichocysts, surface lattice and so forth are all contained within the bounds of a single unit; they are built up of thousands upon thousands of molecules, not hundreds of cells as the skin and muscles of a rat are.

Another large group of protozoa are those which have *flagella* rather than cilia, and which for this reason are called *Mastigophora.* Flagella are almost identical with cilia, but they are much longer. Instead of whipping to and fro, like a cilium, a flagellum moves like a snake, waves passing along it either from base to tip or vice versa. The waves press against the water and move the organism. Some of the Mastigophora are plant-like, and can produce their own food from simple substances by photosynthesis. They have one or two flagella each. But other types, generally similar to these, may be parasitic, living in the fluids somewhere in another animal's body. For Man, some of the most important of these are the *try-panosomes.* These are organisms living in the blood of human beings which cause sleeping sickness, a disease which rendered large areas of Africa uninhabitable in the past. Other close relatives cause *Kala-azar* and oriental sore, serious and common diseases in the tropics: though the use of new drugs usually means that they are no longer fatal.

The phases of the life cycle of the malaria parasite are shown in relation to the body-temperature of a malaria patient. The upper diagram shows the cycle in the mosquito.

Others cause *nagana,* a wasting disease which made it impossible to keep cattle in parts of Africa. Most of these trypano-somes are carried by biting insects; the tsetse flies of Africa which carry sleeping sickness and nagana are good examples.

Parasites

Other Mastigophora live as partners rather than parasites in the gut of some insects, such as termites. These forms have very many flagella and quite a com-plicated body plan, though as with ciliates, all this is in one cell. Their role is to digest pieces of cellulose – the wood on which wood-eating termites feed. Unable to digest it with their own enzymes, the termites depend on the protozoa breaking down the cellulose for them. If the pro-tozoa are removed, the termites die.

Most groups of animals have members which are parasites, and protozoa are no exception. In addition to parasitic Sar-codina and Mastigophora, a whole sub-division of the protozoa, the Sporozoa, are parasitic. Many invertebrate animals, like insects or marine worms, have them in their gut or elsewhere in their bodies. One of these is the malarial parasite *Plasmodium* which lives in the red blood cells and in liver cells of Man. They are passed from person to person by mos-quitoes which infect human beings through the wounds they make before they begin to suck blood. The parasite has a complicated life-history, reproducing in the insect as well as in men. Another parasite, *Eimeria,* lives in the gut of birds and causes a serious disease of game birds being bred for sport. Similarly, *coccidiosis* is a gut infection of domestic chickens

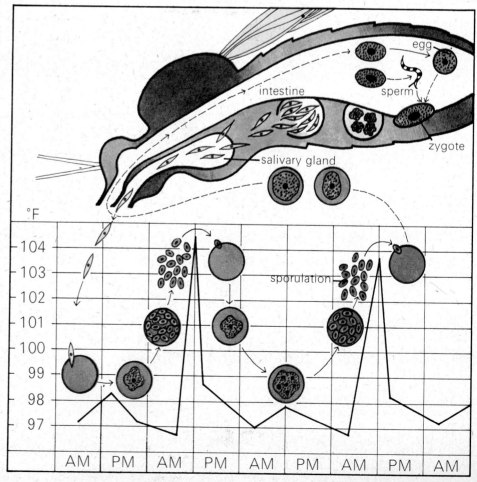

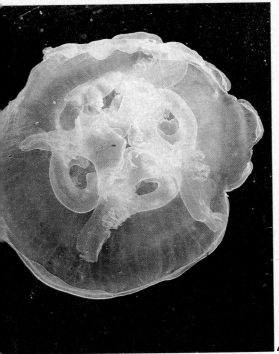

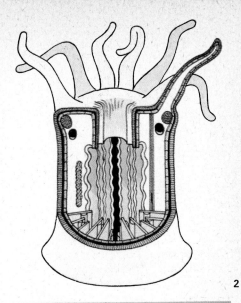

1 Sea-anemones such as this dahlia anemone derive their name from their resemblance to land flowers. The mouth can be seen in the centre of the animal.

2 The vertical division of the gastrovascular cavity in the anemone is revealed by a vertical section. The gullet and cavity are surrounded by a strong muscular body.

3 Corals are the remains of *zoantharians,* and form colonies such as this brain coral in tropical seas. They form hard reefs which are capable of severely damaging the steel hull of a ship.

4 Creatures like this moon jellyfish are often found in the pools left by the outgoing tide. The jelly within the animal consists in the main of water with amoeba cells suspended inside.

5 *Eunicella* is a coral colony which uses the feathery tentacles to catch food which is then distributed among the members.

which can cause great damage in poultry farms.

Some of the single-celled plants form colonies with characteristic shapes, such as the round ball of *Volvox*, but this rarely happens in protozoa. Nevertheless, sponges *(Porifera)* look very much like a slightly later stage of this process of coming together to form a body.

The common bath sponge is the skeleton of a living sponge. The living tissue has been dried off in the tropical sun by the people who dived down to collect the sponges from the sea bottom. Not all sponges have skeletons which are leathery like the fibres of a bath sponge. Some have pointed spicules of silica or calcium carbonate embedded in the living material.

But whatever the skeleton may be like, the living cells are quite simple. They are of two main kinds. The outside of sponges is coated by flat covering cells through which are holes opening into the chambers within. (The numerous holes through the surface of sponges gives them their Latin name which means 'hole-bearers'.) The second type of cell lines these chambers; they are the *collar cells* used in feeding. Like a Mastigophoran, each has a single flagellum whose beat causes water to move past it. Food particles in the water get caught on the collar and carried down to the main part of the cell.

Though sponges look very highly organized, in fact each cell is to a large extent independent of the others. There are no nerve cells, for example, connecting the parts of the body of the sponge together; there is no blood system to carry food and other things about the body. Most important, the cells do not join together to form tissues.

Specialized tissue

When cells are grouped into tissues they become specialized to carry out one main function, they can no longer do everything as a protozoan does. A group of muscle cells can contract but they cannot digest food, so they depend for their food on a supply of sugar brought to them by the blood-stream. But with this loss of some functions comes greater efficiency in doing one; the whole cell can be committed to the one activity.

The sea-anemones, corals and jellyfish are representatives of a group of animals, the *Coelenterates,* which have begun to move in this direction. Their bodies are simple, with an essential plan of an open-mouthed sack, the walls of which are formed of two layers of cells, the *ectoderm*

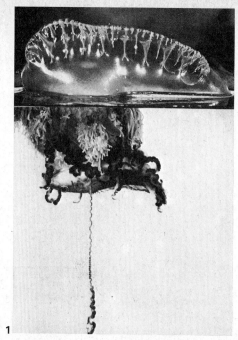

1 This Portuguese Man-of-War has just paralyzed a fish with its sting and is about to ingest it. This is one of the few types of *Physalia* whose sting can be fatal to human beings.
2 The cellular structure of sponges is essential to the taking in of food and oxygen and excretion of waste products.
3 Starting with the simple sponge, this illustration shows three types. In the centre is a more advanced type with a folded wall, while the sponge on the right has a complicated system of canals and chambers.

on the outside and the *endoderm* lining the cavity within. Around the mouth of the sack, which is the animal's mouth, is a ring of tentacles which are used to catch food.

Between the two layers of cells is a layer of jelly-like material, the *mesogloea*. In a sea-anemone this is relatively thin, but it is very thick in a jellyfish forming, in fact, the greater part of the bulk of the animal. The coelenterate body plan is reversed in a jellyfish, for the mouth opens downwards, often on the end of a *manubrium* hanging like a clapper in the middle of the underside of the bell.

There is much greater co-ordination in the bodies of coelenterates than there is in a sponge. Nerve cells scattered about on either side of the mesogloea are joined together to form a network on either side of the layer. There are no nerve trunks as there are in higher animals, but nervous impulses spread over the nerve net like ripples from a stone dropped into a pool. However, conduction is faster and easier in certain directions. This enables an anemone, for example, to shrink up and withdraw its tentacles into its mouth when it is touched firmly, or the tentacles to co-operate in catching food and passing it to the mouth.

Some of the cells of the ectoderm and endoderm have bases which are drawn out into *contractile strands*. These are the muscles of a simple coelenterate like the pond-dwelling *Hydra*.

A lethal sting

Quite characteristic of coelenterates are the *nematocysts*. These are generally found on the tentacles, and each consists of a sack into which is inverted a long thread. Near the tip is a sensitive hair, the *cnidocil*. When the nematocyst discharges, the thread is thrust out turning the right way out as it goes. The threads are of various kinds; they may be long and thin to pierce the prey and inject poison, or coiled, so that they wrap round the spines or hairs of the prey and prevent it from escaping. These nematocysts will discharge when certain chemicals are in the water, or they may be primed by them so that the slightest touch on the cnidocil triggers the weapon off. They are the cause of the unpleasant 'sting' of a jellyfish. In some of the larger coelenterates like the Portuguese Man-of-War the sting may be fatal to a man.

The great coral reefs of the world, so important in warmer seas, are formed by coelenterates. For corals are living animals, often colonies of them, each individual polyp connected to the next by tubes. The stony material of the coral is sometimes laid down in the mesogloea which fill with spicules and so forth; this is the way it is formed in the soft coral *Alcyonaria* or Dead Men's Fingers. But the hard corals form their skeletons of calcium carbonate round them. As the colony grows, so more material is laid down, the living tissue always remaining on the outside. The brain corals *(Madreporine)* make thick mounds of skeleton, each polyp resting in a base whose radiating divisions reflect the arrangement of the animal's body.

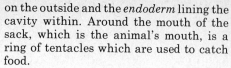

incurrent pores

excurrent opening

Worms - the beginnings of anatomy

Although generally considered lowly creatures, worms display the beginnings of the development of a digestive system, a nervous system and the sense organs familiar in higher animals.

WHEN THE AVERAGE PERSON calls an animal a 'worm', he has usually in his mind a long slimy creature without a very definite head. In all probability he will think of something which is round. But in fact this popular use of the term 'worm' throws together animals which bear only superficial resemblance to each other and which are placed by zoologists in different phyla. At the same time, it frequently ignores the many relatives which do not fit into this general description.

Probably the most familiar worm is the earthworm, a member of the phylum *Annelida*. All the worms grouped under this heading have bodies which are ringed. They represent a level of organization which is considerably greater than that of the *Coelenterates* – the sea-anemones and jellyfish. An indication of this is the relatively active searching life led by the majority of worms, but the real differences lie in the details of their bodies' make-up. Firstly, they have an extra layer of cells in the young state which gives rise to a whole new set of tissues, which no anemone has. As well as an *ectoderm* to cover the body and an *endoderm* to line the gut, they have a middle layer, the *mesoderm*. This can be thought of as taking the place of the jelly layer (*mesogloea*) of the coelenterates. New in an evolutionary sense, this layer is the one which, in every animal which possesses it, forms the muscles and blood system of the adult.

Specialization of function

Indeed, in these worms, not only are cells grouped together for one function to form tissues, but these tissues are grouped to make organs. The gut of an earthworm has, for example, digestive and absorptive tissue lining it, with muscular tissue outside that, and a covering layer around the whole. Now that the body has increased in complexity, transport of oxygen into the body's cells from outside, of carbon dioxide outwards and of food from the gut to the cells by diffusion alone can no longer be sufficient. A transport system has to carry out all these functions. The blood system serves this purpose, passing round the body and carrying with it these materials so vital to the cells in the tissues. Many annelids have, like Man, haemoglobin in their blood.

In addition to these evolutionary innovations, annelids possess a body cavity – the *coelom*. This appears in the developing worm as a split in the mesoderm which enlarges until, in the adult, it isolates the gut from the body wall. The inner part of the mesoderm forms the muscles of the gut and the outer part forms the massive muscles of the body wall. As this cavity is filled with coelomic fluid, it permits the

gut to make the movements necessary to transport food down it independently of the body wall.

These features improve the efficiency of the functioning of the body, but there is yet another factor which aids this – the body is segmented. The rings on the outside reflect divisions within the body. Each segment is to a large extent separated from the next by a muscular *septum* stretching across the coelom from gut to body wall. Within each body division is a set of certain organs which are repeated in each segment throughout the body, so that there are multiple sets of excretory organs, of muscle blocks (the longitudinal muscles stretching from one septum to the next) and of certain blood vessels. In each segment there is a collection of nerve cells (a *ganglion*), connected to those on either side, but with its own set of segmental nerves supplying the skin and organs in its own segment.

Some organs occur in relatively few segments. There are six hearts each of which lies in a segment near the head end. The various organs involved in reproduction are grouped together in another nearby part of the body and occupying six segments. In some other annelids – marine types – very many more segments contain reproductive organs.

Earthworms tend to move in one direction, so that the leading end can be called a head. In fact nerve cells there form a ring of nervous tissue around the gut. On the upper side, this is thickened, showing that there is the beginning of the trend towards forming a brain, typical of animals which have a head-end where sense organs of various sorts are grouped together. The ring of nervous tissue connects beneath the gut with the chain of ganglia which are in the other segments of the body, each joined to its neighbour by a double solid nerve cord.

The movements of an earthworm depend on nervous connections between neighbouring segments. Contraction of the longitudinal muscles of one segment is

1

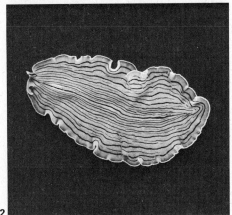

2

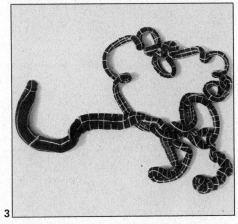

3

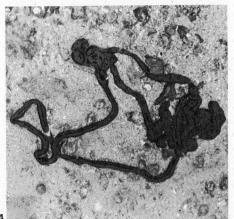

4

1 Flatworms are found in a variety of habitats. These specimens of *Dendrocoelum lacteum* have been photographed crawling on the underside of a piece of wood.
2 This polyclad (*Pseudoceros*), black and yellow in colour, is found on rocks or in colonies of animals (*tunicates*) which it feeds on.
3 An efficient digestive system marks off the ribbon worm, which is a proboscis worm, and is characterized by a long muscular tube which can be projected to catch prey. It also has a fairly efficient sensory system compared with flatworms.
4 The boot-lace worm (*Lineus longissimus*) takes its name from its shape and its ability to stretch.

13

followed by a similar contraction in the next segment, so that a wave of contraction passes down the animal. As the fluid in the coelom is incompressible and none can leak out, contraction of the longitudinal muscles causes the worm to fatten. Similarly, when the circular muscles contract down on the tube of fluid the worm must lengthen. Nervous connections ensure that when one kind of muscle contracts, the other relaxes.

Movement is effected by tiny spines, four pairs of which can be thrust out in each segment. These are the *chaetae,* which give their name to this class of animals. Earthworms and their relatives have few chaetae and are thus called *Oligochaetes.* Other annelid worms have many of them and are called *Polychaetes.*

Most polychaetes are marine animals, some swimming freely, others burrowing, living in a tube, or crawling on the sea bed. Like earthworms they are segmented,

but each segment has a flap-like extension on either side, the *parapondium.* These are large and act as paddles in swimming worms like the rag-worm *Nereis.*

The lugworm, *Arenicola,* is a good example of a burrowing polychaete. In its habits it is like an earthworm of the shore. It burrows down into the sand, swallowing it and discharging the material in a coiled heap at the tail end of its U-shaped burrow. By moving its body it draws water through the burrow from head to tail, causing a circular depression around the head-end. The water contains oxygen which is absorbed into the worm's body through the surface of tufts of gills in segments of the front part of the body.

Many of the tube-dwelling worms have elaborate heads like those of the Peacock Worm, *Sabella.* This has radiating stiffened tentacles covered with cilia. The beating of these cilia moves food towards the mouth and also supplies the particles used for

building the tube. The arrangement of the parapodia is well adapted to holding the animal within the tube. It can retreat into the tube when danger threatens.

Looking, perhaps, unlike relatives of these kinds of worms are the leeches. Despite the fact that they have no chaetae, they are part of the Annelida in a class named the *Hirudinea.* They are segmented, although there are more rings on their bodies than there are segments inside. They live in fresh water and they can be recognized by their two suckers, one around the mouth and the other at the tail.

Other worms have a less complicated body structure than the annelids. One important kind are the flatworms or *Platyhelminthes.* This phylum is unfamiliar because these worms are rarely seen. Some of them are relatively insignificant flatworms, found in ponds and streams. But many others are parasites in Man and other animals.

1 Common lugworms (*Arenicola marina*) display their presence on the seashore by their holes and casts.
2 Differentiation into a head and segmented body is clearly shown in this photograph of *Platynereis dumerili.*
3 The life cycle of the liver fluke demonstrates that both hosts are essential to the worm. At one time, many sheep died because of infection by the fluke, but the disease has been almost eradicated in Europe and North America.
4 This worm hides in rock crevices or kelp holdfasts and forages for food with long tentacles. It is brightly luminescent.
5 The tube-dwelling feather-duster worm is sensitive to light and will withdraw into the tube when a shadow falls on it.
6 Feathery gills extending from the tube of the peacock worm enable it to breathe, and entangle small organisms for food.
7 Tapeworms are parasitic in fish as well as in mammals, as this picture shows. The host often wastes away as a result.

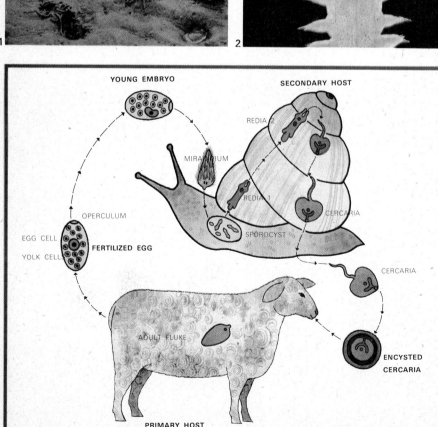

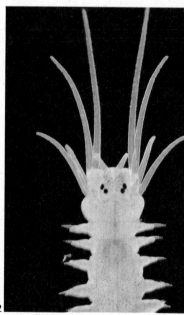

YOUNG EMBRYO

SECONDARY HOST

REDIA 2

MIRACIDIUM

REDIA 1

CERCARIA

OPERCULUM

SPOROCYST

EGG CELL

YOLK CELL

FERTILIZED EGG

CERCARIA

ADULT FLUKE

ENCYSTED CERCARIA

PRIMARY HOST

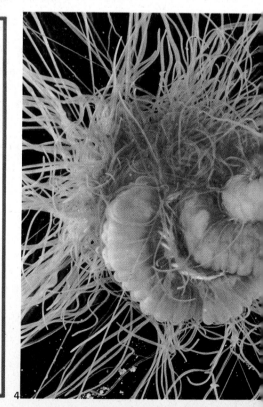

A planarian worm from a pond is not segmented; indeed this is true of all platyhelminthes. Nor do these worms have such clearly distinctive tissues as an annelid, nor have they coelomic cavities. They have heads with eyes; and although there is a certain amount of concentration of nervous tissues at the head end, the rest of the nervous system is simple. The cells which cover their bodies are ciliated and it is the beating of these which enables the worms to move steadily and apparently effortlessly along the mucus trail which each lays. Although they look like leeches, they can be quickly identified by their lack of suckers.

Unsegmented worms

Planaria have guts which have three main branches, one extending forward and the other two backwards from the point mid-way down the body at which the *proboscis* arises. This proboscis is a muscular tube with the mouth at its tip. It can be moved about until it comes in contact with food, which is then passed into the gut. The animals have no blood systems and the space between the outer covering and the gut is packed with cells. The food diffuses from the branches of the gut directly to the body cells.

A few of these worms are found on land, but always in very moist places. Tropical greenhouses, for example, usually have them. Other close relatives are gutless, the space being filled with cells, and others, living in the sea, have many-branched guts. But, to Man, the most important flatworms are those which are parasitic.

The specialization of a parasite for its life within the tissues of another animal nearly always brings about changes from the body pattern of a free-living close relative. This is certainly true of the parasitic flatworms. The process of change has gone less far among the *Trematodes* (the flukes) which in many ways resemble

the free-living *Turbellaria*; it is in the *Cestoda* (the tape-worms) that the greatest change has come about.

The animals in the class *Trematoda* are all flattened in shape and have a gut, although this opens through a mouth at one end of the body and is two-branched; this arrangement is never found in the free-living flatworms. However, the trematodes have suckers by which they fix themselves on to their hosts. Some of them are *ectoparasites,* attaching themselves to the gills of fish. These have elaborate arrangements of suckers which serve this purpose. Others live within their hosts, in the blood or in an organ. They too have suckers; usually one surrounds the mouth while the second is on the underside of the body, about mid-way along its length.

At one time many sheep died because of the liver fluke, a trematode worm which lives in the bile duct of a sheep. Nowadays,

however, it is not so easy to find specimens, so infrequent is this worm as a cause of disease or death.

The life-history of the liver fluke illustrates very well how complex a parasite's may become. The eggs are laid by the adult worm in the liver and pass out through the rest of the gut to fall on the ground. A small ciliated *miracidium* hatches from each; this is a simple organism with light-sensitive eyes and little else apart from cells from which new generations of worm will form. If a miracidium encounters a snail as it swims through the film of water on the grass, it penetrates it and turns into a *redia* larva in the snail's body. Each of the redia larvae can bud off new individuals within itself, and each of these in its turn can continue this process, so that there is a great increase in the numbers of offspring which can arise from the original egg.

But after a time, *cercariae* appear; these

5

6

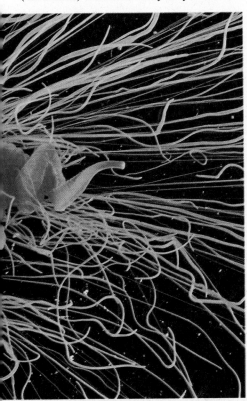
7

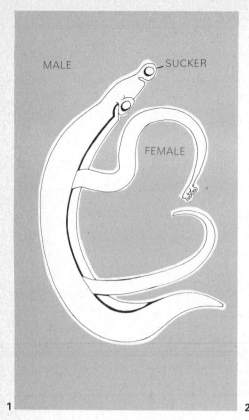

MALE — SUCKER
FEMALE

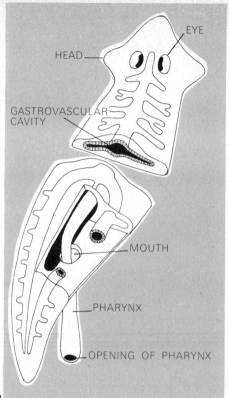

HEAD
EYE
GASTROVASCULAR CAVITY
MOUTH
PHARYNX
OPENING OF PHARYNX

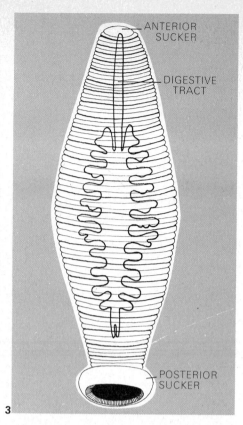

ANTERIOR SUCKER
DIGESTIVE TRACT
POSTERIOR SUCKER

1

2

3

are a different type of larva, able to find their way out of the snail and swim freely using their tails. The cercariae encyst on grass blades. It only requires a sheep to eat this grass for it to become infected when the young fluke breaks out of the cyst and moves into the bile duct. This complicated life-history not only increases the number of larvae, thus increasing their chance of finding a new host, but also distributes them in places where they are likely to encounter a sheep.

Parasites in Man

Other trematodes are the blood flukes. *Schistosoma*, which causes the disease *bilharzia*, is long and thin, well-shaped for moving about the body through the narrow blood vessels. The male worm clasps a female one in a groove along his body, so that both sexes move about together. The eggs have a sharp spike which they use to burst out of the capillaries into the bladder and are passed out with the urine. They too give rise to larvae which enter snails and multiply there. The cercariae which are finally released can penetrate the skin. For this reason, people in the tropics are advised not to wade in ponds or streams barelegged.

Tape-worms are less like turbellarians, for they have no gut and their nervous systems are very rudimentary. Often their head-ends have special attachment hooks and suckers by which they fix themselves into the wall of their host's gut. From this part of the worm, *proglottids* are budded off. These are not like the segments of an earthworm because they are not intimately connected with each other. Each is an egg-factory, and contains little more than the reproductive system. Proglottids packed with fertilized eggs drop to the ground where the eggs hatch and turn into new worms if they are swallowed

PARAPODIUM
EXCRETORY ORGAN
VENTRAL NERVE CORD

4

by the right animal.

Another serious cause of disease are the roundworms or *Nematoda*. These are mainly small worms, pointed at either end and showing no sign of segmentation. Indeed, like platyhelminthes, they have no coelom. Their muscles, formed of a unique kind of contractile cell, are unlike anything found elsewhere in the animal kingdom. Their guts are simple tubes, straight from mouth to anus. Yet although their structure appears simple, they are a hugely successful group of animals which

1 Human blood flukes like *Schistosoma japonicum* cause a number of diseases such as anaemia and blockage of the bile duct. They are often picked up by eating inadequately cooked food.
2 The flatworm *Planaria* has the mouth centrally placed instead of at the head. The pharynx, which is attached at only one end, is extended for feeding.
3 Two suckers and a branched digestive tract are characteristic of the leech. The outside of the body is folded, but not all of these folds correspond with interior segments.
4 Each segment of an *annelid* worm duplicates organs in the other parts. Only the digestive system shows much differentiation between one part and another.

are found everywhere – even in beer mats. They may be harmless, but many are serious pests. Some, called eelworms, are parasitic on plants and cause them to die, while others live in the intestines or the tissues beneath the skin of Man. Typical of the first are the hookworms, *Ancylostoma*, which infect by penetrating the skin of the foot and moving in the blood to the intestine; and of the second, *Wuchereria* which gather in the lymphatic system, block it and cause the vast swellings typical of elephantiasis.

There are other creatures which people would call 'worms', but they are not common and not often seen. However, sometimes beneath a stone on the shore, a boot-lace worm (*Nemertine*) may be found. These very long and thin worms have probosces which they can shoot out to catch prey. A few species are to be found on land, in moist places as are land planarians. They use their probosces for movement; having shot it out, the tip adheres and the worm pulls itself up to it.

Thus, the layman's term 'worm' covers many kinds of animal, very different in structure and habit. Some are useful, but a great many are dangerous to Man.

Life within a shell

Predatory squids and herbivorous snails are both members of the same diverse family — the molluscs. They represent an evolutionary milestone in the development of the senses.

EVERYBODY HAS READ TALES of giant squid locked in deadly combat with the whale. Again, few people have failed to notice the white, crystalline shells of long-dead cuttlefish lying on the beach. The pearl is highly prized throughout the world and is of course produced by oyster and mussel. These animals – like the clam, scallop and whelk – are also prized as a source of food by most of us.

Yet in spite of this background of familiarity, it still comes as a surprise to most of us that all of these animals belong to the *Mollusca,* one of the largest divisions of the animal kingdom. And that their very obvious differences in form and function all arise from the development or adaptation of a basic, primitive molluscan plan.

Soft bodies in a shell

The major factor in the success of any group of living organisms is its ability to adapt its basic plan to meet the challenge and exploit the possibilities, in terms of food and shelter, of many different environments. In the language of the biologist this is called *adaptive radiation,* and the Mollusca provide one of the most graphic and spectacular examples of this in Nature.

The word mollusc derives from the Latin *molluscus* – which means soft – and refers to the characteristically soft body of the animal. The *chiton* is a good example.

One of its two most obvious physical features is the broad, oval foot which is soft but well developed muscularly, and enables the chiton both to move and to cling with great tenacity to the undersea rocks which provide its habitat and on which it finds its food. The rest of the body is likewise soft, and also deformable.

The other very obvious physical attribute of the chiton is the hard shell. It consists of eight transverse plates and provides the animal with useful protection from marauding predators. Immediately beneath the shell is a layer of tissue called the mantle which covers the whole of the inside surface of the shell, but extends slightly beyond the shell edge to form an overhanging lip – like the eaves of a house – around the foot.

Within the space bounded by mantle and foot the vital systems are housed. These are the heart, stomach, digestive equipment, nerves and so on. Recessed under the shell at the front of the animal is the mouth.

These external and internal physical characteristics of the chiton are in most cases shared by the other molluscs, although they may have undergone great development or have been discarded altogether.

But it may be useful to examine the internal mechanics of the chiton. Thanks to its muscular foot the animal is able to move about – slowly – in search of the algae which it takes as food. The method of locomotion is by a peristaltic wave along the foot; or to put it more simply, by a rippling muscular motion rather like that seen in the ordinary caterpillar.

The mouth contains a feeding implement which is itself characteristic of the molluscs. This is the *radula,* consisting of a ribbon of tissue which carries rows of tiny teeth. The chiton employs it like a sort of zoological file. As it moves forward, the mollusc rhythmically protrudes and retracts the radula, scraping up the food as it does so. On retraction, the radula also does duty as a natural conveyor belt, the food being passed to the gut and so to the stomach.

Breathing and feeding

Here it is sorted in terms of size by a complicated system of cilia. These are fine, hair-like appendages, some of which drive the smaller food particles to the tiny openings of the digestive gland, while others push the larger particles into the intestine for excretion. The food which actually reaches the digestive gland is absorbed by the cells which line it.

It is in the digestive system that the chiton converts its food to energy, and it is worth noting that the structure of the digestive tube (with expanded areas forming stomach and digestive gland, and coiling as it progresses towards the hind end) is also characteristic of the molluscs.

Breathing in the chiton – and for that matter most other molluscs – is accomplished by means of gills. The exceptions are certain snails which have graduated to the land, and others which, having once done just that, have later returned to the water. But in the chiton the gills consist of two lateral rows which run the length of the body. They are situated in the cavity between the overhanging lip of the mantle and the edge of the foot, and are therefore in constant contact with the water. It is in the gills that the oxygen is taken from the water and enters the blood, which is itself circulated by a heart situated in the mantle cavity at the hind end of the animal.

The nervous system of the chiton is primitive. It is no more than a nerve ring around the oesophagus (the passage from mouth to stomach) and two pairs of longer nerves. One pair serves the foot, the other takes care of the mantle, digestive system and the rest. In short, the chiton is both blind and brainless.

The *Gastropoda* – the snails and whelks – resemble the chiton in that they also

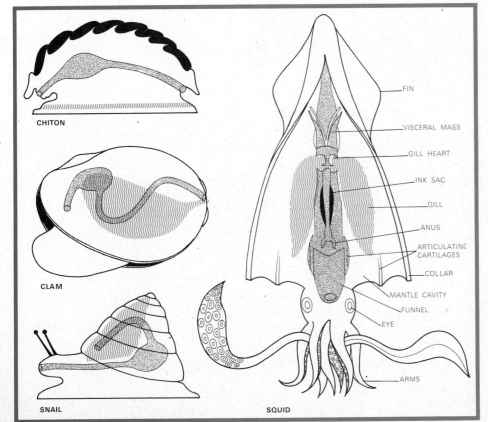

CHITON

CLAM

SNAIL

SQUID

FIN
VISCERAL MASS
GILL HEART
INK SAC
GILL
ANUS
ARTICULATING CARTILAGES
COLLAR
MANTLE CAVITY
FUNNEL
EYE
ARMS

Four examples of molluscs show the development of the various systems. The chiton's digestive tract is a simple tube, while in the squid it is comparatively complex.

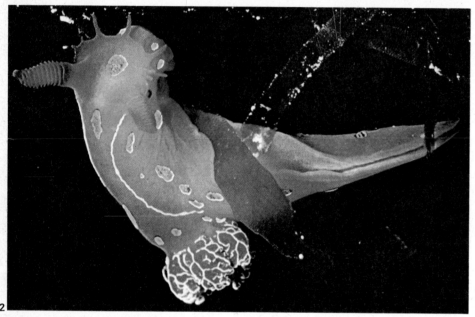

1 Octopuses, members of the class *Cephalopoda,* are among the most highly organized of the molluscs. This class, whose name means 'head-footed', has a foot which is divided into a number of arms arranged about the head.
2 Sea slugs are common, shell-less gastropods. These strange creatures feed on sponges, hydroids and sea anemones.
3 Bivalves include the scallop. This view of an open scallop shows eyes and marginal tentacles. The class to which it belongs, *Pelecypoda,* gets its name from the shape of the foot.

The two halves of the shell are joined by a ligament at the top and held tightly together by internal muscles. But within the shell, the systems of digestion and blood circulation are unchanged from the basic plan. The important differences concern the proportions of the body, in particular the mantle and the gills.

Since the bivalve depends for its existence on drawing in a constant supply of water from which it filters its food and oxygen supply, there are big changes to be seen in both gills and mantle. In most cases the latter has developed so that the edges can be brought together to seal the mantle cavity. But the seal also includes two openings, one to take in water, the other to expel it after use. In some bivalves, the area of the mantle around these gaps is also protrusible, so that in effect the simple openings become tubes of significant size, allowing the bivalve to remain buried with only these life-giving tubes extending to the surface of the sea bed.

The gills have also undergone considerable development. There are two pairs, one on either side of the foot, which as explained earlier is also modified, and the gills extend across almost the whole diameter of the mantle cavity. Gills of this size are required for the oxygen supply, but that is not their only function. The surface of each is covered once again with fine cilia which move the water through the gills but block the suspended food

have a muscular foot, the same internal systems, and a protective shell.

But the gastropod has many differences. For example, although the gastropod foot does not differ in kind from that of the chiton, it is a much better tool for locomotion.

At the same time a head has developed – with eyes, a brain and tentacles which are located above and in front of the mouth (which incidentally also contains a radula).

Specialization

There are, however, more specific developments which have enabled certain members of this group to exploit particular aspects of the environment. Although most of them are herbivores, some have turned to flesh for food. These use the radula to file their way into the shells of other molluscs to get at the juicy meat within, and this different food has led to changes in the digestive system. Types both on

land and in the sea have discarded their shells altogether, and in consequence have become uncoiled both inside and out. Yet another particularly enterprising group within the gastropods, called the *pteropods* (wing foot), have developed the edges of the foot along the sides of the shell into flaps which they use like wings to swim through the water, thus becoming a great deal more mobile than their sea-bed cousins.

If increased mobility has been the goal of the gastropods, the bivalves (oysters, mussels, clams and so on) have developed in the opposite direction.

These animals have in the main abandoned movement. Further, they do not employ the radular feeding mechanism but depend for both food and oxygen on the manipulation of water.

Central to this process is the development of the bivalve shell. This consists of two halves, a right and a left, which extend to cover the whole of the bivalve.

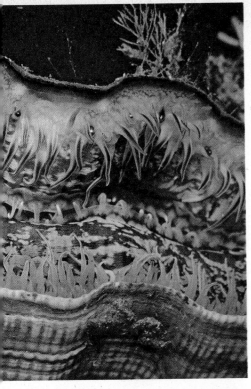

4 The cuttlefish resembles the squid in its general structure. Its ink sac provides a brown pigment which is used by artists. The shell is a hard plate embedded in the mantle.

5 One of the most highly developed invertebrates, the squid, shows an amazingly high degree of adaptation to its life as a predator.

6 *Pteropods* are small molluscs of plankton size. Their discarded shells form a marine ooze in some areas of the ocean. This example is *Spiratella retroversa*.

7 Snails are one of the few land molluscs. Part of the mantle cavity is modified for breathing. They use the toothed radula to cut off pieces from plants, and in this way they can cause extensive damage to some crops.

particles. Other cilia sort the food, driving the smaller particles to the mouth and the larger ones into the outflow tube of the mantle.

The bivalve foot lies most of the time within the protection of the shell, but it has been transformed from a broad base for crawling to a slender blade-like structure. The bivalve can now extend the foot between the shells for use as a digging implement or as a lever by which, from time to time, it can change its position in the mud or sand.

Some organs found in molluscs of the locomotive kind are missing in the bivalves. For example, the bivalve has no use for the radular mechanism and consequently this has disappeared. At the same time, except for the scallop, it has no eyes and no tentacles. This is an animal which has elected to stay in one place in order to live. However, they still adopt a number of habitats. Mussels attach themselves to rocks, submerged roots and wooden piles by means of a self-produced natural plastic thread (the *byssus*), and oysters achieve the same end with a naturally secreted cement. Clams and other bivalves spend most of their lives buried in the mud, feeding by means of the extendible mantle tubes. Another mollusc, the shipworm,

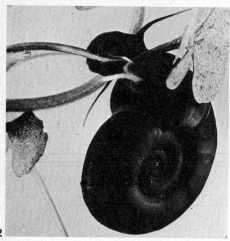

uses the hinged end of its shell to bore into wooden sailing vessels and once again 'communicates' with the outside world by means of its tubular mantle. The Romans called it *'calamitas navium'*, for it riddled the planking of the Roman galleys. Later on it wrought havoc on Drake's *Golden Hind,* and can still be a menace to wooden piling.

The scallop is an interesting example of special development in two directions. The mantle fringe on both shells carries around a hundred tiny green eyes, with which the animal warily surveys its surroundings for signs of predators. It can also swim by opening and closing its shell violently, an action which jerks it forwards and upwards through the water.

Without doubt the most spectacularly developed group of the molluscs is the *Cephalopoda* (squid, octopus, cuttlefish, nautilus). And among the cephalopods it is undoubtedly the squid which is king. Along with the other molluscs, it has a shell, mantle cavity containing gills, and generally the same vital systems. Unlike its lesser brethren though, it actively hunts and kills its food.

Predatory molluscs

Some genera may have tentacles as long as 14 feet and bodies up to six feet in length. *Architeuthis,* the Giant Squid, has the distinction of being the largest living invertebrate animal, and cases have been recorded of specimens being found measuring up to 50 feet (including the outstretched tentacles). This, together with its predatory instincts, has earned the squid its formidable reputation as a sea monster.

Its first requirement is high speed and manoeuvrability, so the squid is fitted with Nature's own jet-propulsion system.

1 This razor shell *(Ensis)* is beginning to burrow into the soft sand. To the right of the picture can be seen the large muscular foot which it uses for locomotion.
2 A large ramshorn snail *(Planorbis corneus)* is seen here feeding on *frogbit,* a common weed. The radula is being used to cut pieces from the leaf.
3 Most chitons, like *Acanthochitona crinita,* are inactive during the day, moving about and feeding in darkness. They are to be found on the underside of rocks on the sea-shore.
4 *Arion ater ater* is a good example of a land slug. These are gastropods which have lost their external shell. They move along a track of slime which they lay in front of them.

The animal is able to draw in large quantities of water through one opening and expel it under pressure through another. The first opening is a slit and the second a nozzle, and both appear to be modifications of the mantle openings noted in the bivalve. The nozzle can also be turned downwards or backwards, an idea which the aeronautical engineers have only just begun to use in some vertical-take-off aircraft.

But although the squid's intake and output apparatus does provide water from which the gills can extract oxygen, the openings play no part in feeding.

The squid's body, although still soft, must necessarily move through the water at speed. It is therefore streamlined and requires stiffening. This is supplied by the shell which runs the length of the back but is situated in a pocket of the body.

It also swims backwards, and further reduces resistance to the water by trailing its ten arms straight out from its head.

The origins of the tentacles – the squid has ten, the octopus eight – are a matter of some argument. Some authorities claim

that they have developed from the simpler tentacles like those found in the head of the gastropod. Others are equally adamant that these powerful tools have stemmed from the molluscan foot.

In any case, the squid uses them for feeding. Two of the tentacles, being longer than the rest, are used to capture the prey. The other eight are employed in holding the luckless captive close to the mouth cavity. A massive beak then tears the victim to pieces, from which it appears that the mouth of the cephalopod has undergone massive adaptation in the long development from the basic mollusc. Surprisingly though, it has still retained its radula, but this is very small and the use to which it is put is not known.

The brain of the squid is large – in relation to body size, the largest possessed by an invertebrate – and this backs a powerful array of sense organs. The animal depends on sight as well as speed to catch its prey and therefore possesses extremely large and efficient eyes. It also has a combined sense of taste and touch which operates mostly through the suckers on the tentacles but also extends to the whole of its body surface.

All in all, the squid is well adapted for its hunting forays through the oceans and it and the other Cephalopoda mark one extreme of molluscan adaptation. But right the way back to lowly chiton, and including the two other classes which have remained unmentioned (the *Scaphoda,* with their tubular shells, and the *Monoplacophora*), the molluscs have adapted their basic make-up in order to make the best use of varied conditions of life which Nature affords. Small wonder then that there are some 100,000 species and that their realm encompasses the world.

Animals with external skeletons

Arthropods live in the sea, on land and in the air. They thrive in almost every conceivable environment. Their success in adapting is due in large measure to their external skeleton.

SCIENCE-FICTION WRITERS often torture their readers with the might-have-been of evolution. There are many stories about what might have happened if human beings had been beaten in the evolutionary struggle. The insects are Man's most effective rivals for control of the Earth. Together with their close allies, the marine and freshwater crustaceans, they make up more than two-thirds of the animal species on Earth. Many of these species are present on Earth in vast numbers, and in some cases there are many more representatives of a single insect species than there are human beings.

Insects and crustaceans between them have conquered every type of environment on this planet. They live on land, on the surface of lakes and the sea, underwater, between the tide-lines, in the air and underground. In fact, there is an *arthropod* to fill almost every available ecological niche. This in itself is a tribute to the tremendous adaptability of the type. Despite the tremendous variety, almost all of them can be recognized as belonging to the same general type of animal.

The name *arthropod* refers to the jointed legs characteristic of animals in this phylum. The arthropods are divided into several major groups, the most important and widespread of which is the insects. The phylum also includes the very large group of crustaceans (lobsters, crabs, shrimps, barnacles, crayfish) and the centipedes, millepedes and arachnids (a group which includes spiders, ticks, mites and scorpions).

Why are the arthropods so successful? The answer to this question is complex, but it can be summed up simply in one word: *exoskeleton*. In Man and other higher animals the muscles and other soft

tissues of the body are supported by an internal core of bones which give the body its shape and make the limbs and trunk rigid. In the arthropods the tissues are supported by a rigid external covering rather like a suit of armour. The exoskeleton makes it possible to maintain a fairly constant internal environment; for example, it prevents rapid loss of water under dry conditions and prevents waterlogging when the animal is wet. It can be fashioned into all sorts of shapes so that the arthropod's shell becomes specialized for various functions suitable for its particular place in the ecological spectrum. This exoskeleton, also called the *cuticle*, is formed from a remarkable protein called *chitin*. Chitin itself is a fairly elastic sub-

1 The hermit crab (*Eupagurus bernhardus*) lives inside the disused shell of other marine creatures. It has sets of legs of different lengths so that it enters the shell with a spiral motion.

stance. Where rigidity is required, it is combined with various salts to make it less liable to bend.

In a typical arthropod the exoskeleton consists of four layers. On the outside is a thin layer of wax which makes the exoskeleton waterproof. Underneath this are two layers of chitin – a rigid layer on the outside and a flexible layer on the inside. Underneath the chitin is the first layer of the animal's cells – the *epidermis*.

The segmented shell

The flexibility of the chitin can be varied in such a way that the arthropod has flexible joints, between which are inflexible areas, thus forming definite limbs and segments of the body. Chitin provides protection without sacrificing mobility. Contrast the hard exoskeleton of the snail, which places grave limitations on its movements.

But although the exoskeleton does much to ensure the success of arthropods, it also imposes grave limitations on them. The larger the animal, of course, the heavier and more restricting the exoskeleton becomes. For this reason, all arthropods are rather small animals, and some are minute. In fact, most of the large arthropods are found in the sea or in fresh water, where the weight of their exo-

2 Barnacles were once classified as molluscs because of their shells, but the chitinous appendage which they use for gathering food identifies them as true arthropods.

skeletons is borne by the water.

The body of arthropods is divided into segments which are frequently grouped together into head, thorax and abdomen. The head of all arthropods consists of six segments, but the number of segments in the rest of the body varies from species to species. Each of the segments bears projections or appendages, but these are generally specialized to serve different functions: some may be sensitive to touch or scent, like the antennae, others may be developed to serve as wings, while still others may become legs. In some arthropods, an appendage may become so large as to be the dominant feature of the body: an example is the male fiddler crab, in which one of the claws is massively developed as a secondary sexual characteristic. The crab owes its name to the to-and-fro movements of this limb during courtship, similar to a violinist's action.

The head of the typical arthropod, as already mentioned, consists of six segments. The first segment bears no appendage, while the second and third together bear either one or two antennae. The jaws are on the fourth segment and vary considerably from species to species depending on the method of feeding. The fifth and sixth segments bear accessory jaws.

Anatomical variation

The other main features of the head are the eyes, which can be simple, as in the spiders, or compound, as in the insects. The simple eye consists of a bundle of light-sensitive cells lying under a single lens. In the compound insect eye, however, each cell has its own individual lens, and the entire unit is separated from its neighbours by pigment cells. A compound eye produces an effect similar to a newspaper half-tone block – the image is broken up by the eye into a series of spots of differing intensities, and the eye sees a mosaic. Such a system is not quite as effective as the vertebrate eye found in human beings, although it is extremely sensitive to motion within the field of view.

The number of segments in the thorax depends on the group involved. The more primitive groups, such as the crustacea and the millepedes and centipedes, have varying numbers of segments. The insects, however, always have three thorax segments, all with a pair of legs each. The second and third thorax segments carry a pair of wings each. The wings and legs vary considerably with the species: the wings may be horny or filmy, long or short, while the legs may be adapted for a number of purposes in addition to walking. In the honey-bee, for example, the legs are modified to hold pollen.

The only appendage on the abdomen is the sexual organ. In the female this is a vagina, and there may also be an *ovipositor* for depositing eggs in the desired position. In the male, the sperm ducts open on to the surface of the body in the abdominal region.

This is only the briefest sketch of the anatomy of the arthropods. The most striking thing about these animals is the way in which this basic structure can be varied and adapted to give rise to such

varied species as the ants and the crayfish, the grasshoppers and the spiders, the centipedes and the shrimps. This alone is an indication of the immense advantages of the exoskeleton and of the insect structure, making it possible for the arthropods to become dominant.

For, from a biological standpoint, the arthropods can be regarded as even more dominant than mankind. Insects and other

arthropods have been able to colonize environments that would be unthinkable for Man. Indeed, in many cases insects have been effective in preventing human beings from inhabiting certain parts of the world. In many areas, until recent years, life was made intolerable by mosquito-borne malaria. In parts of Africa even today sleeping sickness (carried by the *tsetse fly*) is still an almost insuperable

1 The butterfly grows to maturity within the pupa (called a *chrysalis*) and emerges as a fully developed adult. The change from larva to adult is called *metamorphosis*.

2 Fiddler crabs scavenge on sandy beaches. They take their name from the characteristic to-and-fro movement of the male's huge right pincer. In the female, both pincers are smaller.

obstacle to human habitation. Plague, carried by a flea, ravaged the population of Western Europe in historic times, and the battle with harmful insects is by no means over. Insects like the colorado beetle, the locust, the termite and the boll weevil damage and destroy many millions of pounds' worth of food and crops every year. And yet, without insects and other arthropods, large sections of the plant life on this planet would become extinct. Most of the higher plants rely to varying degrees on insects to fertilize and pollinate their seeds. This very fact indicates how ubiquitous insects are and how closely their lives are bound up with other species with which they co-exist.

Their reproductive system is another reason for the great success of arthropods. Again we can see how a relatively simple basic plan can be adapted in an almost infinite number of ways to take account of variations in environment. Arthropods lay large numbers of small eggs and the young usually hatch from the eggs in an immature condition. In order to develop further the young must be viable animals in their own right. The young animal that hatches from the egg is a *larva*. The instincts of the parent insect or crustacean have already led it to place the eggs in a favourable position for the future growth of the larvae. The parent insect may go to great lengths to ensure the right conditions for the growth of her offspring.

The most highly developed of the insects, the social bees, wasps and ants, build highly complex nests in order to care for their young, and the entire colony takes part in a complicated procedure to ensure that the young have the optimum conditions for growth. Specialized members of the colony are developed to provide for defence, construction, feeding, egg-laying and other functions.

1 Lacewing flies live on the juices of small insects and on vegetation. They lay their eggs among colonies of aphids and the larvae feed on these while they are developing.
2 Clusters of barnacles are to be found on rocks, flotsam, and the hulls of ships where they can cause considerable drag and loss of power.
3 Giant millepedes (*Diplopoda*) are classed as *Antennata*. As shown, they are often host to mites, arachnids which are also found on human skin.
4 Scorpions catch their prey with their large pincers and sting them to death with their tails. The prey, spiders and insects, are then sucked dry. The scorpion hunts at night and its sting, though painful, is seldom fatal to human beings.

1 There are almost 20,000 species of rhinoceros beetle, so called from the horns on the thorax. It lives on vegetation and makes its home in palm trees. Despite its heavy shell, it flies very well.

2 South American tarantulas sometimes grow up to seven inches long, and occasionally catch small birds. Smaller tarantulas are preyed on by the *Pepsis* wasp; it lays its eggs in the body of the tarantula, which provides food for the larvae.

3 *Lithobius forficatus*, a common variety of centipede, produces young which hatch with only seven segments, the rest being added as the animal develops.

4 The young of *isopods* develop in a brood pouch and emerge as smaller versions of the adult crustacean.

phosis in many insects may take a long time – in some cases many years – but the insect is heavily protected while it undergoes this change and has the best conditions for becoming an adult.

One of the characteristic features of this type of life cycle is that it allows for a division of labour during the various stages of the cycle. An animal normally has to feed, mate, and distribute the offspring. In the case of many insects these functions are carried out separately by the different stages of the insect's life. The primary function of the caterpillar in most butterflies, for example, is to feed. In some insects, like the dragonfly, the adult is not equipped at all for feeding and has only one purpose, to mate and lay the eggs. This division of labour enables some insects to exploit two totally different environments. The mosquito is an example, the larva living in fresh water and feeding on minute particles. The adult lives on land and in the air, and feeds on blood.

In the most highly developed of the arthropods, the social bees, wasps and ants, specialization has been carried a great deal further. These animals operate as a social community, in which the various members are mutually dependent, and elaborate mechanisms are developed to enable the life of the colony to proceed smoothly. In termite colonies, for example, the sterile workers build the nest, forage for food, and feed the egg-laying queen. The queen is fertilized by specialized reproductives – similar to the drones of bee colonies – whose sole function is to fertilize the queen and establish new colonies. The colony is protected from intruders by specially equipped soldiers which cannot feed themselves.

Instinctual organization

So intricate is the organization of this type of colony that many people have been inclined to treat it as a manifestation of intelligent behaviour. But although the colony as a whole may appear to be organized along highly intelligent lines, and reacts to situations in an apparently intelligent way, the basis for this is not intelligence as known among human beings, but the operation of a complex of built-in instincts which are established even before the insects are born.

The arthropods are very well suited for life on Earth, within certain limits. Their exoskeleton protects them from variations in the environment, and is extremely adaptable for a wide range of specialized functions. Their short life-span makes it possible for their evolution to take place at a rapid rate, and they can thus adapt to gradual changes in their environment. The adaptability of the basic arthropod form makes it possible for them to specialize in thousands of different forms to suit the requirements of particular ecological niches.

The present period of time on the Earth has been called 'the age of the Insects', and we can see that there is a great deal of justification for this view. Perhaps it is as well for human beings that the anatomy and physiology of the arthropods restrict them to small size and short life-spans.

The larvae of most insects are more specialized than the larvae of the aquatic crustaceans. The crustacean larvae are generally free-swimming forms which are rather like smaller versions of their parents. These larvae undergo a gradual change to become adults. In the insects and the higher arthropods, however, the larvae are so different from the parents that it is impossible for them to change gradually into adults. They therefore

undergo a sharp change known as *metamorphosis*. Having gorged itself, the larva, which may be a caterpillar in the case of moths and butterflies, surrounds itself with a cocoon of protective material and changes into a *pupa*. The pupa appears as a quiescent stage in the life of the insect. It does not move around or eat, and it is surrounded by a protective shell. When the insect finally emerges from the cocoon, it is a fully developed adult. Metamor-

The highest invertebrates

Echinoderms and protochordates represent the pinnacle of specialization within the invertebrates. Their structure shows similarities with that of the higher animals, including Man himself.

ASK ANY OYSTERMAN to name his greatest headache, and he will trot out the starfish. And anyone who has seen this brightly coloured predator glide smoothly over the sea bed and stretch its arms around an oyster, will know the reason why. Sooner or later the starfish will force the two halves of its victim's shell apart – and devour the flesh inside.

It may be hard luck on the oysterman, but the fact that the starfish is able to move at all is a matter of considerable interest to the biologist in his study of nature. One of the ways in which the animal kingdom can be divided is in terms of those creatures which can move and those which cannot. Obviously the ability to move has played a crucial part in the development of higher forms of life, and both the starfish itself and the animal group of which it is a member, the *echinoderms*, are particularly interesting from this point of view. For the echinoderms include among their number creatures which are completely stationary; those which begin life in that fashion but later become mobile; and those that are mobile throughout their lives. Since the immobile *(sessile)* types are the root stock from which all the rest spring and representatives of all types exist at the present time, it is possible for the scientist to examine quite easily both the changes which have taken place in these

1 An injured fish falls prey to a slow-moving starfish. Because of the speed with which fish normally move this is a rare event, but starfish often attack and eat oysters.
2 This picture of the sea cucumber clearly shows the rows of tube feet by which the animal clings to rocks. It has five rows of feet, a common number in echinoderms.
3 Tube feet of the sea urchin are long and slender and end in suckers. They extend beyond the spines, which are used both for locomotion and protection from marauders.

animals and which make locomotion possible, and to study the effects of mobility.

Echinoderm is a Greek word which means literally 'prickly skinned'. The group includes not only the starfish but such animals as the equally colourful sea urchin, the sea cucumber (which unlike its salad-bowl namesake is an animal and not a vegetable), the sea star and the sea lily.

The Greeks gave the name echinoderm to both the hedgehog and the sea urchin (the latter was studied by Aristotle and is still called 'Aristotle's Lantern'), and modern science has taken the term to denote this whole group of animals. The reason for this adoption was simply that one of the characteristics which they all have in common is that minute spicules of crystalline carbonate of lime are deposited

in the deeper layers of the skin. These grow together to form plates or prickles in the skin, and resemble a layer of bony net.

The echinoderm which best represents the sessile members of this group is the sea lily (crinoid class). The sea lily consists of a globular body which is rooted to the sea bed by a stalk. The body itself is surmounted by five pairs of tentacles which are radially arranged about the mouth, itself situated on the upper surface of the body.

Five of everything

Before considering the internal systems of the sea lily it is worth examining the tentacles in some detail, for they embody several features which are characteristic of the echinoderms as a whole.

First, there is the fact that the tentacles, or arms, are arranged in *five* pairs. The figure five is something of a magic number in the echinodermic world: most of them have five of everything, except for mouth and stomach (and by an intriguing mathematical accident, incidentally, the number of classes of echinoderms which still exist also amounts to five). In addition to this numerical similarity among echinoderms the radial arrangement of tentacles also represents a form of organization typical of the whole echinoderm family.

Next, the tentacles consist of articulated

plates of calcareous skeletal material. Finally, they incorporate both neuro-muscular systems for movement and a peculiar kind of hydraulic skeleton for support.

In short, they are engineering marvels and of great importance to the echinoderm. Each tentacle carries a myriad of lateral appendages called *pinnules,* and each of these pinnules carries a groove on its upper surface. This groove runs the length of the pinnule and can be considered as a tributary in the food collecting canal of the sea lily. At the tentacle it joins a larger groove which itself runs down to reach the mouth on the top surface of the body. This complex of canals is called the *ambulacral* system, and can extend in total to a quarter of a mile.

Along each side of the pinnule groove are a set of sensitive finger-like protuberances called *podia.* When food particles come in contact with the podia, they whip down towards the pinnule groove and this, combined with the action of cilia (fine hair-like stalks) in the groove itself, drives a stream of food-laden water towards the mouth.

Adaptation for mobility

The podia themselves are supported by the hydraulic system. More properly it is called the water-vascular system and consists of a closed water-containing canal around the oesophagus. From here, five branches lead to the paired tentacles, where they split so that a tube passes up each tentacle. Muscular movement causes the water to move through the branches and so operate the finger-like podia.

Within the globular body of the sea lily there is an oesophagus leading from mouth to stomach, which is followed by an intestine which ends in a vent near the mouth on the upper surface of the body. It is this relative intestinal complexity which separates the echinoderms from animals like sea anemones and jelly-fish, whose digestive systems are little more than internal sacs.

The sea lily, then, is an example of the non-moving type of echinoderm exhibiting the usual characteristics of skeleton, radial organization, what might be called the rule of five, and the water-vascular system. But also to be found among the crinoids is a creature which within its own lifetime demonstrates actual change from sessile to mobile. This is the feather star, one of the most beautiful denizens of tropical waters.

At the start of its life, the feather star is anchored to the sea bed, like the sea lily. But when the stem is about an inch high it breaks and the body and tentacles are free to move. The animal uses tentacles and pinnules to move about as well as to collect the water-borne food. But it also develops short attachments below the body which will allow it to anchor if required.

The fully mobile type of echinoderm is best seen in the starfish (of the group *Asteroidea*). Here, of course, the radial system can be seen more easily, while equally obviously the body and arms are fairly rigid due to the calcareous plates

which are embedded in the tissues.

The starfish differs in many less obvious ways from the sea lily and the feather star. For example, there is the highly efficient manner in which it is able to move about. The chief factor here is that the starfish has ceased to use its water-vascular system as a feeding mechanism. Instead, it is employed as a means of locomotion; in effect it is a hydraulic power system.

This operation is of elegant simplicity. First, the starfish draws water through tiny pores in a sieve plate on the upper surface of its body. From there the water travels around a circular channel from which five channels radiate—one into each arm. Each of these five channels has hundreds of small branches extending to either side, into the 'tube feet' – a special development of the podia seen in the sea lily.

At the free end of each of the tube feet there is a tiny sucker; at the inboard end there is a small chamber called the *ampulla.* When the water reaches the foot, a valve closes behind it, so that it cannot return whence it came. At the same time,

the ampulla contracts and the enclosed water is then forced towards the sucker end, extending the tube and pressing the sucker firmly on to the sea bed below the starfish.

By stretching out its tube feet and attaching them to the sea floor the starfish has thus taken half a step forward. The movement is completed as the ampulla relaxes and the muscles running along the foot contract and shorten the tube once again. The starfish carries thousands of such feet, and when co-ordinated they allow the animal to glide along quickly and smoothly.

Co-ordination is actually effected by a nerve system consisting of a ring around the mouth. Here again the number five reappears, in the form of five nerves radiating from the ring, one to each arm. The starfish, however, has no brain and no eyes. The tips of the arms, however, are light sensitive, and with one of these pointing the way the creature can travel in any required direction.

All of this makes it clear that the starfish does not use its adapted podia for pur-

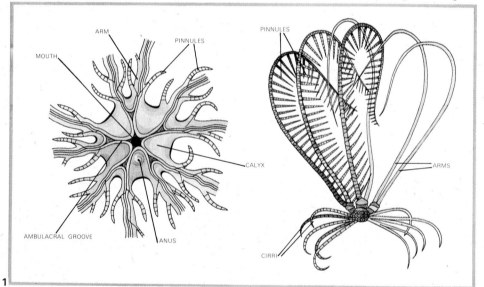

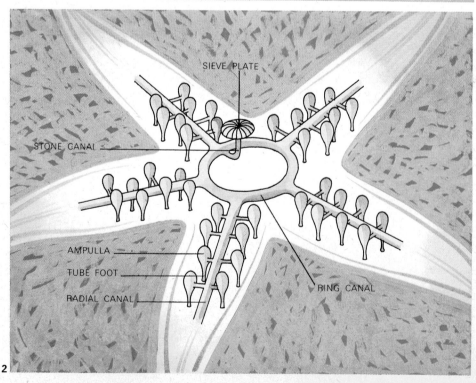

poses of collecting the food drifting down from above. In fact, it has completely transformed its method of feeding. Unlike the sea lily and feather star, which have the mouth and tentacles situated on the upper side of the body, the starfish has turned over so that the mouth, and obviously the feet, are on the under side.

Muscular movement

The animal feeds then on what it can pick up from the sea bed, and its specific method of feeding is to cover its prey and eat directly with the mouth. At the same time, however, the starfish has become a carnivore, or flesh eater, hence its attacks on oysters and other animals. This particular taste often means that the food particles will be too big for entry into the starfish mouth, and so when this happens the animal neatly extrudes the lining of its stomach so that its prey can be partly digested before being taken inside.

The range of living echinoderms is completed by the sea cucumbers *(Holothuroidea),* the brittle stars *(Ophiuroidea)* and

1 Sea lilies or feather stars have a central mouth on the underside *(left)* surmounted by arms which bear fine pinnules as shown on the right. The tube feet are like tentacles.
2 The water-vascular system of the starfish is based on a central ring canal with five radial canals. Water enters through the sieve plate and the rigid stone canal.
3 This sun starfish with 13 arms is less common than the five-armed variety. But individuals with up to 25 arms are found in some waters.
4 Sea urchins are capable of crawling. This one crawling on an aquarium wall clearly shows the mouth with teeth.
5 Serpent stars are so called from the writhing movements which they make. They are also called brittle stars because the arms come off easily whenever they are seized by enemies. Regeneration of the broken limb is rapid, however. The tube feet are used only for respiration and feeling.

finally, the sea urchins and relatives *(Echinoidea).* They are all mobile and represent variations on the starfish theme although most of them look very different. The brittle stars come closest in appearance, usually having five arms, but in contrast they move by muscular action of the arms rather than by hydraulic power. They get their name, incidentally, from the fact that their arms, which are long and spiny, break easily when handled. The sea cucumbers have no radial arms as such, but these are represented instead by clusters of tentacles around the mouth.

Like the starfish, all of these are carnivores. The echinoids, on the other hand, are not. They feed on vegetation which they scrape up with their five pointed teeth. The sea urchin, the most widely known member of the Echinoidea group, also has no arms. However, its body is supported by closely fitting calcareous plates, and these are divided into five vertical sections so that the animal looks a little like a bony ball. In this case the 'seams' of the ball are really the ambulacral grooves described in the sea lily, and

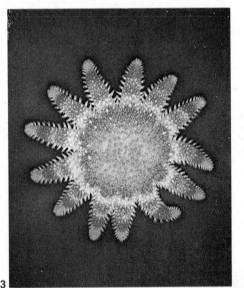

3

they run from the back of the urchin to its mouth on the underside. Particular features of the sea urchin are the long supporting spines which extend from the mass of its body like very fine stilts. The tube feet extend between these spines when the urchin is on the move.

But the echinoderms are not the only animals in the sea which exhibit within one class both sessile and mobile types. There are also the protochordates, the lower members of the great chordate group which includes Man and all other vertebrates as well. Like the echinoderms, some protochordates are able to move – others cannot.

The protochordates themselves are divided into three groups. The largest of these by far are the *urochordates,* most familiar to us as sea squirts. The squirt is the most primitive of the protochordates and is immobile, spending most of its life rooted to some object on the sea bed.

This animal depends for its livelihood on filter feeding. In other words it draws water into its body through an incurrent siphon, and the food is digested. The water is then pushed out again through a second siphon, but on its way out it passes through the squirt's gills where oxygen is extracted. The body of the sea squirt is reasonably flexible, being covered with a layer of an interesting substance called *tunicin* which is almost pure cellulose—one of the few examples of natural manufacture of this material.

Almost a backbone

Taken all in all, there is little here to suggest the sophisticated systems of the higher vertebrates. However, the sea squirts do produce free-swimming larvae which exhibit some of the features which are considered characteristic of the chordates. First, there is an elongated rod, or *notochord,* which stiffens the body and resembles the vertebrate spine. This is also accompanied by a dorsal nerve chord.

4

5

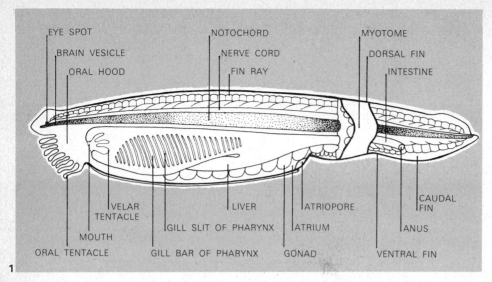

EYE SPOT
BRAIN VESICLE
ORAL HOOD
NOTOCHORD
NERVE CORD
FIN RAY
MYOTOME
DORSAL FIN
INTESTINE
CAUDAL FIN
VELAR TENTACLE
LIVER
ATRIOPORE
ANUS
MOUTH
GILL SLIT OF PHARYNX
ATRIUM
ORAL TENTACLE
GILL BAR OF PHARYNX
GONAD
VENTRAL FIN

1

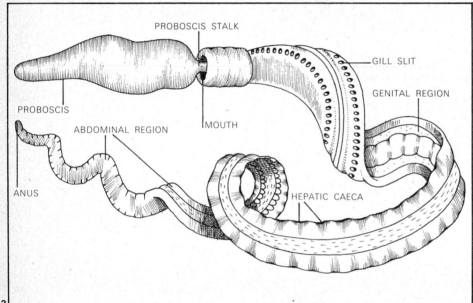

PROBOSCIS STALK
GILL SLIT
GENITAL REGION
PROBOSCIS
ABDOMINAL REGION
MOUTH
ANUS
HEPATIC CAECA

2

The other subdivisions of the protochordates are all mobile, and some of the chordate features already noted are present in these in adult life, while others are absent. The *hemichordates,* for example, include a burrowing worm which has no well--developed notochord, only a rudimentary rod in the head region. For this reason some biologists suggest that they are not true protochordates at all, but are a special case.

Lancelets are the best known representatives of the final protochordate division, the *Cephalochorda.* These animals – 1 to 2½ inches long – both swim freely and burrow in the sand and are truly fishlike. Not only do they have the notochord, so suggestive of a backbone, they also have a number of fins and a tail. The blood system is also fundamentally fishlike.

It is a matter of some argument in the world of biology whether or not the echinoderms and protochordates emerged from the same sessile stock. Nevertheless, together they provide a notable example of the way in which movement has been achieved and also the importance of movement in the development of higher animals. It is true that with the colourful echinoderms, progress has come to a full stop with the brainless and eyeless starfish. But on the other hand the superficially less spectacular protochordates mark the bottom rungs of a ladder which is topped by Man himself.

1 *Amphioxus* (the lancelet), displays some fish-like characteristics, including the ability to swim.
2 Acorn worms provide a link between the chordates and echinoderms. The muscular proboscis is used to drag the animal through its sandy habitat.
3 Two widely different tunicate structures, one of which is the larva of the other.

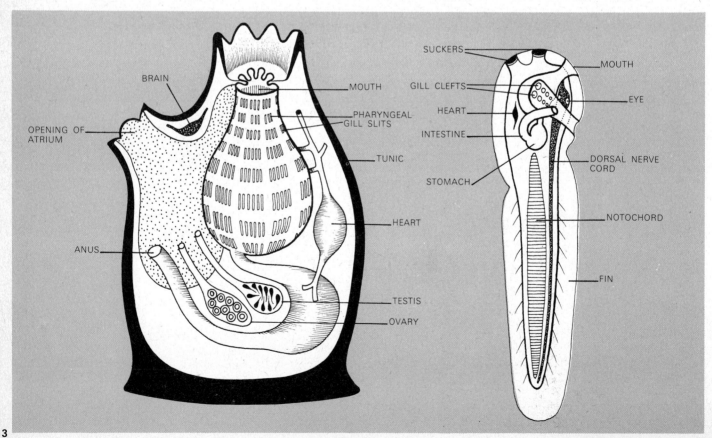

BRAIN
MOUTH
SUCKERS
MOUTH
GILL CLEFTS
EYE
HEART
PHARYNGEAL GILL SLITS
INTESTINE
OPENING OF ATRIUM
TUNIC
STOMACH
DORSAL NERVE CORD
HEART
NOTOCHORD
ANUS
TESTIS
OVARY
FIN

3

28

Fish 1– Evolution and development

Were fish the ancestors of land animals? The evolutionary evidence and study of the existing 20,000 species of fish indicates this. They are the first stage in the development of a skeleton.

FROM THE VERY EARLIEST TIMES the fish has figured largely in the folklore of Man. And the reason is easy to see. Fish exist everywhere in the waters of the world – fresh and salt – in great numbers. This makes them relatively easy to harvest, and once ashore, they provide not only high-quality food, but are also a source of other valuable materials. They supply products like oils, for example, and also fertilizer, meal, glue and fine leather. Again, in some societies their teeth and bones are prized as ornaments, used as money, or employed in the making of spears, arrows and harpoons.

Paradoxically, their very great value and ubiquity may sometimes have led Man to turn his back on the idea of exploiting them. For they have been considered sacred in some parts of the Middle East and Africa, and therefore were hardly exploited at all. Even so, in most areas of the world such restraints have not and do not operate and the fish is of the very greatest importance to the majority of the human race.

At the same time, it is equally important to the balance of nature within the oceans, the rivers and ponds themselves. Fish serve as consumers of small organisms which they convert into food for larger organisms, thus supporting their own food chain as well as contributing to ours.

1 The sting ray *(Dasyatidae)* has well-developed pectoral fins and a sting which is positioned above the tail.
2 Vicious, sharp-toothed moray eels inhabit coral reefs and are a danger to swimmers. Their gills are reduced to no more than pores.

And if all this were not enough in itself to make fish worthy of close study, there is also the fact that they are vertebrates, a class which also includes Man, so their study can add important detail to our knowledge concerning the rise of the 'lord of Creation'.

What is a fish?

In the world at the present time there are more species of fish than any other vertebrate, but in spite of this and their undoubted importance to Man, there is still some confusion concerning what is a fish and what is not. Commonly the name is given to any aquatic creature which employs gills to breathe, moves through the water by means of fins, and possesses scales. But this simple definition will not do. Some fish are finless, some breathe with lungs, some are able to leave the water altogether for a time, and some do not have scales.

Sharks are predatory and live in almost all waters. They produce broods of as many as 30 living offspring at one time.

To define the fish more accurately and usefully it is necessary to be more technical. To begin with there is the characteristic common to all fish which has already been mentioned: the spine. No other ocean animal has a true backbone. It is made up of separate pieces – the *vertebrae* – which fit together to form a structure which, while it is rigid enough to support the body, also allows a great deal of flexibility. The fish typically has lidless eyes. It has a skin containing mucous glands, and a heart consisting of a single folded tube with several chambers.

These then are subdivided, however, into five classes which it is proper to examine and compare since they outline the evolutionary progress of these animals. The fish originally evolved, it is thought, from a type similar to the *Amphioxus* (lancelet) which possesses physiological equipment which seems to foreshadow the backbone and other facilities later found in fish.

The most ancient class of true fish which we know of are the *agnaths*. Their name means 'jawless' which describes their major peculiarity, for indeed that was their condition. The agnaths dominated the fish world for some tens of millions of years before subsiding and finally disappearing as more efficient animals evolved.

One direction in which this develop-

As the chart on pages 30–31 shows, there are five basic classes, and the chain of evolution leading to present-day fishes has been established from the fossil record. However, there are still many gaps that have not yet been filled in.

The fish shown as present-day types are merely representative examples of the various classes. It can be seen that the spiny fish are the most numerous.

Fish are the first vertebrates in the evolutionary scale. The chart shows how the various present-day types have developed from their remote ancestors. The different forms of fish illustrate the changes which have taken place to adapt them to various environments.

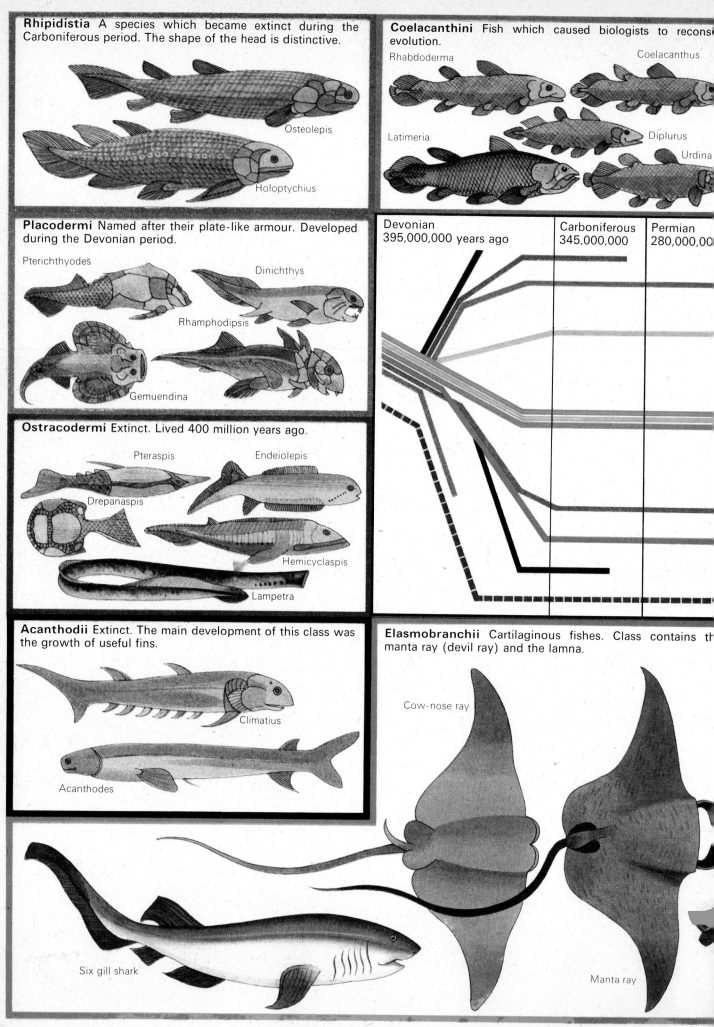

Rhipidistia A species which became extinct during the Carboniferous period. The shape of the head is distinctive.

Osteolepis

Holoptychius

Coelacanthini Fish which caused biologists to recons[ider] evolution.

Rhabdoderma

Coelacanthus

Latimeria

Diplurus

Urdina

Placodermi Named after their plate-like armour. Developed during the Devonian period.

Pterichthyodes

Dinichthys

Rhamphodipsis

Gemuendina

Ostracodermi Extinct. Lived 400 million years ago.

Pteraspis

Endeiolepis

Drepanaspis

Hemicyclaspis

Lampetra

Devonian 395,000,000 years ago	Carboniferous 345,000,000	Permian 280,000,00

Acanthodii Extinct. The main development of this class was the growth of useful fins.

Climatius

Acanthodes

Elasmobranchii Cartilaginous fishes. Class contains th[e] manta ray (devil ray) and the lamna.

Cow-nose ray

Six gill shark

Manta ray

onoi A term reserved for lungfishes and fossil forms by some ...ogists, although others include coelacanths in this class.

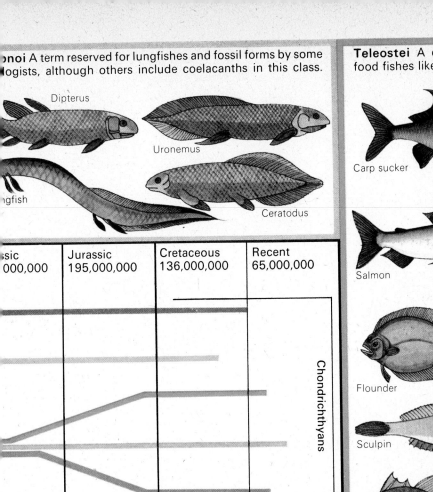

Dipterus

Uronemus

...ngfish

Ceratodus

Teleostei A class which includes many of the customary food fishes like herring and salmon.

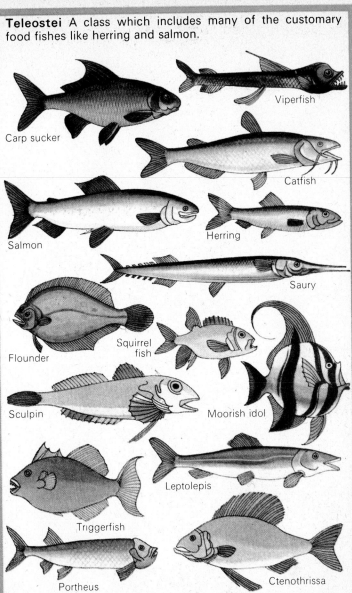

Carp sucker

Viperfish

Catfish

Salmon

Herring

Saury

Flounder

Squirrel fish

Sculpin

Moorish idol

Triggerfish

Leptolepis

Portheus

Ctenothrissa

...sic ...000,000	Jurassic 195,000,000	Cretaceous 136,000,000	Recent 65,000,000

Chondrichthyans

Osteichthyans

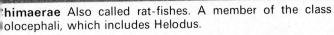

Chimaerae Also called rat-fishes. A member of the class ...olocephali, which includes Helodus.

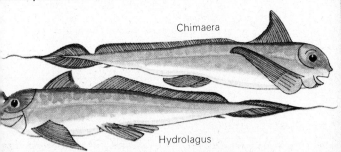

Chimaera

Hydrolagus

Holostei Includes the well-known gar and bowfin fish.

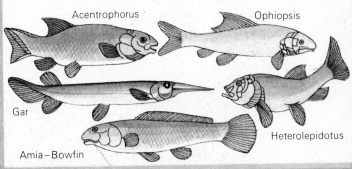

Acentrophorus

Ophiopsis

Gar

Heterolepidotus

Amia–Bowfin

Horn shark

Chondrostei Replaced by more advanced forms of marine life during the Jurassic period. A few survived to the Cretaceous.

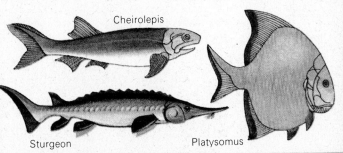

Cheirolepis

Sturgeon

Platysomus

ment took place can be seen in a second class called the *Cyclostomata* which are still much in evidence today in the shape of lampreys and hagfish. Both of these are jawless in the accepted sense and in shape are long and eel-like. For feeding they possess a round sucking funnel lined with teeth, and the technique of both is to attach themselves by means of the sucker to their prey. In the case of the lamprey, the teeth are then used to rasp a way through the skin so that it can suck the blood; and indeed it is no uncommon thing to find other fish which carry the scars of one or more visits from a lamprey. Even more destructive, though, is the unpleasantly named hagfish. Once these have become attached, they eat their way right into and through their prey.

Predators and prey

Another line of development from the agnaths encompassed a truly remarkable evolutionary change – the development of a jaw. Most of the early agnaths probably lived by sucking up the bottom mud and extracting their living from the organic matter which the mud contained. Clearly jaws allow the fish to take a wider variety of foods, and in the third class of fish, the *placoderms* ('plate skin' because many had bony armour plates), hinged gill supports.

The placoderms, however, did not last for long, being replaced by the two remaining classes of fish. These are *chondrichthyans,* which in the shark and ray contain two of the most dangerous animals in the sea, and the *ostychtheians* or bony fish, which include not only most of the world's food fishes, but also some pretty dangerous customers as well – the notorious barracuda, for example, and the aggressive moray eel.

But the two classes also benefit from another interesting comparison. The shark and its relatives were originally developed in order to live in and exploit the salt waters of the Earth, and subsequently only very few have moved into fresh-water habitats. The bony fish, on the other hand, were specialized for life in fresh water. Here they have continued to dominate but have also spread into the seas.

But even though the chondrichthyans have to compete with some 30,000 species of bony fish, they have held their own and have not been wiped out. One reason for this might be their fearsome defensive and offensive equipment as seen in the sharks. But they are also designed in one respect in a much more efficient manner than the ubiquitous bony fish.

This is the mechanism by which their cells are kept supplied with water. This is all a matter of the osmotic pressure of the body fluids within the fish. If this pressure is lower than that of the surrounding water – as it is in the bony fish – then they tend to lose their body water continuously through the gill membranes. So in order, literally, to prevent their cells from dying of thirst, the bony fish must use comparatively large amounts of energy to gulp water continually, thus making good the loss, and then excrete the dissolved salts.

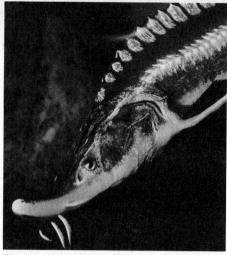
The sturgeon, with its shark-like mouth on the underside of its body, feeds on small marine creatures. Its eggs (caviar) are a delicacy.

In the shark and its relatives, the whole business is carried out in a much simpler manner. In short, the chondrichthyans retain large amounts of urea in their body fluids. In most other animals such a concentration would be fatal but here, together with other salts, it maintains the internal fluids at the same osmotic pressure as the water outside, so the shark, or other chondrichthyan need do much less work in supplying its cells with water.

The other factors which characterize the chondrichthyan include of course its cartilaginous skeleton (indeed the name means 'cartilage fish'); its absence of a swim bladder; and the fact that none of them have lungs.

The bony fish get their name from the fact that most have well-developed bony skeletons. (As mentioned above, the skeleton of the shark is composed of cartilage, the tough gristly material which in bone skeletons is reserved for connective tissue at the joints.) In a few species though, like the sturgeon, the bone has retrogressed and the skeleton consists largely of cartilage.

The most primitive bony fish were equipped with lungs as well as gills for purposes of breathing. This probably stems from the fact that during their fresh-water beginnings they found themselves in semi-

The carp, a native of North American and European waters, has an unusual scale formation. It is preyed on by the pike.

stagnant surroundings in which the oxygen content was very low and gills were therefore ineffective. With subsidiary lungs they would have been able to rise to the surface and breathe air directly.

In most cases the lung has now fallen into disuse in the context of breathing and has become the subject of a particularly interesting adaptation. It has developed into a very important part of the bony fish's equipment: the swim bladder. In most such fish this is a simple gas-filled sac which reduces the animal's specific gravity, and like a pair of internal water wings maintains it at a depth suitable to its mode of life. That, however, is not the swim bladder's only function.

In some fish it operates as a large ear. Sound waves reaching the creature pass through its outer tissues and strike the taut membrane of the sac: from there they are transmitted mechanically to the brain through the small bones of the vertebrae.

But as ever in nature, here there are exceptions to prove the rule. Some bony fish *have* retained lungs, and these not very surprisingly are called lungfish. They are to be found in rivers in Australia and Africa where the water is too foul to support fish having only the more usual gills.

Mammalian forebears

So in all of this we can see the interrelationships of the five classes of fish, but a truer and perhaps more spectacular picture of their range and diversity and the wonderful mechanisms they embody requires more detailed study.

The diversity of forms which the fish adopt provide a number of valuable clues to the ways in which land animals have developed from their aquatic forebears. This is particularly the case in relation to the amphibians and reptiles, whose origins and vestigial fish characteristics are apparent even to the casual observer.

In recent biological research into evolutionary process, the coelacanth has provided a valuable link in the evolutionary chain. But there are many other types of fish which retain their anatomical and physiological forms intact, untouched by the processes of evolution. In many ways, they can be considered as living relics of an age of animals which has long since passed. Their study is a vital part in the completion of the history of the animal kingdom and in the origins of the higher animals, including even Man himself.

Fish 2 – In the waters of the Earth

Bony, jawless, herbivorous, carnivorous – the variety of fish swarming in the rivers, lakes and seas of the world is seemingly endless. How do they relate to each other?

1

2

THE NUMBER of species of fish, approximately 20,000, pales into insignificance when compared with the vast number of insect species. And yet, in their diversity of form, habitats, breeding methods and adaptation, the fish surpass the insects. They range in size from tiny animals to the sharks and rays.

And although they are the Earth's oldest vertebrates, living in their strange environment for many ages before the first of them ventured on dry land to give rise eventually to the mammals, very little has been known about them until comparatively recently. The water which nurtures them and has shaped their physiology and life-cycle has also acted as a considerable barrier between them and investigating scientists.

Despite the diversity of form, all fish are in the end conditioned by their environment. Their watery existence has determined their shape, their means of locomotion, their feeding and breeding habits, and their means of respiration. Furthermore, as many fish live in conditions which make the senses as we know them virtually useless, some of them have developed a sixth sense which has no counterpart among other classes of animal. This alone is enough to make the fish unique among the animal kingdom.

Anatomical development

In most cases fish have moved a long way from the elongated spindly shapes of the first vertebrates. While this may not be so obvious in the cyclostomes (lampreys, etc.), which have become long and snakelike, the cartilaginous fish like the shark have become streamlined for speed, with fins so fleshy that the Chinese are able to make soup from them. Their cousins, the rays, have become flattened and their ventral fins have become extended and winglike. The bony fishes show perhaps the greatest variation in shape of all. They range through almost all shapes – from the long and snakelike moray eel, through the shortened and side-to-side flattened butterfly fish, to the streamlined herring and barracuda.

To return to skeletal matters briefly, it is interesting to note that the fins have a variety of uses apart from propulsion. In some cases they are paired and it is thought that these paired fins in the higher vertebrates have become limbs.

1 The cod family (*Gadidae*) includes a number of food fishes, most of them common in the Northern Hemisphere. Characteristically, they live in shoals.
2 Coral fish have a delicate sense of touch which enables them to dart between rocks which they cannot possibly see. They are also able to change colour very rapidly.

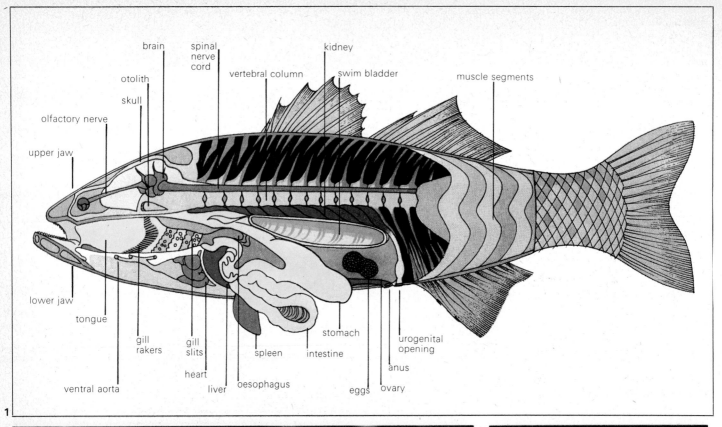

brain
spinal
nerve
cord
kidney
otolith
vertebral column
swim bladder
muscle segments
skull
olfactory nerve
upper jaw

lower jaw

tongue

gill
rakers
gill
slits
stomach
urogenital
opening
heart
spleen
intestine
anus
ventral aorta
liver
oesophagus
eggs
ovary

1

2

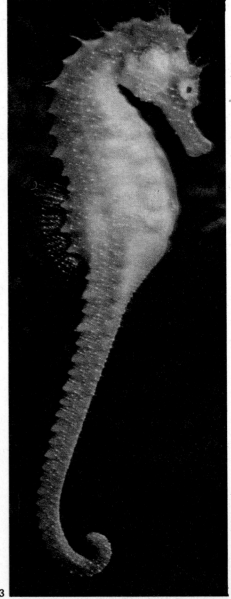

3

1 This drawing shows the anatomy of the fish. The vertebral column is immediately obvious. It is thought that the swim bladder serves a secondary purpose as an organ of sound collection.
2 Mudskippers are able to survive fairly long periods on land by breathing through the skin. They are able to propel themselves by using their fins with a curious walking movement.
3 Sea-horses swim upright as do all the *Austo-midinae*. Their bodies are covered in bony rings, and the males have a brood-pouch located in the tail.

1 The smooth trunk fish has an outer covering made of scales which have fused together. It is a poor swimmer and relies on its armour for protection against predators.
2 Porcupine fish, as shown here, are able to dilate their bodies and erect their spines as a protective device. The spines are not poisonous.
3 Catfishes are mainly found in fresh-water habitats in South America, Asia and Africa.

They often build nests for the protection of their young, and sometimes the eggs are carried in the mouth of the male.
4 Butterfly fish, found in tropical waters, have thin fins covered with scales and brush-like teeth.
5 The lamprey is one of the jawless fishes. It seizes its prey with a powerful sucker in the centre of which is the mouth and teeth. Lampreys cause extensive damage to fisheries.

Some fish, like mudskippers, in fact do use pairs of specially developed fins to 'walk' across the sea bed.

The skin of the fish is a highly complex thing. Mostly it is smooth and flexible and dotted with various glands designed to do various jobs. For example, poison glands occur in the skins of many cartilaginous fish and, needless to say, they are extremely useful as a means of protection, often backing up to sharp spines. In very deep sea forms, there are often *photophores,* or luminous organs, embedded in the skin, and these operate as lures. The other small fry are attracted by the bright glow given out by their bigger brother and usually end up providing a meal for him.

Gills and scales

Then there are the scales. These are divided into five categories, one of which is not found in any living animal and need not concern us here. The others include, first, the *placoids,* which are found in the skins of cartilaginous fish and are spiny and tooth-like – human skin which has been rasped by the pelt of a shark looks much as though it has been treated with coarse-grade sandpaper. Primitive bony fish sometimes carry a second class, *ganoid* scales, which are inclined to be thick and usefully protective. *Cycloid* scales are found on carp and similar fish and are what we usually mean when we talk of scales in everyday life. They are thin, relatively large, and round or oval in shape. They overlap on the skin. Finally, there are the *ctenoid* scales, which occur in the more developed of the bony fish and carry spines or teeth on their free edge.

Even so, some fish are entirely without this kind of protective armour, including the lampreys, and some bony fish, like the eel.

As already noted, most fish have gills and these are extremely important to them, for it is with this equipment that they are able to get the oxygen necessary to life. Gill openings vary in the different groups but inside they are in principle entirely similar. The gills contain finely divided blood vessels which to look at resemble a broad and dense red fringe. Water is continually taken in by the fish through the gill openings and inside comes into contact with the fringes. The fine membranes which house the blood vessels

1

2

3

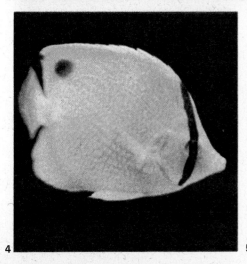

4

5

allow oxygen to pass into the blood-stream where it is distributed to various parts of the body by the pumping action of the heart.

The fish heart is placed behind and below the gills and consists of a folded tube with three or four enlargements. Contractions of the heart drive the blood to a bulb at the base of a main artery, through which it travels to the gills. After the oxygen has been picked up, the blood progresses via capillaries into another main artery – running the length of the fish beneath the backbone – from whence it is delivered to most parts of the body. While giving up its load of oxygen, the blood removes waste products and returns to the heart for recycling.

Colour plays an important part in the life of the fish. They are as colourful at times as the resplendent birds and butter-flies of the tropical jungles. A beautiful if tiny example which is known to every home-aquarium owner is the vivid neon fish.

Some fish can also change the intensity of their colouring. Simply, the mechanism is as follows: the pigment cells in the skin of the fish are comparatively large and when it is necessary for the particular colour to be intensified the pigment floods through the whole of the cell. A lightening of the shade is accomplished when the pigment is concentrated into a tiny dot at the centre of the cell.

Hiding and feeding

Since the fish can also change their colour they are adept at camouflage. This colour-change ability rests upon the fact that the colours of the fish skin are made up by relatively simple mixtures of one-colour cells. By suppressing certain of these cells the animal is able to change its overall colour. Thus a fish, which might normally be seen as green by virtue of sporting a mixture of blue and yellow cells, can become either of these colours by suppressing the other.

Vision is extemely important to many fish and it has been established that most of them are capable of distinguishing between certain colours. There is some physiological evidence to suggest that fish are near-sighted, but some at least are certainly not. The ease with which certain of them distinguish between flies is proof of this, as is the skill of the dolphin which is capable of following the track of a flying-fish when it leaves the water in order to snaffle it when it plops back to the surface. Again, there is the archer-fish which squirts a jet of water at its prey – insects and the like – so knocking them off overhanging branches and into the water where the archer-fish can deal with his meal at leisure.

The hearing mechanism employing the swim bladder has already been covered, but there is another sense-organ system unique to the breed. This is called the lateral-line sensory system. It is thought to be concerned with the apprehension of changes in pressure and is a system of pit organs, or pressure-sensitive cells, usually arranged laterally along canals situated on the animal's head and body.

1 Parrot-fishes are unusual in that they are herbivorous, and they also chew their food. They are equipped with a proper beak to snip off plants.

2 Sterlets are one of the smaller species of sturgeon, most of which periodically ascend rivers to deposit their spawn. They spend the rest of the time in the oceans.

It is possible that the system works as follows. The fish when moving through the water sets up a pressure wave ahead of it. Any solid object in front of the creature would cause this wave to bounce back, and it is thought that the lateral-line system allows the fish to tune into this invisible signal. Now, many fish are capable of emitting sounds at will – as Cousteau, the famous French underwater explorer, has pointed out, the 'silent deep' is anything but silent. In this case it is also suggested that the fish amplify the naturally-occurring pressure waves with sound waves, and thus have an effective echo-location system similar to that used by Man in underwater warfare and exploration. This faculty is often regarded as the fish's sixth sense.

The sense of smell is well developed in fish, particularly those with poor sight. For years men have marvelled at the way in which salmon and other types are able to return to the stream of their birth in order to breed. Now it is thought that they are able to distinguish the specific water course by its smell. Other species, like the shark, apparently locate their prey by the smell which it gives out, and it is also a fact that an injured or distressed fish emits a particular odour which warns its fellows of danger and causes them to disperse or swim about agitatedly.

In size, fish range from the tiny – half an inch long or so – to what is probably the largest of all fish, the whale shark. This can measure up to 70 ft. The largest sunfish and sturgeon may exceed 2,000 lb.

In terms of habitat, there is scarcely any permanent stretch of water which does not carry its quota of fish – from the oceans to the tiniest stream, and again they can exist at great depths and in extremely shallow waters. Finally, there are so many of them that their true numbers can never be known: a graphic example is that it is reckoned the Atlantic Ocean holds some trillion (million million million) of herring.

It is no surprise then that the fish bulks so large in the mind and welfare of mankind, and lucky for the scientist that this important branch on our evolutionary tree is everywhere so abundantly available for study.

A step from the sea

Amphibians – the first animals to leave an aquatic environment, the first to colonize dry land. Today they are a very small but significant remnant of a once much larger family tree.

ANIMALS HAVE ADAPTED in many different ways to fill the various niches in the complex which makes up the natural world. All life began in the oceans of the Earth, but later some animals moved from the waters to the land in order to exploit the way of life which was offered there. The group of animals which bridges the gap between dry land and water is of course the *Amphibia*. And though as a group they have been relatively unsuccessful – a variety of original classes having reduced to just three modern ones – they are extremely important from the point of view of their linking function.

The amphibians are placed somewhere between the fish and the reptiles in the evolutionary scheme of things, and it is necessary to go to the former for clues concerning the way the amphibians developed.

By far the largest class of fish are the *osteichthyans* or bony fish. Among these we find most of the food fish which Man exploits today, but these are only the modern descendants of much more primitive types, and it is with the primitives that we are really concerned. For the early bony fish started up the road of progress as freshwater types; they were possessed of both gills – for breathing when under water – and lungs for breathing air directly at the surface.

Development of breathing

From this point they developed in two ways. Some gave up the use of their lungs and spread into the oceans, where incidentally they have been highly successful. Others moved in the opposite direction, eventually losing the use of their gills and taking up lung breathing completely.

This outline of the process is of course very brief and for that reason gives too great an impression of speed. The truth is that the respiratory change took a great deal of time and was also accompanied by other important changes in the physiology of the animals.

Without doubt the most important of these was the change which came about in the paired fins of these early bony fish. The significant example to take here is a

1 The Alpine newt is a native of mountainous regions of central Europe and some southerly European countries.
2 The Mexican *axolotl* can live in water and remain in the larval stage for years. In this neotic (non-adult) condition they are still able to lay fertile eggs. This particular variety is albino with pink gills.
3 Fish and urodeles have similarly shaped bodies and move in basically the same manner. Breathing patterns vary only in that amphibians possess lungs for life above water.

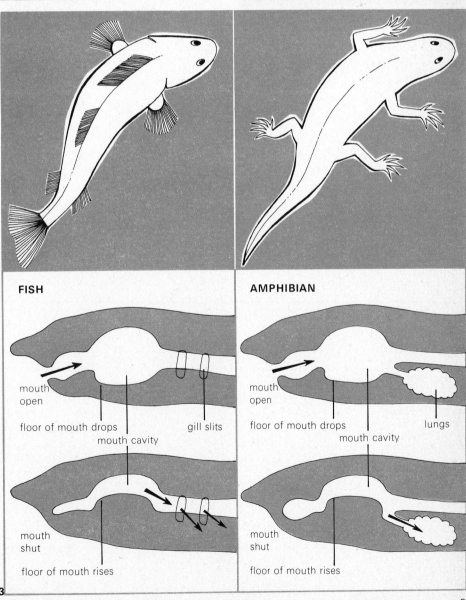

FISH

mouth open

floor of mouth drops
mouth cavity
gill slits

mouth shut

floor of mouth rises

AMPHIBIAN

mouth open

floor of mouth drops
mouth cavity
lungs

mouth shut

floor of mouth rises

type of fish known as the *Crossopterygii*, ('lobe fins'). These lived in large, freshwater swamps and marshes in the period of history known as the Devonian (350 million years ago) and as might be expected possessed the functional lungs mentioned above. They also had paired pectoral and pelvic fins which were fleshy in nature, and it was from these that the limbs of the amphibians are thought to have developed.

Physiological change did not stop here either. The early amphibians were fish-like in shape and were probably only capable of waddling from one water hole to the next. Other changes had to take place before they were capable of existing fully on land and these concerned the nature of the problems which land-life poses, as opposed to those met in water.

First, in water, a body is supported by its natural buoyancy, but when that precious liquid is absent an efficient system of vertebrae and limbs must be developed to support the body. Next there is the requirement of every living cell for drinking water. When any animal is continuously bathed with water then this is little or no problem, but on dry land arrangements have to be made to conserve water in the body and kidneys.

These were the changes which were necessary and which took place in the rise of the amphibians. By the end of the Devonian period some of the fish-like crossopts had developed legs and had crawled from the water. Later, in the Permo-Carboniferous period (240 million years ago) they had developed even further, although they were still ungainly sprawling brutes very different from the modern types. A typical example were *Eryops*, nearly five feet in length, with stubby legs, a tail and a big flattened and triangular head. The Eryops were also *labyrinthodonts*, a name which refers to their teeth and means literally 'labyrinth toothed'. In other words, their teeth were set in an intricate and maze-like pattern.

Fossilized evidence

In historical terms, however, the early amphibians were not long on this world. By the Triassic (180 million years ago, and the period which saw the elevation of the continents, the origin of the dinosaur and so on) most of the early forms had disappeared. The rise of the modern forms of amphibian life are poorly documented in terms of fossils (which are in effect the only real way of discovering the form and function of departed animals) but rise they obviously did, for we still have three modern groups of amphibian.

These are the *anurans* which we know better as frogs and toads; the *urodeles* or colourful salamanders, newts and so on and finally the *caecilians*. The latter are much less well known, being worm-like burrowing animals, almost entirely blind and completely limbless. From this it can be clearly seen that the modern amphibians represent several different types of adaption from the basic plan as shown in the very early types.

Among the living types of amphibians the most successful is undoubtedly the

1 This yellow and black European salamander is a member of the family *Salamandridae*. Like others in the group they may spend most of their lives within an area of a few square yards from where they were born — they are less visually orientated than frogs.
2 The illustration shows a crested newt. The dorsal crest becomes prominent at the stage of the sexual cycle when the male is ready for breeding. A large tail is characteristic of the newt family.
3 Tree frogs possess suction pads on their digits to assist gripping and are particularly good jumpers, but they still spawn in water and the eggs hatch as fish-like tadpoles. This pair are European tree frogs.

1 One of the largest anurans is the giant toad, *(Bufo marinus)* which lives in Central and South America. It has the ability to create an extremely obnoxious smell.

2 A male tree frog calling his mate. The loose skin of the vocal pouch is momentarily filled and emptied of air to produce the sound. Females do not have this vocal ability.

3 The skin surface of the frog is either smooth or warty. It conserves water in the body. Frogs from tropical regions tend to have smooth skin, often very colourfully pigmented.

4 This, the Common Frog, is a largely nocturnal amphibian. Although a poor jumper it can live long distances from water without fear of desiccation.

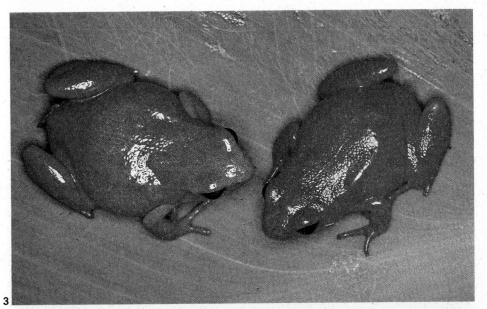

frog. There are some 1,800 species and they vary considerably in colour: red, blue, black, green and yellow in various mixtures. They vary also in habit – there are swimming, digging and also climbing varieties.

But in shape they are generally similar. They have a short squat body without a neck, and they are tail-less. Their back legs are much more powerful than the front ones, the former being used in the anuran's characteristic mode of progress, the leap. Their sense organs include those of sight and smell.

Among the amphibians, the sense of hearing is best developed in frogs, and plays a significant part in the mating ritual of the animals. During the breeding season, which usually occurs after winter hibernation, the males call the females to the breeding areas – the ponds, streams and rivers. Each species of frog has a distinctive call, of which the hoarse croakings of the bullfrog are perhaps most widely talked about, written about and indeed recorded. The females of each species are able, thanks to their hearing, to differentiate between the call of their own species and those emitted by frogs of other species.

Among the amphibians the frogs and toads also occur over the widest area of the Earth's surface. They live north of the Arctic Circle and in the southernmost tips of the continents. Of particular interest is the fact that they have been able to colonize oceanic islands, even though salt water is uncongenial to them. It is thought that they have made the journey to these distant locations on tree trunks and branches carried away during storms. It is also thought that after a particularly heavy rainfall enough fresh water overlays the saline kind to allow the creatures to survive over short distances across the seas.

Pesticide and poison

Because they are carnivores with a voracious appetite for insects, both frogs and toads have also been introduced by Man into various areas in order to rid farming land of insect pests. An example of this is *Bufo marinus* which is something of a monster, having reached as much as nine inches in length. In fact, it is the largest of all toads and has been introduced into sugar fields in the West Indies, Australia, the Hawaii Islands, New Guinea and elsewhere. But even so, insect control is not its only use – in South America at least. Its body contains a very powerful poison which is used by the South American Indians to provide arrows with an extremely deadly payload for their victims.

It is in the larval stage of the frog and toad that its fishy origins can be glimpsed. The larvae – or tadpoles – begin as simple eggs which are laid by the adults in the water. By hatching time, they have developed the same respiratory and circulatory systems as fish; they have four pairs of gills for breathing, supported by a two-chambered heart which circulates the blood through the gills. The tadpole also swims like a fish, using its longish tail.

The change into a land-living animal is

called the *metamorphosis* and it is an extremely fascinating process. The tadpole begins as a vegetarian with horny teeth; as it grows the tail begins to be absorbed into the globular body. At the same time the gills degenerate and the vestigial lungs develop. But this is not all. In the first place back legs form and are followed by the front, the latter breaking through the body wall near the gill chamber.

The horny jaws give way to bony ones which usually carry teeth, and with this the feeding habits of the frog change radically. From herbivore it becomes a predatory flesh-eater, using a long and prehensile tongue to capture its prey.

Now the frog must literally leave the water or drown, having given up its gills for lungs. Once on land the back legs strengthen in the characteristic way, and the reason why the tail disappeared becomes obvious. If the frog retained its tail the appendage would seriously reduce its jumping powers.

One final point, the skin of the metamorphosed frog is either smooth or warty and it plays a large part in the conservation of moisture mentioned above. Again, it also provides a permeable membrane through which the frog is able to breathe as well as through its lungs.

A major difference between the anurans (frogs) and the second large class of Amphibia, the urodeles (salamanders), is that the latter retain their tails in adult life. It is also true that the metamorphosis is less spectacular than that of the frog, but just as complete.

In most cases, the salamanders produce eggs which eventually hatch into fish-like larvae, but some produce living young. In all cases the offspring have three pairs of gills, a tail for swimming and at first are limbless. Just as in the frog, the back legs develop first, followed by the front, while in most species the gills disappear as the lungs expand and grow.

A fish on land

As noted above, the salamander retains something of its fish-like quality in adult life. Its legs are small and weak; they are not very effective in the water and are only just able to lift the body when ashore. All of this has its effect upon the way in which the salamander moves on land. When it wants to get from A to B very quickly it merely wriggles across the ground, just like a fish out of water – it does not use its limbs at all. However, when it does walk it still moves sinuously like a fish.

In short, the salamander and indeed the other urodeles like the newt and mud puppy, are much closer to fish than is the frog. This general characteristic is also to be seen in the breathing equipment of the salamander. It has already been pointed out that some salamanders do not lose their gills. But whatever the particular situation the mechanics of breathing are the same and are basically very similar to the fish.

The creature alternately lowers and raises the floor of its throat by means of muscular action. This means that it gulps in mouthfuls of either air or water and the rising of the throat floor forces whichever is concerned into gills or lungs where gas exchange takes place.

In some other respects the salamander is closer to the frog. For example, its skin is scaleless – either smooth or warty. In some species it also plays a part in respiration.

There are some 150 species of Urodela, all of which are fairly similar in structure, having typically four rather short legs all of about the same size (in contrast with the frogs and toads, where the rear pair are greatly developed for the purpose of jumping). In addition they often have a crest of skin along the upper and lower edges of the tail which are useful aids to swimming.

Newts and salamanders are found almost exclusively in the temperate regions of the Northern Hemisphere; about half of them live in North America.

The final class within the amphibian group is that of the caecilians. This contains about 70 species, all of which are roughly similar in appearance. In effect they look more like earthworms than frog or salamander and indeed were once classified among the snakes.

They spend their lives burrowing in sand and mud and for this reason have a compact head protected by a bony shield. Mostly they are to be found in Central and South America, and parts of Asia and Africa. They are elongated and cylindrical in shape and have no limbs at all. They are to all intents and purposes blind, although they do possess rudimentary eyes. Of much greater importance to them are tentacles, which most caecilians possess, which are situated on either side of the nose. These tentacles are used for both taste and smell.

These then are the Amphibia, one of the groups of animals which marks something of a dead end in one branch of evolution. Nevertheless, grotesque and exotic as they may seem, they do mark the triumphant emergence of animal life from the primeval waters. The changes which are necessary for dry-land existence can be seen in them as also can the clues to their fishy ancestry. They are also the stock from which sprang that much more efficient class of animal the reptile – and ultimately Man himself.

It is a sobering thought that we, so confident of our superiority among the animal species, have very good reason for following St Francis of Assisi in referring to that bloated croaker in the woodland pool as 'Brother Frog'.

1 The *Eryops Permian* was an early amphibian living about 240 million years ago. A reconstruction from fossilized remains shows its numerous teeth and bulky body.
2 Tadpoles swimming near the surface after four weeks of life. As they grow, gills disappear and are replaced by lungs. Tails are absorbed after the little frogs leave the water.

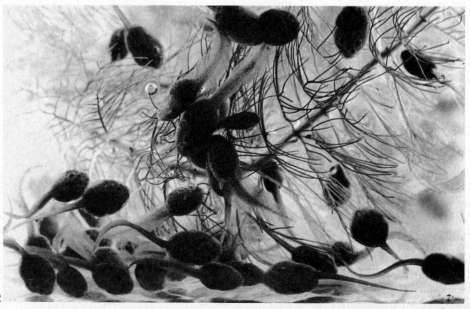

Reptiles 1-Life on land

How they breathe and reproduce, their skin texture and limb development are features which mark the reptiles as one of the most critical stages in the evolution of the higher vertebrates.

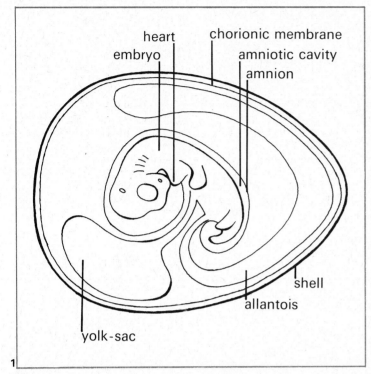

heart
chorionic membrane
embryo
amniotic cavity
amnion
shell
allantois
yolk-sac

1

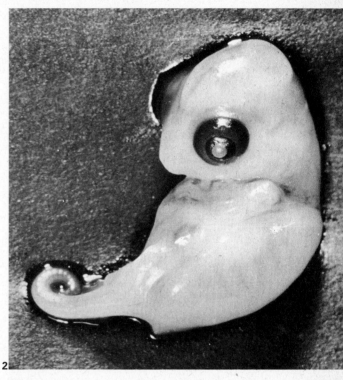

2

LIFE WOULD HAVE no chance of reaching the level which we see around us in the higher vertebrates if it had not adapted in ways to make it possible to leave the water for dry land. The change was not easy, and Nature had two attempts at the job, both involving members of the animal group, the vertebrates.

From the first partially successful attempt, the amphibians, there stemmed the class of animals called *reptiles*. These have become fully adapted for life on dry land, although some still spend a great deal of time in the water. A hundred million years ago this class of animals was dominant, but outside pressures eventually brought the Age of Reptiles to an end. Now their numbers are reduced to a mere handful of types: the crocodiles, turtles and tortoises, snakes and lizards.

But before looking at the extinct or even the living species of reptile in any detail, we should first examine the general physical characteristics which have allowed reptiles their independence of water as a habitat.

From their amphibian forebears, the reptiles inherited lungs. These vary in sophistication, but in general they are superior to the lungs possessed by amphibians. In the case of the latter, the lungs are not efficient enough to supply the animal with all the oxygen it needs for life. Intake has to be supplemented by breathing through the skin. The reptile lung on the other hand has no such limitations.

Again, the reptilian system by which air is actually taken into the body is more advanced. The frog (amphibian), for

1 Diagrammatic representation of a reptilian egg shows the four sacs or membranes, the *chorion, amnion, yolk-sac* and *allantois,* which are essential for the growth of the embryo.

example, gulps in air by expanding the muscles of its throat. These are then contracted and the air is pushed into the lung, the same air being used again and again until the oxygen content is exhausted.

The reptile, on the other hand, possesses a system of muscles which enables it to expand and contract its rib cage. This causes the lungs to work like a pair of bellows and breathing takes place in a more steady and controlled fashion.

This improved breathing apparatus has freed the reptilian skin from its breathing function and allows it to be used for another purpose, water conservation. Since the skin of the amphibian is permeable to air, it also tends to be permeable

2 The two-month-old embryo of a snapping turtle is exposed by removing part of its shell. In later life this variety spends most of its time in water and can be very aggressive.

to water and one reason why frogs and toads are clammy to touch is that they are permanently undergoing a process of evaporation of body liquids through the skin. Constant replenishment of this supply of water in the body is yet another reason why amphibians customarily live close to water. The reptile has overcome this problem by retaining a physiological attribute of a more distant ancestor, the fish. These are scales.

Reptilian scales are overlapping and

3 Crocodilians lay clutches of about 30 eggs. At the end of its snout the emerging crocodile has an *'egg-tooth'* for breaking out of its hard, waterproof shell.

1 Confronted with an adversary, the harmless grass snake puffs itself up menacingly; if this fails, it acts as though dead.

2 Slender European whip snakes are extremely well camouflaged to live in the trees, their natural habitat.

3 The slow-worm, despite its snake-like appearance is a harmless, legless lizard. Here a female is surrounded by her young.

consist of a hard, dry substance called *keratin*, which is virtually impermeable to water. It is therefore both a form of lightweight but effective protection to the body and also precludes loss of body fluids by evaporation. The crocodile or snake, if provided with sufficient drinking water, is unlikely to suffer the fate of desiccation which so often befalls the frog and toad.

However in one other aspect reptiles are not well equipped – dealing with violent changes in temperature. It is obvious that beneath the surface of the water such fluctuations are much smaller than they are on dry land. This is concerned on the one hand with the physical nature of water and its potential for storing and losing heat, and on the other with changing seasons experienced on land where

warm day inevitably gives way to relatively cold night.

Reptiles, like fish and amphibians, are what is generally termed 'cold blooded'. This is a splendidly inaccurate but widely employed term for what in science is called *poikilothermy*. What is really meant is that the blood heat of these animals tends to move up or down until it coincides with the temperature of their environment.

A very wide range of temperature would, however, cause irreparable harm to the delicate mechanism of the animal cells. To combat this possibility the reptile has been forced to develop ways of maintaining a fairly constant body heat.

In this the class has been only partially successful. Some lizards possess a reasonably elegant system by which they are

able to change the intensity of their colouring in response to temperature change. They do so by contracting or enlarging the pigment contained in the cells in their skin. Thus they will become darker – with enlarged pigmentation – on cold days so that their skin absorbs as much of the available heat as possible, while on hot days the pigmentation is contracted and consequently the skin becomes lighter. The effect of this is to reflect the heat in much the same way as the white headcloth of an Arab.

This is only partially effective and most reptiles tend to hide from the sun when it is very hot and even burrow in the ground. In short they are better able to deal with cold than with excess heat, although they do need the average temperature of their surroundings to be fairly high in order to flourish.

Yet another important consequence for animal life of the change from a watery habitat to existence on land is that the body no longer has the support afforded by its buoyancy in water. For the animal to get about it needs limbs strong enough to support and move it.

Most reptiles, therefore, have four relatively powerful legs. (In the turtle these have become adapted for such purposes as swimming; in the snake, the legs have disappeared completely.) These limbs are paired, the forward set being connected to the bones of the pectoral girdle, the rear set to the pelvic girdle.

The legs are thought to be a development of the paired fins found in fish, and in bone structure they resemble the skeletal organization of the fins occurring in some extinct and some modern fish. In both, the fin or limb stems from one basal length of bone; there are two bones in the 'forearm', several smaller bones in the 'wrist', and the system ends with a fan of five articulated bones.

But perhaps the greatest factor in the freeing of reptiles, and thus all the higher vertebrates, from dependence on water as a habitat is to be found in birth and reproduction.

As we saw, the amphibian is forced to return to the water in order to produce its young. This is first and foremost because the infant needs water to support its life processes in both the egg and larval stages. Amphibian larvae are essentially fishlike; the tadpole, for example, has both fins for swimming and gills during its life up to the *metamorphosis* when it changes into the adult form.

On the other hand, reptiles have evolved an egg which can be laid and hatched out on land. There is no fishlike larval stage; the young emerge from the egg as small replicas of their parents. In some cases the egg is held inside the mother until it hatches, and the young therefore come into the world live.

The importance of the development of the land-adapted egg is to make it even more unnecessary for reptiles to live where there are large stretches of water, and it is no surprise that they have been able to colonize, at one time or another, most of the land surface of the Earth.

1 The Indian python is also to be found in the Malay Peninsula. The female coils around her eggs and acts as an incubator.

2 Hermann's tortoise is found almost exclusively on the northern coasts of the Mediterranean even though it is a land animal.

3 The common iguana is a vegetarian and lives in South America. The throat sac, or *dewlap*, distends when the animal is excited.

But what are the requirements for an egg which will be successful on dry land? The first quality needed is without doubt a shell, which at one and the same time must prevent desiccation and also hold the contents together. The egg must contain sufficient food and water for the embryo to go through all its stages of development right up to adult shape before leaving the shell. Finally, it must have some means of storing or disposing of the waste products of the developmental process in such a way as to protect the embryo from poisoning.

All of these requirements are met in the reptile egg, one of the most elegant examples of natural design, a design which the reptiles have passed on to some mammals and birds.

It works like this. The egg is provided with a hard shell – unlike that of the fish and amphibia – and it is made of rigid calcareous material which at one and the same time is rigid enough to support the contents and is also impermeable to water. It is not, however, impermeable to gases.

Within the shell the infant is usually cushioned by a layer of *albumen*, of which almost 90 per cent is water. Next comes the embryo itself with its attached sacs, each of which has an important duty to perform. The *yolk-sac* provides the developing reptile's food; the *amnion* sac contains the embryo's supply of water in which it is constantly bathed. It is from this sac that this kind of egg gets its name. – the *amniotic* egg.

Caring for the embryo

The *allantoic* sac deals with all the waste products of the embryo. First, it holds liquid waste in its interior, and secondly, since it is connected to the circulatory system of the embryo, it is able to carry the gaseous waste to the inner surface of the shell through which it passes to the outside world. By the same means the sac collects in its blood system the oxygen coming in through the shell and passes it back to the embryo. In this sense it is both a respiratory organ and a waste-disposal unit.

Finally, the *chorion* is the sac which surrounds both the *amnion* and the *allantois*. It assists the former in the job of providing the aquatic medium which is so necessary to the development of the embryonic reptile. Further, though the allantois and shell are separated by it, the chorion still allows the gaseous exchange to take place.

The amniotic egg is a complicated arrangement, but although it frees the

1 Lizards are preyed on by snakes, weasels – and human beings. If part of the tail is lost, it will grow again, but with uneven scales different from those of the original tail.
2 Tortoises lay their eggs in the ground. A 'nest' is excavated and the eggs placed in it. The mother then leaves the job of incubation to the warmth of the earth.

reptile from the need to breed in water, it has required one other adaptive change in these animals. The hard shell of the eggs makes it necessary for them to be fertilized before that shell is formed – while the egg is still within the mother. Most male reptiles, therefore, possess some type of intromittent organ, or penis, for the injection of the sperm.

The modifications so far discussed are backed by changes in the nervous and sensory systems. Such changes are necessary for the simple reason that without them the reptiles would be unable to make full use of the other faculties which make fully terrestrial life a possibility.

Crucial among these developments is the sense of hearing. In simple terms the reptilian ear, like that of other land vertebrates is made up of two parts: the sense organ itself and the means of transmission of the sound waves.

The device for performing the latter function is called the *tympanic membrane,* or *eardrum.* In many reptiles this membrane is visible on the side of the head. In others it lies protected in a pit.

What happens is this; the airborne sound waves beat upon the taut tympanum and are then transmitted across a cavity called the *middle ear* by a slender bone, the *ossicle.* Travelling along this the signals

finally reach the second part of the hearing mechanism, called the inner ear. This is where the actual hearing is done in the sense that the sound waves are turned into signals which impart information to the brain.

Again, the eye of the reptile is adapted to do the job of seeing out of water where the refractive index is different and for that reason exhibits significant differences from the eye of the fish. For example, the *cornea* in the fish eye is nothing more than a transparent window. It has no function in focusing the image on the retina. In the reptile the cornea has become curved and plays a considerable part in image formation.

As the reptile eye is now out of water for a good deal of the time its surface must be kept clean by some mechanism in the animal itself. The reptilian eye has therefore developed eyelids – usually three in all. The first two are an upper and a lower lid to each eye, of which the lower is the larger and more mobile. However, it is the third lid which is thought to do the cleaning. This is almost transparent and sweeps backwards from the inner corner of the eye across the surface of the cornea. In mammals this third eyelid has degenerated and exists only vestigially in the inner corner of each eye.

As a footnote, the colour of the reptilian eye is often bright red or yellow, and it has been shown that many of them have the ability to distinguish between colours, although, for some reason, this is thought not to apply to the crocodile.

One per cent brain

The move from water has also brought about the disappearance of the nervous systems associated with gill breathing and also that peculiar organ found in fish called the *lateral line system.* This is generally accepted to be a means by which fish receive information about changes of pressure in the water around them, and by which they may even locate objects in their path and maintain formation with other fish in their particular school. Clearly the terrestrial reptile has no further use for such mechanisms and consequently they have disappeared.

Although the brain shows some development in terms of size from that of amphibia and fish, it remains relatively small in comparison to that of mammals and in comparison to the reptile's own size. It is unlikely to amount to more than one per cent of the animal's body weight. Even in the mighty dinosaurs, some of which weighed as much as 20 tons, it is unlikely that the brain accounted for more than a few ounces and was probably only a few inches long.

All these adaptations have enabled the reptile to survive without dependence on an aquatic environment. Without ignoring the variations and peculiarities which characterize individual types within the reptile family, the physical attributes of this class of animals sets them apart from their antecedents to form perhaps the most important link in the evolutionary chain which has led to the higher vertebrate life on Earth today.

Reptiles 2 – The defeated conquerors

The kings of the Earth, the mighty dinosaurs, have long since faded into extinction. Only four of the original 16 orders have survived, but reptiles still inhabit most corners of the world.

A resting place for a large number of 'grinning' American alligators. The short, broad head distinguishes the family *Alligatoridae* from the slimmer and longer-headed crocodiles.

SAY 'PREHISTORIC ANIMALS' to the average person and they immediately think of the dinosaurs. Yet even then they are not usually thinking of dinosaurs in general but of the giant *Brontosaurus*, merely one of the group. There is little notion of the range and diversity of the reptiles which existed, or that the way the number of species have dwindled is one of the most dramatic happenings in natural history.

The Age of Reptiles – that is the period during which they dominated the land areas of the Earth – was in fact the whole of the Mesozoic era, which began about 205 million years ago, although reptiles did exist in some numbers before that. In fact, they began their climb from origins among the *labyrinthodont amphibians* much earlier in the Paleozoic era.

The dinosaurs were without doubt the most impressive of the reptiles in the Mesozoic era, but they were not only large like the brontosaurus.

The savage *Tyrannosaurus*, about 50 feet long, walked on its hind legs and was a meat eater. Its enormous and powerful head was equipped with sharp sabre-like teeth, but its tiny front legs were rather feeble in marked contrast to the rear ones. The *Stegosaurus* (the name refers to the armour plates which ran down its back and suggest roofing tiles) had only weak teeth and jaws and is considered therefore to have been a vegetarian. Also in con-

trast to the tyrannosaurus it walked on all fours. Some reptiles moved towards exploiting the air; these were the *Pterosaurs* or winged reptiles, which though they did not lead directly to birds as we know them, were certainly successful for a time.

That the pterosaurs could fly was due to the extraordinary development of their forelimbs. In the pterosaur the fourth finger of the forelimb became enormously extended, the fifth finger disappeared and an area of skin stretched from this extension to the sides of the body to form the wing. Some were no bigger than modern bats, although others boasted wing spans of up to 29 feet and were the biggest animals ever to fly.

Birds as we know them also emerged from a reptilian root, the *thecodonts*, which also produced the dinosaurs. In its early life this line progressed less quickly than that which produced the pterosaurs but ultimately it emerged superior.

But what brought about the end of the Age of Reptiles? Why were the number of reptilian species so reduced at the end of the Mesozoic era? At this distance of time it is of course extremely difficult to answer these questions, and many of the reasons given can be dismissed as fanciful. There was probably more than one causal factor.

First, it may be that the temperature of the Earth rose towards the close of the era and all reptiles found difficulty in dealing with increases in temperature. There is fossil evidence that plant life took on a sudden spurt in the later Mesozoic and this

Crocodiles lie submerged with only their eyes above the surface. They can eat in this position – folds of skin inside the mouth prevent them from gulping large quantities of water.

The Egyptian cobra, although smaller and less dangerous than his Indian brothers, is still a man-killer. These snakes kill by ejecting venom into their wounded prey.

1 Almost a 'living fossil', the Tuatara is the only survivor of a group of reptiles common during the Mesozoic era. Today it lives on a few islands near New Zealand and is protected.
2 Tiny hooks on the undersides of the gecko's toes enable the animal to run very fast and cling to almost any surface. The name is derived from the repetitive 'geck-o' call of some species.
3 The Gila Monster is one of only two known poisonous lizards. It lives on small birds, eggs and young mammals, but can fast for long periods after storing food in its tail.

could be accounted for in climatic terms (which would support the temperature-increase theory), but it might also be due to geological changes.

However, if the climate did fluctuate in this way, it may be that the reptiles perished simply because things got too hot for them. With the evaporation of the lakes the animals would be without facilities for hiding from the sun.

The problem of heat

It is likely that the larger reptiles disappeared leaving the relatively smaller forms of life, because the greater the surface area which the animal presents to the sun, the bigger are its problems in terms of resisting overheating. Many could not overcome this inability to deal effectively with temperature fluctuations outside the water.

Modern *Reptilia* are represented by four different orders. The three most common are the *Squamata* (lizards and snakes); the *Crocodilia* (crocodiles, caimans and alligators); the *Chelonia* (turtles and tortoises). The fourth order is the *Rhynchocephalia* and this has only one surviving species, the Tuatara which is found only on small islands of the North Island of New Zealand. Of the four orders, the Squamata is by far the largest. There are over 2,000 species of lizard and about 2,400 species of snake.

The typical lizard has an elongated body with two pairs of limbs terminating in five-toed feet. Some less typical kinds,

however, resemble snakes more closely in that they have no limbs at all, or at best merely rudimentary ones.

The difference between lizards and snakes lies firstly in the distribution of scales. The snake has transverse scales across its belly, while in the case of the lizard that area is covered like the rest of the body in small horny scales. Secondly there is the formation of the jaw. A snake is able to swallow meals much bigger in diameter than itself. This is because the jaws are cunningly articulated, the lower one being split into halves connected by rubbery tissue. The lizard has no such ability.

In one way, however, all lizards are snake-like. This lies in the way their bodies curve as they move across the ground, and is a function of the way the legs are constructed. Where legs do not exist, the lizard gets about in even more of a snake-like style.

Most of the sub-order live by hunting and are flesh eaters. Those that do eat vegetable matter are not strictly vegetarian.

The lizards have an interesting trick or two up their sleeves when it comes to survival. Some can go without water for extremely long periods, slaking their thirst by sucking the dew from stones. Some varieties are able to lose their tail when seized by another animal leaving the lizard to scamper off to safety, apparently unharmed. The reason for this is that such animals have a disc of gristle inserted into the middle of their tails, between two of the vertebrae. The muscles and veins in each part are so designed that they will easily break apart at this point and the damage is minimal. Later a new tail will grow, but it is unusual for it to reach the length of the original. Because of their survival equipment, lizards are to be found all over the world, except in polar regions. However, they flourish most happily along the equator and decrease in numbers progressively towards north or south.

The sub-order of lizard is itself divided into several families, and of these the *monitors* contain the largest types. The

A blue-throated tree agama. The *agamids*, similar to the iguanas, comprise 200 species of lizard found in warm parts of Asia, Africa, Australia and southern Europe.

greatest of all is the Komodo Dragon which can weigh up to 290 pounds and can be over ten feet in length. It was first discovered in 1910, and lives on Komodo Island, which is east of Java and a mere 18 miles long by 12 wide, and a few smaller islands nearby. In spite of their large size, they are capable of a good turn of speed. Usually they remain on land, but can swim, and they burrow a hole in the ground in which to rest at night.

The *Helodermatidae*, another family of lizards, boasts some formidable specimens

Although they have the longest snout of all crocodilians and grow up to 20 feet long, gharials are not dangerous to Man. They keep almost exclusively to their diet of fish.

of its own. These include the only two existing species of poisonous lizard. One at least, the Gila Monster, has a bite which can be fatal to Man and very soon dispatches small mammals. It is a sluggish animal which moves mostly by night, and grows to nearly two feet in length. When disturbed it hisses loudly and froths at the mouth.

Chameleons and geckoes make a pleasant change from the rather unattractive monsters already mentioned. In the former the body carries a sharp ridge down the back and is best known for its ability to change colour to harmonize with its surroundings. In a rage it turns deadly white. The gecko is very common around the Mediterranean and is most notable for its ability to run across the ceiling of a house with its 'hook-pad' feet.

The snake, the second sub-order of Squamata, is a beast for which Man seems to feel an innate repulsion, but only about

Chamaeleo bitaeniatus inhabits the mountains of eastern Africa. Chameleons possess a prehensile tail for climbing, a prehensile tongue for catching insects, and all-round vision.

250 species out of a total of some 2,400 are in fact poisonous to Man. All snakes have the jaw mechanism already mentioned which allows them to take in large quantities of food at one time. This in turn means that they eat at fairly widely spaced intervals.

The teeth of the snake are thin, pointed and tip backwards towards the throat. In the poisonous varieties the venom sac is situated in the upper jaw, and the associated teeth have either grooves running down the outside or a canal running

The leathery turtle is the largest marine turtle. A fully grown adult may be six feet long and weigh up to 1,000 pounds. A female returns to the water after laying her eggs.

through them to carry the poison to the bitten victim.

These creatures, of course, have no legs; however, they do have a great many ribs – commonly a pair to each of as many of 200 vertebrae. They use the tips of these ribs to get them about much as a millipede uses its vast number of limbs. Snakes slough (discard) their skins at regular intervals throughout their lives.

The boas and the pythons are non-poisonous snakes but are well known for the manner in which they kill their prey. Both grow to a considerable length and attack by striking at the victim with their jaws and then squeeze the life out of it. The largest boas are probably the South American anacondas, which have been recorded as growing to as much as 37 feet in length.

The major difference between the boas and pythons is that the former bears its young alive, while nearly all the latter lay eggs, The python, however, provides perhaps the most spectacular example of the snake's ability to eat animals much bigger than itself in girth. One nine-foot Reticulate Python (from South East Asia) was observed to swallow a monitor five feet long; another dealt with a deer weighing 123 pounds.

The crocodilians (crocodiles, alligators, caimans and gharials) are examples of

The European pond tortoise is a strict carnivore feeding on fish, frogs and insects. In autumn it hibernates by burrowing into the mud and remains there until the spring.

A mouse is swallowed whole by a boa. The flexible articulation of the jaws enables the snake to engorge prey of much greater diameter than itself.

reptiles which live most of their lives in water. However, they are fully equipped to move about on the land and commonly do so to find new stretches of water and to lay their eggs.

All species closely resemble one another. They have long heads with powerful jaws and tails for swimming. Their legs carry five toes on the front pair and four on the back and the toes are usually webbed.

Eating under water

The crocodilians are able to lie submerged and yet open their mouths to take in their prey. This is due to a physiological mechanism consisting of a fold in the tongue and a flap hanging from the roof of the mouth. When these are brought together they prevent the lungs and bodies from flooding even though the mouth is open. The largest of the group are probably the gharials (or gavials) of which there is only one species, found in the Ganges. It is characterized by a very long and slender nose which contains teeth finer than those of other crocodilians. Gharials have been known to grow to 21 feet but they do not attack Man.

The true crocodile has a shorter snout than the gharial and exists in most continents other than Europe. It is prepared to attack Man and even larger animals,

should they venture too close.

The alligators and caimans comprise a family of seven species of which all but one live in America. The odd one out is found in the lower reaches of the Yangtse-Kiang River, China, and has been studied relatively little. One peculiarity is that its toes on the forelimbs are not webbed. This may be due to the fact that it spends the winter in a hole which it digs in the mud – presumably any webbing on its front feet would become torn in that process.

The black caiman which is abundant along the Amazon departs from the usual method by which crocodilians get their meals. Instead of seizing the victim in its jaws and dragging it to the bottom, the black caiman stuns the fish or other animal with a swipe of its powerful tail. They have been known to leave the water during the night for hunting trips, killing sheep and small animals.

The Chelonia (tortoises and turtles) are particularly easy to distinguish from other forms of reptiles since they carry a *carapace* or shell which is usually hard but not necessarily so.

They all possess four limbs and breathe in the characteristic reptilian manner through systems of muscles forcing their lungs to contract. The aquatic turtles can take oxygen from the water and emit carbon dioxide through the skin.

Chelonians can live to 100 years old. They live in the tropics, although a few are found in temperate regions. They usually spend the winter in hibernation.

Finally, the Tuatara, which resemble lizards to the casual observer, exhibit internally a number of features which show them to be related to more extinct forms. It is mainly nocturnal in habit and moves about slowly feeding on worms, insects and frogs.

In all of this we can see the decline of a once dominant class of animals and some of the reasons for its decline. However, the modern forms which remain are well adapted to the lives which they lead, and it is likely that without some disastrous intervention by Man they will survive for millions of years to come.

Largest of the monitors is the Komodo Dragon, which can reach ten feet in length. It has an enormous appetite and eats small deer, wild pigs, carrion – and is also cannibalistic.

Birds 1-Feathers and flight

The combination of wings, beaks and feathers sets the birds apart from other animal classes. From reptilian beginnings each has adapted to its own environment — even reverting to flightlessness.

LIFE BEGAN in the oceans; after millions of years of development it progressed to the land and diversified slowly. At this point there only remained one area suitable for the support of animal life, the atmosphere. But progress from Nature's drawing-board to a living flying machine was slower and more complex than any process imaginable in terms of aeronautical engineering.

The birds, a branch of the vertebrates, have their origins among a group of reptiles called the *thecodonts* which were able to run about on their back limbs; the front limbs of one group of animals developed into wings.

Learning to fly

First to appear were the *pterosaurs* which were truly winged reptiles. Their wings were not as sound in aerodynamic terms as those of the true birds and were much more easily broken.

The structure of their legs from fossil evidence seems to suggest that they had difficulty in taking off from flat surfaces, and would in any circumstances have been ungainly on the ground. Though the largest animals ever to fly must be counted among the pterosaurs, they represented something of a blind alley in the progress towards unhindered flight, and died out with most of the other reptiles at the end of the Mesozoic era.

Perhaps the most important acquisition of the animals comprising the second line of development was the feather. It is widely accepted that feathers themselves evolved from reptilian scales, but the change could hardly have been more drastic. The only similarities are that they, like the reptilian scales, are made of *keratin* (a substance produced by the skin, also responsible for hair and horn), and that they both occur in a regularized pattern over the bird's body and wings. The modern bird, incidentally, has retained scales on its legs.

Unlike scales, feathers are enormously intricate in construction and it is worth looking at them in some detail. Each feather has a quill or main shaft from which extend some 600 hair-like barbs on either side. But the resemblance to hair is extremely superficial, for each of the 1,200 offshoots carries about 800 smaller ones, and each of these smaller offshoots carries as many as three dozen tiny hooks.

1 Flying birds have a relatively light skeletal frame with strong and well-developed wings (right). The hen (left) is an almost flightless bird with small wings and a bulky body.
2 White storks, once paired, remain together for life; they build their nests, frequently in exposed places, and return to them each year, gradually adding more and more material.

The whole of this complex is locked together by means of these hooks, and the marvellous interweave which results is so finely meshed that air can only just pass through. If you pick a feather from the ground and handle it roughly all the smoothing in the world will not return it to its original shape. To fit all those tiny hooks accurately together again is just not possible.

Of course in normal life the feathers of the bird do become spoiled. But they, in some unknown way, are able to re-engage the hooks by rubbing the feathers with their beaks. Eventually the feathers become irreparable and drop out during a period which occurs once or twice a year in most birds and is called the *moult*. Since the feather is so important to flight, birds tend to become less active during the moult, which lasts until the lost feathers are replaced by new ones.

Associated with the feathers are muscles which enable the bird to raise and lower them. They are, therefore, important for flight, but more relevantly at this point they also play a vital role in regulation of the bird's body heat.

Living cells are extremely vulnerable to damage by fluctuations in external temperature, so the body temperature must be kept fairly even. In the reptiles, including the extinct pterosaurs, the mechanism of heat control is not very effective; they rely on moving into shade when it is hot and the open when it is cool. Obviously then, outside factors can wreak havoc upon a reptile population; drought can wipe out suitable shade with the sudden destruction of vegetation.

By means of its feathers the bird is able to overcome this heat control problem. The feathers trap air beneath them and, as with the large-mesh string vests used by Arctic explorers, this layer of air becomes heated and proves an effective method of insulation from the cold.

But even so the usefulness of the feathers does not end here. They are vital to successful flight since the way they are distributed over the body and wings produces effective streamlining. The main supporting surfaces of the wings are comprised of long flight feathers. Banks and turns impossible for an aeroplane are open to the bird through movements of particular sections of the wing feathers.

Wind and weather proof

Feather colouring is important both for purposes of camouflage and mating. Feathers are also associated with both waterproofing and the sense of touch. Most birds have two oil-producing glands situated near the tail; the bird when preening presses its beak against the glands, whereby it receives a coating of oil which it then transfers to the feathers, so enhancing their ability to repel water. What is not clear is how other species – some parrots, for example – manage without oil glands at all. As to touch, nerve fibres around the base of each feather provide birds with extensive sensitive areas.

Even though the feathers are crucial to both flight and temperature control, they would have been of little use in the development of the modern bird without other extensive physiological changes from the reptilian pattern.

The wings, as in the pterosaurs, depend upon the adaptation of the bone structure of the reptilian forelimbs. The wing is supported first by the upper arm (the humerus), then by the forearm (the ulna). The 'wrists' are relatively simple and the skeletal system terminates in a much extended second finger. The supporting bones are hollow and reduced to a minimum while still retaining sufficient rigidity for action; lightness is absolutely vital. An indication of the kind of weight saving which is achieved is that the frigate or man o'war bird, although having a wingspan of more than seven feet, has a skeleton which weighs a mere four ounces.

Apart from the wings, the rest of the skeleton consists of light, hollow bones and is suitably adapted to the bird's natural element. The breastbone, or *sternum*, extends along the bottom of the animal's body – from the base of the neck to the tail – like a thick knife-blade. Strengthened also by ribs and backbone, it forms a massive and rigid anchor for the muscle system of the wings.

When not in the air, the bird is able to walk or hop about the ground. It can do so because of the formation and positioning of its leg bones. The legs are toward the front of the body which means the bird's

1 The most common owl in Britain, the tawny owl, has plumage consisting of fine feathers of varying colours which confuse its enemies.

2 In America the swallow is known as the barn swallow because of the bird's close association with Man and his environment. It often builds its nest in man-made nooks and crannies.

3 The strong, sharply curved beak of the peregrine falcon is well suited to the job of killing and dismembering its prey.

4 A coot's nest is built among the reeds, often floating on water. The six to nine eggs are brooded by each of the parents in turn.

5 The family *Paridae*, of which the long-tailed tit is a member, build intricate spherical nests of

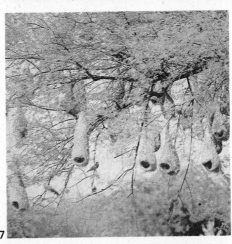

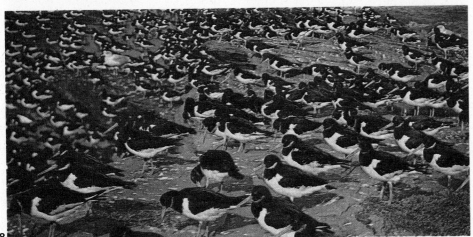

beak, or bill, which is essentially a tool for seizing and handling food. The neck normally carries many more vertebrae than are found in mammals, and consequently has considerable mobility. In fact, such power of movement is essential in conjunction with the bill for the gathering of food.

The bird's muscular system needs to be supported by an equally powerful and efficient system of circulation and respiration. The heart is divided into left and right sections, and relatively speaking is much larger than the heart of the mammals.

Blood, breathing and brain power

The right section pumps blood to the lungs where it takes up oxygen; the left side pumps the oxygenated blood at high pressure to the muscles of the body. The red blood cells – those which actually carry the oxygen – are capable of transporting large quantities of the gas which they are able to give up very quickly, thus keeping high the oxygen level of the tissues.

The lungs of the bird are relatively small, but that does not mean to say they are not highly efficient. The reason is that they are supported by thin-walled air sacs which help once again to lighten the body and even extend into the actual bones of the animal.

The intake of air is greatly increased in this way beyond the capability of the lungs themselves. On breathing out – expiration – it is thought that the air in the sacs passes through the lungs again where further gas exchange takes place within the circulatory system. It also makes sure that stale air is cleared fully from the lungs themselves.

The brain of the bird is well developed; it has very effective senses of hearing and eyesight. Birds react to other bird calls over fairly large distances. Likewise the excellent eyesight of this class of animals can be gauged from the way in which they are able to spot airborne predators, hawks and buzzards, when they are flying very high or a long way off.

On the other hand the sense of smell in birds is not so good. The sense of taste is good in some varieties; most will reject strongly salted food.

A bird's song is one of the greatest pleasures which animal life can give us. The voice-box of the bird is a complicated system of membranes and cartilaginous rings, and these are activated by the column of air drawn down the windpipe.

The sounds which a bird is able to emit are of the utmost importance to it. They enable the adult animals to warn of approaching enemies, to attract mates, and to let intruders know that they are entering a particular bird's territory; the young can keep in touch with their parents and show when they are hungry. The birds have inherited from their reptilian ancestors the kind of egg necessary for successful reproduction on dry land. First and foremost among the requirements is that such an egg should have a hard shell which is capable of holding the contents together. A natural consequence

moss and lichen. Through the round entrance a female feeds her young.
6 Puffins, once on the verge of extinction in Britain, are now protected birds. They are equally at home on land or in water, but are particularly good at swimming and diving for food.
7 Long, pendulous nests hanging in groups from a tree belong to weaver-birds. On closer inspection the intricately woven patterns become more apparent.
8 Oyster-catchers in profusion. Their long red bills are well designed for opening mussels, limpets and, occasionally, oysters. The female lays eggs in the smallest of hollows.

centre of gravity is situated over them; the thigh bones slant forwards and, in conjunction with the muscles of the legs, also help balancing. Thus a bird such as the flamingo is capable of standing easily on one leg, and even of going to sleep in that state.

Feet consist in most cases of four toes, three pointing forward and one back. This configuration makes it easier to move fast on foot and explains the advantage which the modern bird has over the extinct flying reptiles on the ground.

Apart from containing a relatively large brain, the bird's head is dominated by the

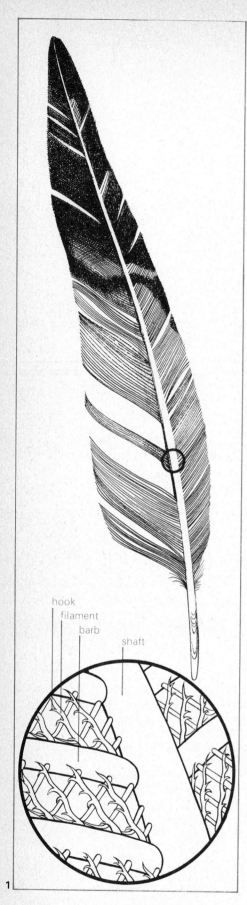

1 The microscope reveals that a feather is not merely a shaft with barbs extending from it. Filaments with minute hooks lock together to form an almost airtight mesh.

2 An outsized baby for this unfortunate hedge-sparrow. The cuckoo lays eggs in the nests of other birds; when the young bird is hatched it pushes out the rightful occupants and continues to be fed even when it grows larger than its 'foster-parents'.

3 Green woodpeckers cling to the tree with their claws and inspect the bark for insects with their long beak and tongue. Nests are built in a hollow tree-trunk.

4 A brooding red-legged partridge is disturbed in the long grass. These birds lay 10 to 16 eggs in a depression in the ground.

5 Found near lakes, the black and white Australian mudlark constructs its nest with mud reinforced with hair, feathers and grass.

hook
filament
barb
shaft

1

is that the egg must be fertilized by the male before it leaves the body of the female, and in some cases the male bird possesses a penis although more usually the sperm is transferred by external bodily contact. Hatching is sometimes aided by the parents sitting on the eggs; sometimes, as in the case of the cuckoo, by other parents. In warm climates, however, the mother may simply leave her eggs behind

and allow the sun and the warm earth to do the job.

Periods of incubation vary enormously. In some smaller birds it can be less than a fortnight; in the larger ones such as eagles and albatrosses it can range from two to three months. The variety of nests built for the eggs is enormous. Some merely use the ground, others build the classic cup shape of mud and interwoven grasses, and yet others rest their brood on nothing more substantial than a pile of twigs.

Clearly the animal which can fly has a number of advantages over his land- or water-locked compatriot. When danger threatens on the ground it can move at high speed to safety. If the right kind of food or vegetation is destroyed in an area, the bird can take to the wing and look for new pastures.

It is, therefore, something of a surprise that some species of bird are flightless, while retaining all or most of the other characteristics of the breed. It might be thought that these were types which had not progressed so far along the evolutionary road, but this is not so. In fact, they have degenerated from types which

could fly but have since lost the ability.

Why this should have happened is not known for sure, it is only possible to guess. For one thing it has been found that many flightless birds occur or have occurred on islands, and the likelihood is that they were not bothered by mammal predators. In New Zealand, where there are no native animals of this type, not only the kiwi but also the duck, owl and penguin are flightless.

Flightless and flying high

For the ostrich, a native of Africa, this theory does not hold true because the continent has perhaps more than its share of predatory mammals. In this case it has been suggested that the large size of the birds, and perhaps their fleetness of foot, has allowed them to live on without the ability to fly.

Whatever the reason for the flightlessness of these animals, they are mavericks or degenerates from the normal. Birds have achieved their extraordinarily wide distribution in the world because they are able to fly. They have conquered the skies in a way that Man, even in a modern aeroplane, can never hope to emulate.

Birds 2 - Soaring far and wide

Almost 9,000 species of bird live in the world today. Through their ability to fly, birds have inhabited almost every corner of the world — even to the edges of the great polar icecaps.

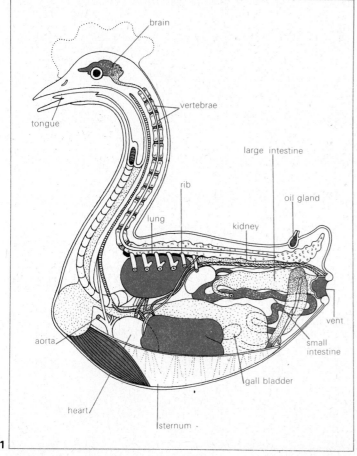

1

brain
vertebrae
tongue
large intestine
rib
oil gland
lung
kidney
vent
aorta
small intestine
heart
gall bladder
sternum

2

'FREE AS A BIRD.' How many times must these words have been used to describe a blithe and carefree state, shorn of all depressing restrictions? In one sense, the expression represents our wistful yearning to be able to get away from it all with as little trouble as these flying vertebrates apparently experience. It also reflects, by implication, the admiration which Man has felt from time unremembered, for the grace and efficiency with which the birds exploit the skies.

Nobody can forget the majesty and power in the wingbeat of a circling Golden eagle or a transitory swan. Smaller birds – in particular the tiny, colourful hummingbird – possess a manoeuvrability which is breathtaking.

The internal structure of the bird is designed for lightness. It has slender and hollow bones, and its lungs are supplemented by air sacs. Similarly its feathers, while important for maintaining body heat, are also light and effectively streamline the bird's body. But it is the wings which really do the job of raising the bird into the air and maintaining it there. They provide lift and propulsion unlike the wings of the aeroplane which provide only lift.

The important wing movement to gain altitude is the downstroke, for it is during

1 The internal structure of a male domestic fowl. Red jungle fowl from Asia were first domesticated about 5,000 years ago. Members of descendant species now outnumber the human race.
2 Dull brown in colour, the emu is the second largest living bird – but it cannot fly. It inhabits the Australian deserts. The male builds the nest, incubates and broods the chicks.

this movement that the under surface of the wing presses down upon the air beneath it. Naturally the air offers resistance to the wide-spread wing, and this levers the bird upwards in much the same way that oars propel a rowing boat.

The most important part of the wing in this context is the tip. Its vertical arc is greater than that of the rest of the wing and, like the blade of the oar, it produces the greatest amount of leverage.

It is important for propulsion. For forward flight, the leading edge of the wingtip is held slightly lower than the trailing one, which means that the tips not only press downwards against the resistance of the air, but backwards as well. The analogy with oars is even more fitting in this case.

When it comes to the upstroke of the wingbeat cycle, the front edge of the wing is raised relative to the trailing edge. As the bird is still moving forward by the

force of the previous downstroke, the air through which it is passing builds up against the underside of the wing. At the same time the wing assumes a delicate curve so that the flow of air across it is smooth and as little speed as possible is lost. This situation cannot last long. In most conditions the bird will be gradually descending and will continue to do so, unless it begins the wingbeat cycle again, with another downstroke. What is called level flight, is nothing of the sort when it comes to bird movement. In fact, the creatures progress in a series of arcs, though these may be so short that the flight path may appear level.

Soaring and gliding

There are important areas of flying which do not depend upon the flapping of the wings, but on spread enabling birds to soar and glide. When gliding the wing is held in the same configuration – that is, with the leading edge held higher than the trailing one - as in the upstroke of level flight mentioned above. But, since in this case there are no downstrokes to maintain height for the bird, it must sink, however gradually, even though it moves forward.

Soaring involves the use of the wings solely as sails. They perform a relatively passive role and are used merely to collect the pressure of air currents which are moving upwards from the surface of the Earth. The upcurrents consist, in one form, of air which is heated at ground level by various means – a town, for example, emits a good deal of heat – and consequently rises. These are called *thermals*. Upwelling occurs when a surface breeze rushing across the ground is deflected upwards by meeting a cliff or other obstruction. Either way, the birds are capable of employing these columns of air to carry them to great heights.

The formation of the wings of a bird clearly reflect the type of flying it does. Creatures like the buzzard and frigatebird have long and broad wings because they spend a great deal of time gliding or soaring. A long wing cannot be moved through its arc as quickly as a short wing with the same expenditure of power, so birds which depend for a living on very quick and agile movement – the sparrow hawk, for example – have wings which are short and broad. Because air will not flow smoothly over a very broad wing at speed, the fast flying birds tend to have narrow swept-back wings.

The highest flyers seem to be found in the region of the Himalayas; the alpine chough, a rather dull-looking black bird, has risen as high as Everest – about 29,000 feet. Other champions from the same area are the lammergeier, which has reached 25,000 feet, and the red billed chough and wall creeper which have attained 21,000 feet.

Fantastic claims have been made for the speeds which birds have achieved in the air. As much as 200 mph has been attributed to the brown-throated spine-tailed swift of Asia, but the observer was not equipped with reliable timing apparatus. In all such cases the claims emerging must be treated with caution. However, it has been proved conclusively that peregrine falcons have achieved as much as 180 mph when swooping on their prey, but here it might be said that they are falling rather than actually flying.

Humming-bird 'helicopter'

In level flight the racing-pigeon has reached a creditable speed of 94 mph. Other speedy birds are the loon (90 mph) and once again the high flying lammergeier (79·5 mph). Most birds, of course, never exceed 40 mph, but an interesting exception is the ruby-throated hummingbird, which can hover like a helicopter – maintaining its position with 55 wingbeats a second – and fly at 60 mph.

Some birds habitually cover enormous distances on their migratory flights, the journeys which are, it is thought, prompted by changing climatic conditions. 'One swallow does not make a summer', but when there are plenty of them around it usually means that the British summer is well under way. Few people realize, however, that these relatively tiny birds have flown all the way from Africa. The Manx shearwater has been known to travel 3,000 miles and the white-fronted goose commutes from Greenland to Ireland, a distance of some 2,000 miles across the choppy featureless surface of the Atlantic.

There is some evidence to suggest that birds navigate by the sun during the day and the stars at night, but exactly how the brain uses this positional information as a basis for action is not at all clear. At other times it is known that the creatures do depend upon visual clues from the ground below. They have been seen following the indentations and outcroppings of shore lines. No doubt they also find the meanderings of rivers valuable from a navigational point of view since these make strong visual patterns against the green, brown or other colour of the land.

There are about 8,600 living species of bird and there is no area of the world which does not support some avian life. Some areas, however, are more abundantly populated than others. The North Pole

1 To discover migration routes and other bird movements, ornithologists ring the legs of selected specimens – in this case it is the common black-backed gull.
2 The male whinchat calls for a mate after returning to England from winter migration. A female that likes the bush the male has chosen will nest with him beneath it.
3 Flamingoes in Europe and Africa live in large flocks in shallow water. They possess a beak for filtering food from the water and can stand for a long time on one leg.
4 The great crested grebe flies poorly and is unhappy on land. If the female is disturbed on her nest she covers her eggs and then dives into the water.

5 The delicate wings and fantail of the Chinese bluepie are beautifully depicted in *Birds of Asia* by the famous British ornithologist, John Gould.
6 Long-tailed macaws from Central and South America, the largest and most colourful parrots, are good 'speakers'. Note the nut-cracking beaks.
7 A circling vulture is the sign of impending doom. The king vulture from South America is a scavenger feeding on carrion. Its wing span can reach over six feet.

has been visited by at least four species of bird, but only skuas visit the South Pole. The Antarctic continent supports 16 species of bird, mostly along its shores and on its islands but also many miles inland.

Other poorly endowed areas are oceans, deserts, or systems of islands (archipelagos). Few birds inhabit islands because remoteness has made them difficult for the birds to reach from the larger land masses, and thus colonization has been restricted.

The number of species increases considerably in the temperate areas of the world – Great Britain and Ireland, for example, have about 450, Japan has 425. But the really big counts are reserved for the densely forested areas of the world like the Congo and the Amazon belt of South America. The country with the largest share of the world's bird life is Columbia, where a total of 1,700 bird species have been noted. In their splendid and comprehensive guide to ornithology, *The World of Birds,* James Fisher and Roger Tory Peterson call Columbia 'the heartland of ornithological variety on our planet'.

This distribution pattern has naturally required considerable special adaptations in the animals; it is instructive to look briefly at the subdivisions of the class from this point of view.

Some 600 living species are adapted for life on or in water. They include the beautiful and stately flamingoes. These birds stalk through the shallows of the warm African lakes repeatedly dipping their strongly curved bills into the water to feed. They suck the liquid into their beaks in a steady stream and eject it from the corners of their mouths. On its way it passes through a filter system which collects the food content. Similarly, the heron moves about in the shallows on its stilt-like legs, but is able to spear luckless fish and other small animals with rapier-like thrusts of its sharp beak. Webbed feet are another modification for life in water – to be seen commonly in the swans, geese and ducks.

Life without land

Most of the water birds of this type feed by poking their heads beneath the surface of the water; others bob right under or use their webbed feet for swimming beneath the surface. They may be carnivores or vegetarians; an interesting example of the former, and one which is specially adapted, is the oyster-catcher. Its bill is so constructed that it can be used like a powerful chisel to knock limpets and molluscs from the rocks.

Most of these birds confine themselves to fresh water but there are about 260 further species which have taken to life at sea. In some instances adaptation has gone so far that they drink only sea water and spend many years without touching down on dry land at all. An example of this is the albatross, but the majority, such as puffins and gulls, live at least part of their lives ashore. The cormorant is one of these but this bird has taken to the water with such relish that is uses its wings like giant fins to swim about beneath the surface in search of food. In the East, incidentally, these birds are used to catch fish for fishermen. The bird is attached to a thin line so that it can be recovered once it has dived; and it is prevented from eating its catch by a ring placed around its neck which stops it swallowing.

The birds of prey are divided into two groups: the day hunting types, or *Falconiformes;* and those that operate at night, the *Owls.* These predators generally have very powerful talons, with which to grab their prey, and sharply hooked beaks with which to tear it up if it cannot be eaten whole.

The daylight hunters are broad winged and soar to great heights, dropping like stones to take their victim on the ground, or in some cases, if it is a smaller bird, while still in flight. The daylight group includes eagles, ospreys and falcons, but there are others less well endowed with talons – vultures, buzzards and the like – which feed on dead meat, carrion. The group varies greatly in the size of individual species. Apart from the large ones already mentioned it also includes the tiny falconet, which employs all the fierce skills of its bigger cousins to seize and kill insects.

The owls dispose of their victims in the same way as the daytime predators, that is with beak and claw. But obviously they have eyesight which is adapted to seeing in the dark and their hearing is extremely acute, allowing them to assess the range and direction of sounds.

The most brightly coloured of all the birds are to be found in the equatorial forests, and a great many of these belong to the fruit and seed eating group. They exist in great numbers because the forests provide a never-ending supply of their dietary requirements. Seeds and nuts often have hard shells so the nut-cracking species, which include some parrots, have a strong beak with sharp edges to do the job. Much more remarkable are the birds which live, at least in part, on honey. Among these are the humming-birds, which carry out their feeding while still in flight; they push their beaks into the flower as they hover above it and suck out the honey. The sword-billed hummer is found in the Andes and has a five-inch bill which is longer than the rest of its body.

A further division in the family of birds is provided by the *omnivores* – those that will eat vegetable matter, insects and even small mammals. In Britain, for example, the skylark eats both insects and the seeds of weeds, a relatively sedate diet; but the scarlet-rumped tanager from Central America is much more adventurous. Its intake ranges from bananas, through spiders, to mice and eggs.

Birds which feed on insects also occur in great numbers. Many of them hunt on the wing and are capable of great speed and manoeuvrability. Among these are the swifts and swallows, both of which fly enormous distances back and forth over the same area during a day's feeding. Most birds give the wasp a wide berth when it comes to eating, but not so the shrike, which has learnt how to pluck the sting out of the insect before it is eaten. This is, of course, a behavioural adaptation rather than a physical one. Also of interest here, are those birds like the South American ant pipit and tanager, which follow the ant armies and feed on both the ants themselves and the other insects which the marching column disturbs.

Next, there are the *ratites,* or flightless birds, of which there are 46 living species. The ostrich, emu and kiwi are included in this group.

Birds for food

The game birds are much hunted by Man as a source of meat. They include the pheasant, partridge, grouse and quail, and the turkey. Some of these are able to fly efficiently but others are less well equipped for aerial manoeuvring. Most of them are very quick on their feet and often use this method combined with short flights to evade danger.

Other birds used for food were long ago domesticated by Man. Most of these have been bred specifically to provide meat and are ill-adapted for life in the wild.

The ability to fly has enabled birds to conquer both land and ocean throughout the world. They have adapted in many different ways to meet the challenges of colonization, but there are many qualities which even now we do not understand.

1 The northern gannet lives around the northern shores of the Atlantic. It hunts fish and is an excellent diver and flyer. Although nesting in colonies each pair has only one egg.

2 Reminiscent of a sentry dressed in the traditional uniform of some exotic state, the Californian tufted quail also keeps watch for enemies, its plume erect on the crown of its head.

1

2

Mammals 1 - The lower orders

From duck-billed platypus to Man, the variety in size and structure of the mammals is astounding. Even the egg-laying monotremes and pouched marsupials have the ability to suckle their young.

HUMAN BEINGS, together with most of their domestic animals, belong to the class of animals known as *Mammalia,* or mammals. Members of the group range in size from the gigantic blue whale, the largest animal ever known on Earth, weighing up to 120 tons, to the tiny tree shrews, not much more than an inch long and weighing about three grams. Mammals are found all over the world – polar bears and arctic foxes have been found close to the North Pole, while whales, seals and dolphins are adapted to life in the cold oceans. Generally regarded as the most advanced animals, mammals are *craniates;* that is, they have skulls and backbones, but differ from the amphibians, reptiles and birds, by possessing a larger brain, hairy skin and an ability to suckle their young. It is this last ability that gives the mammals their name (Latin, *mamma,* breast). Like the birds, mammals have a four-chambered heart – venous blood flows into the right side of the heart through the right atrium and ventricle and to the lungs. The blood then returns from the lungs bearing oxygen and is pumped to the tissues by the left ventricle. Apart from three species (the platypus and two ant-eaters) the mammals produce their young alive. All are warm-blooded, like the birds but unlike the reptiles, and have elaborate internal mechanisms for maintaining body temperature within a very narrow range.

Learning how to live

A large brain means that a much greater proportion of behaviour is learned than is the case with other animal types. In birds, for example, the brain is smaller and less developed than the typical mammalian brain. This restricts the bird very largely to instinctive behaviour. The young mammal requires a considerable period of protected life while its parents and other members of the species teach it to cope with enemies, to find food, to seek a mate. The role of instinct decreases in the higher mammals, playing a relatively minor part in Man.

Control of body temperature means that the body processes take place in a constant environment. The kidneys and lungs ensure that the acidity of the tissues is maintained within a narrow range; the kidneys are also responsible for conserving the salt content of the body. This temperature stability makes it possible for mammals to develop a more sophisticated biochemistry than is possible for lower animals.

As soon as they are born, the young are fed with milk manufactured inside the mother's body. This makes them to a large extent independent of the availability of food in the environment and they can rely

1 Domestic cats have litters of five or six kittens. They are fed from eight abdominal teats and at birth are blind and completely dependent on their mother for food and protection.

2 The common opossum is the United States' only marsupial. It has two litters of nine each year; the young stay in the pouch for three months, then travel on their mother's back.

on the mother to provide the essentials of life until they are able to feed themselves. This period of dependence is essential for animals that must be trained by their parents.

The four-chambered heart is an extremely efficient way of ensuring that the blood is washed completely free of carbon dioxide in the lungs, and that all the oxygen accumulated by the blood in passing through the lungs is made available in the tissues throughout the body.

More than 8,500 species of mammals are at present alive on the Earth. The history of mammals is unclear, but it is certain that they are descended from reptiles. One group of reptiles, the *Synapsida,* appeared on the Earth about 60 million years ago. They were heavy animals, some reaching the size of large dogs. These animals were abundant in the Permian period, about 30–40 million years ago. The bone structure of fossilized specimens shows that they were extremely similar to primitive mammals. It is difficult to be certain about the ancestry of the mammals because the only evidence of the early reptiles is in fossils. There is no way of knowing whether these animals suckled their young, had four-chambered hearts, were hairy or warm-blooded. However, the weight of evidence suggests that mammalian origins were among the Synapsida.

The difficulty of determining the early history of the mammals makes it difficult to classify modern mammals according to their evolutionary history, but zoologists are now generally agreed on the basic classification of the mammals. The living mammals can be divided into three sub-classes.

The sub-class *Prototheria*, which is now largely extinct, has three surviving species. All three are *monotremes*, and are extremely primitive. All are confined to Australia and New Guinea and are very different from the rest of the mammals. Although they have milk-glands, hair and a relatively large brain, they lay eggs. The platypus, commonly but inaccurately referred to as 'duck-billed', is the best known representative of this sub-class. It is confined to Australia, and lives in pools and streams. Although the platypus has some ability to control its body temperature, this ability is not well developed; its temperature often falls by as much as 15 °C. Its close relatives, the spiny anteaters or echidnas, are found in New Guinea and Australia. They live on ants, lay eggs like the platypus, and have no teeth; the upper part of the body is covered with stiff spines, and the skeleton, like that of the platypus, is very different from other living mammals. All three monotremes have probably been able to survive because they have few natural predators and are highly specialized for their particular habitats. The platypus was at one time hunted almost to extinction because of its fine fur, but it is now rigidly protected by the Australian government.

The sub-class *Allotheria* is now entirely extinct, but it is thought that this group of mammals evolved independently of the modern mammals. They existed for almost 70 million years, and fossil evidence shows that they were quite successful. Their ecological position may have been similar to modern rabbits.

Competition for space

The sub-class *Theria* contains three groups, one of which is totally extinct. The other two groups are the *marsupials* and the *placental* mammals. The latter contain the vast majority of mammalian species and are the most highly developed.

The marsupials are now confined largely to Australia and South America. They are basically similar to the placental mammals, but their young are born in a less developed condition and usually finish their development inside the mother's pouch. Some marsupials, however, do not possess a pouch; in others the development of the young before birth is very similar to reproduction in placental mammals.

The oldest fossil remains of marsupials have been found in Canada, but the animals were fairly common all over the world until about 15 million years ago. In the Old World they have been eliminated by competition with the more highly developed placental mammals; in Australia, however, marsupials had few competitors until the arrival of Europeans and they have developed a considerable variety of species. Although they have evolved separately from the mammals of Europe, Africa and Asia, the marsupials of Australia and New Guinea have in many cases developed species which have close counterparts in the Old World. This phenomenon, known as *convergence*, is a striking illustration of natural selection. Some marsupials came to fill the equivalent position of mice, cats and moles, and many remarkable resemblances between these animals and their marsupial counterparts can be found.

Even in Australia, isolated by the sea

1 The duck-billed platypus is an egg-laying mammal. It is about 20 inches long with webbed feet for swimming, a beak for grubbing for food but no pouch. The young are taken into a fold in the mother's skin where milk is discharged.
2 A New Forest pony suckles her young foal. The composition of milk varies from mammal to mammal — cow's milk is the most balanced.

1 The dark-grey fur seals are protected from the cold by a thick layer of fat. These aquatic mammals look after their young for four months — but many do not survive their first year.

2 On the alert for danger — a lioness and her cubs. Two or three cubs are born at a time and are weaned at six months. After five months they accompany the male on his hunting trips.

3 The dingoes are believed to be the descendants of domestic dogs brought to Australia in prehistoric times. Today they prey on sheep and in this case a not-so-agile wallaby.

4 The offspring of an opossum still in the pouch. They crawl there a short time after conception when only half an inch long and feed from internal nipples.

5 Like the platypus, the echidna or spiny anteater is an egg-laying monotreme. It has strong claws and a sensitive snout to search out termites and ants. When alarmed it can roll into a prickly ball or burrow into the ground. It lives in rocky areas of Australia and New Guinea.

accidentally displaced from the pouch.

The largest of the kangaroos is the great grey kangaroo which reaches a height of six feet; the smallest is the rat-kangaroo, about the size of a hare.

In the same general zoological grouping as the kangaroos are the Australian possums, the flying phalangers, the wombats and the koala bear. The large family of possums includes a number of tree-dwelling species. Some, such as the sugar glider, have long feathery tails and webs linking their front and hind limbs. They are able to glide from tree to tree. The possums were once extensively hunted for their beautiful fur, but are now protected and have become much more common.

The wombats, heavy and rather sluggish vegetarians, live in underground burrows and emerge at night to feed.

The koala bear, the original 'teddy bear', is a sluggish tree-living animal, and not a true bear at all. It will only eat the leaves of a few species of eucalyptus tree. It never drinks, but absorbs sufficient water from the leaves on which it feeds. It does, however, eat earth, presumably in order to obtain essential minerals. The pouch of the female koala is downward facing and the young are born only 34 days after conception. They have to make their way without assistance to the pouch; after eight months the baby emerges as an eight-inch youngster. For some time afterwards, the baby koala is carried around by the mother, on her back or in her arms.

'Playing possum'

The Tasmanian wolf is representative of a large group of flesh-eating marsupials found in Australia. Some of these are similar to the cat family, and include the so-called tiger-cat. These animals are easily able to hold their own against 'imported' cats and dogs, but are hunted down where possible because of their ferocious raids on poultry farms.

The South American marsupials are somewhat removed from the Australian species although both groups probably arise from a common stock. The American species have undergone a process of selection in competition with placental mammals. At one time there were marsupial 'bears', carnivores rather like the modern grizzly bear, but these were ousted by similar placental species. There are also fossil remains of a marsupial superficially similar to the sabre-toothed tiger.

The best known of the American marsupials are the opossums. They occur all over the American continent, live in trees and feed on insects. Some of the species of opossums in America have the remarkable habit, not shared with their Australian counterparts, of shamming dead when threatened. This is the origin of the expression 'playing possum'.

The survival of these animals that have not achieved the level of development of the true mammals is certainly due to geographical isolation in the case of Australia and New Guinea. In all probability South American varieties have not been extinguished because of the late arrival of true mammals to the continent.

1 The 'badger' of Australia is the common wombat. It is a nocturnal, herbivorous animal which digs burrows up to 100 feet long. The female raises one baby at a time.
2 The kangaroo licks her fur to aid the migration of her newly born young to the pouch. After two months it can leave the pouch to find food but returns at all other times for a period of up to a year. Only one offspring is born each year.
3 The Australian possums resemble dormice or squirrels and their habitat is the trees. This is the long-tailed Leadbeater possum.

from the rest of the world, the marsupials were not entirely left to themselves. Bats flew into the area, while rats and other rodents arrived, perhaps on pieces of drift-wood. These rats flourished and gave rise to a large number of native species. They probably eliminated some of the smaller marsupials by competing with them for food and living-space. Originally, there was a marsupial species similar to the wolf, but by the time Europeans arrived on the Australian mainland, the marsupial wolf was extinct, having been ousted entirely by the dog or dingo. In Tasmania, however, there were no dogs, and here the marsupial wolf still flourished at the time of the European colonization. The Tasmanian aboriginals themselves are now extinct, but a few of the marsupial wolves have survived.

Agile kangaroos

The best known of the marsupials are the Australian kangaroos and wallabies. These animals are adapted for swift travel over land. They are vegetarians, equipped with powerful hind legs with which they move in a series of long jumps. Most have large pouches, or marsupiums, in which the females carry their young after they are born. At birth the baby kangaroos are extremely small, in some cases not much bigger than a man's thumb-nail, and are almost incapable of any independent activity. The kangaroo assists them into the pouch by licking her fur in a broad band from her vagina to the pouch. The tiny babies then 'swim' up the bank of wet fur. They remain in the pouch for as much as a year feeding on milk from nipples inside the pouch. Once the tiny foetuses become attached to the nipples they swell, thus ensuring that the offspring do not become

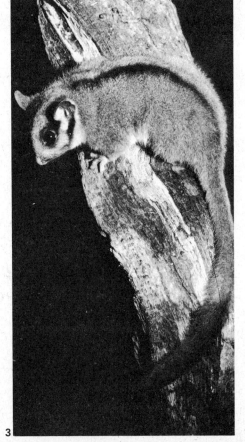

Mammals 2 - Man's closest relatives

At the summit of the animal kingdom are the true mammals. Their young are born in a more advanced condition than any other group — a common feature which classifies a wide variety of creatures.

THE PLACENTAL or true mammals form the largest and best developed group of Mammalia. They are generally regarded as the highest point of the evolutionary tree. Man is a placental mammal, as are the great apes, the whales, all the mammals of the Old World and most of the mammals found in the Americas.

This group of animals are called 'placental' because their young are carried in the mother's womb and born alive, the blood circulation of the unborn young being linked with the blood-stream of the mother by a complex of membranes. These membranes, bathed on one side by the mother's blood and on the other by the blood of the offspring, transmit substances required for the growth of the offspring, and carry away its waste products. This system of membranes is called a *placenta*.

Ancestors of the mammal

The early placental mammals appear from fossils to have been rather similar in appearance to today's shrews. Zoologists believe that these early mammals lived in trees, as indeed some of the shrews do today. For reasons that are not fully understood, the dinosaurs and large reptiles disappeared rather rapidly from the

1 Barely two inches long, the harvest mouse is an agile little mammal which uses its prehensile tail to perform fantastic balancing feats.
2 Deer have less developed hooves than other ruminants and are still four-toed. This red deer stag is 'in velvet' — growing new antlers.

Earth, while at the same time there was a rapid development of the mammals. They spread quickly across the surface of the Earth and diversified into a large number of species and types.

The early mammals probably lived largely on insects, as moles and ant-eaters do today. Modern mammals feed on an astonishing variety of foods: *carnivores* like dogs and cats eat the flesh of other animals; *herbivores* like cows and elephants eat grass, tree leaves, and other vegetable matter; *rodents* – rats, mice, squirrels – also live mainly on vegetable matter but obtain their food by gnawing rather than by chewing; *omnivores* such as Man will eat almost any food available. Of the aquatic mammals, seals eat fish, sea cows eat only sea plants, others like the whalebone whales, live on plankton.

Adapting to their needs carnivores have become well equipped for catching their prey with sharp claws, strong teeth for tearing flesh, and an ability to run faster than their prey. Most have developed good eyesight or sense of smell for tracking down the animals they wish to eat. Herbivores, on the other hand, often require special internal adaptations in order to digest their food. The four stomachs of the cow, for example, make it possible for it to digest cellulose, the main constituent of grass. Cellulose is normally indigestible for carnivores because they lack the necessary enzymes to break down this substance in their stomachs.

Escaping the killer

Other vegetarian animals are well adapted for flight from their predators. The gazelle, which is preyed upon by the lion and hyena, has long legs and quick reflexes to enable it to escape. Other herbivores, like the elephant and the hippopotamus, are large and powerful enough to deter any meat-eater.

The carnivores alive today are generally separated by zoologists into two main groups. One group contains cats and similar animals; the other, dogs, bears, weasels, and animals like them. The cats are extremely pure examples of carnivores; their teeth are adapted solely for tearing flesh and they have no equipment for chewing their food. This restricts them entirely to flesh, because flesh can be swallowed whole and digested, whereas vegetable matter cannot. Cats tend to be individualists, unlike dogs, and do not hunt in packs. They cannot run for long distances and catch their prey by stalking and springing on them. Lions and tigers are the best known big cats. Lions and tigers have been successfully interbred, notably at the Paris Zoo, producing 'tigons' with some characteristics of both. These artificial hybrids are, however, sterile. A mammal closely related to the cat is the hyena. This animal was once thought to be a scavenging species; but detailed studies of hyenas in African national parks have shown that these animals do not generally scavenge. They catch living prey, such as antelopes, by hunting them down.

Unlike the cats, the dogs, foxes and wolves have retained some chewing ability and have some molar teeth. They tend to hunt in packs and can run for long distances. Some of the wild forms found today, such as the Australian dingo, are probably descended from domesticated dogs that have reverted to the wild state. The bears are closely related to the dogs and are also capable of eating a mixed diet. The only purely carnivorous bear is the polar bear, which has little choice in an area where fish is the the only available food.

The marine carnivores are probably descended from land carnivores of the dog type. They include the seals, which live almost exclusively on fish, and the walrus, which uses its huge canine teeth or tusks to open the shellfish on which it feeds. In these animals, the legs have become adapted for swimming.

The most adaptable and successful of all mammals are not the carnivores, but the rodents, the gnawing mammals. Best known are the rats and mice, but the family also includes squirrels, porcupines, rabbits, chipmunks and guinea pigs.

1 Lemurs, or 'half-apes', are the most primitive primates. The ring-tailed lemur of Madagascar prefers thinly wooded country to thick forest.
2 The 'tiger' of South and Central America, the jaguar, hides during the day and hunts at night. This ferocious big cat can be a man-eater.

3 The 'white' rhinoceros is, in fact, a muddy grey in colour. Despite its four tons weight and menacing horns it is quite placid unless provoked.
4 The American black bear is a quiet animal, a good climber and is partial to fish. Protected in national parks, it is elsewhere hunted as a pest.

Rodents are found in every part of the world, and some live in close connection with Man. The rodents are almost entirely vegetarian. Characteristic of the group are prominent incisors or front teeth which grow at a rapid rate. If the animal for some reason ceases to gnaw for a period, the growth of the incisors tends to force the jaws apart and the animal may die.

Many rodents dig burrows in the ground; some, such as beavers and musk-rats, are partially water-dwelling. Others live in the trees, and while there are no flying rodents, some of the squirrels can glide long distances using webs of skin between their limbs and trunks. The extraordinary ability of rodents to adapt is shown by the rats. These animals were the only placental mammals to enter Australia unaided by Man, and have developed a number of forms well suited to their new environment.

The guinea pig and the porcupine are representatives of a group of rodents which penetrated into South America

when North America was a separate land mass. They include the largest living rodent, the capybara, or water-pig, which grows as large as a domestic pig. Hares and rabbits although successful are unlike the other rodents because they have four upper incisor teeth.

The *ungulates* contain the mammals which are most useful to Man. This is a large and diverse group of animals developed from different evolutionary lines. Almost all the large herbivorous mammals are ungulates: cows, horses, sheep, elephants, camels and other animals domesticated by human beings. The ungulates are not a single group and are classified together more for reasons of convenience than because all the animals are closely related. All, however, have certain similarities, which are chiefly related to their method of feeding.

5 Shrews are very small insectivores and have a three-hour cycle of sleeping and feeding. The common shrew, like other species, lives alone.

6 Common red foxes generally live in burrows, or earths. During daylight they lie low and at night hunt birds, rabbits, mice and moles.

5

4

6

The obvious similarities are in the teeth of the ungulates. Their food is generally grass or vegetable matter which must be thoroughly chewed before it enters the animal's stomach. This has given rise to molar (grinding) teeth of large size and surface area.

Swift-toed horse

The ungulates are usually highly mobile, either to escape from carnivores, or because they must traverse a wide area to find food. Many African species, the antelopes for example, may travel thousands of miles in the course of the year and migrate from winter feeding grounds to summer pastures. The horse is a typical example of an ungulate well adapted for rapid motion, but a fallen horse finds it difficult to rise. The horse's legs are typical of many fast-running ungulates; the first part of the limb is relatively short making it possible for the second, longer segment of the limb to move rapidly, giving a powerful muscular thrust to the drive of the leg. The third section of the horse's leg corresponds with the hand or foot in Man. In animals like the horse, the bones of the foot are lengthened and the animal really runs on its toes. The horny hooves are adaptations of the claws found in the early primitive mammals. Claws, where they do persist among the ungulates, are generally blunted and have the function of protecting the feet.

The horn is typical of the defence mechanisms developed by the ungulates against hostile predators. Another defence, developed, for example, in the pig family and by the elephants, is the elongated tusk. In reality this is a canine tooth, valuable as a weapon of defence or attack.

The ungulates are divided into odd-toed and even-toed; typical of the former is the horse. It runs on the middle toe, the other toes being reduced in size and no longer used in running. Three-toed horses are found in fossil remains, but today this type

1 The incisors of a beaver are used for gnawing; flaps of skin prevent wood chips from entering the mouth. Teeth grow quickly to compensate for wear.
2 At night, the Brazilian tapir feeds on leaves and fruit with the aid of its prehensile muzzle. It is an odd-toed ungulate having four toes on each front foot and three on the back.
3 Wild rabbits are smaller than hares; they live in large groups in complex warrens.

of foot is found only in the rhinoceros. The only truly wild horse now living is the rare Prezwalsky horse of the Mongolian steppes, although there are other species, like the native ponies of the British Isles, which have reverted to a semi-wild existence. The other major representative of the odd-toed ungulates is the tapir of Malaya. This animal retains a very primitive foot formation; four toes on the front feet and three on the hind feet.

The even-toed ungulates are represented by a much wider variety of living species than their odd-toed relatives. They include the diverse cattle family, with such wild species as the buffalo of North America. To these are related the deer and camel families and the giraffes. They form a large group of *ruminants,* pure vegetarians with a complex arrangement of stomachs for digesting grass and leaves. After being taken into the mouth, the food travels into one of the stomachs where it is partly digested and then regurgitated to the mouth to be chewed over again. The camels and their relatives the llamas are descended from North American species and there were native camels in the United States until quite recent times. The giraffe is another ruminant; the formation of its long neck does not involve the addition of any bones to the animal's skeleton. Almost all mammals have seven neck bones; the giraffe is no exception, its bones are just extremely long.

The elephants belong to another group of ungulates, or more properly sub-ungulates. Their group, the proboscidians, was originally widespread in the Northern hemisphere where mammoths were once

common animals. Well-preserved mammoths are found regularly in the frozen bogs of Siberia; it has been reported that the flesh is often still edible. The proboscidians also include another bizarre species of mammal – the dugong or seacow. These belong to the *sirenians,* so-called because the appearance of these vegetarian beasts off tropical coasts probably gave rise to legends about mermaids. Despite their specialized habits, the seacows are closely related to the elephants.

Whales are the largest group of aquatic mammals and the best adapted to life in water. They are able to withstand the major pressure changes involved in deep diving and are insulated against cold by a thick layer of fatty blubber. They are also streamlined for fast and efficient movement. Some of the whales appear to have a very high degree of intelligence, and species like the dolphin are friendly towards human beings, easily learn complicated 'tricks', and appear to have a well-developed method of communication.

Primates – born in the trees

The most intelligent of the land mammals are the primates, the group to which Man himself belongs. The lemurs, monkeys and apes are derived from tropical tree-living forms, and indeed most of the present-day primates still live in trees. They are omnivorous, eating both flesh and vegetation, although many species rely more or less exclusively on vegetable food. Their mode of life in the trees has given rise to a well-developed sense of sight, and the necessity for quick reactions and muscular coordination in order to swing around the forest has given rise to a highly developed brain. The lemurs are generally considered to be the most primitive of the primates. The monkeys are divided into Old and New World types. The New World monkeys are less advanced from an evolutionary point of view than the Old World monkeys and are chiefly distinguished from them by their flattened snouts. The Old World monkeys include the great apes and Man. The most developed of these are the gibbon, orang-utans, chimpanzees and gorillas. Of these, the last two have relatively large brains and a fair degree of intelligence. Both are large animals, and both have begun to move out of the trees and on to the ground.

But the highest form of primate, *Homo sapiens,* is another story altogether. . . .

Dead and dying species

The history of life on the Earth is punctuated with examples of animals which have become extinct. Extinction remains an imminent threat to many species which may need protection to survive.

'AS DEAD AS THE DODO!' What could be more final than that? Everyone knows that the dodo is an extinct animal, but very little is known about it and the other animals which have disappeared for ever from the face of the Earth. Certain species alive now are also in danger of extinction.

Animals are fitted to survive and prosper in a given set of natural circumstances. As long as these circumstances remain the same the success of the animal group continues. But if the situation changes, perhaps in only a very minor way, the animal comes under pressure from nature. It is then no longer the right kind of machine to deal with its environment.

Unless the animal can adapt to the new circumstances it will perish. Animal groups which are narrowly specialized – those which are designed to deal with one specific type of environment – are particularly prone to extinction.

The death of the dodo

The dodo is a dramatic example of this theory in practice. This strange bird, which was larger than a turkey, succumbed to the arrival in its environment of a larger and intelligent animal which preyed upon it mercilessly. That new animal was Man.

Until 1598, the dodo existed in considerable numbers on the island of Mauritius. Although it was flightless and therefore particularly vulnerable on the ground, it was able to exist simply because there was no animal large enough to attack it.

At the end of the sixteenth century the island was discovered by Van Neck, a Dutch admiral, and subsequently became a station for merchantmen bound for India and the East Indies. Apart from water and fruit, Mauritius also had a ready supply of meat – the dodo.

1 Cow and calf of the North American bison. Huge herds of these animals once covered the Great Plains but they were massacred for their meat and hides during the nineteenth century.
2 Orang-utans are shy retiring animals found in remote jungles of Borneo. They are threatened by the advance of civilization, and the Borneo government is trying to protect them.
3 The trumpeter swan, now rare and threatened with extinction, once ranged over a wide area of North America. It is now limited to a small part of the continent.

In 1644 the Dutch decided to colonize the island completely. The newcomers brought with them their own domestic animals. These included dogs and pigs, and together they finished the job of extermination which Man had begun.

Some dogs and pigs escaped from their owners and took to the forests, living wild. The dogs slaughtered the dodos, while the pigs ate their eggs.

In under 100 years, from the first discovery of the island by Europeans, the dodo had disappeared for ever. The only way that it could have escaped its fate was to have redeveloped the ability to fly; but the onslaught was too great and too fast.

Man has made considerable attacks on the animal kingdom, but they are nothing when compared to the changes wrought by non-human agencies through history.

The great age of extinction was the Cretaceous period, the latter part of the Mesozoic era, which ended about 63 million years ago. This saw the destruction of almost all the reptiles, which had been the dominant creatures of the Earth. The most likely reason for this 'great death' seems to be that climatic conditions gradually became unsuitable for these animals.

The only way that we can form any idea of the nature and variety of these creatures is from fossils left in the ground. Careful research in this direction has revealed an enormous amount of fascinating information about the reptiles, great and small, which trod the Earth, swam in the waters, and even flew in the sky.

The *Brontosaurus* is easily the best known of the extinct large reptiles. It lived its life in and around swamps in the Jurassic period (mid-Mesozoic) and it was easy meat for the carnivorous reptiles which also abounded. It had no body armour and its only defence was to take to the water.

It was extremely large, weighing as much as 5,000 lb and is known to have achieved some 65 ft in length. The *Diplodocus* resembled the Brontosaurus but was often much longer; the bones of the longest specimen found measured 97 ft in length. It fed on aquatic plants in the main, but also preyed on some of the smaller animals – molluscs and crustaceans.

Both of these reptiles moved on all fours. Not so the savage *Tyrannosaurus rex*. As much as 50 ft long, this terrifying beast stalked about on its highly developed back

legs and reached a height of 20 ft. Its front legs were comparatively puny, but it was able to dispatch its prey with powerful jaws equipped with a large number of sharp teeth. A specimen of its footprint was discovered in a coalmine. The foot was about 2 ft 6 in. long.

Long extinct

It was not only the reptiles which suffered extinction during prehistory. Many types of fish were able to adapt to the changing conditions – some developed so far that they were able to leave the water for short periods altogether. But many were unable to adapt.

One of them was the *Xiphactinus*. A fossil discovered in the chalk beds in western Kansas, U.S.A., is truly spectacular. It is 16 ft in length and thus is the largest fossil of a prehistoric bony fish yet discovered. The specimen has the fossilized skeleton of another fish still inside it.

Among the mammals, the list of departed species is great indeed. Mammoths, the contemporaries of early Man, were protected from the rigours of the Ice Age by thick coats which covered even their

1 *Tyrannosaurus rex,* a giant carnivorous dinosaur. Twenty feet high and 50 feet in length, *Tyrannosaurus* became extinct with other dinosaurs in the Cretaceous.
2 Reconstruction of a Siberian woolly mammoth. A contemporary of early Man, this sub-Arctic elephant is sometimes found buried intact in the frozen soil of Siberia.
3 Reconstruction, based on fossil evidence of a sabre-tooth tiger. The sabre-tooth may have

died out because its canine teeth grew longer as the species developed.
4 The extinct Irish elk is closely related to the American moose. The elk died out in Ireland only a few thousand years ago, and this illustration shows a reconstruction of its appearance.
5 Female of the giant Australian stick-insect. This remarkable insect grows to a length of ten inches, and feeds on desert plants. It is now rare and threatened with extinction.

1 Extinct fish found fossilized in Italy. The three large fish are *Myripistes* (sea-bottom fish) and the smaller fish are *Clupea* which are similar to present-day sardines.
2 The London Zoo's giant panda, Chi Chi. Attempts to mate Chi-Chi with Moscow Zoo's An-An focused attention on the rarity of the giant panda, found only in a small area of China.
3 Human hunting reduced the Hawaian or néné goose population to a low point of 30 in 1951; since then, breeding of specimens in captivity has raised the number of birds to 400.

trunk. They had comparatively small ears, but closely resembled the modern elephant.

Remains of mammoths have been discovered in Europe, Asia and North America, but the most spectacular finds have been uncovered in the harsh and frozen soil of Siberia. It is not uncommon to find complete skeletons and even bodies in this great natural deep-freeze.

Scientists are able to discover exactly what the mammoths lived on because the contents of the stomachs are often preserved. The animal had a thick layer of fat beneath its skin to supplement the protection afforded by its covering of hair, and a large hump of fat on its back that provided a store of food when the blanketing snow and ice made other food impossible to obtain.

Thanks to the fact that conditions in Siberia have remained so severe, the museum of the Academy of Science in Leningrad is able to boast of a unique specimen. This is nothing less than a *stuffed* mammoth. In fact, the body was discovered in 1907 on the banks of the River Berezovka and an expedition was specially mounted to save it from the depredations of the local population who could sell mammoth tusks at a great price.

It is possible also that Man, or his ancestors, shivered in the night at the roar of the great sabre-toothed cats. These are commonly called sabre-toothed tigers but in fact were not tigers at all, although they did stem from the same root as the modern cats.

The difference can be seen in the now extinct *Machairodus*. It lived in Europe and preyed upon antelopes, gazelles and ancestors of the horse. It was covered in fur and had a short tail; its paws were equipped with razor-like claws. But the most outstanding features of this creature were its teeth.

In the true cat (Felinae) the canines became smaller as the breed evolved, but in the sabre-toothed cats (Felidae) the very opposite happened. Among the last generations of *Machairodus* these teeth grew to 6 in. in length. When the mouth

closed they projected outside and when used for attack they naturally needed strong roots. The roots of each tooth continued right through the upper jaw to the lower rim of the eye socket.

It has been conjectured that the sabre-tooth cats became extinct because, though their teeth may have been excellent for making the kill, they rendered difficult the actual process of eating. But the real truth of the matter is lost in the past.

So far, all of the animals mentioned, with the exception of the dodo, have been extinct for thousands of years. But a number of other animals have become extinct more recently, and an alarming number are threatened with extinction right now.

Man, the greatest hazard

Today, the greatest hazard to wild life is Man himself. He has exterminated a great many species directly by hunting, and indirectly by industrialization, intensive agriculture and the introduction of particular species to areas of the world in which they were not previously found.

Hunting, for example, has put paid to the great auk, a flightless bird which was once found in the North Atlantic area. The major centre of population was a small group of islets off the coast of Iceland, and there, after the discovery of the birds in 1534, they were killed in great numbers. They were killed not for food, but for their feathers which were highly prized for decoration. Now every single bird of this type has gone.

Food requirements of native workers and the need for hides for various purposes led to the wholesale slaughter of the curiously named quagga in South Africa. Before the Boers arrived, these animals, which were actually a species of zebra, existed in herds numbering many thousands. They, too, are now extinct.

A dramatic example of the dangers inherent in the introduction of species to new areas arose in the late nineteenth century in Jamaica. The crops on the sugar-cane farms were seriously threatened by a plague of rats – themselves accidentally introduced – and somebody came up with the idea of decimating the rat population with mongooses. Consequently, large numbers were imported

1 The Tasmanian wolf or thylacine. This is the only existing photograph of this very rare marsupial carnivore. The thylacine is threatened by more efficient competitors.
2 Until the arrival of Europeans on the island of Mauritius, the dodo, a large flightless bird, was fairly common. Within 100 years of colonization by Man, it was extinct.

from breeders in London and released in Jamaica.

The experiment proved a total flop, for the London-born mongooses refused to attack the rats. So the next step was to import the animals from India.

The new variety spread like wildfire and the rats began to disappear. Such was the population pressure that the mongooses were forced to turn elsewhere for food and promptly wiped out a number of reptiles and birds. Now they are firmly established in Jamaica and are only controlled at considerable expense.

Threatened animals

The list of animals threatened by extinction at present is large, and makes sombre reading. Quite recently the Survival Service Commission of the International Union for Conservation of Nature and Natural Resources and the International Council for Bird Preservation published such a list; it contained 204 mammals and 312 birds.

Choosing almost at random, we find that these species include the mountain gorilla,

of which only a few thousand are left in the eastern Congo and Uganda, and the orang-utan, which exists only in some areas of Sumatra and Borneo.

No less than seven species of whale have been sadly depleted by hunters; the North Pacific right whale has almost reached vanishing point and only a few hundred blue whales still exist.

Although whale fishing is now closely controlled by international agreements, many leading zoologists feel that present protection is inadequate. Each country's whaling fleet is allowed a quota of whales, classified according to species, to limit the amount it can catch in any one season. But some species are now so diminished that the fleets can no longer catch their full quotas. The northern seas are now very depleted, and the advent of modern industrial whaling ships, which are more like floating factories than anything else, is opening up the Antarctic to the full effects of exploitation. Relatively little is known about the breeding habits of these mammals and some marine ecologists fear that the depletion of some species is already so far advanced as to set in motion an irreversible process of decline for the whole species.

From the very large underwater to the very large on land: the Ceylon elephant has been greatly reduced in numbers. It is now protected and the population, although small, is stable.

Breeding rare species

The importance of the breeding attempts made in London and Moscow with the giant pandas Chi-Chi and An-An can be readily understood when it is realized that the species is threatened with extinction. Population estimates are not available but there is little doubt that few remain in the high bamboo forests of central and western Szechuan, China.

Numbers of the Javan rhinoceros, which is a survivor from the Pleistocene era and the rarest large mammal in the world, had dwindled to the desperate level of 24 in 1964. And so the list continues – the African cheetah, the Manchurian tiger, some kinds of seals, and, of course, many species of birds. But why should we care about the disappearance of life forms from the planet Earth? This is perhaps best answered by quoting the words of Professor J.L. Cloudsley-Thompson, a distinguished zoologist. There are, he says, three reasons why Man should care about and therefore conserve wild life. 'The first is to provide material for research purposes, in particular with regard to ascertaining the economic potential of the land. The second is purely economic; because the natural fauna has been selected over such a long period that it is inevitably more productive than introduced, exotic forms. Finally, the conservation of variety is an insurance against ecological imbalance with the attendant risk of pestilence, plagues and soil erosion.'

To this one thing alone could be usefully added. That is the fact that the beauties of wild life can also provide us with great visual stimulation, and that in itself is an enriching experience.

Inside the breath of life

A fish gulps air at the pond surface. Man's breath on a frosty morning steams from moisture in the lungs. The dividing line between air and water dwellers is less sharp than it looks.

IN WINTER, worms are commonly seen on lawns and in gardens. But where do they go in summer? After a spell of hot, dry weather, they are extremely difficult to find because they are deep down in the soil where there is still plenty of water. Worms have to live in the damp because they breathe through their skin. Oxygen dissolves in the slimy moisture on the skin surface and diffuses into the worm's body. In this way, the worm uses its skin as a *respiratory membrane*.

A large land animal, however, could not possibly breathe through its skin. Its surface area is nowhere near large enough to absorb the amount of oxygen its body requires. Its skin would also need to be thin – and therefore practically defenceless – and it would have to stay moist the whole time. Evolution has solved the problem for large land animals: they have their breathing apparatus tucked away inside their bodies in the form of lungs. The skin is then free to play its protective role and it can stay dry. The development of an internal

Drawing in a deep breath, the goldfish pumps oxygen-rich water over its gills, *above*. The gills, which are basically not very different from lungs, contain a thin skin surface which is folded into filaments to save space in the animal's body. Blood, running close to the surface, picks up oxygen from the water, *right. Top*. The structure of the bronchial arches, which lie between the gill slits and which do the job of absorbing oxygen, is in the diagram, *bottom right*.

respiratory membrane is an evolutionary triumph. The only connection to the outside is through the windpipe, nose and mouth. This means that the wet lung surface can be made large enough to absorb sufficient oxygen for the animal's needs, without losing too much precious water vapour to the atmosphere.

Thin and delicate lung tissue forms countless folds and pockets which enormously increase its surface area. The tissue in a man's lungs, if spread out flat, would cover about a thousand square feet of area. Any land animal with an outer skin of that area would be at the mercy of

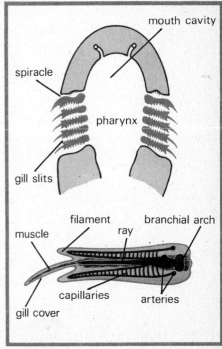

the environment. It would lose water at an alarming rate and soon be as dry as a crisp. So we can see that, for large land animals, an internal respiratory membrane is essential.

Apart from an efficient oxygen absorption mechanism, animals require other systems. The gills of a fish and the lungs of an animal occupy only a part of the body. There must also be a means of transporting oxygen from the gills and lungs to every other part of the body. Blood is the transport medium which does this. The blood circulates round a system of blood vessels (or blood spaces in molluscs and arthropods) under the pumping action of the heart.

Blood which arrives at a respiratory surface is poor in oxygen: it has recently returned from body cells which have taken up most of its supply. But the water on the outer surface of a lung or gill is rich in oxygen. If we plot a graph of the amounts of oxygen in the various cells, from those of the blood to those of the respiratory membrane, we get a sloped line which runs down from the higher 'gill' or 'lung end' towards the lower 'blood end' of the graph. We say, therefore, that there is a *gradient* of oxygen concentration. Oxygen diffuses from the oxygen-rich gill or lung through the thin membrane to the oxygen-poor blood, along the oxygen gradient.

Steepening the gradient

A respiratory surface becomes more and more efficient as the diffusion gradient across it becomes steeper. That is, the greater the difference in concentration of oxygen on one side of the membrane in comparison with the concentration of oxygen on the other side of the membrane, the more quickly and easily it can be made to flow to where it is needed. This, then, is another way of overcoming the problem of large size. First, an animal can evolve in such a way as to increase the area of a particular part of its body and make a respiratory surface of it. Second, it can evolve in such a way as to maintain a steep diffusion gradient across this surface. As we shall see, there are several ways of doing this.

In an animal, the blood is continuously moving past the respiratory surface. In other words, as the blood picks up oxygen, it moves away and makes room for blood poorer in oxygen. In just the same way, air or water moves continuously over the other side of the respiratory surface so that the steepest possible diffusion gradient is maintained across it. Blood is moved along by the action of the heart. Water or air is drawn over a membrane, usually by muscular actions known as respiratory movements.

In primitive molluscs, which use gills, the respiratory movement of water is maintained by the action of thousands of hair-like cilia. But more highly evolved molluscs, such as squids and octopuses, drive water over their gills by muscular respiratory movements.

Crustaceans such as crabs and lobsters use their legs to create water currents over their gills. Fishes use the muscles of their mouth and throat to pump water

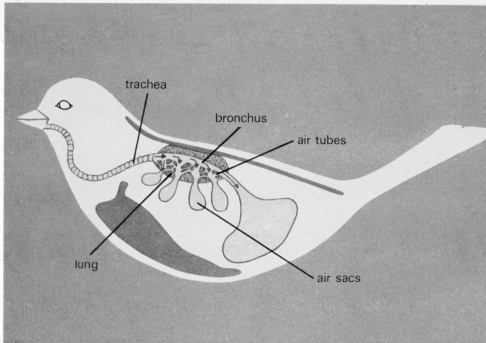

1

Birds, **1**, use energy at a faster rate than mammals, so their respiratory system gives their lungs two chances to take oxygen from the same air. As the bird breathes in, air passes over the lungs into air sacs. As it breathes out, the air sacs deflate, passing air over the lungs a second time. Man's inability to breathe water hampers his exploration of a major part of the Earth's surface, **2**. But the barrier between air- and water-breathing creatures is not so great as it might appear — even in air-breathing animals, oxygen dissolves in the water which forms the moisture of the lungs. In the human lung, **3**, muscular action pumps air in, while the heart pumps blood past the respiratory surface to collect the oxygen. Though aquatic animals, the playful dolphins, **4**, are mammals and must surface periodically to replenish their lungs with air, but the shark, **5**, is a fish and must pass large quantities of water over its gills to extract oxygen. The frog is equipped with lungs, but can breathe through its skin as well. A closed network of blood vessels just below the surface of the skin, **6**, gathers in the oxygen for transportation to other parts of the body.

4

over their gills and out through their gill slits. In bony fishes, the mouth pumps water into the gills, and the *operculum* (gill flap) sucks it out. Sharks and rays do not have the 'suction pump' part of this system, and some sharks have to swim all the time to pass enough water over their gills. If they stop swimming, they quickly suffocate.

Gills are generally on the outside of an animal's body, although they may be covered for protection. As a result, water is able to pass over them and between the many gill filaments. Lungs, on the other hand, are bags inside the body; to renew the air in them, they must be continually emptied and refilled. For instance, frogs and toads gulp down air and blow up their lungs like balloons.

Other backboned animals with lungs use a different system. By moving their ribs, they cause the space around the lungs to get larger and air is sucked in. More precisely, they lower the pressure around the lungs by increasing the volume of the

rib-cage, and the air pressure forces air down into the lungs through the windpipe.

Reptiles rely on movements of the ribs alone, but mammals have a *diaphragm* which converts the rib-cage into a closed chamber. Birds have a slightly different system. They have extra air sacs connected to the lungs. When a bird breathes in, air passes over the lungs and into the air sacs. When the bird breathes out, the same air is passed over the lungs a second time, giving two chances for the lungs to pick up oxygen. This system is more efficient than that of mammals, and means that birds can use energy at a faster rate than their earth-bound brethren. Indeed, if it were not for the extraordinarily efficient respiratory system, birds would be unable to muster enough energy to get off the ground.

If we compare this mechanism with that of the air-breathing spiders and land snails, we see that snails empty and refill their lungs just as higher animals do. But spiders do not. The oxygen merely dif-

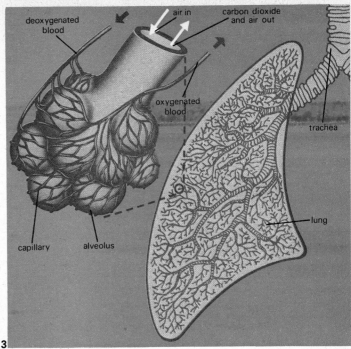

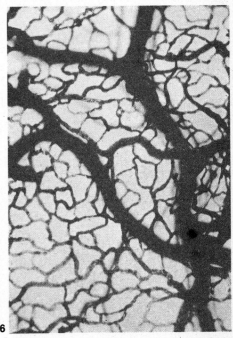

fuses through the book-lung. Fresh air enters as the air in the lung becomes depleted with oxygen.

We have seen how, in higher animals, an increased surface area is formed and a steep diffusion gradient is maintained across it. An efficient blood system is also developed, and blood has special properties which make it a very efficient carrier of oxygen.

The blood of most animals is coloured. This colour is due to a material in the blood which is used to carry oxygen. It is called a *respiratory pigment.* Actually, the colour is not important – it is just one of the properties of the compound concerned. Backboned animals, and some insects, have red blood with haemoglobin as the respiratory pigment. The blood of crustaceans and molluscs has a different pigment called haemocyanin, which is blue. Some worms have green blood pigment called chlorocruorin.

Although they have different colours and chemical structures, these respiratory pigments all serve the purpose of carrying oxygen. They combine chemically with any oxygen present near them at a high concentration, and the compound formed releases oxygen when its surroundings are low in oxygen. In practice, this means that oxygen is picked up in the lungs or gills, which are surrounded by a relatively high concentration of oxygen, and released in the tissues, which are poor in oxygen. The presence of a respiratory pigment means that blood carries much more oxygen than it could if the gas were merely dissolved in solution.

Oxygen is only one of the gases in air or water. Others include nitrogen, carbon dioxide and rare gases. Each gas exerts a pressure. The contribution to the total pressure made by each gas is known as its *partial pressure,* and the sum of the partial pressures of all the gases equals the total pressure of the air – the atmospheric pressure. The gas with the highest partial pressure is the one which is most abundant in the air.

Respiratory pigments pick up oxygen when the partial pressure of oxygen is high, and release it when the oxygen partial pressure is low. Each respiratory pigment works within its own particular range of oxygen partial pressures. These vary with the ways of life of the animals concerned and the different amounts of oxygen available in their environments.

Exertion requires oxygen

Respiration must be able to keep pace with the muscular exertions of an animal. The harder a muscle is working, the more energy it is using, and so the faster will its food be broken down by tissue respiration to release energy.

Tissue respiration needs a supply of oxygen and involves the production of carbon dioxide. As the oxygen content of the tissue is used up, more oxygen leaves the blood, and more must therefore be supplied by the respiratory surface.

There are many ways in which the need for this increased supply is met by the

71

When the bat, *left,* hibernates, his breathing and temperature drop to a minimum. The bird, *above,* has a different kind of problem. Feathers, unlike bat skin, retain heat. To prevent overheating, cooling air is diverted to spaces within the bones as the bird breathes.

body. The carbon dioxide produced by tissue respiration is carried in the blood, and certain areas of the blood vessels are sensitive to the amount of carbon dioxide in it. These areas 'inform' the brain of the concentration of carbon dioxide in the blood. As the concentration increases, the brain acts to boost the rate at which oxygen is made available in the tissues. For example, the rate of lung ventilation or the rate of flow of water over the gills can be increased to make more oxygen available at the respiratory surface. At the same time, the rate of the heart beat can be increased, and oxygen is moved more quickly around the body by the circulatory system. Also, the blood supply to areas of the body not actually being used can be reduced, making more of the oxygen-carrying mechanism available to the muscles and the brain.

The energy needed to make muscles contract comes from the breakdown of ATP to ADP. ATP is a high-energy compound important in all kinds of cell reactions which need a shot of energy to make them 'go'. But ATP is not the only energy-rich compound in muscles. An-

other one, called *creatine phosphate,* is present in much greater amounts. It is the muscle's store of energy. When muscles contract, they use up ATP. The ADP formed is quickly recharged to form ATP by transferring high-energy phosphate radicals from creatine phosphate (which ends up as creatine). As soon as the muscles relax, the creatine phosphate store is built up again from fresh ATP made by glycolysis and the Krebs cycle.

Anyone who has ever run long and hard knows the agony of muscle fatigue. As a person starts to run, the ATP in his muscles breaks down, and the muscles contract. The ADP is recharged to ATP from the reserves of creatine phosphate, and his muscles keep going. Eventually, however, the creatine phosphate runs out. The muscles must now draw their supply of ATP directly from tissue respiration. Most of this ATP comes from the Krebs cycle, and the Krebs cycle runs on oxygen. But the blood cannot supply oxygen fast enough to a muscle that is working at maximum capacity, and so the system begins to seize up.

Fortunately, the first part of tissue res-

piration – the conversion of glucose to pyruvic acid – can work without oxygen and, although not much ATP is made during these reactions, the muscles will continue to work. But the pyruvic acid is not allowed to accumulate; it is converted by muscle cells into lactic acid. If a person is courageous or desperate enough to keep running flat out, the lactic acid in his muscles piles up, the agony starts, and he stops!

Paying the 'oxygen debt'

The accumulated lactic acid must now be removed. Part of it is re-converted to pyruvic acid, which is shunted round the Krebs cycle to make ATP. This ATP is used to push the remainder of the lactic acid along the glycolysis pathway to glucose. ATP is also needed to recharge the creatine phosphate store. Manufacture of these large amounts of ATP requires oxygen, since it is made by means of the Krebs cycle. That is the reason why the person goes on panting for air a long time after he has staggered to a stop. He is repaying his 'oxygen debt'.

Although higher animals have developed very complicated methods of obtaining oxygen from their environment, their cells and tissues still respire in much the same way as does the most primitive protozoan. Although respiratory mechanisms may differ markedly from one organism to another, the basic need for oxygen has remained the same throughout the plant and animal kingdoms.

The beat of the blood

Animals emerged from the prehistoric oceans to conquer the land millions of years ago, but they never lost their need of a liquid environment. So they learned to carry it with them – as blood.

PLANTS AND ANIMALS need energy to maintain their life and growth. The chemical reactions involved in supplying this energy generally take place in solution, so that living cells which are not in direct contact with fluids, especially water, must be supplied by some mechanism of the body. In higher animals, particularly those which are not aquatic, this 'distribution system' can become quite complex, but the function is always the same, to supply the living cell with vitally needed materials to carry on life processes.

The simplest system is found in the single-celled protozoans. Their minute size gives them a very high surface area in proportion to their volume, which enables them to absorb oxygen from their watery surroundings by passive diffusion. Similarly, food and excretory products in solution can diffuse in and around the whole animal. It has been estimated that an animal of up to 1 millimetre in diameter can maintain a high metabolic rate by this method.

Blood carries fluid

But in larger animals, the ratio of surface area to volume is inadequate for passive diffusion, so they must either reduce their oxygen and food demands and become less active, as do sponges, or they must develop an efficient internal transport system. In more highly evolved animals, diffusion is replaced by convection and by a circulatory system. A *blood system* is developed, which aids the continuous and fairly rapid movement of fluids to all parts of the body.

The first rudiments of a circulatory system is found in a group of worms called the *nemertines.* Each of these worms has two vessels running along its length, with cross-connections joining the ends of the vessels. The main vessels have in their walls circular muscle fibres that can contract and expand and 'pump' fluids along the vessels. In nemertines, the system is probably used only for the transport of metabolic, cell-building substances, because it is located too deeply to be used for respiratory purposes.

The group *Annelida,* which includes the earthworm, the marine ragworm and many other related forms, shows several advances over the nemertines. They have a well-developed body cavity (*coelom*) and gut-like tissues (*mesoderm*). The circulatory or vascular system is derived from mesodermal tissue, and it is not surprising to find a circulatory system which has become associated with the uptake and transport of oxygen and carbon dioxide. In the earthworm, for instance, blood vessels lie just beneath the thin moist *epidermis* (outer skin), enabling gases to diffuse freely between the blood

Blood not only transports nourishment and waste products to and from body cells. In the case of the dragonfly, *top,* pressure created by blood is essential in freeing a new adult from its pupal shroud. Pressure then aids the insect to unfold its moist wings, *above,* for drying in the sun.

system and the body surface.

The circulatory system of the earthworm consists basically of a contractile vessel running dorsally (along the length of the animal's back) and acting as the main collecting vessel. In it the blood flows forwards, propelled by rhythmic *peristaltic* waves of muscle contractions. Blood is distributed via a non-contractile ventral vein in which the blood flows backwards. The anelid body is made up of a series of segments, in which blood flows from the ventral (lower) to the dorsal (upper) vessels through capillaries in the body wall.

Near the front end of the gut, dorsal and ventral vessels are directly connected by five pairs of muscular transverse vessels. Those act as hearts, pumping blood through the ventral vessel. Blood is prevented from flowing the wrong way by valves in the hearts and in the dorsal vessel. Transverse segmental vessels supply the segmentally arranged kidneys and the musculature of the body-wall with blood which is then returned to the dorsal vessel. This flow is reversed in segments 7 to 11, where blood flows down from the dorsal to the ventral vessel through the hearts. Blood supplies the head region and also flows back from the hearts to supply the transverse vessels. The gut is supplied by branches from the ventral vessel. In this way, absorbed food material is transported up to the dorsal vessel and then around the body.

The annelid circulatory system is known as a *closed blood system,* because the blood is always enclosed within definite walled vessels such as arteries, veins and the capillaries which join them. The blood flow in the invertebrates is generally forwards in the dorsal vessels and backwards in the ventral vessels; but in the vertebrates it is reversed, being forwards in the ventral vessels and backwards in the dorsal vessel.

Insects have hearts

A second type of circulation, found in many invertebrates, is called an *open blood system.* Here, the blood is pumped forwards in the dorsal vessel, which has a series of contractile hearts incorporated into it, and out into body cavities where it bathes the organs of the body. Blood returns to a large cavity (*sinus*) surrounding the dorsal vessel and is drawn into the hearts through paired lateral apertures called *ostia.* The open blood system is characteristic of arthropods, such as insects, spiders and crustaceans, and of molluscs, such as garden snails and marine shell-fish.

Insects are unusual in that their respiratory demands are met by a system of tubes which are ingrowths of the hard exoskeleton. These tubes carry oxygen directly into the tissues. As a result, the blood system plays little or no part in the transport of oxygen and carbon dioxide (except in a few aquatic forms). Insect blood is called *haemolymph* and is made up essentially of plasma and *haemocytes,* which are cells capable of *phagocytosis* (the ingesting of tissues and micro-organisms) and stabilizing the effect of chemical metabolites in the blood.

Insects also have accessory circulatory organs which meet special demands. For instance, organs which pulsate rhythmically are found at the bases of the antennae of certain butterflies and cockroaches.

The 'heart' is composed of from one to 13 serially repeated chambers in the dorsal vessel.

Other important functions of the blood of insects include transporting hormones (the chemical regulators of the body functions), maintaining the body fluids at a constant concentration, and assisting in egg laying and moulting. In the case of the last two, blood is used to create a pressure and is particularly important in enabling the insect to break out of its old cuticle at moulting and in expanding the wings after pupation. The blood also acts as a water storer.

Blood is essentially a suspension of cells in a liquid tissue called *plasma.* The plasma is predominantly water containing proteins, inorganic salts (mainly sodium chloride and sodium bicarbonate) and substances being transported from one part of the body to another. The proteins include albumen, globulin, prothrombin and fibrinogen. Each has a high molecular weight, and in mammalian blood in solution they exert a high osmotic pressure. The proteins provide an emergency supply of food, and help to give the blood its viscosity and facilitate blood clotting (particularly prothrombin and fibrinogen). They also prevent major changes in the level of acidity of the blood.

Glucose, some fats and amino acids are also carried in the blood. But unlike plasma proteins, they have relatively small molecular weights and can pass directly into the tissues and cells where they are used to provide energy and form structural proteins.

Waste products are found in the plasma during their passage from the cells to the excretory sites. Carbon dioxide is usually carried combined as sodium bicarbonate, nitrogenous wastes are found as either uric acid or urea, and some lactic acid may also be present. In addition to these substances, various amounts of hormones and enzymes are found in the plasma.

An important function of the blood is to transport oxygen to the tissues; but plasma can absorb only very small amounts of the gas. More oxygen can be carried when it is chemically combined with a *respiratory pigment.* Such pigments are found in most animals, and may be present in the blood plasma (as in many invertebrates), or in the red blood corpuscles (as in vertebrates). A respiratory pigment consists of a metallic ion (iron or copper), a porphyrin group (haem) and a protein group (globin). The best-known pigment is *haemoglobin,* which is found in the blood of vertebrates and some invertebrates. Other pigments found among the invertebrates include *haemocyanin, hae-*

The lowly earthworm (1), a member of the Annelida group, contains within it a circulatory system exhibiting most of the fundamental parts of more advanced designs. The cutaway diagram (2) reveals the dorsal and the ventral vessels, plus the five transverse blood-pumping vessels, or 'hearts'. Very much further along the scale of complexity and efficiency is the heart of a sheep (3), the four-chambered mammalian design. The two upper chambers, or auricles, receive the blood; while the two lower chambers, or ventricles, pump it throughout the body (4), carrying food and oxygen to the billions of living cells. The actual work is carried out in the countless networks of microscopic capillaries (5), sometimes so small that the blood cells have to queue up in order to reach their destination. 1

2
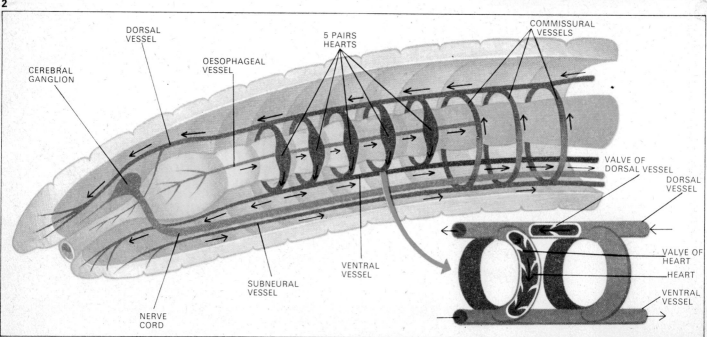

CEREBRAL GANGLION

DORSAL VESSEL

OESOPHAGEAL VESSEL

5 PAIRS HEARTS

COMMISSURAL VESSELS

VALVE OF DORSAL VESSEL

DORSAL VESSEL

VALVE OF HEART

HEART

VENTRAL VESSEL

NERVE CORD

SUBNEURAL VESSEL

VENTRAL VESSEL

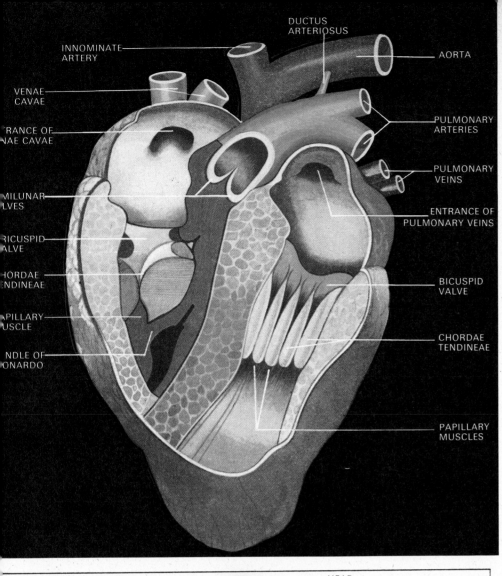

INNOMINATE ARTERY

DUCTUS ARTERIOSUS

AORTA

VENAE CAVAE

PULMONARY ARTERIES

RANCE OF NAE CAVAE

PULMONARY VEINS

MILUNAR LVES

ENTRANCE OF PULMONARY VEINS

RICUSPID ALVE

BICUSPID VALVE

HORDAE ENDINEAE

PILLARY USCLE

CHORDAE TENDINEAE

NDLE OF ONARDO

PAPILLARY MUSCLES

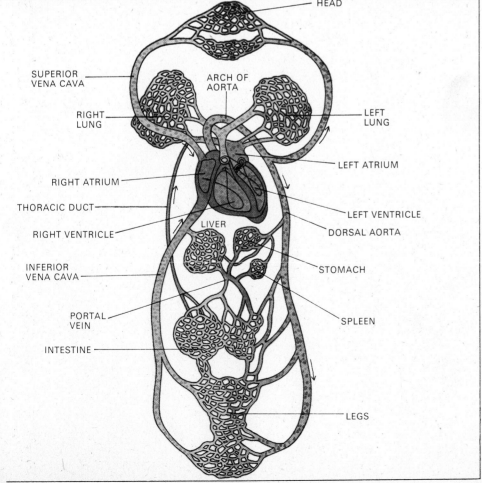

HEAD

SUPERIOR VENA CAVA

ARCH OF AORTA

RIGHT LUNG

LEFT LUNG

RIGHT ATRIUM

LEFT ATRIUM

THORACIC DUCT

RIGHT VENTRICLE

LEFT VENTRICLE

DORSAL AORTA

LIVER

INFERIOR VENA CAVA

STOMACH

PORTAL VEIN

SPLEEN

INTESTINE

LEGS

5

merythrin and the green *chlorocruorin*.

An important advance shown in vertebrate circulatory systems is the development of a chambered heart. In its most primitive form, it consists of four successive chambers. Starting from the back, these are called *sinus venosus, atrium, ventricle* and *conus arteriosus*. Contraction of the primitive heart begins in the sinus venosus and spreads forward towards the conus arteriosus. The musculature of the sinus acts as a 'pacemaker' for the rest of the heart. The arrangement becomes slightly more sophisticated in higher vertebrates but the basic pattern remains the same. In advanced vertebrates, only the atrium and ventricle retain their identity and these are subdivided to give the four-chambered heart. The heart lies ventral to the gut and remains 'free' in the body cavity, attached only at the points where blood vessels enter or leave it. This enables it to constrict and relax – that is to beat – without hindrance.

The heart's own blood supply

In all higher animals, the heart is surrounded by a *pericardial membrane*. The heart 'wall' has three layers; the predominant one consists of connective tissue and muscle and is called the *myocardium*. A series of powerful valves prevent backflow, and in advanced vertebrates these may be furnished with tendons and muscles. The heart receives its own blood supply from the coronary artery. Fibres of the autonomic nervous system modify the heart rate, but heart muscle is able to beat without stimulation for a considerable time even after removal from the body.

In the embryonic development of lower vertebrates, the heart curls to form a compact S-shaped structure. Blood enters and leaves the ventricle on the dorsal plane, enabling it freely to perform vigorous contractions. In the primitive gill-breathing vertebrates, all blood leaving the heart flows forwards in the ventral vessel or *ventral aorta*. This vessel has paired branches which arch upwards towards the gill-slits where they break

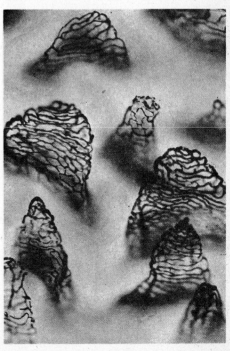

into capillaries at the sites of oxygen uptake. The capillaries then come together to form arteries near the animal's back, which run into the *dorsal aorta* and from there to the various tissues of the body. The paired vessels which supply and drain the gills are called aortic arches. There are generally five gill-slits and a spiracle, giving a total of six pairs of aortic arches.

The arterial arches of all other vertebrates are based on this six-fold pattern, although the development of lungs causes fusion, loss and specialization of the vessels, and the basic arrangement becomes heavily disguised. For instance, in adult mammals only three pairs of arches are found, one of them forming the pulmonary supply to the lungs.

Let us consider now the changes in the vertebrate circulatory system which enabled this group of animals successfully to conquer the land.

In fish, the heart is essentially a muscular tube pumping blood forwards, into the aortic arches, through the gill capillaries, and round the body. This process involves the blood passing through at least two sets of capillaries before returning to the heart, and requires a considerable pressure.

Circulatory systems

To add to the problem, nearly all fishes have portal blood systems (a portal vessel is one which has capillary systems at both ends). The *hepatic portal* vessel carries blood directly from the gut to the liver, and the *renal portal* vessel runs from the tail and hind limbs to the kidney. These systems put an even greater demand on the blood pressure. In fish, blood passes through the heart only once during one circulation around the body; this condition is known as a *single circulatory system*.

With the evolution of lungs in the amphibians and the loss of paired gill-slits, a more efficient circulatory system developed. The lungs are provided with a separate circulatory route, so that after the blood has been oxygenated in the lung capillaries it is returned to the heart before being pumped round the remaining tissues. This reduces the number of capillaries through which the blood must flow. The renal portal system is retained, and the ventricle remains undivided so that oxygenated and deoxygenated blood is mixed. In reptiles, the renal portal system is reduced and the ventricle becomes at least partially divided.

Birds require a very quick and efficient method of oxygen transport to meet the high demand of their very active flight mechanisms. To fulfil this need, the heart is relatively large and beats considerably faster than that of most mammals. The blood contains an increased number of red blood corpuscles to enable more oxygen to be absorbed, and the arteries supplying the flight muscles are greatly enlarged.

But the highest circulatory efficiency is found in mammals. The mammalian circulation has no renal portal system and the ventricle becomes completely divided into two. This results in the typical four-chambered heart with which we are

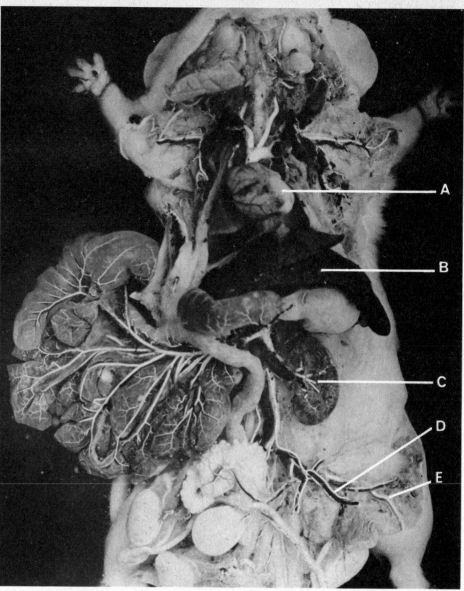

In mammals, such as this mouse, the circulatory system is differentiated into several distinct organs. The heart (A) is of course the pump, the veins (D) and arteries (E) are the transport tubes. The liver (B) and kidneys (C) act to filter waste products carried in the blood.

familiar, composed of left atrium, right atrium, left ventricle, and right ventricle.

The mammalian circulation, of course, shows slight variations to meet the needs of animals as varied as mice, bats, horses, whales, monkeys and men. But the fundamental arrangement remains the same. Basically there are two pumps at work (the right-hand side of the heart and the left-hand side) and two sets of vessels in series (the systemic and pulmonary circulations). The systemic circulation supplies the body muscles and organs, and the pulmonary supplies the lungs.

Blood enters the right atrium in two large collecting veins, the *superior vena cava* from the head and neck region and the *inferior vena cava* from the trunk and limbs. The auricle contracts and blood is forced through into the right ventricle (back-flow is prevented by valves and the closing of the openings of the collecting vessels). The blood is then pumped by the right ventricle into the pulmonary artery to the lungs, where it is oxygenated and then returned to the left auricle via the pulmonary veins. From the left auricle blood is pumped into the left ventricle, which is more muscular than any of the

other chambers. From there it is pumped out into the aorta. The aorta divides, carrying blood forwards in the carotid artery to supply the head and neck region and backwards in the dorsal aorta to the remainder of the body. The arteries of the systemic system therefore supply the head, trunk, limbs and main organs (except lungs). The pulmonary artery contains deoxygenated blood, and the pulmonary vein contains oxygenated blood. This is the opposite of the condition of blood circulating in the systemic vessels.

The connection between an artery and a vein is a system of capillaries. These carry gases, food materials and wastes between the blood and tissues. A vessel which has a system of capillaries at both ends is called a portal vein, for example the vein that carries blood rich in absorbed food materials from the intestine to the liver is called the hepatic portal vein.

The evolution of an efficient and well-developed vascular system has enabled animals to reach considerable sizes and to maintain a high rate of activity. It has overcome many of the limitations imposed on animals that rely on diffusion or on only a poorly developed transport system.

Network of the nerves

Most animals are made up of millions upon millions of different cells, all of which must work together to maintain life. The nervous system co-ordinates and controls this vital activity.

WHEN WE sit on a pin, our reaction is immediate – we leap up. We do not consciously think: 'I have a pain; I must have sat on something; I must get up.' The reaction is completely automatic.

Such automatic responses are common to all animals, from the highest to the lowest. If a simple amoeba is pricked, it automatically shies away; if a torch is shone on an earthworm at night, it automatically dives back into its hole. What sets Man and other higher animals apart from amoeba and worm is the complex bodily organization required to control their responses. This complex organization is known as the nervous system, and its primary function is communication – receiving messages from one part of the body and sending messages to another part.

Like all vertebrates, Man has a tube of nervous tissue running the length of his body. This tube, called the spinal cord, is responsible for the co-ordination of nerve actions. The brain has evolved from the specialized front end of the spinal cord and constitutes a central control system. But such a system exists in relatively few animals.

Bypassing the brain

The spinal cord and the brain together make up the central nervous system (CNS, for short). All sensory nerve fibres (which detect stimuli) run *to* the CNS, whereas all effector nerve fibres (which cause muscular actions) run *from* it. In most animals, the links between the sensory nerve fibres and the effector (motor) fibres occur inside the CNS, either in the brain or in the spinal cord.

A *reflex* is a nervous response that does not require a brain, or bypasses the brain. A familiar reflex reaction is used by doctors to test the functioning of part of the nervous system in humans. This is the knee-jerk reflex in which the lower leg jumps forward and the leg straightens in response to a blow just below the knee-cap. There is a straightforward communication link between the stretch receptors in the ligament below the knee-cap and the muscle above the knee-cap which pulls on this ligament.

How does this reflex work? In the very short space of time between the tap and the jerk, a 'message' in the form of an electrical impulse passes up a nerve from the knee to the base of the spine and back down again – a distance of about three feet – causing the knee to jerk.

Such a simple type of reflex is called a

spinal reflex. It involves at least three nerve fibres: one *to* the CNS, one *from* the CNS, and one connecting these two *within* the CNS. It is the range and complexity of the connections between the incoming and outgoing signals which determines the number of responses possible for a given stimulation – the bigger the telephone exchange the greater the number of calls it can handle.

In lower animals with a simple nervous system, it is possible to understand much of behaviour in terms of nervous connections. For example, sea-anemones are simple animals which have no central nervous system. Instead they have nerve cells which connect with one another to form a simple intermeshing *nerve-net*. These cells conduct in all directions, so that stimulation of the animal's body in any one place causes muscular contractions to spread outwards in a circle from the point of stimulation, rather like the way ripples spread out from a stone dropped into a pool. With no central system, these animals have an extremely simple direct form of behaviour, and different parts of their bodies can react to different stimuli at the same time. Even so, conduction along the nerve-net is

faster in some directions than in others.

Slightly more complex animals, such as the annelid worms, have longitudinal nervous systems. As a result, the nerves from the various segments are co-ordinated to a certain extent but the 'brain' is poorly developed, with little overall control.

In higher animals, the nervous system has evolved into something more than merely simple point-to-point communication links. It has become a network complete with complex exchanges and switchboards capable of controlling their own operation. In Man, where the whole of the part of the brain called the cerebral cortex may be involved, the connecting pathways between incoming and outgoing systems become incredibly complex. We experience the millions of correlation processes as memory and insight.

A nerve consists of a bundle of fibres. The fibres are made up of nerve cells or *neurones*. Long thin branches called *processes* radiate from the main cell body. A neurone can therefore be thought of as a special type of cell which in some way can conduct a 'message' from one side to the other.

The 'message' actually takes the form of an electric current. The conduction of a

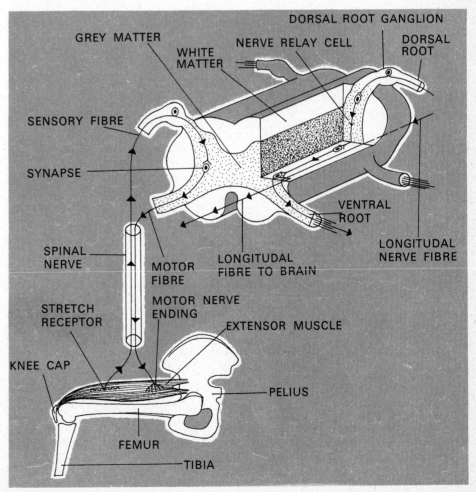

Even in higher animals, many body actions are not controlled by conscious thought. In a reflex arc, a message is sent through a sensory neuron to the spinal cord and out to a muscle through a motor neuron, bypassing the brain.

'message' is brought about by a brief change in the electric potential of the neurone, when a positively charged electric pulse passes along it. The change in potential is caused by a brief influx of positive sodium ions (Na^+), which are normally kept out of the cell by the continuous osmotic activity of the cytoplasmic 'pump'. The stimulation of the neurone causes its membrane to become permeable to sodium ions, the electric potential changes, and the next neurone along the fibre is stimulated. The actual value of electric potential involved is about 100 thousandths of a volt (written as +100 millivolts).

Because the energy used to transmit the electric pulse is contained within the relaxed nerve, it is called the *resting potential*. An impulse travels from one side of a neurone to the other without losing any of its strength. The nerve can transmit only one sort of information – a brief pulse of positive charge. There can be no variation or gradation in the size of the charge or in the duration of the pulse, although of course a rapid or a slow series of pulses may be transmitted (up to 500 impulses a second are possible). In other words, all nervous impulses are of exactly the same type whether they originate from the eye, the ear, or the skin where we sit on a pin.

Most nerves conduct in only one direction, although some can conduct both ways. When an impulse reaches the end of a neurone, the 'message' is passed across a space to the receptive end of the next neurone. This space is known as a *synaptic space* and the junction between neurones is a *synapse*.

Transmission of the message across a synapse is thought to be a chemical and not an electrical phenomenon. The arrival of a nerve impulse causes the ends of the nerve fibre to produce a chemical called acetyl-choline. This substance diffuses across the synaptic spaces and either excites or inhibits the receptive ends of adjacent neurones. Many nerve cells have thousands of synapses reaching them and branching out from them. Since thousands of such cells may be interconnected, giving millions of possible pathways, the complexity becomes very great. And by varying the proportion of stimulating and

Below, owls fly and hunt at night, so they have a keenly developed sense of sight. In general, the higher an animal on the evolutionary scale, the more specialized are its nervous responses.

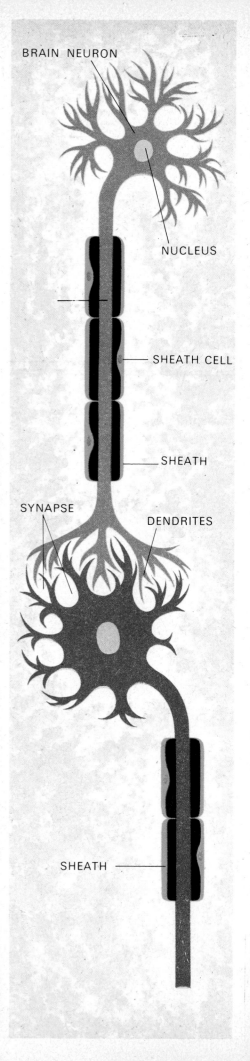

BRAIN NEURON

NUCLEUS

SHEATH CELL

SHEATH

SYNAPSE

DENDRITES

SHEATH

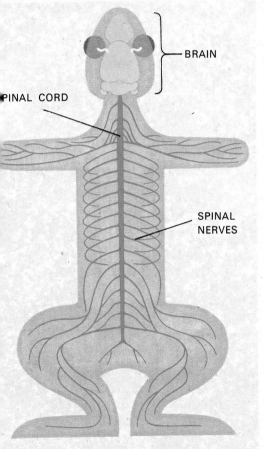

Left, nervous impulses are transmitted from the axon of one neuron to the dendrites of a second neuron across an open synapse. The two neurons do not actually touch one another, but relay the message by producing chemicals which flow across the synaptic gap. *Top left,* some animals are almost completely helpless at birth and must have time until their nervous system and other organs reach maturity. *Top right,* for other animals, it is imperative that they be ready to defend themselves almost at once. A foal can stand and run almost immediately after birth. *Above,* a diagram of the central nervous system of a rabbit is typical of most higher animals. The brain acts as a complex communications exchange, receiving messages from – and routing messages to – nerve endings throughout the body.

BRAIN

SPINAL CORD

SPINAL NERVES

inhibiting impulses, a very fine balance can be achieved.

The single unalterable electric pulses passing along nerves are very similar to the 'language' used by a computer. In both cases, an 'all or none' binary system is at work and information is passed as a series of either 'on' or 'off' pulses. And in both cases the components making up the system are comparatively simple; the complexity and flexibility come from the ways in which the simple components are assembled to form the various interconnections inside the system.

We saw earlier how a spinal reflex arc can cause a stimulus to give rise to the same response every time. We can now understand how more complicated responses are possible. Imagine that most of the impulses passing to the spinal cord of a man can travel along branch connections to the brain. Then at any one time, the number of nervous impulses passing round the co-ordinating centres in the brain will be enormous. The pattern of these impulses will give a sort of 'picture' of the condition of the man at a given instant. But the situation will be continually changing as environmental changes alter the pattern of the incoming signals.

Sensory inputs will also influence what messages are sent out to activate the various muscles. It is the overall complexity which makes the study of animal behaviour so difficult, and in higher animals there is often no obvious or direct relationship between stimulus and response. The same stimulus may evoke quite opposite responses under different conditions.

Even in a thinking animal such as Man there is still a great deal of co-ordination and 'decision making' which completely bypasses the conscious parts of the brain. Instead they depend on the way in which the nervous system is built. For example, control of breathing rate, heart rate, movement of food along the gut, and so on, all take place without any conscious effort. Indeed, most of them are *beyond* the control of the conscious mind – we cannot alter our heart rate merely by thinking about it.

The special part of the nervous system which deals with these 'automatic' activities is called the *autonomic* nervous system. It has its own co-ordination centres in the brain and its own network of nervous fibres which largely lie outside the central nervous system. The autonomic nervous system acts as a very complex series of reflex actions and keeps the machinery of the body running without involving any conscious thought. Imagine the nuisance of having to remember to breathe every few seconds. This leads us to realize that these automatic actions are the fundamental ones, and conscious thought is a much later development of the nervous system.

Life without thought

Nerves that carry messages to activate muscles under the control of the conscious mind form the *voluntary* nervous system. The nerves of the voluntary and autonomic systems are made up and 'work' in much the same way. Most of our daily activities are of the voluntary type. Whether we are brushing our teeth, running for a bus, or doing our daily work, most of our actions are controlled, not reflex or instinctive. In terms of stamina, strength, or agility, Man is not an extraordinary nor a particularly outstanding animal. Where he does score is in his ability to think and translate his thoughts into conscious actions.

If we can imagine life without any conscious awareness of anything at all, then we are probably close to the state which exists in simple animals. Our own sophisticated nervous system, awareness of ourselves and things around us can easily trap us into the error of anthropomorphism – that is, assigning to all animals attributes and emotions requiring conscious thought.

Discussing the ability of animals to think can lead to profound philosophical arguments; but it is necessary to try to envisage life without 'thought' in order to be able to assess the advantages which conscious thought gives to an animal. Conscious thought allows an animal to translate information about its real

1 The whiskers of a cat are sensitive to touch, but felines also rely on night eyesight and mental agility to make their way in the world. **2** Sensory acuity in moths has reached a very high stage of development. These leaf structure antennae are the principal receptors. **3** The dog's acute sense of smell is well known, and is put to good use in hunting, as the criminal whose scent this police dog is following well understands. **4** Many activities of birds appear to result from conscious thought, but are really reflexes or 'species memory'. This mother bird reacts to anything with a gaping mouth, be it her own young or, in this case, hungry fish.

environment, given by its sensory organs, into a language of nervous impulses. By this simplification it is possible to record events in the memory and to call on these – that is, to use experience – in making new decisions.

The further ability of being able to pass on experience from animal to animal seems to have developed in only a few instances. It reaches its peak in Man where the 'language' of the nervous system is further simplified to the languages which we speak and write.

Perhaps the best contrast with the condition reached in Man is provided by the complex behaviour of many birds. Whereas Man and some mammals have developed the powers of thought and individual memory, birds have tended to develop a set of 'species memories'. Many of the complex activities of birds are completely instinctive and are fixed at birth as surely as are factors such as the colour of their feathers or the sizes of the beaks.

This is not to say that birds are incapable of learning, but most of their essential behaviour is controlled by instinct. This is the fundamental difference between the bird type of behaviour and the type found in higher mammals. Perhaps the greatest consequence of conscious memory in mammals is that mammals are capable of behaviour modifications from generation to generation, whereas birds can change only by evolution over many hundreds of generations.

Windows on the world

An astonishing diversity of eyes is found in nature, from the primitive eyespot to the insects' compound eyes. How do they work, what can they see, and how are they suited to their owner's way of life?

THE VERTEBRATE EYE is like a camera. Light enters it through a transparent 'window' at the front, known as the cornea. It is focused by a lens (which in the case of Man is flexible, and in the case of fishes is not) on to a layer of light-sensitive cells, which collectively form the retina. The amount of light passing through the lens to the retina is controlled, as in the camera, by the iris – a muscular ring overlaid with light-absorbing pigment which closes when the light is bright and opens when it is dim. The eye's shape is maintained in the same way as a football's: fluid inside the eye, at carefully regulated pressure, pushes against the tough fibrous 'husk' of the eye, known as the sclera.

The 'simple' eye

This extremely complex camera-like organ is known, seemingly ironically, as a 'simple' eye to distinguish it from the compound eye of insects. That the vertebrate eye is, in fact, complex, is not in itself surprising – most things in nature are complex if you look at them closely enough. The puzzling thing is how such an eye developed. For the various parts of the eye are not related structurally or embryologically to each other; the retina develops as an outcrop of the embryonic brain; the cornea develops from transparent ectoderm at the surface of the embryo; the sclera is mesodermal. Yet each part of the eye is – apparently – useless without the other parts. How could a sophisticated, flexible lens evolve, unless the animal already possessed a retina capable of picking up and interpreting the image

Built for night vision, this owl's eyes reflect an image of the photographer. The large pupils catch as much as possible of the incident light so that the owl can hunt in darkness.

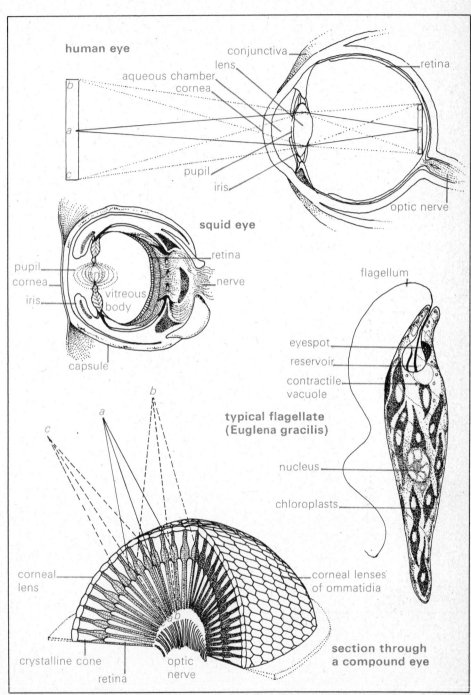

Four different types of eye. The most primitive, in *Euglena*, is a simple light-sensitive spot, while the compound eye is highly complex. Squid and human eyes look similar but develop differently.

projected on to it? And, conversely, how could such a retina develop unless the animal stock already possessed reasonable lenses capable of focusing light? It is the chicken and egg problem all over again. Nor is this the whole problem. We can see that the vertebrate lens is very useful. But what use would a lens be that was only half evolved? What were primitive lenses like before they were sophisti-

cated enough to focus light properly – what function did they serve the primitive animals that possessed them?

Before we seek to answer these questions, let us make the problem still more complex. The things that we 'see' around us – solid objects, each with a definite form, each standing separately from all the other objects – bear very little obvious relation to the 'image' that is focused on our retinas. For this image – a mere patch of light – is distorted (since the retina is a curved surface); it is granular (since the retina is composed of separate cells, not all of which are functional at any one time); and it is two-dimensional. And this image, in turn apparently bears very little relation to the flurry of electrical impulses that travel from the retina down the optic nerve, to the visual cortex of our brains.

For these impulses do not travel down the nerve like electrodes rushing down a cathode-ray tube in a television, to re-create the retinal image on our brain as if it were a television screen. And even if a retinal-type image were re-created inside our brains, this would not explain vision; for we would still need some means of interpreting the image projected on our brain; we would need a second eye in the brain to see that image. In fact, of course, both the retinal image and the nerve impulses that arise from it are part of a rarefied and stylized visual code, just as the printed words on this page are a stylized code of the thoughts they are intended to convey.

Half-way eyes

Thus even when we have explained how all the various components of our eye might have come into being (which is the theme of this chapter) we have told only half the story. To glean meaningful information about the outside world through the medium of light energy, it is not enough simply to have good eyes. Graft a man's eye into an earthworm (if such a thing were possible) and it would 'see' no better than it does now, for it lacks the nervous equipment needed to make sense of the esoteric and very individual code of nervous impulses that would come from the eye. Eyes and brains have evolved in concert, just as have the various components of the eyes of higher animals.

If an animal is to respond to light it must 'know' that the light is there. The first requirement, then, is that light should produce some chemical change in the animal. The simplest animals – like amoebae – can respond to bright light (generally by shunning it) simply because the large amount of light energy hitting the animal produces somewhat generalized chemical changes in much the same way as heat or sound energy would.

The next stage in perception is for the animal to possess special chemicals that respond to light much less intense than that needed to produce generalized chemical changes – and furthermore, that are reversibly alterable, so that having once been changed by the light they can then be restored in their original form, and thus become capable of responding to the light a second time. Several such chemicals exist in nature. Of necessity, they absorb light. They therefore appear coloured and are known as pigments.

Even very simple animals possess blobs

1 The almost human eye of the conch peers out from under the animal's shell. This type of eye is probably capable of forming a reasonable image of undersea objects.
2 The hawkmoth caterpillar keeps its predators at bay by simulating an 'eye' on its trunk. The 'eye' is simply a form of camouflage.
3 The squid, a very advanced mollusc, has a number of eyes which appear superficially very similar to those of vertebrates. In fact, the squid has well-developed vision.
4 The loris, a nocturnal primate distantly related to Man, has large round eyes which take up a considerable portion of its face. They help it see in the dark.
5 In the snail, a primitive mollusc, the eyes are projected on the ends of the animal's antennae. A pit of light-sensitive cells is sunk into the tip beneath a layer of transparent cells.

of visual pigment. The flagellate protozoan *Euglena* has such a light-sensitive spot – an 'eye' spot – near its gullet. *Euglena* also possesses chloroplasts, and can photosynthesize. Unlike amoeba, *Euglena* moves towards light stimuli.

Euglena with its single eyespot, can learn very little about its environment beyond the fact that the prevailing light intensity suddenly decreased – as when a shadow fell over the animal; or that it pulsed a signal only when the light suddenly increased, signifying that the shadow had passed. Already we would have

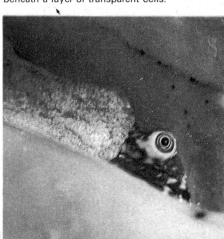

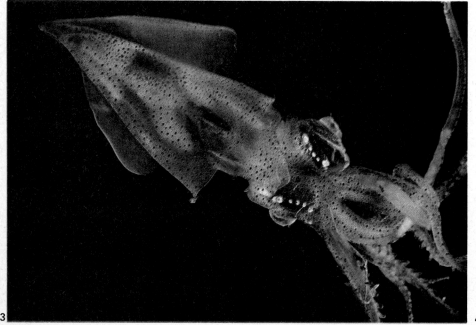

a coding system that could tell an animal with a suitable nervous system that something in the environment is moving.

Animals whose bodies are made up of many cells – the *Metazoa* – generally have specialized light-sensitive cells. In the simplest conceivable situation, these cells are scattered over the body surface. Thus the flat-worm *Planaria* – besides having recognizable eyes at its front end – also has light-sensitive cells scattered over its body surface. The earthworm's light-sensitive cells are similarly scattered, but it is doubtful whether this should be regarded

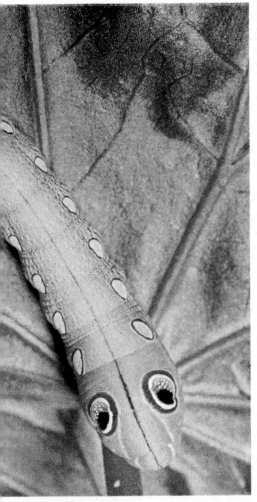

merely as a 'primitive' feature. The earthworm is a burrower, and it generally surfaces only at night. It needs to know only if it is dark or not. Animals more primitive than the earthworm – like *Planaria*, and like *Nereis*, a marine segmented worm that hunts its food – have perfectly good eyes.

But in most animals, even in primitive things like *Planaria*, the light-sensitive cells are mostly grouped together into recognizable eyes. This is no accident; most mobile animals move in one direction only, and there is obvious selective advantage in having light-sensitive cells at the front: it is better to have information about where you are going than where you have been.

Eyes front

That light cells became grouped at the front of the animal might seem obvious and of no great significance. But the point is that *unless* light-sensitive cells had become grouped together then they could never have been used co-operatively in the way that is necessary to form images. Yet they originally became grouped together long before any animal had a brain big enough to cope with images, and long before animals even had means of focusing light on to the cells to make image formation possible. A very primitive retina – which at its simplest is no more than a patch of light-sensitive cells – might have evolved simply because animals tend to move in one direction only and it is best to have the receptors at the front.

In fact, even lowly *Planaria* uses its

The cat is another vertebrate with good eyesight, to suit its nocturnal habits. The pupil in this case is slit, and can be widened to accommodate more light when it is dark.

very elementary group of light-sensitive cells to tell it from which direction the light is coming. The whole eye lies beneath a patch of specially transparent surface ectoderm. Each group of light-sensitive cells whose ends project directly into the 'brain' is surrounded by a bowl of black pigment cells, which shade the receptor cells from light coming from all directions but one.

Usually, however, the light-sensitive cells in lowly animals are not buried beneath epidermis; they generally are at the surface. A common arrangement is seen in the limpet, where the light-sensitive cells line a shallow pit on the body surface. Possibly light-sensitive regions became pit-shaped so as to protect the light-sensitive cells from mechanical damage. But having cells in pits also has a visual advantage. The ancient Greeks found that they could look at the stars in the daytime by looking straight upwards from the bottom of deep pits, because that way the view of the stars was not obliterated by the glare of the sun. Similarly, light-sensitive cells sunk in pits are shielded from glare, and so the possibility of image formation is enhanced. Again, limpets probably cannot form images; but if their eyes were wired to a better nervous system, possibly they might perceive some sort of image.

And indeed, very similar eyes in the

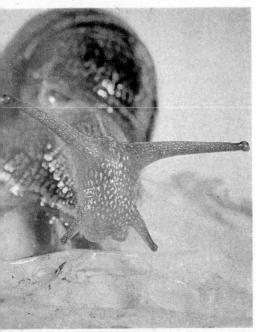

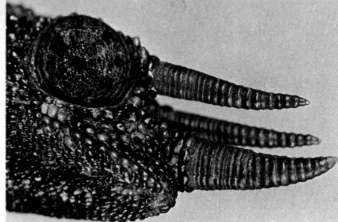

The eight eyes of a spider. Not every animal has only two eyes — many insects have numerous light-sensitive organs. In this case, the eyes give the spider an all-round view.

The horned chameleon has a turret for its eye — rather like the turret of a tank. By swivelling the turret round, the chameleon can look round without turning its head.

head of the cephalopod *Nautilus* (primitive relative of the squids and octopuses) undoubtedly serve to form respectable images. The eye-pit has deepened in *Nautilus,* and the edges of the pit have closed over, leaving only a small hole. In fact *Nautilus*'s eye is exactly like a pin-hole camera, which though primitive can produce images which are extremely sharp – though not very bright.

You have only to combine the very primitive features of limpet and *Nautilus* eyes – the deep cell-lined pit of one and the protective and refractive transparent covering of the other – to produce eyes like those of spiders or scorpions – predatory animals that use their eyes in hunting. In these animals, the thickened secretion that has come to serve as a lens is on the surface. In the predatory marine worm *Nereis* development has gone one step further; the cup of light-sensitive cells, with the lens secreted over them, has sunk beneath a transparent cuticle. In the snail there is a similar arrangement, except that the external transparent cuticle is replaced by an external cell layer.

Snail eyes

Snails are in many ways primitive molluscs: squids and octopuses (which, like *Nautilus,* are cephalopods) are very advanced molluscs. No one is saying that squids evolved from snails; but they do belong to the same phylum, and it is easy to see how a snail-like eye could be modified into a squid-like eye. And the squid's eye, though in detail very different from the vertebrate eye, bears a strong superficial resemblance to it; it is of comparable efficiency, and, like the vertebrate eye, it works on the camera principle.

The vertebrate eye, though it has all the components of a squid's eye, is in detail totally different. And, of course, vertebrates are totally unrelated to squids – their evolutionary lines diverged when the Earth was still young. The most striking difference between vertebrate and squid eye is that the vertebrate retina, compared to that of the squid, is inside out. The nerves running from the squid's retinal cells run directly from the back of the retina. The nerves from the vertebrate's

The head of the dragonfly is dominated by an enormous pair of compound eyes, bulging out to give almost all-round vision. This type of eye is very sensitive to tiny movements in the field of view.

retinal cells actually run forward, so that the nerve fibres lie inside the retinal cells, between them and the light.

Thus we see how the complex and closely interrelated components of the camera-like eyes of squids and vertebrates are reflected in more primitive creatures. But there has been one important evolutionary diversion that has produced eyes that work totally differently. This diversion led to the compound eyes of the primitive trilobites and the modern insects. We can see how camera-like eyes may have evolved by looking at simplified versions of them in simple animals, but the compound eye apparently appeared complete in the trilobites which lived more than 500 million years ago. There are no fossils older than these trilobites, so the origin of compound eyes is uncertain.

The compound eye has a great many – sometimes hundreds – of separate vase-shaped components known as *ommatidia.* Each ommatidium consists of a cluster – usually seven – of light-sensitive cells, surrounded by a hexagonal pattern of six pigment cells. At the outside of each ommatidium is a thickened piece of cuticle that serves both as protector and lens, and is called therefore a 'corneal lens', or a lens facet. Behind this corneal lens lies a

second lens, the so-called lens cylinder. Now, the vertebrate lens – like those of pretty well all other animals – works as a lens by virtue of its shape. Not so the lens cylinder. The refractive index of the centre of the lens cylinder is greater than at its edge; thus light is funnelled down the cylinder, in a way that is unique.

One of the silliest misconceptions about insect eyes is that each ommatidium forms a separate image; according to this idea the fly sees a thousand views at once, as if it were looking through the dimpled glass that is used for bathroom windows. This is impossible on anatomical grounds; for each group of light-sensitive cells in each ommatidium is served by a single nerve fibre, and single nerve fibres, though more versatile than one might think, cannot form images. In fact each ommatidium works on an on/off basis – the ommatidium probably signals only when there is a sudden change in the intensity of light hitting it. In fact, the insect eye is primarily adapted to detect movement – and very efficient it is too, to judge from the speed of a fly's reaction to the swatter.

Evolution of vision

Thus animals glean information from light stimuli in a remarkable variety of ways, and the information they glean differs markedly in quality. At the most primitive level, only the presence or absence of light can be detected. More advanced animals can detect light's direction; then movement was detectable; then eyes and brains combined to form images; and finally, of course, animals became able to detect the subtlest differences in the quality of light in the images they formed: they developed colour vision. We cannot know how the vertebrate eye developed – the most primitive vertebrates have quite good eyes and the fossil relics of the pre-vertebrate line are virtually non-existent – but we can infer how the functionally similar eyes of squids, for example, might have been built up from simple components, and presumably vertebrates' ancestors showed a similar step-wise progression. But the early development of compound eyes, the hallmark of insects, remains something of a mystery.

Making sense of sounds

Most animals respond in some way to sound. In higher animals, special sense organs — ears — concentrate and sort out the various sounds around the animal. Many species rely heavily on their ears.

ALMOST EVERY MOVEMENT that takes place on Earth leads to some kind of noise. The ability to detect sounds and react correctly to the disturbances they produce is thus an asset of considerable value to living beings.

Response to the vibrations of sounds is found even in very primitive forms of life. Earthworms retreat into their holes when they feel the vibrations of footsteps through the earth. They are able to respond even though they have no 'ears' as such.

In the same way, an amoeba would not be regarded as 'seeing' light, although it will move away from bright light. But hearing is generally associated with special sense organs which have developed the ability to respond to vibration to a higher degree than the rest of the body's tissues.

The basic plan of all sense organs is sufficiently similar to show a common origin. Each consists of a *receptor cell* or cells specially modified to receive a stimulus. These initiate an impulse through nerves to the brain or spinal cord where the impulses are 'interpreted' and acted upon.

This basic model of receptor, nerve and brain is found not only in the eyes, the ears, and the organs of taste and smell, but also in the cells in the skin dealing with touch and pressure senses, and in the muscles. The ear is designed to convert the energy of sound, that is, the energy of the movement of air or water molecules, into electrical energy that can then be detected by the brain.

The human ear, a fairly typical example of the type of organ required to detect sounds, acts not only as a *transducer* – turning sound energy into electrical energy – but is also able to amplify the energy received.

The external appearance of the ear is of a flap, the *pinna,* which is designed to concentrate sound into the cavity, the *meatus.* In Man the pinna is rudimentary compared with that found in animals like the horse or the rabbit, which rely far more on their sense of hearing than do human beings. But the pinnae do serve a useful purpose in so far as they tend to cut out sound coming from behind the head and help locate the source of a sound more accurately.

The meatus of the ear is really a tube in the bone leading to a stretched membrane, the *ear-drum.* Behind the ear-drum is a cavity, the *middle ear,* which is normally closed, except during swallowing. The cavity acts as a resonant chamber to increase the efficiency of the ear-drum. The outer and middle ears are solely concerned with the transmission of vibrations, and act merely to pick up sounds and pass them on their way to the inner ear. For this purpose, the ear-drum is connected to the inner ear by a train of small bones, the *ossicles* (*malleus, incus* and *stapes*), which are so arranged that they give added leverage to the small membrane which covers the entrance to the inner ear. The inner ear itself is safely concealed

1 Hares – like this East African species – live close to the ground and require acute hearing. Ear pinnae are well developed and can be swung round to catch sounds from all directions.
2 The hippopotamus has small ears but like the eyes they are set close to the top of the head so that the animal can listen to its surroundings without raising its body from the water.
3 Diagram contrasting the human ear with the ear of a bird. The bird has no pinna and its outer ear canal is broader than Man's. The ear-drum is relatively larger and the middle ear shorter.

Human ear

pinna
auditory ossicles
bone protecting ear
semi-circular canals
nerves
external auditory meatus
ear-drum
middle ear cavity
vestibules
Eustachian tube
cochlea

Bird ear

ear-drum
labyrinth
outer ear canal
cochlea
columella

1 In the green crested lizard (*Calotes cristatellus*) the membrane covering the ear-cavity shows up on the side of the head as an oval brown spot with a central depression.

2 Wild dogs in Murchison Falls Park, Uganda, show the well-developed external ears of hunters. Their acute hearing enables them to detect their prey at considerable distances.

3 The large membranous ears of the African elephant are chiefly concerned with temperature regulation. Blood flowing through the pinnae is cooled by the air.

4 The ear of this occipital vulture can be clearly seen behind the eye. The form of the ear in birds betrays their reptile ancestry, although in birds the ear-drum has sunk below the surface.

inside the bones of the skull so that it is unlikely to be damaged except by a major catastrophe.

The vibrations which reach the membrane of the inner ear are transmitted to a fluid which fills the cavity of the inner ear. This fluid communicates with a spiral cavity, the *cochlea,* where the real work of the ear is carried out.

The *cochlea* is lined with nerve cells which have hair-like projections. As the vibrations in the fluid set these 'hairs' in motion, they cause the nerve cells to set up impulses which are transmitted through the auditory nerve to the brain.

The shape of the cochlea is such that sounds of different frequency set up vibrations in different parts of the cochlea. This is the basis of our ability to distinguish notes and to hear the pitch of sounds falling on the ear.

The human ear is not equally sensitive to vibrations of all intensities. In fact, we hear only in a comparatively narrow band of frequencies spanning about ten octaves from 20 to 20,000 cycles per second. Below this level, if the vibration is strong enough, it is detected by feel, whereas above 20,000 cycles the sounds are outside our senses altogether.

In fact, human beings have only a moderately developed sense of hearing compared with many other animals. We rely far more on our eyes than on other sense organs. No doubt this is related to the mode of life of the ancestors of human beings who were probably tree dwellers. Good vision was obviously more important than well-developed hearing under these circumstances.

Every dog-owner will have noticed his pet pricking up its ears even when human beings in the vicinity have noticed nothing. This is because dogs have a larger range of hearing than Man. This property is exploited in the so-called 'ultra-sonic' whistles, which emit notes too high for the human ear to detect, but which are readily audible to dogs. The same ability to hear sounds outside the human range is found in many insects. One American research team set out to study the sounds made by crickets. They took tape-recorded imitations of the crickets' chirps, but even when they played these in an area full of crickets, they were apparently unable to get any of the crickets to reply. The reason for this is that the crickets communicate with sounds that are far higher than the human ear can detect: the sound made by the crickets in scraping their wings is entirely incidental to the real communication.

The human ear becomes less sensitive to high notes with increasing age. The ear-drum graduallly grows thicker and the tiny bones which link it to the inner ear become less flexible and tend to fuse together. The loss of sensitivity can be charted, and it has been found that in middle-aged men, the loss runs at a rate of about 160 cycles per second lost every year.

The human ear is most sensitive to sound in the range of about 3,000 cycles per second, about four octaves above middle C. This sound is about the same pitch as a woman's scream.

The fact that the ear is relatively insensitive to very low-frequency vibrations is important in preventing hearing being swamped by the sounds of ordinary bodily activity. Some of the problems this might pose can be found by stopping up both ears with the fingers. The low humming sound one can then hear is caused by the continual tiny contractions of muscle cells in the arms.

Hearing aids

Stopping the ears, and thus shutting out the airborne vibrations shows that the air is not the only medium that transmits sound to the inner ear. With our ears stopped, we can still quite clearly hear ourselves humming. In this case, the energy of the sound is transmitted through the bones of the head. Because the inner ear is surrounded by bone, it is able to detect easily vibrations passing through the bone. This principle is exploited in the treatment of some types of deafness, particularly those due to damaged ossicles (middle-ear deafness). Hearing aids for these types of deafness amplify the sound and apply the vibrations to the bone just behind the ear, thereby by-passing the middle ear.

The ability to hear is the basis of language and this form of communication is widespread throughout the animal kingdom. Many bird songs and animal cries are familiar sounds but until recently the sounds made by fish and sea creatures were almost unknown. In fact, water is a better medium than air for carrying sound. One startling demonstration of this fact was the picking up by a microphone off the American coast of the sound of the explosion of four pounds of TNT off the coast of South Africa.

The sound-transmitting properties of water are used to the full by fish and other marine and freshwater animals. If a microphone is lowered into an aquarium, the fish are found to be making a cacophony of sounds. Some species of fish have specially developed muscles surrounding their swim-bladders which cause the taut surface of the sac to vibrate like a drum. Others rub their gill arches together to make sounds which are meaningful to others of the same species. Fishermen trying to sleep in their thin wooden ships off the coast of China have long found that the noise from certain types of croaking fish keeps them awake at night. The same noises disrupted American anti-submarine defences during the Second World War. These defences made use of microphones under the water connected with loud-speakers above ground. The sound made by large shoals of croakers was almost deafening, and the apparatus had to be redesigned,

Fish are not the only marine animals with the ability to communicate with one another by sound. Dolphins, the intelligent friendly marine mammals which follow ships and can be trained to perform tricks,

1 The ear of the bullfrog (*Rana catesbeiana*) is covered by a stretched membrane continuous with the skin of the head. The bullfrog ear is particularly sensitive to low notes.
2 The fennec is the smallest known fox, being only 16 inches long. Its striking external ears reach a length of four inches and serve mainly to regulate temperature in its desert habitat.
3 Bats have extremely sensitive hearing, particularly for high notes, and navigate in the dark by emitting squeaks and picking up the echoes with their large external ears.

are now known to have a well-developed language and seem to be able to express a wide range of feelings. Dolphins are also accomplished mimics; captured species can imitate the human voice.

One question which puzzles many people about hearing is why it should be necessary to have two ears. The reason for this can be more readily appreciated by considering the ears not only as sound-receiving devices but also as direction-finders. When a sound is heard, the head turns slightly to find out where the sound is coming from. But even if the head were fixed in one position, it would still be possible to detect where the sound is. With only one ear functioning, however, and in the absence of other clues, it is hard to tell where a sound is coming from.

The brain can detect very small differences in the time of arrival of a sound at each ear. Differences of as little as 1/10000 of a second can be easily detected, an ability which enables Man to place the

source of the sound. The illusion of stereophonic noise can be simulated by a device which delivers sound to one ear and then to the other after an almost imperceptible delay. By varying the delay, the sound can be made to appear to come from various points around the listener.

Blind people are forced to develop the ability to respond to sound to a very high degree. Many of them claim to be able to 'feel' objects through the pores of their skin. In fact, however, they make great use of the direction-finding ability of the ears, and are extremely sensitive to echoes which most people do not notice.

The echoes produced from objects along the side of the road during the course of a car journey are probably familiar to most people. The sound is a regular hiss normally, but passing a car or a pedestrian produces a more pronounced note for a split-second. Much of the time, our ears ignore the echoes produced when we make noises. For example, if you shout in a

forest, the echoes are scarcely noticed, if at all. On the other hand, if the sound is recorded and then played backwards it becomes clear that there is really quite a loud echo, and one which is somewhat higher in pitch than the original sound. It is the presence of these echoes that enables blind people to locate objects and to avoid obstacles in their path.

This ability to navigate by ear is found in certain bats. These animals have small mouths which produce a note far outside the human range of hearing, with frequencies up to 130,000 cycles per second. Almost all the smaller bats can use this very high-frequency note as a form of 'radar' to detect obstacles in their path. Their ears detect the reflections from even quite small objects, and they are able to take avoiding action. This ability depends on being able to emit a note at very high frequency: only at this sort of frequency are the echoes from small objects really detectable. Lower notes, with longer wavelengths, need larger surfaces for adequate reflection. To give an efficient echo, the object acting as a reflector needs to be about three times as wide as the wavelength of the sound being reflected. In the case of a note like middle C, for example, the wavelength is just over four feet, so only an object larger than 12 feet by 12 feet has a reasonable chance of producing a good echo. This explains why the spectacular echoes are generally found either in large buildings with big reflecting areas or in mountain districts, where walls of rock act as natural reflectors.

Not many animals can hear as well as the bat but there are few animals that are totally deaf, and no fish has yet been found which lacks completely the ability to hear. Hearing, in fact, is probably the basic sense for communication between members of the same species.

The feel of things

The sense of touch, widespread throughout the animal kingdom, plays a predominant part in many animals' lives. In human beings, its potential for communication is only now being explored fully.

THE ABILITY of animals to detect and react to objects with which they come into physical contact is so widespread that it may almost be classed as a fundamental property of living matter. Every animal shows this property in some way, even the simple one-celled amoeba; while among plants it is also found in many species.

The living cell consists of a complex chemical structure which is constantly undergoing change. Objects in contact with the cell will clearly affect the way in which chemical change proceeds in the cell.

In most lower forms of life response does not rise above the level of a simple reaction. A typical example is the one-celled animal *Paramecium*, a tiny organism found in ponds. The paramecium swims by means of a cilia or tail which it moves convulsively to force its way through the water. When it encounters an obstacle to its progress, the animal 'back-tracks' and approaches again from a slightly different angle. The organism can clearly notice in some way that its path is blocked and take some form of avoiding action.

Sea-anemones not only pull in their tentacles when they protrude above the level of the tide – a necessary reaction if they are to avoid becoming dehydrated by

1 Spiders rely heavily on their sense of touch to tell them when insects land on their webs. The spider's reaction varies according to the magnitude of the vibrations of the web.
2 Ant-lions lie in wait for their prey at the bottom of shallow pits in sand. When an ant (**3**) blunders over the edge of the pit, the ant-lion throws sand over it and drags it down.

1

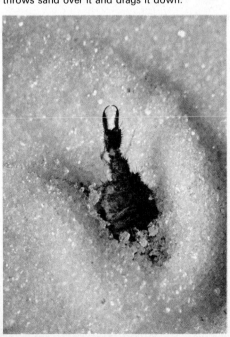

2

3

being left high and dry – but they also seem to be able to distinguish food from other underwater objects. The anemones which 'ride' on the back of hermit crabs are frequently bumped against rocks by the movement of their 'chargers', but in these cases they scarcely bother to contract. They pull in their tentacles actively only when they feel the motion of a small fish or shrimp that brushes against their fronds. Thus they can tell 'touching' from 'being touched'.

Privileged fish

This distinguishing ability is even better developed in one particular anemone. *Actinia quadricolor*, a Red Sea species, works in close conjunction with the common small fish *Amphiprion bicinctus*. The fish drive away the anemones' enemies, while the anemones will not open out if they do not feel the frequent touches of the fishes passing and repassing over them. In normal circumstances the anemones make no attempt to sting the fish, which pass through the fronds unharmed. However, if the fish is passively pushed on to the anemone's tentacles, the anemone can no longer tell it from food and will sting and eat it if it is small enough.

The catfish of the Mississippi, like the cat itself, relies heavily for information on the whiskers fringing its mouth. In the case of the catfish, the whiskers droop on to the bed of the muddy river, trailing over it and warning the catfish when they come into contact with anything unusual. Unlike those of the cat, however, the catfish 'whiskers' are not hairs. Instead they are fleshy outgrowths of the face, but they serve the same function.

Shrimps, too, make use of their antennae as probes. The tropical barbershop shrimp keeps its extensions in constant motion, probing the surrounding water with them. Each of its antennae is two or three times its own length, and they clearly provide it with a great deal of information.

Touch is particularly developed where the senses of sight and sound are unable to operate effectively. In the cat, a nocturnal hunter, the face is fringed with sensitive whiskers which provide instant information about the whereabouts of small prey that may have been tracked down into a dark corner. If a mouse touches its whiskers, a cat will react with hair-trigger speed, and is instantly aware of the mouse's position.

Feeling ability

The sense of touch is capable of giving accurate information, particularly of a comparative kind. In human beings, for example, it is sufficiently well developed to make it easy to tell a smooth pane of glass from one that is etched to a depth of only 1/2500 inch. This ability has been put to professional use by 'cloth-feelers' whose job it is to feel cloth to tell its quality and type. Many of these men can tell the exact type of a cloth merely by rubbing it with a stick. Others can distinguish a particular type of cloth even if the only contact they have with it is a momentary tap with a fingernail.

Unlike that of the primitive paramecium, but like that of most higher animals, Man's sense of touch is linked with and mediated by a complex nervous system. Cells within the skin are capable of reacting to touch, pain and pressure. These are linked with fine nerve-endings which transmit messages back to the brain. The activity of the brain itself influences what is felt. We have all seen the person, who, absorbed in some task, suddenly starts looking for his spectacles, which are all the while on his nose. This situation is in fact evidence that our nervous systems profoundly influence what we can feel. The central nervous system, after a while suppresses our consciousness of objects which we are constantly touching. Thus we do not, after a short while, feel our clothes on our bodies unless they get in our way. The brain stops 'telling' us that we are wearing them. At the same time, however, the touch cells in the skin are

still sending out their messages whenever our clothes rub against them.

For human beings, of course, touch is not the most important sense. It plays a large part in the minutiae of our lives, but has relatively little survival value.

One stage of life in which touch plays a predominant part, however, is in the very young child. A baby gets most of his information about his restricted world from the things he touches. His contact with his mother is even more important. Unless he is nursed and fondled during

these early months and years, his development will be impaired. During his childhood, he will feel a need to take part in rough play with other children, involving considerable amounts of touching and contact.

Experiments with animals have shed light on this problem. A third of the rats in one experiment were left in their cages without being handled at all. Two other groups were placed by hand at intervals into special boxes, where one group was given mildly painful electric shocks regu-

1 The baby macaque monkey in this experiment faces a choice between two 'mothers' – one cloth-covered, one made of chicken-wire. Though feeding from the wire doll, he prefers the cloth one, and runs to 'her' when in danger.
2 These armoured catfish find their food in murky water by trailing their fleshy barbels along the river floor. The barbels are outgrowths from the face, but they serve the same purpose as whiskers.
3 Books written in Braille, a code of raised dots, can be read quickly after practice by blind people. Many blind people acquire a remarkably acute sense of touch.
4 The queen bee, top, determines what sort of egg to lay in a particular honeycomb cell by feeling the cell's dimensions with her antennae. In large cells, she lays unfertilized eggs that later become drones.
5 These fish swim unconcernedly around the fronds of an anemone. The anemone ignores them so long as they are not pushed passively against it. If they are it stings and kills them.

larly while the others were merely left alone once inside. The interesting result was that the two groups of rats that had been handled, both those that had been shocked and those that had not, were friendly and 'tame' when they grew older. It was the third group, the unhandled, unstimulated rats, that showed a difference. As they grew up, these cowered timidly in the corners of their cages, showing all the signs of fear and anxiety. When they grew older, they underwent brain surgery which turned them into

2

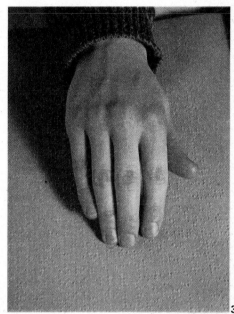

3

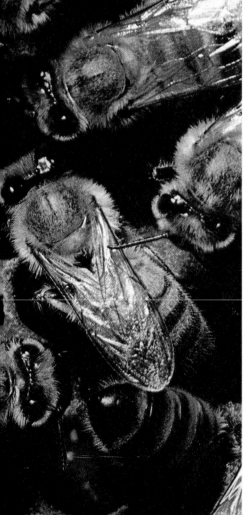

5

Play, involving touch and mock fighting as well as affectionate gestures, is essential to the full development of the young animal. Here a kitten and a Shetland sheepdog pup play together.

extremely vicious rats. The other rats after similar surgery remained comparatively tame. It appeared that the presence of stimulation rather than its quality was the vital factor.

This experiment, with emphasis on the role of the sense of touch in the development of sociability, leads on to consideration of the role of the mother in raising normal children. Here again animal experiments throw some light on the intricacies of this problem. A group of scientists at the University of Wisconsin under the leadership of Dr Harry Harlow took new-born macaque monkeys from their mothers and put them into cages at the age of two days with a dummy mother, a life-size doll fitted with a teat delivering milk. One type of doll was made of chicken wire, while the other was covered in soft cloth.

Gained confidence

The baby macaques fed from the nipples of either type of parent, but only the cloth-covered doll gave rise to any affectionate feelings. The chicken-wire mother was treated solely as a source of food, while the babies placed in cages with cloth-covered mothers also came to regard them as a source of protection and would run to them if threatened. The reactions of the two groups of monkeys to unfamiliar objects thrust into their cages was also different: The 'chicken wire' babies, frightened of anything new, cowered in the corners of their cages for long periods without venturing to examine the objects, while the 'cloth' babies ran first to their 'mothers' and seemed then to gain sufficient confidence fairly rapidly to venture out and examine the objects.

This illustrates the powerful part that touch plays in the development of maternal love and in the normal development of the infant.

All parts of the body surface are not equally sensitive to touch. The palms of the hands, which we use constantly in touching, are among the most sensitive parts. Under the skin of the palms is a maze of nerve-endings. This heavy *innervation* is reflected in the cortex of the brain, where the nerves eventually terminate. The part of the cortex which deals with conscious touch sensations can be represented as a distorted image of the body, in which the parts are not life-size, but are scaled according to their innervation. The fingertips and the lips are among the most sensitive areas of the body. These are the parts of the body with which babies constantly explore the world around them.

A remarkable example of touch in insects is the ant-lion, an insect common in the southern deserts of the United States. The ant-lion lies at the bottom of a pit of sand and waits for ants to land on the edge of the pit. A few grains of sand falling on the ant-lion triggers off its sensitive nervous system, and the insect begins to shower the ant with grains of sand. In its state of confusion it becomes easy prey for the ant-lion.

The activity of the queen bee is also triggered by touch. She wanders over the face of the honeycomb, weighed down by her enormous egg-filled abdomen, feeling the cells of the honeycomb to decide what type of egg to lay in each. If the cell is small, a reflex of her nervous system releases a valve inside her reproductive organs and allows a few sperms to pass through to fertilize the next egg. Shortly afterwards, she deposits the egg in the small cell, where it will eventually become a worker bee. If the cell is large the reflex does not operate and an unfertilized egg is deposited which can develop only into a drone.

Many species of spider extend their sense of touch by building webs so that they can detect instantly any insect which lands on the web. In the spider, the sense of touch is especially well served by sense organs on her legs, and she is able to sit at the edge of the web and sense what is happening over a wide area.

When the tide goes out, the shore-line animals like these anemones, feel the lack of water and draw in their tentacles to prevent loss of body water from the action of wind and sun.

The female spiders which build webs are sensitive to the size of the movement of the web. If the vibration is too small, the spider will not respond. On the other hand, if a large insect, a beetle for example, becomes caught in the web, the spider will cower in a corner of the web while a considerable part of it is destroyed by the beetle's struggles.

Braille

Touch thus plays a predominant part in the lives of many insects, enabling them to find food and guiding them in many other activities. In human beings, while touch is important, and vital in early life, it is not as powerful a sense as sight. But for specialized purposes it can be immensely useful. In blind people, for instance, training and experience combine to develop enormously the sense of touch, and the language of Braille gives a clear example of the way in which touch can be used for communicating abstract information.

Scientists are now studying new ways of communicating by the use of touch. One such device makes use of a vibrator attached to the chest, which sends out a form of Morse code. The recipient can distinguish different vibrations and can use the results to form a mental image of what is being 'said'. Such a device would be extremely useful for people to communicate rapidly in situations where the noise level is too high for hearing. Airline pilots are now testing such devices.

With the increasing noise involved in many occupations, and even in everyday living, such devices utilizing touch sensations may become even more common.

It has also been suggested that similar devices might be of considerable value for spacemen, who need to be able to take in large amounts of complex information very rapidly and whose sensory channels might otherwise be overworked.

Taste and smell

Taste and smell are less important for human beings than sight and hearing. Many animals, however, use chemical senses to seek their mates, find their food and keep out of the way of dangerous predators.

SMELL AND TASTE are very much bound up with each other, and when we talk of 'tasting' a substance particularly something with a lot of flavour, we very often mean that we are 'smelling' it. We have only to have a heavy cold, or to hold our noses while eating to find our food with little taste. The reason is simple; the tongue can only distinguish between four main classes of flavour – sweet, sour, bitter and salt – the other flavours that we taste are in fact selected by our noses.

Although most of us can tell between good and bad smells, a sense of smell is not as important for Man as sight or hearing. The aroma of good cooking or a subtle perfume will certainly arouse us, but we will not, like the dog, be able to track down our food simply by sniffing the ground or air. In fact Man, together with the apes and most marine mammals, is somewhat exceptional among the higher animals in having a relatively poor sense of smell.

Powers of smell

Animals with poor or non-existent vision rely heavily on their senses of smell and taste. Using their olfactory powers (*olfaction* is the sense of smell), they learn to recognize their territories, can track their food, and avoid predators. Sometimes, too, mating is contingent on the male being able to smell when the female is ready and receptive for him; the cat on heat, for example, releases a strong sex attractant. Some animals have extraordinary powers of smell. The salmon can find its way back across miles of ocean to the freshwater

Snakes and lizards use their tongues to touch and sense the surroundings. The tongue is flicked back into the mouth and inserted into a sensory pit behind the upper lip.

river where it was reared. It is believed that once back at the mouth of the river the salmon finds its way back to the spawning ground by remembering the smells of various parts of its outward journey.

Even the lowest forms of animal – the single-celled protozoans – can react to changes in their environment, and they will either be attracted towards a pleasant stimulus like food, or try to escape a noxious one. Thus, squirting a drop of dilute acid near to the protozoan *Paramecium* makes it swim furiously away. Every substance is basically chemical and therefore capable of reacting with other chemical compounds. The ability to detect such a change in the environment depends on a process called *chemoreception*: the most elaborate forms of chemoreception are the sensory cells of taste and smell.

The simplest animals to have these sensory cells are the coelenterates – the sea-anemones, the jelly-fish and hydra. Their chemoreceptors are modified nerve cells, and their structure is very similar to the receptor cells of mammals.

Insects have probably developed the most sophisticated ability to smell and taste. Very often communication between one insect and another is effected by means of substances that are liberated by one insect and picked up by another. Thus bees and ants depend on smell and taste to recognize members of the hive or nest, and any intruder is promptly dealt with. The sense of taste is very often on the tip of the proboscis; the housefly is able to sense the presence of sugars or salt through special receptors on its feet. Sometimes the antennae are used for taste, as in the wasp; more often, they are used to distinguish smells. A cockroach can therefore

smell its food with its long, pointed antennae and will follow the trail to a piece of cheese. A few insects, like the cabbage white butterfly, smell with their *palps*, which are small projections on their mouths. Whether they are for taste or smell the sense organs have very similar structures and they are, in fact, derived from the same cells, the *ectodermal* cells. As in the coelenterates the receptor cells are connected to nerve fibres which run to the insect's brain, and the insect's behaviour can be completely governed by what it smells. For example, the male silkmoth is endowed with large feathery antennae, and these are so sensitive that they can pick up the scent of a female silkmoth that may be several miles away.

Phenomenal ability

It has been calculated that only a few molecules of the scent need strike the antennae for them to be stimulated. This phenomenal ability to smell the female is one way in which reproduction is ensured. The adult silkmoth does not feed and at most only lives for about nine days after emerging from the cocoon. In that short span of time the silkmoth must mate and lay its eggs. To attract the male, the female thus secretes a volatile substance into the air from special glands on her abdomen. This substance – called a *pheromone* because it is a secretion of one animal that can change the behaviour of another animal – is the substance the males are so sensitive to, and once they have picked up the scent their sole object in life is to find

This colt's foster-mother accepted and nursed him after he was encased in the skin of her own dead colt. Smell clearly plays the predominant part in the mare's recognition of her offspring.

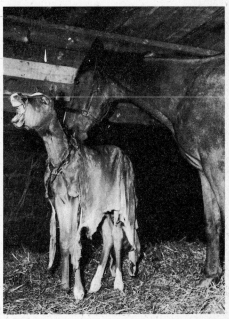

the source and mate with the female.

Cockroaches live for much longer than the adult silkmoth and they go through several reproductive cycles. The female only mates at certain times when she releases a pheromone and only then is she attractive to the male. If a filter paper touched by a receptive female is put into a cage containing male cockroaches, they immediately go beserk and clamber over each other to get to the source of the pheromone. The secretion of the pheromone is under the control of hormones and these hormones are released from glands associated with the brain of the insect. There is thus a tie-up between the season, the year, the animal's reproductive state, and the animal's behaviour – and as we have seen smell plays an important part. The gypsy moth produces a pheromone known as gypsol and this has now been synthesized by chemists. In the United States plagues of gypsy moths are controlled by putting out containers of synthetic gypsol. The male moths are attracted to the containers, where they are trapped and can be destroyed.

Female mammals on heat, also produce substances to attract the males. It is believed that women release a special substance when they are at the most fertile periods of the menstrual cycle. If they do, it is unlikely that men have sufficiently good noses to know.

Olfactory lobes

We think of the nose primarily as an organ through which we breathe, but the origin of the nose and nostrils was undoubtedly for smell. If we look at fishes, particularly the sharks which have a very good sense of smell, we see that the nostrils lead into a small blind-end chamber – all the breathing in fishes is done through the mouth and the gill slits. Inside the chamber the *surface epithelium,* which is the skin layer that has the olfactory cells, may be in a series of folds. By this means the number

1 Salmon leaping a waterfall on their way to spawn. Smell may play a considerable part in guiding these fish in their long and perilous journey to the spawning grounds.

2 The feathery antennae of the male silkmoth are sensitive to minute concentrations of the female sex attractant. Only a few molecules of this volatile scent alert the male to the female.

3 The housefly tastes with the tip of its proboscis, the trunk-like organ it uses for feeding. By brushing objects with its proboscis it can taste whether they are sweet or salty.

4 Taste and smell in human beings. Food on the tongue can be smelt by the olfactory organ at the top of the nose as well as being tasted by the taste buds on the tongue.

5 Plagues of gypsy moths in the United States are controlled by 'fooling' the male moths with a synthetic female attractant, gypsol. The pheromone draws the males into traps.

6 Otter hunting is almost entirely based on the hounds' well-developed sense of smell. Here, the otter has tried to throw the hounds off the scent by swimming a river.

7 Giraffes licking salt from the edges of a dried water hole. Many animals when short of salt exhibit a craving for salty-tasting foods and will go to considerable lengths to satisfy their needs.

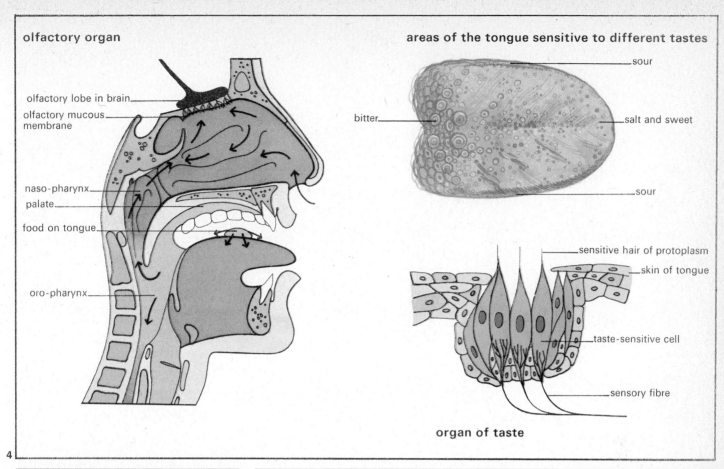

olfactory organ

olfactory lobe in brain

olfactory mucous membrane

naso-pharynx

palate

food on tongue

oro-pharynx

areas of the tongue sensitive to different tastes

sour

bitter

salt and sweet

sour

sensitive hair of protoplasm

skin of tongue

taste-sensitive cell

sensory fibre

organ of taste

4

5

6

7

of sensory cells that can be contained is increased enormously. The cells are also very well supplied with nerves from the olfactory lobes in the brain. These lobes lie at the front of the brain and they are relatively large in animals with a good sense of smell, like the man-eating shark, the blacktip, where they are clearly the largest portion of the brain.

In the amphibians the nostrils connect with the roof of the mouth. As the animal breathes it is taking in at the same time a sample of air to be tested for any interesting smells. Frogs, and most reptiles, are, however, lacking a 'true palate' and the air and food intermingle in the mouth. The true palate, where the air is almost entirely shut off from the mouth and filters through a network of fine porous bones, is only found in the mammals. However, amphibians and many reptiles have developed a small pouch called *Jacobson's*

The erect siphon of the common whelk draws a current of water over the animal's organ of smell. In this way, the whelk can smell out its prey and proceed to catch it.

A skilled wine-taster also makes considerable use of his sense of smell. 'Nosing' is the technical term for the preliminary examination of a wine's bouquet.

organ leading off from the main respiratory passages. This small organ contains many olfactory cells. The tongues of some snakes lie on pads in the mouth. When testing their environment these snakes flick their tongues out of their mouths and pick up traces of scent. When they retract their tongues the scent is brushed off on to the pads, from where it passes into Jacobson's organ.

The sensation of taste in many vertebrates can be confused with that of olfaction. The catfish has a number of antennae-like barbels projecting in all directions from its head. These barbels contain assemblages of taste and touch sensors, and using them the catfish can follow a food source upstream. However, in most vertebrates the sense of taste is confined to areas within the mouth.

How man tastes

In contrast to catfish, adult Man has 100,000 taste buds, some 9,000 taste receptors, placed mainly on the peripheral parts of the top of the tongue. In children the taste buds may be much more numerous and distributed widely over the tongue and even on the cheeks. The taste bud is an oval structure consisting of a thin receptor cell surrounded by supporting cells like the staves of a barrel. Each taste cell ends in a hair process which projects upward through a small pore on to the surface of the tongue. The four main flavours of taste are distinguished for the most part in different areas of the tongue. Thus sweet tastes are most easily perceived at the tip of the tongue, bitter at the back, sour at the edge and salt both on the tip and the edge.

How we taste is not really known, although it has been suggested that a substance which has a characteristic taste somehow depresses or excites the activities of enzymes – biological catalysts – which

are known to be secreted by the cells surrounding the taste buds.

There has been some attempt to discover if a sensation of taste can be tied in any way to appetite. The association is certainly tenuous, and one of the main factors in feeling satiated is undoubtedly when the stomach is full. Nevertheless, if animals are deprived of certain basic substances like salt they will in preference choose to drink water that has a high salt content; it is well known that miners and other hard-working labourers who sweat a great deal like to drink salty water to replace the loss of salt. There are some strange anomalies with taste. Although all normal people can taste the four basic flavours, some people are unable to taste substances which to others have a distinct flavour; this is governed by inherited characteristics. Substances like saccharin, which we think of as sweet, are very bitter to the cat, which cannot taste sweet substances. Animals are often sensitive to the smells of their own species; the dog, like the tom cat that goes round its neighbourhood spraying musk, leaves its 'visiting card' to warn other dogs in the area of its presence. In one sense the dog is staking out his territory. Many animals use musks or scents to indicate their presence.

Scent is also very important to colonies of animals. We have already mentioned the insects. Rats, too, live in colonies, and each member of the colony has a distinct smell of the colony by which he is recognized by his fellow rats. Should he be an intruder or have his scent masked in some way, he is likely to be driven away or even killed.

Some social insects, like the ants, when they have found a food source, leave a pheromone trail as their abdomen brushes the ground on the return journey to the nest. This trail attracts other ants of the nest to the food source; they themselves leave trails, and by this method maximum ant-power can be brought to play in the search for food. Bees also taste the food brought back by foraging bees, and this stimulates them to join in an all-out effort

to bring back food for the hive from the source. Bee communities depend on substances being passed all the time between one bee and another. The smell and taste of these substances determine the social behaviour of the hive. Indeed, the queen bee retains her status by secreting a special substance which is tasted by all the bees of the hive.

The sense of flavour

The close relationship between smell and taste means that it is often more accurate to speak of a single 'sense of flavour'. Certainly, people who lack a sense of smell (anosmics) seem to have a different sense of taste from other people.

In recent years, there have been considerable advances in research into the mechanism of smell. One of the centres of this research is the University of British Columbia, where Dr James Wright has recently put forward a theory of smell based on the observation that there are seven 'primary' scents. Receptors in the nose are shaped to receive molecules of these primary scents, and the extent to which a particular molecule fits a receptor determines how much of that smell we detect in it. Dr Wright's theory explains a number of hitherto puzzling facts about smell, though it may not be the whole story.

Smell and taste are part of the same phenomenon, and Man depends very much on both operating at the same time for the sense of flavour. A sprinkling of salt on our food often makes it taste better, although much of what we are tasting is perceived in the nose. Throughout the animal kingdom taste and smell have a certain universality – the bee seems to be able to recognize the same perfumed scents, such as tincture of orange, as Man, but there is a difference – the bee can smell it a thousand times better.

Teeth, beaks and tentacles

Animals cannot draw sustenance directly from air or soil. They must derive it instead by eating plants or other animals and are therefore equipped with suitably adapted mouthparts.

PLANTS MAKE their own food supply within their tissues; by means of photosynthesis, they convert carbon dioxide and water into sugars. Animals cannot manufacture their own food supply from simple substances within their bodies. They cannot make proteins, carbohydrates or fats directly, but depend on plants to supply the starting materials. In other words, all animals ultimately use plants for food. Some animals, *herbivores,* eat plants directly; others, *carnivores,* eat the flesh of animals that have eaten plants.

The food of animals therefore consists of the flesh and juices of other living things, either plants or animals. For digestion to take place, this food must be in a form in which the enzymes in the animal's digestive system can attack it and break it down into soluble compounds that can be absorbed. Juices are easy to digest, although there are special means for collecting and imbibing them. Large pieces of plant or animal have to be broken up or torn apart before they can be digested. This is one of the functions of the teeth in animals.

Fish, reptiles and mammals

But structures that can be used for cutting and tearing flesh are equally useful as weapons, and teeth in many animals have the dual purpose of killing the prey and breaking it up. The backward-facing teeth of snakes and the scales which serve as teeth in dogfish and skates aid in swallowing the prey whole as, once grasped, the prey cannot slip out of the mouth again.

The teeth of vertebrate animals are formed mainly by the sub-dermal tissues. The epidermis secretes on to the surface of the teeth a layer of protective enamel. In vertebrates other than mammals, the lower jaw is formed from a number of bones. But the teeth are borne only on the *dentary,* which is the only bone in the lower jaws of mammals. In the upper jaw, it is the *maxilla* and *premaxilla* bones which bear the teeth.

Generally the teeth grow in sockets of bone and they are rarely fused to the bone of the jaw. Some animals, such as amphibians, have teeth in other parts of the mouth – on the *vomer* bones in the roof of the mouth, for example. The teeth in a lizard's jaw are all alike, and this is also the case for most reptiles, all amphibians and all fish. As the teeth in reptiles wear, they are replaced from below.

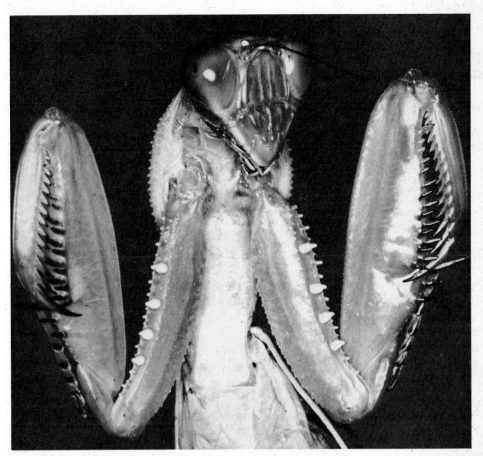

Above right, the praying mantis presents a formidable sight as it rears up, displaying the highly modified pincers it uses to grasp its prey. *Right,* because the mandibles of the locust are extremely hard, it can eat almost any kind of plant. A single swarm may need 3,000 tons of food a day.

The bones of the jaw and palate of snakes such as the boa constrictor are loosely hinged, so that the jaws can gape wide apart to allow the snake to swallow very large prey whole. There are teeth in the *pterygoid* and *palatine* bones which, like those on the maxilla and on the lower jaw, are long and backward-pointing. The hinge of the jaw can be moved forward, allowing the jaws to part very widely, and at the same time thrusting forward the teeth on the palatine and pterygoid. This accounts for the ability of many snakes to swallow whole animals. One example is the boa constrictor, which first crushes its victim to death before swallowing it. Another is the African Egg-eating snake, which is able to open its mouth amazingly wide. Such snakes take one very large meal and then rest somewhere and digest it. In a poisonous snake, such as a rattlesnake, the action of slinging the jaw-hinge forward swings out the fangs on the mandibles. Venom is injected through the fangs into the prey.

In mammals, special kinds of teeth have evolved to function with various diets. The main kinds of teeth are the *incisors* at the front of the mouth (generally chisel-like), the *canines* (pointed and dagger-like), and the *pre-molars* and *molars* (mainly stubby, and used for crushing and grinding).

The original number of teeth in early mammals was three incisors, one canine, four pre-molars and three molars on each side, top and bottom, giving a total of 44 teeth. But this arrangement has altered in the process of evolution of special dentitions. For example, Man has two incisors, one canine, two pre-molars and three molars on each side of each jaw, giving a total of 32 teeth.

Fangs, grinders and bills

Carnivores have long pointed canine teeth, sometimes called *fangs*, for tearing at their prey. Sabre-toothed tigers, now extinct, used to open their lower jaws until they were almost at right angles to the upper jaws, and use their canines for stabbing. The incisors of flesh-eating cats and dogs, for example, are relatively unspecialized, being small and chisel-shaped; it is in the teeth farther back along the row that real adaptations occur. The upper fourth pre-molar forms a blade-like *carnassial* which, with the first molar of the lower jaw, acts like a pair of scissors, shearing flesh from the prey. These are the real cutting teeth and their position explains why a dog bites at a bone with the back of its mouth. And since these teeth are near the hinge of the jaw, great force can be applied when they are brought together.

If the carnassials were not precisely aligned, they would lose their effectiveness, just as a pair of scissors with loose blades is useless for cutting paper. Alignment is assured by the shape of the hinge of a carnivore's lower jaw. The socket on the skull fits round a protuberance on the lower jaw, restricting movement to a vertical direction.

However, in herbivores, such as cattle and horses, the hinge is looser and the

1

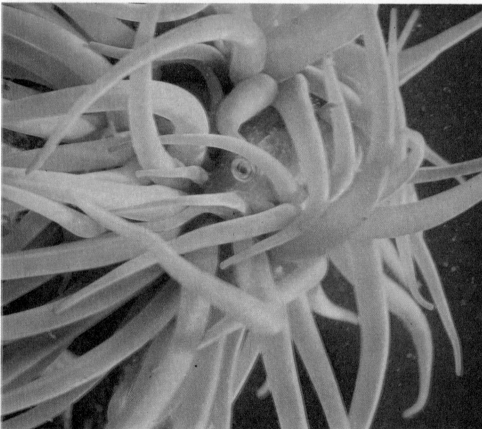

2

lower jaw can move both up and down and from side to side. This results in a grinding action of the molar and pre-molar teeth of the lower jaw on those of the upper. Each molar tooth in the upper jaw has been squared-up, as it were, by the addition of an extra cusp to the three original ones. In the lower jaw, each tooth has one cusp fewer and so a large grinding surface is formed. The side-to-side movement of tooth on tooth soon tends to wear down the cusps to a level surface. Some cells in grass contain deposits of silica which can act as a strong abrasive. But in grass-eating animals such as a horse, the wear is compensated for by a great elongation of the tooth into a high-crowned form. A thick layer of cement that covers a horse's molar teeth fills in the depressions between the greatly enlarged cusps, and reduces wear. This arrangement is in effect self-sharpening. A horse's grinders will

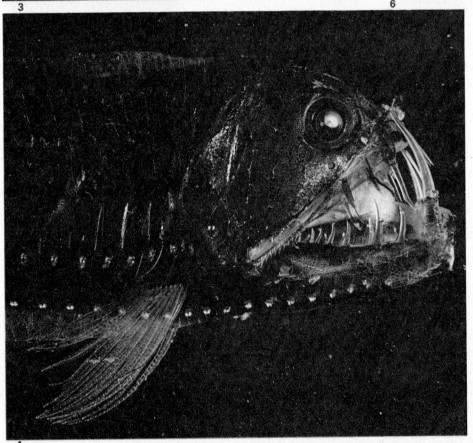

1 The squid normally swims with its long arms withdrawn among its eight tentacles, but throws them out to seize a small fish or shrimp.

2 The tentacles of the Snakelocks sea-anemone twine tightly round a tiny wrasse which is already paralysed by the poison injected into it.

3 With its powerful hooked end, the beak of a bird of prey, such as the eagle, is able to tear away hide and flesh with ease.

4 A deep-sea carnivore swims silently in search of food. Its razor-sharp incisors seize its victims, which are then cut to ribbons by its other teeth.

5 The shape of a bird's beak is often the clue to its diet – the gannet lives entirely off fish, and uses its pointed beak like a spear.

6 The vividly-coloured saffron finch has a short stubby beak – the force it can exert is powerful enough to crack open even the hardest seed.

remain rough, no matter how much grass it chews.

Plant-eating animals have no canines. There is instead a toothless gap in the upper and lower jaws between the pre-molars and incisors, called the *diastema*. The incisors are used to crop food from the ground or off trees. Many ruminants, such as deer and cows, have evolved without incisors in the upper jaw, their place being taken by a gristly pad. The incisors on the lower jaw act against this in much the same way as a knife on a chopping-board. Plants are grasped between the lower incisors and this pad and torn off by a movement of the head. But horses have retained all their front teeth, which cut off the grass that they eat. An elephant's tusks are greatly enlarged incisors.

The forms of dentition just described are only two examples from a whole range of adaptations among mammals. Man's own teeth are characteristic of an omnivorous creature; his canines are small and his molars have individual cusps. Neither kind of tooth is specialized for a diet of flesh or of plants, so that Man is able to include many different kinds of food in his diet. But in some mammals, all the teeth have become similar, returning to the undifferentiated condition found in reptiles. For example, a sperm whale has teeth that form a row of simple pointed pegs, which are quite adequate for grasping squids, on which it feeds.

One whole group of vertebrates – the birds – is toothless. Many prehistoric birds of the Cretaceous period had teeth, but no modern birds have any. Their function has been taken over by the beak, which is a horny covering on upper and lower jaws. The shapes of birds' beaks are very varied, and give a good indication of the animal's diet.

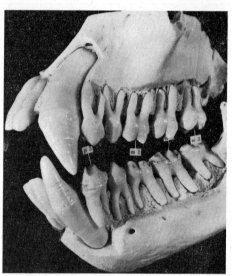

The stubby beak of many common seed-eating birds is strong and short and can bring a great deal of force to bear to break open seeds. A parrot has a beak adapted for manipulating and cracking nuts. The hooked beak of a bird of prey is used to tear pieces of flesh from the bodies of animals they catch or find dead. Insectivorous birds generally have longer beaks better adapted for extracting insects from crevices. A number of wading birds have long bills with which they probe about in mud for their animal food. These are often fringed at the edges to filter out mud and water while retaining small animals and pieces of plant matter.

The earliest insects had jaws with which they chewed solid food. Today, many species still have jaws of this sort, though many modifications of the basic form of insect mouthparts have occurred to enable them to take liquid food from many sources. Insect jaws, called *mandibles*, are pivoted so that they move sideways across the head; they do not move vertically as do the jaws of vertebrates. They are strongly thickened with hardened cuticle, often having the thickest cuticle of the body. The edges of the mandibles have raised teeth in patterns that may be characteristic of the species.

Insects, crabs and sea-anemones

The mandibles of an insect move in what is almost an open box below the head. The front side of the box is the flap of the upper lip (*labrum*). And behind the jaws lie the *maxillae,* which have appendages called *palps* that are sensitive to chemicals in food and which manipulate the pieces. Behind these, forming the back of the box, is the lower lip (*labium*), which also bears sensory palps. With jaws like these, locusts can lay waste great areas of cultivated ground by eating all the green plants; predatory beetles can feed on other insects; and scavenging beetles can clean the bones of a dead mouse.

Crustacea are remarkable for the many different forms of appendages that they have, often one pair to each segment along their whole body. Some species, such as crabs and lobsters, have mandibles which are used for chewing. The food is carried to the jaws by the great pincers or *chelae* on the first pair of walking legs. The food is also manipulated and passed to the mouth by the *maxillules,* and other appendages on the thorax may also help in dealing with food. Crustacea are arthropods; they have thick exoskeletons and, like the insects, have strong, hard jaws.

Some of the marine bristle-worms, called *polychaetes,* can deal with pieces of food. A rag-worm has a proboscis which it pushes out and at the same time exposes at its end jaws with which it can grasp food. Another worm which lives in the shell of a hermit crab will emerge and take food from beneath the mouthparts of its host crab.

Prey is also captured and dealt with by *coelenterates* (sea-anemones and corals). They possess stinging cells, called *nematocysts,* which form a long pointed needle that can penetrate and immobilize prey. Other kinds of nematocysts are coiled structures that act as lassoes and trap the prey by twisting round its hairs or spines. Mild stimulation of a few tentacles of a sea-anemone by touching them with a straw causes them to bend towards the mouth of the animal. But more vigorous stimulation, such as happens when a prey struggles as it becomes attached to the nematocysts of the tentacles, involves more tentacles, and the whole of one side of the disc of the anemone folds over. This action pushes food into the mouth, which has already been stimulated into opening by tissue fluids from the prey.

Jelly-fish catch their prey in a similar way, and the tentacles hanging round the edge of the bell are also covered with nematocysts, which automatically come into action when touched.

Top left, the python illustrates the typical arrangement of teeth in non-poisonous snakes. Since they all point backwards, it is virtually impossible for prey to escape. *Top right,* because Man is omnivorous and eats both meat and plants, his teeth are not specialized in any one direction. *Above,* the gorilla is one of the primates most closely related to Man and his teeth are very similarly arranged. *Below,* the genet has the cat's characteristic pointed canines; the large carnassial teeth act as scissors, shearing flesh from its prey.

The particle eaters

The sea is a pasture for many creatures. From great whales to tiny mussels, they graze like animals on land, filtering millions of tiny organisms to provide a continuous intake of food.

THE WATERS of the seas are full of nutrients in the form of chemical substances washed into them by rivers. Animals cannot make direct use of all these substances. But in the upper layers of the sea, there live millions of single-celled plant organisms which can photosynthesise and build the nutrients into proteins, fats and carbohydrates. There are several kinds of these organisms, which are called *phytoplankton,* including *diatoms* with their silica-containing cases, and flagellates such as *dinoflagellates.* There are also enormous numbers of the very tiniest flagellates, called *nannoflagellates,* which are so small that they escape capture in the normal nets used for catching plankton. Despite their small size, these creatures are the main source of food for other larger creatures in the plankton. The phytoplankton is the pasture of the sea.

Filters and filaments

There are many small animals in the plankton; some of the young creatures which grow to be adults who live elsewhere, feed on the phytoplankton. The whole collection of small animals and tiny plants are an almost limitless source of food for animals that can collect them. But to be able to sieve these forms of food out of the water requires special adaptation quite different from the jaws and teeth of animals that take food in large pieces. For example, the whalebone whales, unlike sperm whales and porpoises, have no teeth. In their place, they have horny strips with frayed edges hanging down the sides of their mouths. After taking a mouthful of sea-water, the whale uses its tongue like a piston to drive water out of its mouth through the whalebone sieve which traps small shrimp-like creatures called *krill* on the inner sides of the strips. Krill occur in swarms in the Antarctic seas and provide the food for these huge mammals. To provide enough energy and proteins, the intake of food must be as continuous as in the feeding habits of many land herbivores.

Filter-feeding involves straining food from large quantities of water, and is found only in aquatic animals. Since most invertebrates live in water, filter-feeding is well developed in many of them. A good example is the peacock worm *(Sabella pavonina).* This worm builds an erect tube which stands six to twelve inches high on the seabed. The worm lives inside the tube, moving to the top to display a fan of tentacular filaments which give the worm its name. Each filament sticks out radially from the head-end of the worm and the worms use them to catch the tiny food particles which swim by or which come raining down on them.

The filaments of the peacock worm are

The lovely branching filaments *above* belong to the peacock worm. But not only are they very beautiful; they provide one of the finest examples of a filter-feeding apparatus in an invertebrate. They act as a gill, sifting minute particles from the water, and then passing them on to the mouth.

arranged like a funnel, with the mouth of the worm at its base. Each filament has a row of tiny branches called *pinnules* sticking out on two sides. The rows of pinnules on neighbouring filaments interlock near the bases, but higher up they are free from each other. Hair-like *cilia,* are borne on these pinnules and produce a water current which carries food to the worm. The cilia beat towards the tips of the pinnules, bringing water into the funnel. Other cilia on the upper and lower sides of the pinnules beat cross-ways at right angles to the cilia on the outside. This action creates eddies in the water on the inner side of each pinnule and also deposits food particles inside the worm's 'funnel'. More cilia, beating towards the base of the funnel, convey food particles downwards and towards the mouth.

Notice that this mechanism catches particles and conveys them regardless of their size or of their usefulness as food. Some of the particles may be silt, without any food value at all, and others may be small diatoms and so on which can be used as food. It is typical of filter-feeding that at first the creature makes a random collection of particles. There then follows a period of sorting when some particles are retained and others are rejected. Generally the choice is based on size, and this is the case with the peacock worm which retains only the smaller particles as food. The largest particles are rejected, and those of intermediate size used as building material for the worm's tube. How is this sorting done?

Towards the base of each filament, the pinnules are replaced by two continuous folds that rise from the axis to enclose a space between them. The width of this space is not equal from its base to the upper open side: it tapers towards the bottom. Cilia on the outer surfaces of the folds carry particles upwards to the edges. Cilia inside beat in the same direction and there are two additional tracts down the length of the filament leading to the worm's mouth. There is not enough room for large particles between the folds and they are therefore carried along the top to be rejected at the base of the filament. Intermediate-sized particles travel along one of the tracts and the smallest particles fall to the bottom to be carried to the mouth.

Selecting particles

The worm's mouth is surrounded by three lips, one dorsal and two lateral. Each has two ciliary tracts on its surface, which coincide with those on the basal folds of the filament. Sorting which has taken place on the filament is maintained by the lips, whose tracts lead the medium and small particles to their appropriate places. The smallest are taken into the mouth as food. The medium particles are also important, although they are not used as food. They pass instead to two expansions of the lateral lips called the *ventral sacs*. Here they are mixed with mucus to form a string which is manipulated by special folds and added to the upper edge of the tube which encloses the worm's body. In this way, the particles collected by the crown of tentacles are used not only for feeding but also for building.

Mucus 'glues' together particles to form larger pieces and sheets which can be moved more easily; the particles for building the tube are held together in this way. The largest particles, due for rejection, are also trapped in mucus on the lips so that they can be discarded more easily. This material, mucus, is found throughout the animal kingdom and is frequently associated with cilia in filter-feeding mechanisms. Its sticky properties, its ability to form sheets and strings, and the ease with which cilia can move it make it ideal for its function. Mucus also poses interesting problems, such as: why the material in which small food particles become stuck does not also tangle the cilia which move it? In a similar way, the mites which inhabit the gills of freshwater mussels move about in mucus without becoming entangled.

Mucus is particularly associated with filter-feeding in molluscs. But it is used in different ways in other worms, such as *Chaetopterus*, which lives in a U-shaped burrow in mud. Its tube is as thick as a finger, and the worm itself has various flaps and appendages on its body with which it creates a current of water through the tube. The circulating water is the worm's source of oxygen and is also its source of food. On its tenth segment, the worm has a pair of appendages which can be held out like arms against the walls of

Attached to each waving, hollow tentacle of the freshwater polyzoa, *top,* are hundreds of little hair-like cilia. These pick up the microscopic specks of organic matter on which the polyzoa feed, before they are carried into their mouths.

Above, when submerged again by the incoming tide, each one of these massed gooseneck barnacles will open its hinged shell and start sweeping the water for little plants and animals with its feathery *cirri,* or feeding limbs.

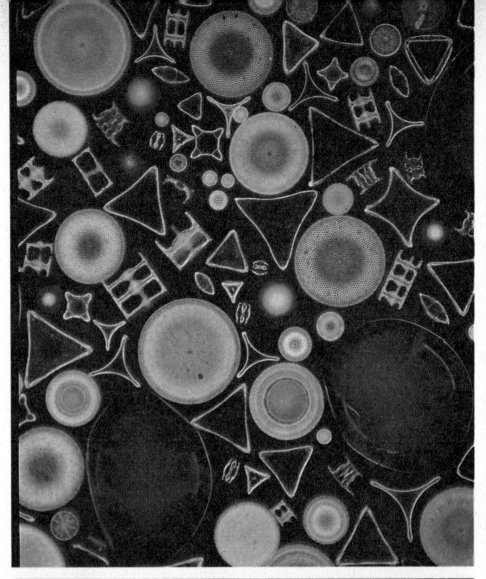

Left, a fantastic pattern is made by tiny, unicellular diatoms. They occur in plankton in such numbers they are justly termed the seas' 'pasture'. *Below,* the sponge is virtually a living machine, constantly pumping water in, and out again, while filtering precious food particles *en route.*

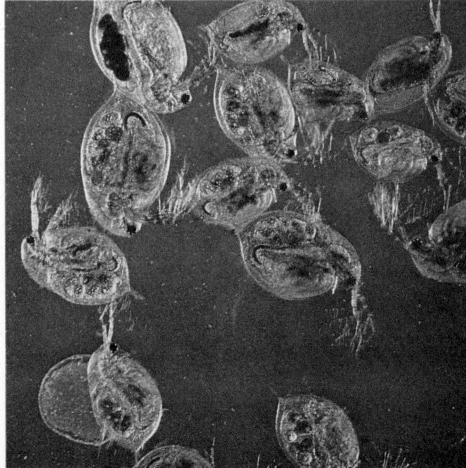

Above, although the mussel looks drab and lifeless when exposed, once surrounded again by water it opens up its two shells and displays one of the most elaborate filtering arrangements of all. *Left,* tiny water-fleas—*Daphnia ulex*—dart through the water searching for the minute plants they feed on. These are filtered from the surrounding sea by means of the *Daphnia's* complicated limbs.

The sea-squirts, *above,* feed by drawing water in through one entrance and then across a large gill chamber where particles become trapped in mucus. The sea-fir, *right,* is made up of thousands of little polyps, each housed in interconnecting tubes, equipped with its own feeding filaments.

the tube. From along their edges, they secrete mucus in a continuous sheet. The bottom edge of the mucus-sheet, next to the body, ends in a small ciliated cup in the middle of the underside of the body (as the worm lies on its back, this appears to be the upper surface). In this way, the sheet of mucus forms a bag which is held open by the 'arms' and which ends in the ciliated cup. The mucus is produced continuously, and the bag is continuously gathered in by the cup. The water current passes through the mucus net and particles are trapped. Then the whole lot, mucus and food, is gathered in and passed forward along the body to the worm's mouth. In this way, food is removed from the water stream as it passes through the tube.

Of all creatures, molluscs have the most elaborate arrangements for sorting and rejecting particles. Most bivalves – the two-shelled molluscs such as oysters, clams and mussels – feed by filtering their food from the surrounding water or from the sediment on the sea bottom beside them. Most of these creatures remain in one place for a long time, often buried in sand or mud. Some of them are capable of moving with ease and speed, but even these remain still for most of the time. The cockle, for example, burrows its way deep into the sand, using its muscular foot as a scoop. Clams, which prefer to lie in mud, are found particularly on the shores of North America, and can weigh up to six or seven pounds. Mussels like to adhere to rocks, between the lines of high and low tide, doing so by means of sticky

hairs called the *byssus.*

It is characteristic of these animals that they maintain a stream of water into and out of their shells. The water is impelled by the beat of cilia to enter through the *inhalant* opening of a siphon; after bathing the animal's body within the shells, the water leaves through the *exhalant* opening of the siphon. The shells are hinged along the animal's back. Beneath the animal hangs the muscular foot by which it moves, and at each side of the foot are the gills which are the food-gathering organs of the animal. On the inner side of each shell lies the *mantle,* a thin layer of tissue whose edge forms the shell.

Fine cilia and mucus sheets

The common shore mussel, for example, has a pair of gills on each side of its body. Each gill is folded back on itself, so that in cross-section the pair resembles a letter W. But the gill is not a continuous sheet of tissue; it is made up a series of filaments which run from the point of attachment to the fold and then to the edge. Each filament is attached to the next by a pad of interlocking stiff cilia, so that the gills are virtually sheets of tissue perforated by many small holes through which water can pass.

The *lateral* cilia on each side of the outer surface of the gill filament draw water into the shells and, by their beating action, pass it between the filaments and into the space within the gills. Just in front of these cilia, standing on the angle

of the gills in a perfect position to guard the entrances between the filaments, are the *latero-frontal* cilia which beat towards the outer surfaces of the filaments. In this way, food particles in the water stream are caught by the cilia and thrown on to the surface of the filament. This outer surface has, in turn, a set of cilia called the *frontals* which beat in yet another direction, downwards towards the fold in the filament. These cilia move a sheet of mucus downwards over the gill, and in this sheet the particles become trapped. The mucus from both sides of the gill moves into a food groove along the fold. There, ciliary tracts move the food towards the mouth, where further sorting of particles takes place. This is achieved by a series of overlapping folds. In the gutters between them, ciliary tracts beat outwards while another stream crosses the crests going towards the mouth. Heavier particles tend to drop out of the mucus into the gutters where they are swept away and rejected. But the lighter particles are passed from crest to crest and reach the mouth. This sorting is purely by weight and size; actual food value is not a consideration.

Mucus and cilia are not essentials for filter-feeding. Shrimps, crabs and lobsters characteristically lack both cilia and mucus, and they strain their food from the water by using complicated arrangements of appendages fringed with fine hairs. These sweep the food from the water, and the particles are carried along to the mouth by eddies which form among the moving limbs.

Predators and prey

Many animals, including ourselves, are predators, hunting and killing other animals for food. Man is the most dangerous of all, because his activities destroy the natural balance of Nature.

THE CONCEPT of ecology has probably been one of the most fruitful developments in biological science over the past 50 years. By taking a broad view of the relations between various animals in an area and by noting how the species interact, the ecologist is able to draw some conclusions about the likely effects of changes in the environment on the intricate links in the life-chain.

Nowhere is this interaction more apparent than in the relations between predator and prey. Human beings are accustomed to see this relationship in moral terms, but this view is of little value. Darwin's famous definition of survival of the fittest is far more applicable than the type of moral considerations often imposed on natural events. What the moral view fails to see is the fact that both predator and prey benefit from the relationship in a balanced ecology, and that the system often operates in the best interests of both species.

Meat-eaters and plant-eaters

All animal life in one way or another is dependent on plants. Only the plants can make the complex carbon molecules, the sugars and the amino acids, that are required for life. Many animals feed wholly or in part on plants, while other animals eat the plant-eaters. The animals which eat other animals are called *carnivores* (meat-eaters) and unlike the plant-eaters they have to track down and overcome their animal prey, unless they happen to find their meat already dead.

Because of the relationship between plants and animals, the meat-eaters have a much more limited supply of food than the plant-eaters and there are therefore

1 A larva of the great diving beetle holds a tadpole clamped between its powerful mandibles. The larva is well built to capture and kill its defenceless prey.
2 The elongated snout of the giant South American ant-eater equips it for eating the termites which form its staple diet. The ant-eater is itself camouflaged against its predators.
3 The end of the hunt for an otter. A number of mammals have taken to life in or around water, which contains a plentiful supply of food. The otter's streamlined body aids its swimming.

fewer of them. This general rule can be seen in operation in many different types of habitat. Every fisherman knows that while there may be many tiny minnows in a river, there are likely to be few large pike. The same is true of the relative numbers of foxes and rabbits in hunting country, or of the numbers of golden eagles compared with herbivores in the Scottish Highlands. The predators, in other words, tend to come at or near the end of a food-chain, where much of the energy originally taken from the plants eaten by the plant-eating animals has already been spent on keeping the plant-eaters alive. An additional reason is that the predators must not eat all their prey – if the pike were to eat all the minnows no more minnows would be reproduced and the pike would rapidly die of starvation.

These basic considerations, then, condition the relations between predatory animals and their prey. No predator can afford to exterminate the whole of the species it preys on without undermining the condition for its own existence.

At the same time, the predatory animal must be able to catch sufficient of the prey to remain alive, and for this may require

certain special attributes to enable it to make sure of catching and eating enough.

For these reasons, predators are generally larger than their prey, although this is not an invariable rule, and they tend to be isolated animals rather than vast flocks or herds. It is estimated, for example, that there is only one grizzly bear to every 40 square miles of the Canadian Rockies. Like many other predators, these animals tend to be solitary in habit and highly jealous of their territory. If another grizzly enters into their domain they are liable to fight it out with the intruder, which will often retreat rapidly over the 'frontier'.

There is therefore a social adaptation among predators which allows them to exploit their prey most efficiently without too great competition between members of the same species.

But predators also need to be specialized in other ways. In many cases, like the predators which feed on the giant herds of antelope in the African veld, their prey is fast-moving and congregates in herds for protection. The predators must be able to stalk their prey so as not to give too much warning of their presence and to be able to catch the prey on the run. For this reason, animals like the lion are capable of considerable turns of speed, at least over short distances, and are well equipped with sharp claws and powerful limbs to strike down and kill their victims once they have caught up with them. The ability to run fast in pursuit of prey is even more highly developed in the cheetah. This animal can run faster than an express train over short distances, and is well equipped to catch an antelope on the run.

Birds of prey also need to be able to make speedy captures. The kestrel is a typical example. This bird feeds mainly on small rodents and insects, and hovers high above them, swooping down with great speed to catch the prey before it has had time to escape. The kestrel's powerful beak and strong talons give it the power to kill and grasp its prey while carrying it off through the air.

Teeth and jaws

Predators must also be able to eat their food after they have killed it, and for this they require specially adapted teeth and powerful jaws. The dog family of animals have well-developed canine teeth for ripping the flesh of their prey and powerful jaws for cracking its bones.

Not all carnivores are solitary animals; some have evolved the social mechanism of the pack to help them to catch and kill their prey. The dog family is an example, and wolves frequently hunt in packs, enabling them to bring down animals larger than themselves, extending the scope of their predation.

By no means all animals prey on the larger herbivores, however. There are many species specially adapted for eating insects or fish or birds. The various species of ant-eater, for example, are highly specialized for eating ants, and the giant ant-eaters of South America, with their elongated heads and mouths, are virtually incapable of eating anything else. Their success in this activity is testified to by their large size. The termites which form their main food live in huge mounds which tower above the plain, and the ant-eaters can generally find a plentiful supply of ants.

Other animals, both mammals and birds, have made fishing their niche. The otter, like the beaver and the water-rat, will swim underwater in order to catch large fish in their native environment.

The seals have carried this adaptation even further than the otter and spend all their time in the sea, except for a short period before and after breeding.

Other species have become adapted to other forms of predation. The blood-sucking insects provide a good example. There are many different types of blood-

1

1 The genet, a small cat-like carnivore, is found in Africa and southern Europe and feeds mainly on small mammals and birds. It lives in trees and on the banks of streams.
2 A dead vapourer moth caterpillar surrounded by larvae of the ichneumon fly. The larvae, laid inside the caterpillar, have eaten away its tissues and thus killed it.
3 A chain snake forms the food for this king snake. Snakes usually eat small reptiles and mammals and devour their prey whole. Their teeth are set backwards to help them swallow.

2

3

sucking insects, and by no means all are adapted to feed on Man. Within the blood-sucking varieties there is considerable specialization, which goes so far that, in the case of the tsetse fly *Glossina*, the insect is unable to ingest blood corpuscles more than 18 microns in diameter. Other blood-suckers, attracted by certain scents or by other forms of chemical attraction, will only drink the blood of a single species.

The blood-sucking bats are highly adapted to take advantage of their prey while it is asleep. Though their activities bear only a tenuous relation to those of the legendary vampire, some blood-sucking bats display remarkable ingenuity in getting at their victim's blood. They attack only at night, while the victim is sleeping, and search out uncovered areas of the body, such as the soles of the feet. There they make small incisions through which the blood seeps out and the bat licks it up rather like a cat lapping up milk. Not all vampires attack human beings – some prey largely on cattle and other large mammals.

How does predation affect the popula-

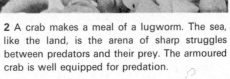

1 The leopard has dragged its prey, a dead antelope, into the branches of a tree to prevent other predators from eating its kill. Many large predators have prodigious strength.

2 A crab makes a meal of a lugworm. The sea, like the land, is the arena of sharp struggles between predators and their prey. The armoured crab is well equipped for predation.

3 The sparrowhawk, a bird of prey, takes the bodies of its victims to a specific spot – the plucking post – where it discards their feathers or hair before eating them.

tion of prey? Naturally, too much predation tends towards the extermination of the prey, and no doubt this happens to some species when the balance of their relationship with their predator is seriously upset. Often the introduction of a new predator into the set-up can menace the survival of a species. Man is easily the most dangerous predator in this respect.

The annals of zoology are littered with examples of animals killed off by the activities of human beings. One thinks of the almost-extinct American buffalo, the dodo and the passenger pigeon. But in undisturbed circumstances, the activities of the predators can have a strengthening effect on the population of prey as a whole.

One reason for this is that the very act of predation, particularly on a herd of animals, tends to select the least hardy animals as prey. The old animals, those unable to run as fast as the others, and the animals rejected by the herd are likely to fall prey to the predators first. Indeed, this type of selection occurs all the time in the antelope herds which form the staple reservoir for the predatory activities

1 Man as predator. The rabbits in the wire enclosure were rounded up in Idaho in order to keep down the population and protect the surrounding farmland.
2 A kingfisher with a captured fish. Many types of birds have taken to fishing as a way of life, both in fresh-water rivers and, like the gulls, in ocean waters.
3 The shrike feeds on small animals and birds, which it kills with a blow of its pointed beak. It bears the bodies off to a thorn tree, where it impales them on thorns until ready to eat.

mates with her and gets away as best he can.

Cannibalism is not confined to the spiders and is fairly common among animals, and even more common among insects. Sharks are another group of animals noted for their cannibalistic tendencies – they will tear an injured comrade to pieces as readily as they will tear a piece of carrion.

Wolves are noted for the same type of behaviour, and are not averse to a bit of cannibalism when the supply of other food is low.

Many predators change their prey if they are forced to by hunger. Foxes, which usually feed on small mammals, will eat berries and other plant foods if they are faced with starvation. In fact, most predators have fairly catholic tastes, because their food supply is less assured than that of their prey. An over-finnicky predator would not be able to survive for very long.

Many predators are subject to cyclical variations in the availability of their food supply. Many small mammals undergo a cycle of some years duration, during which the population reaches a peak and then declines. The predator population tends to decline with the cycle and rise again as the glut of prey increases.

Man – the most harmful predator

Human activity is having highly deleterious effects on many of the most important predators, particularly the birds of prey. Some years ago, there were 12 breeding pairs of golden eagles in Wales, but in 1968 there was only one pair. Similar falls in the number of large carnivorous birds have been found in other parts of the world. The reason for this fall is the spread of the use of persistent insecticides. These poisons have a particularly harmful effect on the reproductive system, and eggs with a high concentration of substances like DDT are frequently sterile. The effect on the predators, right at the top of the food-chain, is most marked because the insecticide residues persist for many years in animal fat and are thus passed up the food-chains and retained in the tissues of the animals at the top of the food-chain. The immediate effects are felt among the insects at the bottom of the food-chains, but the effects are in fact far more catastrophic among the few beautiful birds at the top of the chain.

This damage to the most beautiful predators, the birds of prey like the eagles, hawks and owls, is entirely in line with the rest of human disruption of the natural ecology. The plight of many rare animals stems directly from human activities. Whaling has almost exterminated a number of species of whale, while other animals, like the giant panda and the mountain gorilla, are in grave danger of extinction. Man is in fact the most widespread, the most persistent and the most harmful of all predators. His ability to spread death and destruction in the animal kingdom has already had disastrous results in many cases and is likely if continued unchecked, to do still more harm. If there is a moral in predation it is surely in this and not in the activities of other predators.

of the African lion and his family.

Even in cases where this type of mechanism can only operate less directly, predation still has a beneficial effect in maintaining the population of prey within acceptable overall limits. Where a predator is removed altogether, catastrophic effects can result. Lack of the customary predators was probably one of main reasons for the enormous and rapid spread of the rabbit after its introduction into Australia. The animals' formidable breeding system was able to operate without hindrance and within a very few years the whole continent was covered with millions of rabbits, an almost uncontrollable pest. Similar dangers have been found with other species introduced from abroad, particularly with insect pests. One species of ladybirds introduced into America to control cotton pests itself became a serious menace in the absence of its natural predators.

Despite the benefits to the species and to the general balance of nature which predation provides, many animals go to great lengths to avoid falling victim to predators. Among insects many bizarre and often attractive forms have resulted from attempts at protective coloration. Camouflage, like that of the stick insects, provides one obvious type of protection, and hundreds of examples from among the insect community could be found. But less well known are the insects which have developed warning colours to mimic some distasteful or noxious insect which a predator would be likely to avoid.

The various pseudo-wasps have solved some of their problems in this way, matching their colours to those of real wasps in an attempt, often successful, to discourage birds and other insects from tackling them.

A more serious problem is posed for the males of some kinds of spider, which are likely to become the prey of the females if they approach while the females are unreceptive. The male is smaller than the female in many spider species, and has to resort to subterfuge in order to make sure of escaping with his life.

The male spider shakes the web before venturing on to it and judges the female's receptivity by her response. If she comes thundering down the web towards him, he flees, whereas if she gives signs that she is not hungry, he gingerly approaches,

Blood-suckers and hangers-on

Parasites obtain nourishment in a multitude of ingenious ways. While some tap the sap of trees or the blood of animals, others wallow in the luxury of digested food in their hosts' intestines.

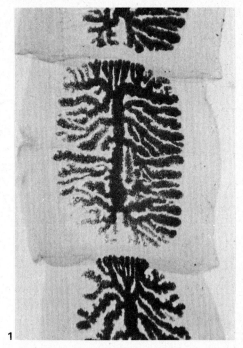

FOR AS LONG as he can remember Man has come up against parasites which concern him especially because of their attacks upon him and upon his domestic animals. Records of parasites date back very far. Ancient Chinese physicians described malaria in fine detail and the Bible provides other possible references to parasites. The fiery serpent of the Book of Numbers may be none other than the guinea-worm, *Dracunculus medinensis,* a scourge common in Africa and parts of Asia.

In the course of their excavations archaeologists are now finding evidence of human parasites. In 1910 Dr Ruffer discovered the eggs of a type of liver fluke, *Schistosoma haematobium* in Egyptian mummies. This parasite causes bilharzia, a terrible disease which can be fatal and is still widespread in many parts of the world, including Egypt. Close inspection of fossilized human faeces has revealed on occasions the eggs, often extraordinarily well preserved, of intestinal parasites such as the roundworm – Ascaris – and of several types of tapeworm.

Although many of the common parasites have been known and endured for many hundreds of years, until recently very little was known about the parasites themselves. Parasites have a unique and complicated relationship with the organisms they attack as well as with their environment. They are, therefore, difficult to study although they are often a source of morbid fascination.

What do we mean by the term parasite? In nature we find all kinds of associations between animals; when the association is loose and both species are able to

1 By adding new segments to its body, a tapeworm can reach a length of 60 ft or more in the intestine of its host. When ripe each segment contains thousands of eggs.
2 Barnacles are usually associated with rocks and ships. But the sac barnacle parasitizes the shore crab and when mature produces a huge egg mass on the underside of its host.

live independently of one another – like the association of a sea anemone and a hermit crab with one animal being transported by the other which itself gains protection from predators – this association is described as *commensalism.* When both species are dependent on each other but obtain some mutual benefit – as when certain *unicellular plants* (species of algae) live in animal cells such as those of the coelenterate hydra, and in return for nutrients such as amino acids, photosynthesize and produce carbohydrates which they share with their host – this association is called *symbiosis.* But when one species is highly dependent on the other species and is unable to survive if separated permanently from its host, it is called *parasitism.*

Parasitism is not a freak of nature but a way of life adopted by many different animal types. Indeed almost every major branch of the evolutionary tree in the animal kingdom has some parasitic members, although very few of these are able to infect human beings.

Because parasites have had to evolve a special form and physiology to enable them to lead their special way of life, they have come to look very different from their free-living non-parasitic relatives. For example, a close relative, *Ler-*

naeocera branchialis, of the crustacean water mites looks quite unlike its near relatives when, as an adult, it is attached to the gills of sea fish that are its natural host. The female has three functions: to remain attached to the gills, to feed on the tissues of the host, and to reproduce.

Whereas *Lernaeocera* cannot move around on its host, fleas are highly mobile. The dog flea, *Ctenocephalides canis,* which also infects cats, does not remain long on Man. It is laterally flattened, enabling it to move about easily amongst the host's hairs. The well-developed jumping legs and the lack of wings are characteristic of all fleas. On the other hand the mite, *Demodex folliculorum* has short, stumpy legs, which it does not use to carry it about for *Demodex,* causing mange in Man, lives in the hair follicles, into which it conveniently fits owing to the elongated shape of the body. The whale louse, *Paracyamus boopis,* has three highly developed pairs of clawed legs, which are used for attachment to the skin. It also has a flattened body and biting mouthparts.

The Lamellibranch molluscs, *Anodonta cygnea,* or swan mussels, common in many streams and lakes move about very little and have evolved a cunning method of dispersing their young. The parasitic larvae are specially adapted for attachment to the gills or skin of the fish with which they come into contact. The larvae remain with the fish for many weeks assimilating tissue which is induced to grow around them. Eventually they drop off and take up a free-living existence as young adults.

Leeches, relatives of the earthworms,

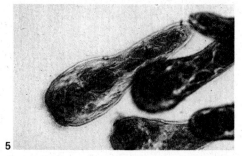

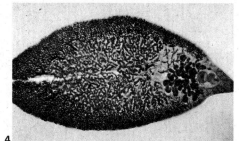

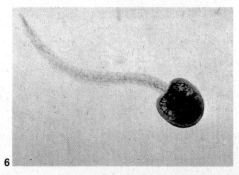

1 Certain fungi, like *Ganoderma,* grow on the bark of trees. By infiltrating the wood with their roots they may cause considerable damage.

2 Another fungus, black smut, parasitizes the head of mature barley. When the infestation is severe an entire crop can be ruined.

3 Mildew is a parasitic fungus that grows like a coat over the surface of its host. These rosebuds will never be able to blossom properly.

4 The liver fluke, which causes liver rot in sheep and cattle, lives in the large portal veins in the liver of its host. The fluke has a large sucker on its head to prevent it being swept away in a torrent of blood.

5 Before being able to infect a sheep, the liver fluke must pass through an intermediate host, a snail. The larvae, which infect a snail, reproduce many times into these tiny redia larvae.

6 The redia larvae also reproduce into mature larvae called cercaria. These then burst out of the snail and swim on to nearby vegetation, where they encyst until ingested by a browsing sheep. The cercaria then matures into a fluke.

7 Nearly all species of mammal can harbour ticks. These hang on to long grass until an unsuspecting mammal brushes by. Once on the mammal the ticks, like these on a hedgehog, bury their mouthparts into the skin and suck blood.

are common in many waters and are well known for their blood-sucking habits. They are highly developed for blood feeding, with biting jaws and sucking apparatus. The two strong suckers and their slimy nature make them very difficult to remove once on the host.

Parasites which live on the skin and outer tissues, have evolved all kinds of fascinating adaptations. But many of the more economically important parasites live right inside the tissues of the host. The most devastating and important, as far as man is concerned, are the malarial parasites, and *trypanosomes* (the parasites responsible for sleeping sickness). Both are single-celled protozoa, living in the blood, and humans are infected through being bitten by the insects which act as intermediate hosts. As well as being adapted to living in humans, these para-

sites are adapted to living in mosquitoes and tsetse flies.

The amoeba, *Entamoeba histolytica,* which causes a severe type of dysentery, is a parasite of temperate and tropical areas. It, too, is a protozoan, but has no intermediate host and the infection is maintained by unhygienic conditions. The reproducing form of this amoeba is passed in the faeces. The amoeba can pass unharmed through the intestine of flies and thus get transmitted to food when carried on the feet of flies.

The flukes or *schistosomes* which live in the blood-vessels of Man and other mammals, need to pass through a snail as an intermediate host. A variety of freshwater snails harbour the larval stages. The infective larvae escape from the snails and penetrate the human skin. They then travel to the portal blood-vessels of the liver where they become adult. They are always found in pairs, the female living in a groove formed by folds of the male body. Sophistications of this sort are not uncommon among parasites and are always of some advantage, either for reproduction or transmission, for all parasites have extremely efficient methods of reproduction.

The beef tapeworm, *Taenia saginata*, of Man demonstrates the ultimate in parasite egg production. It can reach a length of 80 ft with 2,000 or more segments, all capable of producing enormous numbers of eggs. The adults live in the intestine, holding on to the gut wall with four strong suckers, and release ripe segments, which pass out with the faeces. Cattle act as the intermediate hosts to the parasite and Man is infected by eating contaminated raw or undercooked beef.

Eelworms are threadworms (nematodes) that parasitize a wide variety of bulbs and other economic crops. Potato rot, for example, is due to *Heterodera rostochiensis,* and once the eggs of this parasite are present in the soil they are very difficult to eliminate. Several diseases of Man are caused by nematodes, like *Wuchereria bancrofti,* which is carried by mosquitoes and manifests itself in Man by the gross enlargement of the lymph nodes, a condition known as elephantiasis. The guinea worm, *Dracunculus medinensis,* uses tiny crustacean copepods living in drinking water as the intermediate hosts. The adult worm may be up to one metre long and can be extracted from under the skin by winding it slowly on to a stick, an unpleasant method, but still the most successful.

If the biology of a parasite is to be understood the zoologist must unravel its fascinating mode of life and especially its passage between one host and another. This transmission is perhaps a parasite's largest hurdle, for failure would prove fatal to any parasite species.

The liver fluke, *Fasciola hepatica,* which causes liver rot in sheep and cattle, is a common parasite in Britain. It is responsible for losses of thousands of pounds to the farmer and thrives in low-lying areas where there is often standing water in which lives the intermediate host, an amphibious snail, *Linnaea trunculata.*

Multiplication

In sheep, the adult fluke lives in the bile duct of the liver and moves around by the use of two suckers on its ventral surface. Here it feeds, causing extensive liver damage (rendering it totally inedible) and produces many thousands of eggs. These eventually find their way out with the faeces, and if they are deposited in water, the eggs develop and hatch, releasing a very small mobile ciliated larva which swims around in the water, and has a sensory system enabling it to detect chemicals released by the snail. Once the larva finds a suitable snail it penetrates the skin of the snail – the integument – by secreting enzymes.

Then follows two larval stages within the snail, called the *sporocyst* and the *redia,* both of which are purely for the multiplication of individuals. Each sporocyst gives rise to large numbers of redia and each redia in turn produces many other individuals called *cercariae*. These

escape from the snail either when it dies or by bursting out into the water. Somehow each cercaria must get back into the sheep to complete the cycle, and it does so by swimming up nearby vegetation, using its tail for propulsion, and encysts there. The cyst is amazingly resistant to water loss and only hatches when a sheep eats it while browsing on the vegetation. The process is extremely wasteful at both stages, for not every larva finds a snail and only some of the cercarial cysts are eaten by sheep.

Most people, at one time or another, have kept a pet cat and watched it meticulously wash and preen itself. Few realize that this habit has helped the tapeworm *Dipylidium caninum* to infect nearly a third of the cats in Britain. The adult worm lives in the intestine of cats and dogs. Although this is an excellent site for readily available food, it tends to be somewhat turbulent, and therefore the tapeworm is armed on its head with four strong suckers and a small protuberance around which is arranged rows of hooklets. The whole apparatus is used to anchor the worm to the gut wall and prevent it from being swept away. Unlike the beef tapeworm, *Dipylidium* is very much shorter and has fewer segments, but they both lay their eggs in a mobile pocket or *proglottid* which breaks away from the end of the worm. This is passed down the intestine and may be expelled with the faeces or crawl out of the anus. As it moves along it leaves a trail of eggs upon which larval fleas feed. These larval fleas become infected with the cysticercoid stage which remains with them through-

it uses the *opisthaptor*. This organ is similar in shape to a feeble sucker, but is armed with a most impressive array of hooks – two large hooks, separated by a bar, near the centre of the opisthaptor and eight pairs of smaller hooks arranged round the edge. The entire organ acts as a most efficient anchoring system. *Gyrodactylus* moves along by a curious looping movement, alternately using the opisthaptor and the oral method of attachment.

Gyrodactylus is unique amongst its fellows in that it is mostly *ovoviviparous* (does not lay eggs); the larvae develop within the adult uterus. By the time the larvae are ready to leave the adult they themselves may have a developing larva within their own uterus. The number of *Gyrodactylus* on the fish in winter-time is fairly low, but during the spring larvae are rapidly produced and in overcrowded conditions the numbers may reach a pathogenic level very quickly, resulting in extensive gill damage and sometimes death.

Ways of reinfection

The nematode *Enterobius vermicularis,* or common pinworm, uses precisely the same crowded conditions for its dispersal, for it is a characteristic parasite of schools and institutions. The adults live in the lower part of the intestine of Man and at night the female partially crawls out of the anus to lay her eggs on the skin. At the same time an acid secretion is produced which causes irritation and induces the host to scratch the area. The eggs are prone to drying out, but at night conditions in a bed are warm and humid and they can survive for some time. They are also very sticky and remain on the fingers and under the nails. People with *Enterobius* often show certain nervous symptoms, such as biting the nails, and in this way reinfection takes place when the eggs are ingested. The sticky eggs may, however, be transferred to doorknobs and railings where they soon dry out and die, unless quickly picked up by the next host.

Despite the multitude of parasites and their successful adaptations we can be cheered by the thought that not all living creatures are weighed down under a heavy burden of worms or festooned from head to tail with ectoparasites. Indeed, it is only under exceptional circumstances that parasites gain the upper hand, for a dead or chronically sick host is no use to a living parasite.

The very nature of parasitism requires the parasite to maintain a finely balanced relationship with its various hosts, for the host must not eliminate it or prevent the continuation of its cycle. We, therefore, have a very effective tool with which to attack the parasite, for by simply looking for the weakest link in the cycle we have some control.

An ever-increasing number of chemicals are being developed for the control of insects, molluscs and the parasites themselves. It is because of this, together with a better understanding of the mechanisms of parasitism and particularly their ecology, that we are now, to a certain extent, able to control and contain infections.

1 Mistletoe grows as a parasite on the bark of trees. By burying its roots into the bark it can draw the sap of its host.
2 By secreting a special substance the growing gall wasp makes the oak leaf form a protective hump around it.
3 In earlier times physicians made use of the medicinal leech to .bleed feverish patients. The leech is endowed with two large suckers, one for hanging on and the other for burying in the skin of its host. The leech also secretes an anti-coagulant to stop the blood clotting.

out their development into adults. Cats and dogs accidentally ingest the fleas while washing themselves and become infected.

In this situation a host has two species of parasites, fleas and tapeworms, in which one, the flea, is acting as host to the larval stages of the tapeworm. Although this is unusual it is not a unique relationship amongst parasites. *Dipylidium* is merely taking advantage of the association between fleas and their cat and dog hosts for its own transmission.

Dipylidium only has a brief phase outside a host and the eggs have a thick shell to prevent water loss. Parasites in the aquatic environment do not have to prevent dehydration, and transmission is therefore less hazardous. For this reason fish have many species of ectoparasites living on their skin and gills, such as *Gyrodactylus elegans,* a common parasite of the goldfish in garden ponds.

Gyrodactylus is a direct parasite; it relies on bodily contact for its infection and distribution and flourishes under crowded conditions such as an overstocked garden pond. It is able temporarily to attach itself by means of the cement gland, situated at the oral end, which exudes a sticky secretion, but for permanent or semi-permanent attachment

The fuel of life

All life on Earth depends on the sun's energy. Plants can use this directly, but animals cannot. Complex 'food-webs' of prey and predator among animals have developed to overcome this.

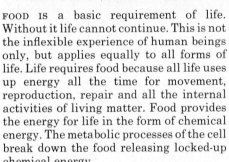

1

2

FOOD IS a basic requirement of life. Without it life cannot continue. This is not the inflexible experience of human beings only, but applies equally to all forms of life. Life requires food because all life uses up energy all the time for movement, reproduction, repair and all the internal activities of living matter. Food provides the energy for life in the form of chemical energy. The metabolic processes of the cell break down the food releasing locked-up chemical energy.

The basic types of food for most living matter are *proteins, carbohydrates* and *fats*. These three types of compounds serve different functions in living matter. The proteins, which consist basically of long chains of smaller molecules called *amino acids,* are the fundamental 'building blocks' of the cell. In animals, they are closely involved in the reproduction of the cell and control of its development. Most animals can make protein from its constituent amino acids, but require protein in food to obtain the amino acids from which to manufacture further protein.

Sources of energy

Carbohydrates, such as sugar and starch, are composed of longer or shorter sugar molecules, in much the same way that proteins are chains of amino acids. The carbohydrates are ready sources of energy for the activities of living cells. They are used by some living matter to provide structural material as protein is used by animals. The cellulose which makes up the cell wall of many plants is a form of

1 A privet moth caterpillar feeding on privet leaves. Caterpillars are voracious eaters – indeed, they do little else. Some eat many times their own weight of food per day.

carbohydrate.

Fats are another energy source. For human beings, and many other animals, fats are an essential part of the diet because they carry certain vital substances which are required in small quantities if the metabolism of the cell is to proceed normally. These substances, particularly vitamins, form an essential part of food because without them the cell cannot break down other foods to provide

2 A willow tit picking a caterpillar out of the bark of a birch tree. Caterpillars and grubs provide food for a large number of species of birds and animals.

energy in the correct way. In other cases, vitamins are required to take part in the construction of the structure of the cell and other organs.

An apparent paradox is suggested by this description of the relationship between life and food. If all living matter is using up energy throughout its life, the sources of energy-containing foods must be rapidly exhausted. How then is life able to continue? All the energy of

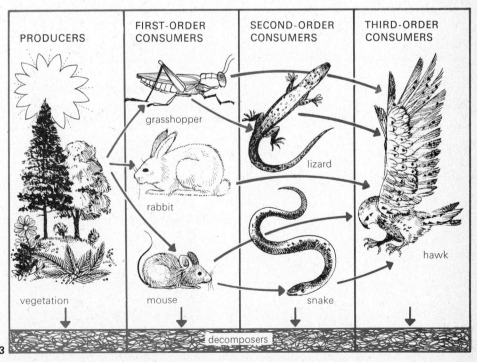

3 Scheme of a typical food-web. The first-order consumers are vegetarians, feeding on the green plants. Second- and third-order consumers are carnivores.

3

living matter on Earth can be regarded as coming from the sun. Living matter can be divided into two types. The first, which forms the bulk of living matter on Earth, consists of those organisms which are able to make direct use of the sun's energy. This group of organisms is known as the *autotrophs*. The green plants, which are its main constituent members, are machines for turning the sun's energy into complex chemical compounds in which energy is locked up. The basic process involved in the green plants can be summarized as:

$$\text{carbon dioxide} + \text{water} + \text{energy} \rightarrow \text{sugars} + \text{oxygen}.$$

This synthesis or fabrication of energy-containing substances takes place every day on a vast scale. One has only to look at the countryside with acre after acre of green plants stretching as far as the eye can see to understand that the scope of *photosynthesis*, as this process is called, is vast. But of course not all life consists of green plants. The reverse process, the breakdown of energy-containing compounds, also takes place on a very large scale. This is the fundamental equation of the *heterotrophs* – those forms of life which cannot synthesize their own energy requirements:

$$\text{complex molecules} + \text{oxygen} \rightarrow \text{energy} + \text{carbon dioxide}.$$

Plants – an energy bottleneck

Animals, which have no means of making use directly of solar energy, depend on the green plants to provide the basic requirements of life. As green plants are the basic source of energy-giving food for other forms of life, there must be a greater quantity of green plant life than any other form of living matter. The autotrophs are the basic source of all foods, but they also form a bottleneck in the process of energy utilization. All the energy available to life on Earth must, as we have seen, flow through them. The rate at which living plants can create new energy by turning the sun's rays into chemical energy is thus a fundamental limitation on the amount of life that the Earth can support. Estimates of how much of the sun's energy is converted by

green plants are hard to make, but there is no doubt that the figure is only a small fraction of the energy radiated on to the Earth from the sun. It is almost certainly less than one per cent of the energy falling on the Earth in the form of light.

There is a very much larger mass of green plants than of animals and other organisms living off their products. But in addition to the animals which live directly on green plants, there are others that feed on the plant-eating animals. There may be several links in a chain of this type. Thus, tuna fish from Japan which is canned for human consumption, probably fed on smaller fish, which in turn ate green plants. Man is not the final link in the chain, for human tissues will sooner or later be food for bacteria.

The situation is much more complicated than this simple example would make it appear. One species of plant may provide food for a large number of different types of organisms, and each may be the prey of a number of other animals. Instead of a simple chain there is in fact a web inter-connecting many different species which are thus rendered mutually dependent. It is this fact which has led biologists to the concept of *ecology*.

Ecology is the branch of biology concerned with the interactions of the different species inhabiting the Earth. Ecologists have to pay a great deal of attention to the food chains in the areas they are studying. They see life not merely as the life of the individual or species but as the life of the entire mass of living organisms.

One example of the complicated inter-relationship between food and the life of animals is the tragic story of the Kaibab deer of Arizona.

In an attempt to improve the natural balance in favour of the deer, a campaign of extermination was waged against the pumas, wolves and other animals that preyed on them. The grasslands were unable to support the increase in population of deer and the herd began to starve to death, at the same time permanently damaging their grazing grounds.

This story illustrates the fact that the relationship between the various parts of the food-chain is a complex one, and that

1 The energy cycle in the ocean. Surface plankton provides the basic source of energy, utilized by whales and fish. Dead plants and animals feed lower-living forms.
2 An immature kestrel uses its claws and beak to tear apart its prey. The kestrel, a bird of prey, is the summit of a chain involving plants and other animals.
3 A praying mantis devours a fly. Among the insects, as well as in more developed forms of life, there are complex energy cycles based on food-chains.
4 A grizzly bear and a puma share the remains of an elk. Both animals are carnivores and are close to the top of their food-chains. They are thus competitors for food.
5 Two green hydra feeding on water fleas. The short hydra has engulfed its water flea, and is in the process of digesting it, while the longer hydra is paralysing a water flea using the stinging cells in its tentacles.

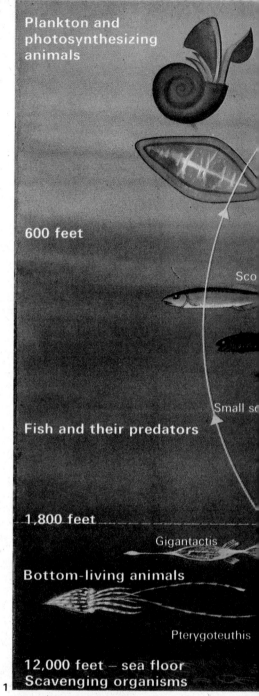

Plankton and photosynthesizing animals

600 feet

Sco

Small s

Fish and their predators

1,800 feet

Gigantactis

Bottom-living animals

Pterygoteuthis

12,000 feet – sea floor
Scavenging organisms

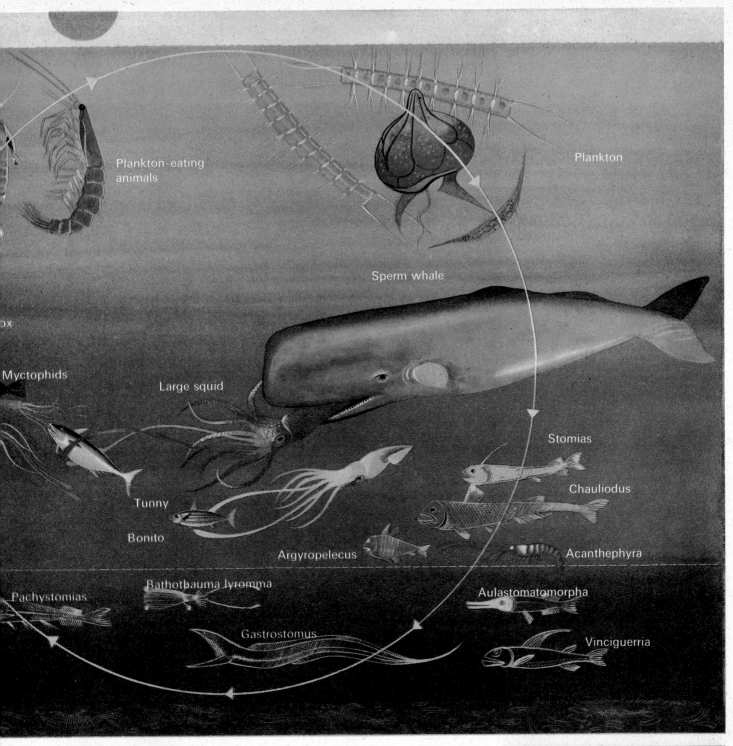

Plankton-eating animals

Plankton

Sperm whale

Myctophids

Large squid

Stomias

Chauliodus

Tunny

Bonito

Argyropelecus

Acanthephyra

Pachystomias

Bathothauma lyromma

Aulastomatomorpha

Gastrostomus

Vinciguerria

4

5

it is unwise for human beings to bring about major changes without understanding the links in the chain.

Competition for food shapes the nature of many animal species. The classic example of this is Darwin's study of the finches of the Galapagos Islands. The three main species of Galapagos finches are *Camarhynchus parvulus, C. pauper* and *C. psittacula.* On Chatham Island, where *parvulus* alone is found, the size of its beak, though small, is larger than that found in species of *parvulus* on Charles and Albemarle Islands. The reason for this is that on Chatham Island the species has no competitors, while on the other two islands, *parvulus* has to face competition from *pauper* on Charles and *psittacula* on Chatham. The possession of a shorter beak enables it to eat a slightly different selection of insects from its competitors. Competition for food has shaped the bodies of the animals concerned.

Devious links

The requirements of two species which live in the same area may be so different that the two species are not in competition. But they may still be linked together by more devious routes. A humorous illustration of this is the story of the origins of roast beef put forward by one of Darwin's early supporters. England's greatness, so the tale went, was based on roast beef from cows nourished on clover. The clover was pollinated by bumblebees, which were attacked in their nests by mice. The mice were kept under control by cats, and the cats were raised by old maids. Thus, went the argument, the greatness of England was due to her old maids. The legend illustrates the links which bind together apparently unrelated, uncompeting species. These links through food-chains show that there is a constant circulation of biological material from plants to animals and thence to other animals.

Investigations of the links in food-chains have shown conclusively that there is a pyramid based on the green plants. The green plants cannot supply food continually to more than a small proportion of their own mass in the form of plant-eating animals. Again, the number of carnivorous animals is limited to a relatively small fraction of the number of herbivores. This explains why the number of eagles in a given area of Scotland is much less than the population of game-birds. Again, in the plains of Africa, there are vast herds of deer, antelope and other plant-eaters, preyed on by a relatively small number of lions and jackals.

A measure of the quantities involved has been made in various specialized habitats. Measurements of the masses of the various levels of producers and consumers in a lake in Wisconsin in the United States have shown that the masses (in kilograms per hectare) of the various levels of food-chains in the lake were: mass of green plants – 1,700; mass of herbivorous animals – 220; and mass of carnivorous animals – 23. The amount of energy at each level was found to vary in a similar way. Since the animals at the top

A nest of blue tits at feeding time. A brood this size requires a small army of caterpillars and grubs to feed it. Birds help in this way to keep down insect pests.

of the food-chain tend to be larger than their prey, the effect is even more striking when we come to consider the numbers involved. In another study, this time of prairie land, the ratio was something of the order of 6,000,000 : 700,000 : 350,000 : 3. Here a more complex structure of four levels was involved.

Large ants clearing up the remains of a dead frog. Dead organic matter provides food for many different species of scavengers, from bacteria to fungi and insects.

The circulation of energy-containing material, of course, involves movement from place to place as well as from animal to animal. A good example of this is found in the oceans. It is obvious that the plants and animals of the great ocean depths cannot obtain energy directly from the sun, for no light penetrates to these areas. But in the oceans, as on land, there is a constant circulation of material which enables the animals at the bottom of the sea to obtain food.

In the illuminated zone below the surface of the water, there is abundant plant and animal life. The diatoms and algae which convert solar energy into food are eaten by the many herbivorous fish at this level. Many of these small animals become very abundant and such animals as the *copepods* (tiny shrimp-like organisms) provide food for the whalebone whales.

Below the illuminated level, the organisms have to rely on the debris of life above. Plankton sinks when it is dead and fish from the upper reaches of the sea may venture further down. The animals at this level tend to be voracious and every animal has some predator. At the bottom of the sea there are many organisms living in permanent darkness and re-using the dead matter that has fallen from above.

Circulation of energy

Water circulates between the surface of the sea and the ocean depths; the cold water from the sea bottom is raised by currents which return the dissolved nutrients to the photosynthetic zone at the surface. The fertilizing effect of this water gives an impulse to the growth of plankton and restarts the cycle.

The constant circulation of organic matter is not confined to the sea. It is characteristic of all types of community. Life on the Earth has evolved to a constantly changing balance. The green plants synthesize the energy which provides food for the animals. The animals preyed on by other animals become in their turn food for some other species. Man must beware of interfering too much with this natural cycle, for to do so could endanger the whole of life on the Earth.

Animal behaviour

The complex and sometimes bizarre behaviour patterns found in animals enable them to survive, find food and procreate. How far are these patterns inborn and how do they adapt to environmental changes?

THE STUDY of behaviour concerns animals in their interaction with the environment, and particularly with the activity of locomotion.

According to Bernard Campbell in *Human Evolution*, 'broadly, it is concerned with how animals come into contact with their environment – how they breathe, how they touch and move on the ground, how they eat the portion of the environment that constitutes food, how they escape from that portion that constitutes predators, and how they communicate with and copulate with the portion that constitutes their own species.' Behaviour describes the way that an animal is related to the environment, and much of the interaction between the phenotype and the environment occurs through the medium of behaviour.

All behaviour is hereditary in the sense that it is an expression of genetic information coded in the genes.

As the nervous system develops in the embryo, definite behaviour patterns are provided for in its structure.

Nervous organization

Insects and spiders exhibit this nervous organization to a high degree; it is found to be well developed also in fishes, birds and other animals. In some vertebrates (particularly mammals), in some molluscs (soft-bodied unsegmented animals usually having a hard shell) and in various other groups, the structure of the nervous system makes allowance for flexible responses and learning. But this does not mean an animal's behaviour is either completely fixed in pattern or completely flexible: mammals, in addition to intelligence, also possess instincts; perhaps far more than has been suspected: similarly insects, despite their repertory of stereo-

Like many other animals, the oribi, a species of antelope, marks out its territory by means of the secretions from its scent gland. Many forms of behaviour are based on protection of territory.

typed instincts, can learn some things.

Behaviour can be either innate, or, to varying extents, learned. In practice it is difficult to draw a line between innate (inborn) and learned behaviour – the problem is that since innate behaviour develops as a result of the interaction of internal and environmental influences, it is, like learned behaviour, to some extent determined by the environment. For this reason the distinction is not clear-cut, and the term unlearned is often preferred to the terms innate and inborn.

The young cygnets of this mute swan inherit an instinct to follow the first large white object they see after they are born. The inherited behaviour keeps them close to their mother.

The best example of innate behaviour is provided by birds. In fact the discovery of extensive and varied innate behaviour in birds has literally revolutionized the attitude of scientists towards their behaviour. It is now recognized, for example, that hawks, gulls, ducks and most of the familiar passerine birds will defend a certain area shortly before mating and while mated. This territory-defence behaviour appears to be a trait inherited from the lizards, from which birds descended.

The characteristic bird song serves notice to others of the same species that a certain piece of territory is claimed. This is the message conveyed when one male bird, whether wood thrush or barnyard cock, answers another. To a female the song may indicate a male and a possible mate.

The actual song in some species is inherited, and this has been demonstrated by rearing the birds by hand in the complete absence of others of the species. It was also found that male canaries so raised will sing a typical, although somewhat simple, canary song; for the development of the flourishes, apparently, the example of other males is necessary. Female canaries injected with the male sex hormone will sing as long as the hormone lasts.

Territorial behaviour

Scientists studying the behaviour of birds have found that in defending their territories against intruding males of the same species, male birds respond to definite features that are characteristic of their rivals – even when these features are combined in some object only slightly resembling a rival bird. Thus male bluebirds will attack a ball of blue and reddish feathers. When male birds attack their own images in window panes or mirrors,

they are usually trying to defend a breeding territory against intruding males.

The building of nests is also under the control of instinctive responses. Captive birds that have been reared out of nests for several generations will construct the proper kind of nest, which they have never seen, when they mature and are provided with the necessary materials.

There are three different ways of learning: by trial and error, by imitation and by instruction. The trial and error method is found in all animals that can learn and is the sole means of learning in invertebrate animals. Compared with other methods, it takes a long time and can be dangerous. It is the method usually referred to in discussions of learning and in experiments testing learning ability.

For example, rats can learn to find their way through a maze by trial and error so long as a reward is offered. Learning by trial and error, however, reaches its highest development in mammals.

Learning by imitation

Learning by imitation is a speedier and much more sophisticated means of building up behaviour patterns. In the first place imitation depends on the ability of an animal to recognize and copy another member of its species, usually its mother. A very good example of this is seen in certain species of birds within a few hours of hatching. Normally, young ducklings follow the mother duck, but if they are raised in an incubator and the first large moving object they see is a large ball, then after that they will always follow the ball, and not a female duck, even if the latter is shown to the ducklings later. Imitation is a short cut to learned behaviour, but it introduces a certain inflexibility in the behaviour pattern that is not found in trial and error learning and is therefore more valuable when behaviour is concerned with the more constant features of the environment.

Instruction is, of course, a uniquely human way of creating behaviour patterns, for it involves conscious thought and intent.

In addition, a great deal of behaviour in animals, from jelly-fish to birds and mammals, falls into one of two general categories: *appetitive* behaviour or *consumatory* behaviour. Appetitive behaviour is more or less a series of actions performed at random, often an apparently aimless wandering, which may nevertheless serve to disseminate the species or bring an animal that is hungry into contact with food. Appetitive behaviour is usually, and perhaps always, due to some motivation,

1 This mass of caterpillars all display marked degrees of appetitive behaviour. As soon as they hatch from the egg, caterpillars are driven by instinct to search out food.

2 A belted kingfisher about to swoop down on a fish. Despite the difficulties of spotting the exact position of fish underwater, kingfishers are able to track them down.

3 A sparrow placed in front of a mirror will try to fight its own image. Many birds behave in this way towards real or fancied rivals. Threat behaviour is often well developed.

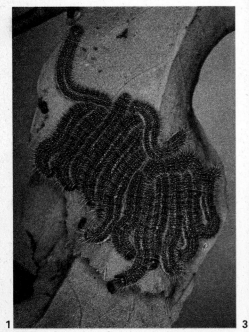

1

3

1 A blue tit stealing milk from a milk bottle. This is an example of learned behaviour. The tits learn that milk can be extracted from the bottles by a process of trial and error.
2 Beavers have a highly developed behaviour pattern, partly inherited and partly learned. Their persistent nibbling at trees in order to build their lodges is an example.
3 Another example of territorial behaviour. The dog-fox on the log in the photograph is threatening a strange dog which has invaded his territory. In the foreground the vixen waits.

drive, or 'need'.

One usually finds that a large number of caterpillars must spend a certain amount of energy in walking before they will settle down and spin a cocoon. A hawk that is hungry will fly in irregular lazy circles. A male spider that is sexually mature will wander at random until it comes into contact with the web of a female.

Consummatory behaviour is the act or series of acts that end, or at least inter-

rupt, the generalized appetitive phase and results in satisfaction of the drive.

The classic type of primitive response is the so-called trial and error behaviour found in one-celled animals, e.g. the paramecium and other ciliates. When a paramecium collides with a solid object it reverses the beat of its cilia, backs away, turns through a small angle, and moves off in a new direction. A series of such responses will enable the ciliate to avoid the obstacle. At the moment there is no

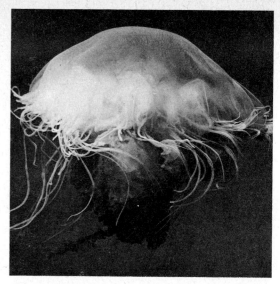

Even plants can show primitive forms of behaviour. Here, the sticky secretions of a sundew leaf have trapped a gnat, which will eventually serve the plant as food.

The lion's mane jelly-fish is a stinging variety. Like most of the open-sea jelly-fish, this species floats at a certain depth fairly near the surface catching small marine creatures.

convincing evidence that learning takes place in a paramecium. But the trial and error response does occur in a host of different animals, and the successful trial may result in learning.

A cat or a man making an attempt to get away from a confining puzzle box will resort to random trial and error by pulling, pushing, turning, squeezing, lifting and depressing the door handle until he stumbles on the correct answer and opens the door.

Coelenterates – jelly-fish and sea-anemones – are thought of as having the most primitive type of nervous system – a network of nerve cells. The jelly-fish behaves in an instructive way which shows how the behaviour of animals is characteristic of the species and adapted to the type of environment in which animals live. Jelly-fish also illustrate the continuous state of activity common in many kinds of creatures. *Cassiopea,* a jelly-fish that lives in very shallow water around the Florida Keys in the United States of America, spends its time lying on its 'back', mouth up, while languid pulsations of its bell-shaped body keep a current of water passing over its tentacles. In this way it catches small fish and other animals.

Sinking jelly-fish

Jelly-fish that act very differently from *Cassiopea* are *Aurelia,* usually studied in laboratories, and *Dactylometra,* the sea nettle, both of which live in coastal waters. These jelly-fish usually swim very slowly to the surface of the water, turn over, and then drift to the bottom, catching any small creatures that become entangled in the tentacles. As soon as the animal gets to the bottom, the muscles begin to contract; these contractions have the effect of sending the jelly-fish up to the surface again, and this is repeated again and again. Jelly-fish of the open sea, for example *Liriope,* behave in marked contrast. They swim very quickly at a fixed depth. If they allowed themselves to sink to the bottom, which in the open sea can

often be much more than a mile from the surface, they would be in waters in which there are very few living things small enough for them to capture.

The kind of prefabricated answer to life's problems that instincts provide for their possessors can be profitably studied in the water flea *Daphnia,* the honeybee and birds.

Daphnias are small crustaceans that live in ponds, and instinctively swim to the surface whenever the concentration of carbon dioxide (CO_2) in the water increases appreciably. This is a very useful response, because close to the surface the concentration of CO_2 is low owing to diffusion into the air, and the concentration of oxygen is relatively high. In the laboratory it is easy to show that this reaction is really a response to light, the response occurring whenever the water becomes sufficiently acid, which it does in nature when the CO_2 concentration rises.

The long sticky tongue of the chameleon claims another victim. Though largely instinctive, the chameleon's behaviour requires considerable muscular and eye co-ordination.

The lion's mane jelly-fish is a stinging variety. Like most of the open-sea jelly-fish, this species floats at a certain depth fairly near the surface catching small marine creatures.

As is often the case with instinctive behaviour, no single stimulus is sufficient to elicit or release the response. In the above example, the acidity becomes the 'releasing' stimulus, and the light the 'directing' stimulus.

In their famous 'language' honeybees exhibit a remarkable combination of learned and innate responses. Von Frisch (1950) has shown conclusively that a worker bee that has discovered a new source of food will, on returning to the hive, perform a dance on the face of the honeycomb.

Flexibility of behaviour

This dance is known as the 'waggle dance'. It is known that if the waggle part of the dance is vertical, the source of the food is directly towards the sun. However, if the waggle is done at an angle of 45 degrees to the left of the vertical, the food source is in a direction of 45 degrees to the left of the direction of the sun. The direction of the waggle taken in relation to the direction of the food source is not learned in any normal sense of the word, because bees do not have to be taught the correct signals to make on their return to the hive. Nor do the bees in the hive have to be taught or have to learn by trial and error what these signals mean.

The purpose of the dance then is to transmit information to other worker bees about the direction, distance and nature of the food source, and is thought a rare example of a descriptive language among animals. This descriptive information is in condensed, coded form and accurately enables other bees to find the flowers described.

This innate behaviour is not flexible, and in an environment that is changing quickly it could be disastrous for the species, since it could be changed only by the slow processes of variation and natural selection.

Learned behaviour, however, is expensive in time and danger but is much more flexible and allows readaptation to occur in every generation.

Why the worm turns

The intriguing and ingenious mechanisms which control the behaviour of primitive animals can provide a clue to the laws which govern the behaviour of higher animals and human beings.

IN ORDER to survive the changes of any environment animals must be able to react to stimuli. The responses an animal makes are generally designed to protect it from harm, to allow it to reproduce and to maintain it in favourable conditions. The sum of these activities is called the *behaviour* of the animal.

Much of the behaviour of lower organisms like amoeba, sea-anemones and hydra consists of responses to stimuli from the environment that cause the animal to remain in an environment to which it is adapted. This class of behaviour is referred to as *orientating responses*. These responses are divided into two main classes, *kineses* and *taxes*.

Kineses are a form of locomotory behaviour in which there is no orientation of the axes of the body in relation to the source of stimulus. The stimuli eliciting such responses cannot usually guide an animal directly to their source, in the way that a beam of light can. Humidity, pressure and diffuse light are examples of such stimuli. To make responses to such stimuli the animal only requires receptor organs sensitive to variations in stimulus intensity, because it is the gradient of intensity of the stimulus, and not the source, that the animal responds to. There are two types of kineses, *ortho-kinesis* and *klino-kinesis*. In both types movement appears at first to be random, but this is not really the case.

An example of ortho-kinesis is seen in the behaviour of the common woodlouse, *Porcellio scaber*, a small creature that lives in damp areas beneath stones, boards and leaf matter. Woodlice lose water from their bodies fairly rapidly and unless they remain in a humid environment soon die due to desiccation. If woodlice are placed in a situation with a variable humidity they appear to move about in an undirected fashion, but it is found that the speed at which they move depends on the humidity. In dry air they move at a greater speed than in moist air where they may stop altogether. This variation in their speed of movement has the effect of causing the woodlice to spend a greater proportion of their time in moist areas than dry ones.

One of the effects of this behaviour is to cause woodlice to aggregate in damp areas. The way in which this comes about is similar to the way the density of motor cars on a stretch of road often depends on the speed at which the cars can travel. If the cars slow down they tend to come closer together. In the case of the woodlouse this behaviour ensures that the animal remains in the moist environment to which it is adapted. This is done without the necessity of complex sense organs; the act of walking can be thought of as a reflex action in response to dryness. The drier the air the more the animal walks.

In klino-kinesis the speed of locomotion remains constant but the rate at which the animal changes direction depends on the intensity of the stimulus to which it is responding. If a planarian worm is watched it can be seen to change direction every so often as it crawls along. If the light

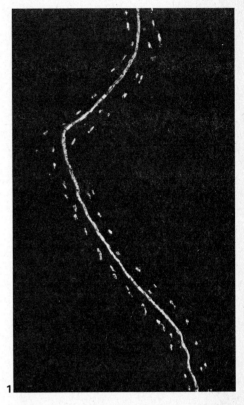

1 Track of a maggot larva moving on smoked paper away from a light source. Note the marks of the side-to-side head movements. The light position was changed during the experiment.
2 'Head' of a maggot larva showing the receptor structures. The progress and side-to-side head movements of a larva, right, in response to a change in light direction (indicated by arrows).

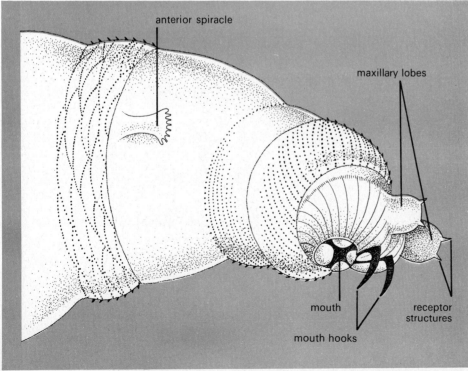

anterior spiracle

maxillary lobes

mouth

receptor structures

mouth hooks

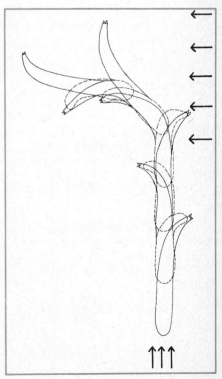

intensity above the animal is increased it changes direction more frequently but moves at the same speed. This is an example of klino-kinesis. The increase in rate of turning falls after about 30 minutes as the animal's photo-receptors become adapted to the increased light. A further increase in illumination will repeat the process. This type of behaviour – negative photo-kinesis – has the effect of causing the animal to move somewhat erratically from areas of high light intensity to areas of lower light intensity.

Kinesis is also found in the behaviour of plankton – the microscopic animals found in the sea. Some of these creatures are adapted to live near the surface, but as they are heavier than water they tend to sink when inactive. As this happens the pressure exerted on their bodies increases, and the plankton respond by increasing their activity and swimming towards the surface. This type of behaviour is called *baro-kinesis*.

Some animals, such as the cockroach, react to touch in a similar manner. If their body is in contact with something there is a decrease in activity and the animal will remain still. If there is no such contact the animal tends to move about rapidly. This is known as *thigmokinesis* and means that the animal spends most of its time in the crevices in which it lives.

Inefficient behaviour patterns

Because of the undirected nature of the response, kineses tend to be an inefficient form of behaviour. Directed responses where the animal moves more or less directly towards or away from the source of the stimulus are known as taxes. A beam or steep gradient of intensity are necessary for this type of orientating response. To perform taxes an animal must have a more highly developed receptor system than needed for kineses.

In the simplest type of taxis, *klino-taxis*, the animal is able to orientate itself either towards or away from a source of stimulus although possessing only a single intensity receptor. If the maggot larva of the blowfly (the gentle used as bait by anglers) is placed on a surface illuminated by a beam of light, it will move away from the source of light in a more or less straight line. This is negative photo-taxis. During locomotion the maggot usually keeps its body straight, but every so often it will put its head down alternately to the left or right of its body.

When the light is first switched on, these lateral deviations of the head are more pronounced and occur more often. The maggot has a single light receptor at the anterior end of its body. Its primitive receptor is incapable of precise discrimination of direction; if the head is stationary it provides no clue to light direction but only to its intensity. However, by raising its head from one side to the other, the maggot can determine the intensity of the light first on one side of the body and then on the other. If the intensities are equal then the animal's body must be orientated along the beam of light. When this is the

case the animal moves forward. As the anterior end of the maggot's body is smaller than the rest, the receptor will be in the shadow of the body when the animal is facing away from the light. By comparing successive light intensities the maggot is able to orientate itself so as to crawl away from a source of light, and to make periodic lateral head movements to ensure that it is still heading in the correct direction.

Maggots do not always show this photo-negative response. They perform it most readily shortly before they pupate, and the mechanism enables them to locate a dark place in which to pupate. Immediately after hatching, however, they will move towards light, a photo-positive response which has the effect of dispersing the larvae from where they hatched. This behaviour may vary according to an animal's stage of development.

Another form of taxis, *tropo-taxis*, requires a more elaborate receptor system. In this case the animal must possess paired intensity receptors such as primitive eyespots, positioned to enable the animal to make simultaneous comparisons of stimulus intensity on each side of its body. It can then orientate itself along the beam or gradient of intensity of stimulus according to the balance struck between the two receptors. Orientation is more direct than with klino-taxis. Once orientated no further deviations are required. This form of behaviour is widespread among animals with pairs of simple eyes such as woodlice, planarian worms

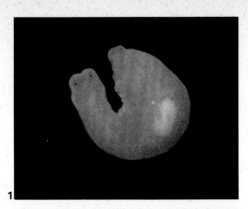

1 The planarian worm *Dendrocoelum* periodically turns in its tracks and doubles back. When the light intensity is increased, the worm turns more frequently.
2 Diagram of the track of an ant returning to its nest. At *X* the ant was shut in a dark box and held until the sun had changed position by 37 degrees. The ant's track changed by the same amount.
3 Plankton respond to increased pressure by swimming towards the water surface. This response, a baro-kinesis, keeps the animals at or near the surface of the water.

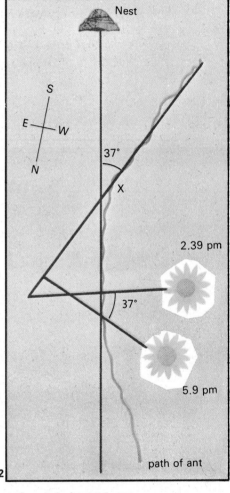

and certain insect larvae.

With the development of more complex eyes a third type of taxis is seen. This is *telo-taxis* and orientation to a stimulus is attained directly without any deviation. It is known only as a response to light and requires receptor organs composed of a number of receptive elements pointing in different directions, such as the compound eyes of insects. A characteristic of telo-taxis is that the animal can orientate itself as efficiently with one eye as with two. The way in which a bee released in a room flies directly for the window illustrates the speed with which this type of orientation can occur.

Kineses and taxes are orientating responses that result in the animal moving either towards or away from the stimulus sources. There are, however, two other ways in which certain invertebrates use light stimuli as a means of orientation. Dragonflies in flight and when resting orientate their bodies so that the dorsal surface is at right angles to the light

1

2

3

4

5

1 A giant Madagascar cockroach. When it feels the enclosing walls of its burrow, the cockroach stays still, but moves rapidly when the stimulus of touch is removed.
2 The fish leech orientates itself towards its host by making use of a combination of the fish's vibrations in the water and chemicals released from the fish's body.
3 The damselfly keeps itself the right way up while in flight and resting by keeping the dorsal surface of its body at right angles to the direction of the sun's light.
4 Snails withdraw into their shells when subjected to sudden movements. If the movements are continued, however, the snail may become habituated to them and cease to react.
5 The fairy shrimp swims on its back by keeping its underside nearest the light. If illuminated from below, the shrimp swims with its back towards the surface.

source, usually the sun. This is known as the dorsal light response and keeps the animal the correct way up. The animal does not move towards or away from the light but at right angles to it and, for this, it requires paired intensity receptors. The water flea *Daphnia* swims with its dorsal surface nearest the surface. If illuminated from underneath the daphnia will orientate itself to the new light source and swim upside down.

Navigating by the sun

Under natural conditions light from the sky is always present though the direction varies in a constant way. Some invertebrates can use the sun's rays as a means of navigation. This is known as the *light compass reaction*. Ants use this response to find their way back to their nests. In one experiment ants returning to their nests were retained in a light-proof box for a period of time. On being released they set off on a path different from their original one. It was found that the new

path deviated from the original at an angle corresponding to the change in the angle of the sun's rays during the time the ant was in the box. The track of an ant could also be altered by using a mirror to change the direction of the sun's rays falling on the animal.

Many invertebrates respond to heat stimuli. This is of particular importance in the orientating responses of animals that are parasitic on warm-blooded animals. The warmth is only a 'token' stimulus of the host's presence as the parasite is not seeking warmth but food. Many blood-sucking ectoparasites do not remain on the host once they have sucked enough blood to satiate them. They only respond to the stimulus of the host's warmth when hungry.

The temperature range to which certain parasites respond is often quite specific. The stories of lice and fleas deserting the body of a host before it dies are an example of this. The parasites are attracted to the host by its normal body temperature, but

if this temperature rises due to a fever the parasites no longer receive the stimulus to which they are adapted and leave the host.

Chemical stimuli are used by many parasites to locate their host. A fish leech senses the presence of a fish by the vibrations caused by the fish as it swims. But before the leech can attach itself to the host a secondary stimulus, a chemical secretion given off by the fish, must also be present.

The solitary wasp *Idechtha* is parasitic in its larval stage on the larva of the flour moth. The wasp lays its eggs in the eggs of the moth. A danger of parasitism is that if too many parasites are present in one host the host may die and so will the parasites. To ensure that this does not happen the female wasp will not lay in eggs that have the characteristic odour left by another wasp. If the eggs are washed free of this odour the wasp will begin to lay in the eggs but will detect the presence of the other eggs with her ovipositor and stop laying. *Idechtha* can locate a culture of the flour moth from a distance of 800 metres.

Certain moths are renowned for the ability of the male to locate a female even when released at as much as four kilometres from the female.

The responses of certain invertebrates

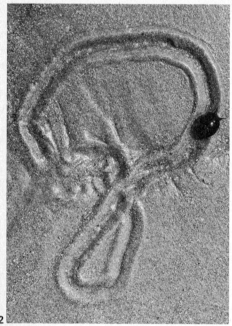

1 The woodlouse shows an ortho-kinesis. It moves more slowly in damp areas than in dry areas, thus ensuring that it spends as much time as possible in damp places.
2 The light compass reaction. The winkle maintains its position on the sand by periodically changing the direction of movement in relation to the direction of the sun's light.
3 Hydra's tentacles are very sensitive to touch. Once the sequence of cell activity that follows touching is set in motion, the hydra is unable to prevent it going to completion.

to the stimulus of food give further illustrations of simple behaviour. Amoeba feeds by moving towards its prey, wrapping itself round its prey, and slowly engulfing it completely inside its cell where ingestion occurs. This response occurs most readily to minute organisms providing a stimulus both to touch and to a weak chemical sense. A hungry amoeba will ingest a grain of sand providing the tactile stimulus only; but a well-fed amoeba will ignore such an object. This is an example of how the physiological state of an organism, in this case, can affect the behaviour of the organism.

Sea-anemones and hydra belong to a class of animals known as coelenterates. They have a tube-like body with a mouth at one end and surrounded by a circle of tentacles by means of which they catch their food. The other end of the body is used to attach them to the substratum and for locomotion. The tentacles are very sensitive to touch so that if one touches the tentacles of a sea-anemone it responds by rapidly withdrawing its tentacles. The tentacles have specialized cells called nematocysts which are thought to be able to respond to stimuli of certain chemical substances and touch without control from the animal's nervous system. These cells shoot out barbs that paralyse the prey and long threads that wrap round it. As soon as the prey touches a tentacle other tentacles move over and grasp it, and it is then moved to the mouth and swallowed. Once this pattern of responses has started, removal of the food and even a change of water will not necessarily cause the animal to stop completing the pattern. This is an example of an external stimulus 'triggering' off a pattern of responses which the animal then executes in the absence of the original stimulus. A hungry hydra will respond to a tactile stimulus only, but a satiated one requires a tactile and chemical stimulus to trigger off the response.

An animal will sometimes be seen to make an alarm reaction to a stimulus which, although not potentially harmful to it, is strange. If it persisted in making such responses to all strange stimuli whenever they were perceived the animal could not perform efficiently. In order to eliminate such useless responses some animals exhibit a type of behaviour known as habituation, by which the animal becomes adapted to a strange stimulus and no longer responds to it. If a common snail (a mollusc) is placed on a board which is frequently jerked up and down, it will at first react to the sudden movements by withdrawing into its shell. After a number of presentations of the stimulus it will no longer react in this way. It has become habituated to the stimulus which although strange did not prove to be harmful.

The various types of behaviour described can only give a brief illustration of the very varied methods by which invertebrate animals, possessing a very simple nervous system, respond to stimuli from their environment. These simple forms of behaviour play an important part in ensuring the animals' survival in an environment that is potentially and may well be actually hostile.

How the bee sucks

Bees, butterflies, mosquitoes and spiders are among the many small creatures which feed on plant or animal juices, extracting them with mouthparts ingeniously evolved for this purpose.

A WEB of fine threads, beaded with dew, spans the space between a plant's leaves. A fly unwittingly blunders into the sticky meshes. In an instant, it is the victim of a waiting spider. Paralysed by venom injected into it, the fly is quickly wrapped in a cocoon of web filaments. Rather than devour its victim piece by piece, the spider will instead suck the precious body fluids, leaving, in the end, only a dry lifeless husk.

The juices of animals and plants provide one of the best sources of food for other creatures. Plant juices, which are rich in sugars and contain some amino acids, can be easily digested. But whole plant tissues, which contain a high proportion of cellulose, are indigestible to most animals. Animal juices, that is animals' blood, are solutions of proteins with less carbohydrate than a plant's juices, but they are nevertheless a good food supply. In both cases the animal using these liquid foods has to eliminate a great deal of water which it 'eats' with the food. Some animals, such as aphids, which suck up the contents of plant cells, also have to eliminate the large amount of sugars they consume in excess of their nutritional requirements. In aphids, excess sugar is excreted as *honeydew,* which serves as food for ants. Plants also produce special secretions which are attractive to insects, for example *nectar,* the sweet juice to be found in many flowers which must be insect-pollinated if they are to reproduce.

Crushing, sucking and chewing

The simplest way for an animal to feed on juices is to crush the prey and suck up the juices which exude from it. This is how many *arachnids* (spiders, scorpions and so on) feed. A scorpion, for example, may chew its food, which it holds with large 'pincers' called *pedipalps.* The chewing is not so much to break up the prey into small pieces as to release its fluids. These are sucked in by the scorpion's *sucking pharynx.* This is the fore-part of the gut and has a number of muscles attached to it. When the muscles contract, the pharynx expands and lowers the pressure inside it, drawing the liquid in through the mouth. Spiders suck their prey in a similar way.

But apart from these relatively crude ways of feeding on liquid food, insects, more than any other animal group, have specialized in using liquid sources of food. Insects are a biologically successful group of animals, judging by their wide distribution and the huge variety of their species. No other group has equalled them in diversification, and at least some of their success stems from their ability to adapt and use, thanks to their extremely ingenious mouthparts, food sources which

A honey bee, enlarged until it looks like some terrifying monster, leans forward to drink. Its slender glistening 'tongue' is fully extended as it sucks the sweet liquid up the hollow centre.

other animals have not exploited.

In insects, the mouthparts are essentially the paired appendages of the mandibles, and maxillary and labial segments of the head. Although insects are arthropods (which in their original form probably had two pairs of appendages to each segment), they have lost many of these appendages in the course of evolution. But like the appendages of crustacea, for example, which have become modified for many different functions, the insect's mouthparts have similarly evolved into a variety of forms which are perfectly designed to carry out different kinds of highly specialized feeding functions.

The pattern upon which these changes are made can perhaps best be seen in the mouthparts of a chewing insect. The essential parts are the large thickened *mandibles,* the main jaws, with their teeth for biting, the paired *maxillae* (auxiliary jaws), each with a long sensory *palp,* or 'feeler', and the *labium* (lip) formed by the fusion of a pair of appendages. This was the form of the mouthparts of the first insects which appeared in the evolution of life on Earth.

The evolution of flowering plants took place step by step with the evolution of insects and their rapid increase in numbers. Flowers need pollinating, and insects are most important agents for doing this. Indeed, the form of many flowers has evolved in such a way that the insect visitor cannot help but leave pollen behind and carry some to another flower. The colours and scents of flowers have their part in attracting insects, but they could only serve this purpose if insects were 'rewarded' when they visited a flower. It is nectar which is the real attraction and which brings insects to flowers. This is a liquid rich in sugars (mainly sucrose, glucose and fructose – all attractive in themselves).

The bee's amazing tongue

Bees of all sorts collect nectar and some bees change it into honey, which is stored in the nest for feeding the young. (The main change which takes place when nectar becomes honey is an increase in sugar concentration through the evaporation of water.)

The bees' 'tongues' are specializations of their labial mouthparts. Some species of bumblebee are short-tongued, while other bumblebees and honeybees are long-tongued. The tongue is formed from the *glossa* (lobes) of the labium, which are long and hairy and end in a spoon-shaped *flabellum*. In addition there are two large labial palps. A honeybee's maxillae form blade-like structures called *galeae* on each side; the maxillary palps are very small.

When the bee sucks nectar, it extends its tongue by the pressure of blood forced from the head into the cavity. Under a microscope, it can be seen that the tongue is not flat but has its edges rolled over until they nearly meet in the mid-line to form a tube. The bore of this tube is small enough for liquid to rise up it by capillary action,

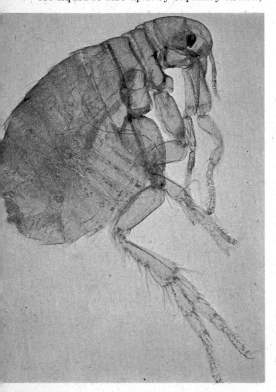

Above, the human flea first pierces its victim's skin with razor-sharp mandibles, then injects saliva to stop blood clotting as it feeds.

Top, held fast in the spider's fatal grip, a fly has already ceased to struggle. Paralysed and helpless, its body is slowly sucked dry.

Normally, the proboscis of the Tomato Sphinx moth, *above*, is coiled – but at the slightest smell of nectar, it springs into a long probing tongue.

Top left, the horse-fly needs its saw-tipped mandibles to puncture tough hide; it then laps up the blood which oozes from the wound. *Top right,* a bee perched on the centre of a daisy is gathering nectar through its dipped proboscis. Its apparatus operates in marked contrast to the fly's searching labella, *left.* The fly is unable to penetrate flowers like the bee, but can liquidize its own food by bathing it in saliva. *Right,* aphids, since they live entirely off plant sap, have mouths specially adapted not only for piercing cellulose, but for penetrating deep inside to gather precious juices.

and the movement of the liquid is aided by a shortening of the tongue which forces liquid higher up. All this is further aided by the sucking action of the pharynx which has special muscles to increase its volume.

When the tongue is in action, it is enclosed by the maxillary *laciniae* (inner lobes) and by the labial palps, so that it is effectively a tube within a tube. Mandibles are still present, although they are small; honeybees use them for moulding wax in building combs. But short-tongued bumble-bees use their mandibles to chew their way into flowers from the side in order to reach nectar, when their tongues are too short to reach the nectar through the normal entrance. For this reason, incidentally, the insect does not make any contact with the anther or stigma of the flower it is visiting and so does not contribute to pollination.

Butterflies and moths are almost as efficient at collecting nectar as are bees. Their mouthparts, however, are different in form, for the main part is derived from the maxillae and not from the labium. The galeae are greatly elongated, each forming a half-tube which makes a complete tube when they are locked together. Each galea is also hollow, and so constructed that it tends to coil up into position beneath the head, where the sucking proboscis can generally be seen in butterflies and moths.

A tube springs into action

The stimulus to extend the proboscis is often the sensing of sugars by hairs on the fore-feet. The signal from these sense cells causes a rise in blood pressure which uncoils the proboscis. As the two halves are held close together by a neat arrangement of overlapping pieces and interlocking hairs the tube is watertight, and the liquid nectar can be sucked up by the action of the pharyngeal pump. The insect probes with the end of the extended proboscis, which suggests that it can use the tip for sensing the right place from which to collect food. Most moths and butterflies have no mandibles, and the labium is no more than a small plate situated on the underside of the mouth.

But there is a great deal more food available to an insect which can pierce through the surface of a plant and penetrate its cells. Each cell is virtually a nutrient-filled bag of liquid which can be tapped. There are many plant bugs of one sort and another which can digest away plant-cell walls to permit their piercing mouthparts to enter, for example, leaf-hoppers, frog-hoppers, scale insects, cochineal insects and cicadas; some of the commonest are the aphids.

All species of this insect feed on the contents of plant cells. Their mouthparts are in the form of fine needles which can be pushed through the outer layers of a leaf, root or stem. When the mouthparts are in the tissue, they make a tube through which the food can be extracted. The two maxillae form the core of the needle, each one being shaped like a letter E in cross-section. The E's face each other and interlock to form two channels. Through the lower one, salivary juices are injected into the plant to digest away the cell walls, and the liquid food is sucked up through the upper channel. The mandibles are half-tubes which enclose and support

127

the maxillae; all four mouthparts are contained in a labial sheath.

Such a delicate, flexible set of mouthparts could not be inserted into tough tissue without buckling, but this is prevented by the sheath, whose tip is held close to the plant's surface, and grasps within itself the mandibles and maxillae. Then one of them is inserted a short distance into the plant, followed by the second for the same distance, then the third, and finally the fourth. The tissue now keeps the tips together so that the process of penetrating a short distance at a time can go on until all four are fully in. The way in which some plant bugs do this is even more remarkable, for their mouthparts are sometimes so long that they are looped or coiled in a sac beneath the head. Yet they can be inserted a long way into plant tissue.

Aphids may carry viruses from one plant to another, as well as taking their juices. Having fed on an infected plant and taken in virus particles with the cell contents, they then pass the viruses into the next plant along with the saliva which they inject to break up the cell walls.

Blades which pierce

Blood-sucking flies such as mosquitoes and insects such as the bed-bug and 'kissing bug' have similar feeding habits. Not only are their mouthparts superficially similar, but when these insects inject saliva into a wound to prevent coagulation of the blood in their mouthparts, they may transfer various disease organisms. For example, *Anopheles* mosquitoes transmit the malarial parasite in this way, while other species of mosquito carry the organisms of yellow fever and encephalitis. These insects are usually thought of as 'biting', but in fact their mouths are not equipped to do so – they can only pierce.

The mandibles and maxillae resemble fine blades; they are responsible for piercing the flesh and making the wound. But in these flies, the upper lip (which is relatively unimportant in aphids) is as long and almost as fine as the maxillae and mandibles. On its under surface it bears a hollowed channel through which the blood is drawn into the mouth. The open underside of the channel is closed by the long fine *hypopharynx,* through which runs the duct for the anti-coagulant saliva. It is as if the opening of the salivary ducts, generally situated just behind the mouth, had been pulled out to make a long fine tube. All these tubes and blades are wrapped by the labium, which acts as a proboscis sheath. At its tip are two small labella which are used as feelers and enable the mosquito to select the appropriate part of its victim to attack. These mouthparts are fully developed only in the female mosquito, and it is therefore only the females who feed on blood.

This kind of piercing-sucking mouthpart can be found in a less developed form in many other types of 'biting' flies, such as the tsetse flies responsible for transmitting the trypanosome which causes sleeping sickness.

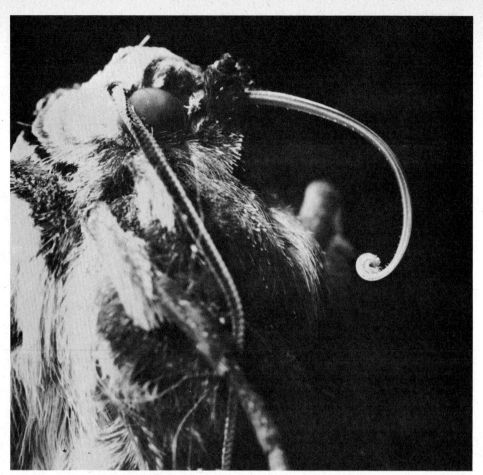

Top, stimulated by the smell of food, a moth's blood pressure has risen sharply with excitement and his proboscis uncoiled like a spring. *Left,* this enlargement of the head of a female

In other flies such as horse-flies, the maxillae and mandibles are much shorter than those of the tsetse fly or a mosquito; they are flattened and blade-like with a minutely toothed saw tip. The labrum is also sharp and the hypopharynx is long and slender. All these piercing mouthparts are again sheathed by the labium, but the labella are much bigger and more like those of a house-fly. They form pads, the outer surfaces of which contain a series of food-channels passing from the outer edges to the middle. These channels are strengthened and kept open by almost complete rings of cuticle. When the pads are put down into a liquid, this can be sucked up through the walls of the channels into the space within and then passed

bluebottle shows clearly her flat, pad-like labella. *Right,* the male mosquito's mouthparts are a study in detail. He is not a bloodsucker; his wife is, carrying diseases from one victim to another.

to the mouth.

The labella of a house-fly are particularly large and this insect lives solely on food which is already liquid or which has been made so by saliva ejected on to it. A house-fly lacks the cutting weapons of the mouthparts of a horse-fly; this uses its labella to lap up the blood which seeps from the wound it makes in its victim.

The detail of the 'engineering' of insect mouthparts is most perfect; the cuticle-covered mouthparts dovetail together or slide smoothly upon one another. They represent the remarkable end-result of evolution, aided by the very great biological advantage to be gained by being able to tap sources of liquid food.

Living world on the move

The movement of an animal can be either fast or slow, jerky or smooth, graceful or clumsy; but in all cases it admirably suits the animal for its niche in the world, be it predator or prey.

ONE OF the often-quoted differences between animals and plants is that animals can move from place to place and most plants cannot. Although this is a sweeping generalization and is not strictly true, it does pose an important question: Why *do* animals move? Like so many apparently simple questions in biology, it has no simple, straightforward answer. We can get a long way towards reaching the answer by saying: 'Animals generally move in search of food.'

When food in one place becomes scarce, animals must move on to a region where food is more plentiful. Vast herds of plant-eating animals *(herbivores),* such as deer, antelopes and zebras, roam the plains in search of good pasture and water. Meat-eaters *(carnivores),* such as lions and leopards, follow them and have to be able to move swiftly to hunt and catch their prey. Scavengers, such as hyenas and vultures, move in to finish up what the hunters leave.

Other factors also influence and necessitate movement. The climate may become unfavourable, either by directly affecting an animal or by affecting its food supply. For this reason, every winter large flocks of birds leave northern countries for the warmer climates of southern Europe and Africa. For instance, swallows migrate in the autumn and fly from Britain to Africa.

Action in earthworms

In the breeding season, animals search for a mate. For many mammals and birds, movement is often required for their complex courtship behaviour. Movement enables a species as a whole to disperse and occupy a wider range of favourable regions.

But whatever the motives, in biological terms, movement in higher animals can be regarded as the conversion of chemical energy into a muscular contraction – which is then transformed into motion.

A contracting muscle must act against something. In the soft-bodied lower metazoan animals, such as worms, shell-fish and starfish, which have no skeletal elements, the muscles act against the body cavity *(coelom).* The coelom here takes on the function of a skeleton. Muscles bring about changes in pressure which are converted into movement. The coelom is said to act as a *hydrostatic skeleton,* and its function can be understood by considering the movements in an earthworm.

Like all worms, the earthworm has a body made up of a chain of segments. Each segment contains a portion of coelom separated from the neighbouring segment by a wall or *septum.* The body wall around the coelom contains muscles running the length of the body. Other circular muscles running around the body control changes

The way an animal moves must be adapted both to the medium through which it moves and its reasons for moving. *Top,* the predatory lion must be swift and agile to catch its prey. The prey, of course, must be even swifter and more agile to avoid becoming the lion's dinner. *Above,* webbed feet and powerful hindlegs are the frog's special adaptations for movement in the water.

in body diameter. The worm anchors itself to the soil by means of small 'hairs' or *chaetae* on its skin.

An earthworm moves forward either in its burrow or along the ground by withdrawing the chaetae of the front segments and by contracting their circular muscles. As the circular muscles contract, the pressure of the coelomic fluid causes the segment to increase in length which, in turn, forces the head end of the worm forward. The segments immediately behind the head now increase in diameter as the circular muscles relax and longitudinal muscles contract. The chaetae on these segments are now stuck out to complete

the anchorage of the head end. Chaetae of the rear segments are now retracted and the posterior segments drawn forward by contraction of longitudinal muscles.

The essential features of this type of locomotion are circular and longitudinal muscles working against each other (when one contracts the other relaxes) – these are known as *antagonistic muscles;* the coelomic fluid acts as a hydrostatic skeleton; and there is a means of anchoring the stationary segments to prevent the body from slipping backwards.

Hydrostatic skeletons are found in many other invertebrate animals and are particularly well suited to the act of burrowing. Bivalve shell-fish, such as razor-shells, which burrow in the sea bed rely on antagonistic foot *retractor* and *protractor* muscles acting against the coelom of the foot. The two shell valves are used to anchor the body while the muscular foot probes into the sea bed. The foot is pushed down into the sand and expands at its tip to provide anchorage. The shell closes tightly and is pulled down as the foot muscles contract. As the shell opens to anchor the animal, the foot probes further into the sand, swells at its tip, and the body is again drawn down with the shell closed deeper into the sea bed.

A skeleton of levers

A starfish crawls by means of hundreds of tiny tube 'feet' on each of its arms. Each tube foot contains a part of the coelom, upon which antagonistic longitudinal and circular muscles act. The end of the foot also acts as a minute suction pad, enabling the starfish to cling to rocks and seaweed.

In animals with a hard skeleton, muscular movements are transmitted into motion by a system of levers. The levers are the bones or plates of the skeleton. In the invertebrates we find animals such as insects, millipedes and crustaceans (crabs and lobsters). These *arthropods* have hard outer skeletons and are characterized by jointed appendages. For example, a typical adult insect has three pairs of legs. Each leg has *flexor* muscles within the joints, and the movement of a land insect is typified by that of the common ground beetle. Of its six legs, only three are in contact with the ground at any one time. The front and back legs of one side are balanced by the middle leg of the other side. In this way, the beetle has a triangle of contact with the ground. A similar but

Below, the humming-bird's tiny body and its ability to flap its wings at a dazzling rate give it exceptional manoeuvrability: it can hover, fly backwards, and dart through the air much as a lizard scampers across the ground. *Right,* a lash of its powerful tail launches this hungry fish skyward after an unusual morsel for dinner.

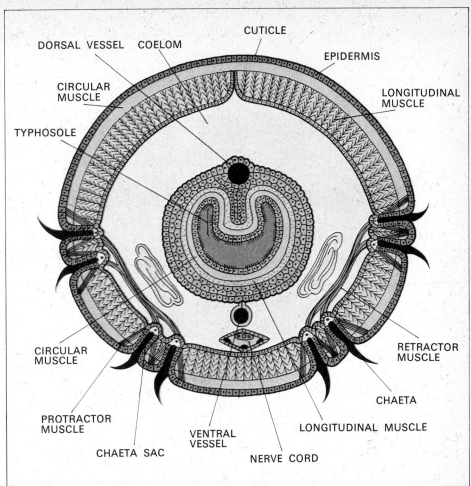

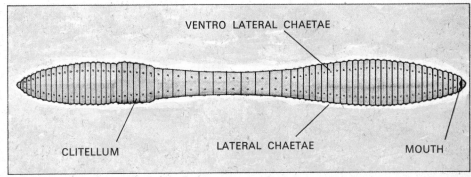

Above, birds, fish and aeroplanes in a sense are cousins, because their bodies incorporate similar design elements. The sleek, flowing lines of their shapes minimize friction with air and water as they pass through. The wings of the bird and the aeroplane are essential in keeping them aloft, but they also function to stabilize motion, as do the fins of the fish. *Diagrams*: the earthworm, in cross-section, *top,* shows the muscular structure which allows it to inch along. Contraction of the circular muscles elongates the segments, pushing the head end of the worm forward. *Above,* the diagram shows a worm in the process of motion, the elongation of the middle segments clearly exhibited. The process is slow, but it serves the purpose. The prominent area shown in yellow, the *clitellum,* is for reproduction, not for locomotion.

opposite triangle is made when the other three legs make contact. This quick alternation of a three-point 'undercarriage' produces a zig-zag forward movement, each leg acting as a lever against which muscles are pulling.

Vertebrate animals have an inner skeleton. The backbone, girdles and limbs provide a highly efficient system of levers by which the voluntary muscles act to produce movements. Once again, we find antagonistic muscles involved in the movement of a limb – the bones are the levers, and the joint between them is the pivot. In the human arm for instance, the biceps and triceps are two such antagonistic muscles (lying either side of the humerus bone in the upper arm); the elbow joint is the pivot. When the biceps muscle con-tracts, the triceps relaxes and the forearm is raised. The opposite applies when the arm is lowered. In this way, the musculo-skeletal system provides a rigid support for the body, while at the same time allowing the jointed bones to remain flexible for movement.

Streams and streamlining

Water is a relatively dense medium which surrounds some animals and provides support by buoyancy. An animal as large as a whale, for instance, could not live on land – the effort required to lift its weight off the ground would be too great. Even the ancient dinosaurs probably spent much of their time in water in order to 'take the weight off their feet'.

The propulsive forces that move a fish through water are usually produced by the wriggling action of longitudinal muscle fibres along the back. The fins are sometimes used to help forward movement, but more often they act as stabilizers, rudders and brakes. Fast swimmers have streamlined bodies which offer a minimum resistance as the fish pass through water.

Aquatic mammals, such as whales and dolphins, have fish-like forms with an elongated head, no neck, a streamlined body and a powerful tail. Whales have a horizontal tail fin and the swimming mechanism depends on its up and down movement. The fore-limbs have a paddle-like appearance and are used as stabilizers.

Many animals have webbed feet, which increase the swimming efficiency of the limbs. The hind limbs of frogs and toads bear webbed feet, as do the legs of many aquatic birds, and a few mammals such as the beaver whose hind feet are webbed. The uniformity in such animals is well shown by the penguin, a bird which is perfectly adapted to its aquatic environment. Once again, we find a streamlined body with a short neck region. But unlike most water birds, a penguin swims with forelimbs which are modified into flippers; the feet are webbed.

The first prehistoric land animals were confronted with problems very different from those which their ancestors had so successfully overcome in water. Air friction is negligible and so no highly developed streamlining is required.

Legs for land animals

The main problem is how to overcome gravity and lift the body from the ground with no buoyant water to help. This was accomplished by the evolution of paired limbs, and by fusion of the backbone and limb girdles. The paired limbs of all four-legged animals are thought to derive from the paired fins of an ancient group of fishes represented today by the coelacanth, which has survived for at least 50 million years.

The earliest land-walking amphibians and reptiles were still very fish-like in appearance and relied on undulations of the body assisted by clumsy limbs held outwards. Many modern amphibians such as newts move in this way, and when frightened they seem to 'swim on land' with their bellies on the ground.

Evolutionary trends have led to a more efficient way of locomotion in reptiles and, particularly, in mammals. In mammals, the limbs are tucked in beneath the body, taking the full weight in a less strenuous way. The work required to hold the body up is now switched from what was the front of the animal to the back surface. In mammals which can walk erect, such as apes and men, all the weight is transferred to two limbs.

In the mammals, we find a wide variety of forms and some interesting comparisons. There is the sloth, which hangs upside down in the forests of South America and moves at a rate of 14 feet a minute – when it is in a hurry. On the other hand, a cheetah or an antelope may reach speeds exceeding 50 miles an hour. Nevertheless, the sloth and the antelope are each well adapted for its own way of life. The sloth remains still and inconspicuous to avoid predators; an antelope needs high-speed movement to escape from its predators.

Three types of walking limbs are found in mammals. The first is called *plantigrade,* for the animals which walk with their feet flat on the ground – for example, a polar bear, which pads across the arctic ice. The second is *digitigrade,* for the animals which walk on 'tip-toe' – for example, a dog, which leaves only the imprint of its toes as it walks along. And the third is *unguligrade,* for animals whose limbs become stilt-like with hoofs – for example, a horse, which clops along on what are virtually single toes. The unguligrade condition is also found in all the fleet-footed herbivores, such as deer and antelopes.

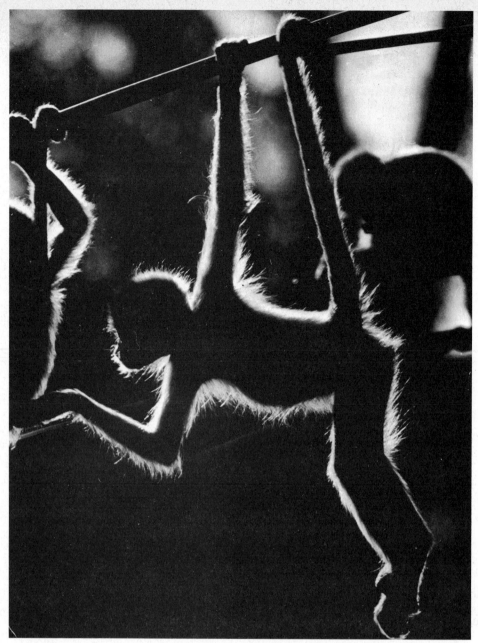

Many animals spend much of their time in tree tops. The gibbon, for instance, is well adapted to this mode of life; it has extremely long forelimbs and digits. The orang-utan is another tree dweller, with special adaptations to allow it to take a firm grip on tree branches.

Bats are a group of mammals that have joined the birds in conquering the air. Bird flight has been studied in great detail. The wing acts as an *aerofoil* – that is, when it moves forwards through the air with its surface slightly inclined, two forces are set up. A *lift* force acts upwards, and a *drag* force acts backwards, tending to oppose the movement. Movement of air over the wing causes the pressure above it to be less than that below. As a result, the wing is pushed upwards into the region of lower pressure by the higher pressure under it.

Into the wide blue yonder

A small wing area is necessary for efficient flight (to keep drag to a minimum), but has disadvantages since the wings must be flapped continuously to maintain lift. This, in turn, limits the size of the bird. Flapping flight is typical of the pigeon, and

The monkey shows a variety of adaptations for motion. Its four limbs allow it to scamper across the ground; its human-like hands allow it to climb trees; its long, limber tail gives it the ability to swing from branch to branch.

is taken to an extreme in the hummingbird where the wings beat back and forth as fast as 200 times a second. Some fast-flying birds, however, have a large wing span, their higher speed giving their wings more lift and compensating for drag. This allows them to glide without losing much height, thereby saving energy. An albatross is an example of such a bird.

Soaring flight, shown by many birds of prey such as the eagles and vultures, makes use of rising hot air currents. These birds can often be seen rising in a spiral fashion with no effort from their wings, soaring like a kite in a breeze. Large broad wings are needed for this type of flight.

From the simple wriggling of worms and tadpoles to the complex movements made by apes and men, creatures have evolved in such a way as to equip them for their survival in their own particular environment, on land, sea, or in the air.

Animal travellers

Each year hordes of animals migrate from one part of the world to another. Some species seek warmth in winter, some swim oceans to breed, others leave their birthplace in search of new land.

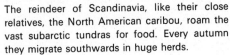
The reindeer of Scandinavia, like their close relatives, the North American caribou, roam the vast subarctic tundras for food. Every autumn they migrate southwards in huge herds.

TO MOST PEOPLE the word 'migration' means the seasonal movements of some species of bird – such as the swallow which in Britain heralds the spring, or the wild goose which flies dramatically across the skies of the United States in its arrow-shaped formations. Comparatively few people are aware that bird movement, although in some ways the most dramatic aspect of migration, is only part of the picture.

Many other creatures, on land and in the sea, behave similarly and do so for similar reasons. They deliberately seek changes of climate and scene in order to achieve better living conditions. This may be designed to protect the adult population, to weed out the old and infirm (by the rigours of the trip), or to provide an environment in which the young have a better chance of survival.

The migration of birds like swallows and geese, implies regular seasonal trips back and forth over roughly the same route in an endless cycle. And indeed, for some zoologists this is the only definition of migration which is acceptable. On the other hand, there are many species of animals which set out to find better conditions and thereby maintain the standing of their kind, yet make no return trip to their point of departure. This may be left to their young, or indeed no return trip may be made at all – the travellers just settle where they land and colonize.

Later their offspring may be moved by one circumstance or another to make their own revitalizing journey.

When considering the migrant creatures we find that the regular commuters across the face of the globe – the animals with two addresses, as it were – comprise a comparatively large part of the whole. Of the bird population of the world, nearly half (more than 4,000 species) migrate regularly.

Following the sun

In the northern hemisphere, this is most likely to be a southerly movement on the outward trip in the autumn, and a return northwards in the spring (although some species, such as wigeon, do travel east–west and vice versa). The reasons for this general similarity are not hard to find. In arctic regions, for instance, the climate is insupportable during winter except for a handful of specially adapted creatures. The rest must leave.

In Greenland of the 64 species common to the island, 36 leave totally for the winter. The rest migrate to its southern edge. When the short Arctic summer begins, the birds return to their former haunts.

In the temperate zone, the picture is similar but the climatic conditions are not so extreme. Yet even so, the winter means difficulties in finding food – the ground is hard, hours of daylight dwindle and there is little fruit. Birds, such as swallows and starlings, leave northern Europe to winter in the south and thus maintain their strength. Then they return for the northern summer to breed.

The autumn has come. No longer living in territories, these martins have forgotten their individual aggressions in preparation for the long flight from Britain to Africa.

Even in the tropics, some seasonal changes takes place. They are likely to be in wet or dry seasons and they, too, may cause migratory movements.

Some bird migrants customarily clock up enormous distances. A case in point is the Arctic tern. Breeding during the short summer of the far north, it leaves in the winter for a marathon journey south – to the southernmost tip of the African continent and sometimes even to the northern edge of Antarctica. One specimen ringed in Greenland in 1951 was retrieved some four months later in Durban, South Africa, having covered a distance of 9,000 miles. But at least one shearwater is known to have bettered this feat. Ringed in Wales, it later turned up in South Australia, a record distance for a marked bird. The sea route is about 12,000 miles.

In the southern hemisphere some species make winter migrations to the north for similar reasons as their cousins in the northern hemisphere. However comparatively few land birds actually cross the Equator; though some sea birds do so in considerable numbers.

At least one southern bird migrates not on the wing, but in the water. Penguins congregate in enormous numbers in Antarctica for breeding purposes during the fine weather. Afterwards they disperse and have been known to make trips of many hundreds of miles entirely by swimming. An emperor penguin killed by members of an American exploration party in 1840 was found to have stones in its gizzard, although there was no known land within 1,000 miles in any direction. The explorers therefore reasoned that there must have been some uncharted land closer to them. Heartened by this thought they continued and reached Antarctica.

Many marine creatures migrate regularly. Among fish, the tunny of the Mediterranean and Azores follow a well-defined route to the Dogger Bank area and back. Plaice and cod make similar journeys. In these cases the search for optimum breeding conditions, directly or indirectly, give impetus to the movements.

Eel migration is a case which clearly shows the actual effect that migration has on the eel population. Unlike the birds, the eels complete only one migratory cycle in their lifetime. As the eels come to maturity in the rivers and streams of Europe and America, they begin to journey down to the sea. They make for their breeding grounds which are the waters of the Sargasso Sea, a vast area of the Atlantic to the east of the West Indies. In these turgid waters, largely unruffled by wind or current, a great carpet of seaweed thrives and it is thronged with animal life as well. The adult eels reach the Sargasso in the spring, when the summer abundance of food is about to begin.

Breeding takes place and millions of eggs are laid. Within a matter of weeks these have hatched into larvae. The adult eels then die, leaving the larvae to rise to the surface where they become part of the surface life. They spread out towards the edge of the Sargasso Sea until eventually they come into contact with the great ocean current. Then their great journey begins: in the case of the European

eel it stretches over 2,000 miles and takes more than two years.

Growing all the time the eels first drift with the currents and later they swim towards the shores from which their parent eels came. On the way this vast horde of immature eels is constantly preyed upon – only the strongest and most agile survive.

The migration of salmon runs in the opposite direction. The salmon are spawned in individual rivers and streams and move down to the salt water where they come to maturity. Then they return, often to the same waterway in which they were born, to continue the breeding cycle.

Two-way migrants

Examples of two-way migration are extremely common among mammals. They include the springbok of South Africa, the Californian seal, whales and no less than three species of bat in the United States. (Self-protection against the hardships of the winter more usually takes the form of hibernation among bats.)

The caribou of North America move south in the autumn after mating has taken place. Then in the spring they move northwards again, prompted, it has been suggested, by the hordes of mosquitoes which appear in the warmer weather and which harry the caribou unmercifully.

Journeys which are likely to guarantee the survival of many of the young, play havoc with the old. This has been graphically described in relation to the once great herds of American buffalo. When these animals moved to new pastures, as they did in both spring and autumn, they were attacked along the route by hungry wolves. The attack was inevitably launched from behind, and by some natural instinct the older buffalo congregated at the rear of the herd. Likewise any injured

beast would take up its position there.

Thus the predators pulled down the beasts which the herd could most afford to lose – the aged and the infirm. That the mechanism of migration worked well for the buffalo is evidenced by the numbers in which they existed at one time on the American plains.

The nomads are the second group of animals within our definition. They are those that are in a state of almost permanent migration, and cover the same ground twice only by accident. The need for fresh sources of food is probably the main triggering factor here.

The army ants of South America move about in very great numbers. They have voracious appetites, and any living creature which cannot get out of their way is trapped and dies in a particularly horrible way. A million tiny but powerful jaws will tear small pieces of flesh from their bodies until nothing is left but the clean, white bones.

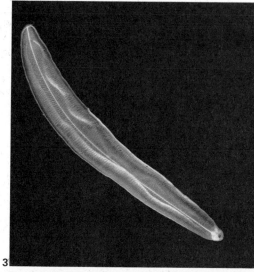

1 In prehistoric times the nine-banded armadillo was a native of South America. Since then it has migrated north to the United States, where it is now considered a pest.

2 Whooper swans nest in far northern countries like Greenland and Iceland. As soon as the autumn comes they migrate south in V-shaped formations.

3 After hatching in the Sargasso Sea, the tiny eel larvae are carried by the ocean currents to the rivers of Europe and America. There they mature before returning to breed.

4 The rhinoceros is a nomadic migrant constantly searching for good grazing. By travelling with the rhinoceros certain species of bird have an excellent supply of insects.

5 Caribou crossing a glacial stream in Alaska on their way south in the autumn, after mating. The young are born after the migration.

6 The common eel makes the journey from the Sargasso Sea and back once in its lifetime. The arctic tern makes its huge migrations every year.

7 The African buffalo, with its herds of as many as 1,000 animals is a nomadic migrant well adapted to living in forest or savanna.

5

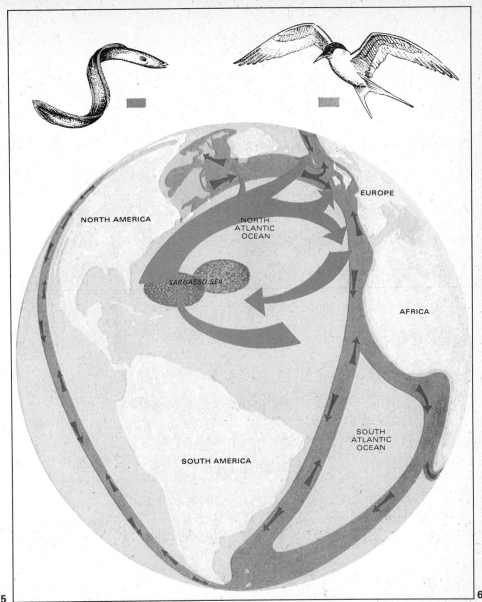

EUROPE

NORTH AMERICA

NORTH ATLANTIC OCEAN

SARGASSO SEA

AFRICA

SOUTH AMERICA

SOUTH ATLANTIC OCEAN

6

7

The ant species, *Eciton hamatum*, which thrives in areas of Panama, searches for food on the march for about 17 days and then halts for a further 19 or 20. The respite is for breeding purposes. At this time, the queen lays her eggs and the party waits until the larvae which hatch from them are strong enough to travel. Then each larva is picked up by a worker and carried in its mouth until the next stop. At each stop, the queen lays more eggs, but the larvae carried by mouth from the previous breeding-halt take the opportunity to spin cocoons and emerge before the new start as adult ants. Thus the population level is maintained during the permanent migration.

The elephants of both Africa and India are generally nomadic. But their feeding habits often impart some kind of regularity and pattern to their movements. The elephant eats a vast quantity of vegetation during a day in order to fuel its vast bulk. At the same time it is fastidious, has definite likes and dislikes concerning food and therefore moves about constantly in search of titbits, often returning regularly to the spots where it knows the goodies can be obtained. It was reported by a nineteenth-century zoologist that the elephants of Ceylon were very partial to the taste of the palmyra palm's fruit. When the fruit ripened, the natives kept an expectant eye open for the herds, and they were seldom disappointed. Similarly, in Africa it has been noted during the first two months of the year, that the elephants move up the slopes of Mount Kenya to feed on mukaita berries which ripen at this time.

Very little will deter elephants from reaching food of their choice. Fire and firearms may, but the stoutest fence or stockade will shatter before them, and water, however deep, is no problem. If the latter is deep enough to cover the creatures but they are still able to reach the surface with their trunks, they will walk across the bottom using trunks as natural 'snorkels'. If the water is too deep for this, then they swim.

The gorilla, fierce of feature but gentle by nature unless frightened or attacked, shares at least one of the problems of the

elephant. This is its great size – a male can weigh as much as 40 stone – and its need for food in large quantities keeps it on the move. It is a vegetarian like the elephant, subsisting on sugar-cane, fruit and nuts, but it roams over a much smaller area than does the elephant.

The colonizers

The final group of migrants are those which should be called the colonizers. Their one-way and spasmodic journeys account for the spread of the particular species and its consequent growth in numbers.

The cattle egret, so called because it is found in association with large herds, was originally a native of India and some parts of West Africa. It still exists in these areas, but relatively recently the birds have moved into new areas far removed from the old. By 1930 cattle egrets had turned up in South America; by 1948 they had reached Australia; and 1952 was the year in which they were first spotted in the United States.

The cattle egrets have set up home in large numbers in the areas within these countries which are hot and where cattle exist in quantity. Guyana (formerly British Guiana) must have seemed a particularly attractive spot to the egrets when they arrived. Not only is the climate very similar to that of parts of India, but the country also carries some herds of Brahman cattle.

The arriving birds would, however, have been unable to draw these parallels, even if they were capable of powers of reasoning. They would just find the conditions to their liking. It is very unlikely that the birds which reached Guyana had ever been in India, for colonizing migrations of this kind are much less direct.

In the homeland at the time initial dispersal began, the triggering factor was

population pressure. And as a matter of course adult birds drive their young away when the latter reach maturity. Although the treatment may seem harsh, congestion is relieved in this way and it ensures that the colonizing flights are undertaken by the young and strong. They are best suited to make the flight to new grounds and to survive new problems which may arise there. Generation after generation of cattle egrets would be hatched and dispatched by their parents in a slow territorial spread. There is little chance that any colonist actually reached South America direct from India, but came instead from some intermediate colony.

There are several mammals which figure among the colonizers. An interesting example is the nine-banded armadillo. In prehistory the animal is known to have been a native of South America. But the freezing of sea-water to form polar ice-caps caused a drop in the level of the world oceans. What had once been the *island* of South America was now revealed as being joined to the northern land mass by a previously submerged strip of land, the Isthmus of Panama.

The small but tank-like armadillo was one of the first adventurers to cross to the north. But for thousands of years its progress must have been very slow. For example, it was not until the last quarter of the nineteenth century that it was noticed in Texas. But since then, and in particular since the 1930s, it has spread dramatically. In some states it is now even considered a pest.

One reason given for this spread of population has been that intensive agriculture has also spread rapidly across the United States during this period. The armadillo finds it easier to root out the insects upon which it lives, if it is working in cultivated ground.

In short, this is yet another example of the way in which an animal species can maintain or even strengthen its numbers by moving from one location to another. It makes no difference whether the journey is one- or two-directional, regular or irregular. It is to migration of all kinds that we owe the present distribution and multiplicity of wildlife forms.

Born navigators

Many animals and insects travel long distances and are able to find their way with remarkable accuracy. How they navigate remains a baffling problem, still the subject of intensive scientific investigation.

SOME STORIES seem to get into the newspapers time and time again, never losing curiosity value. One such story concerns an individualistic tom-cat which, having been moved with the rest of its owner's belongings to a new home, promptly disappears – only to turn up days or even weeks later at the old address. And it may have travelled over 100 miles in the interim.

Some species of birds migrate, or travel great distances seasonally, in order to enjoy a warmer climate and more plentiful food. Arctic tern, for example, have been known to cover as much as 9,000 miles (Greenland to South Africa) during a migratory trip.

These are among the more spectacular examples of long-distance travel by animals. But it is also true that most animals at some time during their lives accomplish some long trip, although it may be considerable only in relation to their size. Again, like cats and birds, some larger animals seem to be capable of aiming themselves towards a specific geographical location; but among many smaller animals, particularly the invertebrates, the goal is not a specific place but a set of conditions.

These creatures wander aimlessly until they encounter some external stimuli, like a taste or smell which appeals to them, and then they home on to the source. In

1 Salmon leaping a waterfall on their way up the River Conway, Wales, to spawn. Mature salmon navigate hundreds of miles to their birthplaces to lay their eggs.

2 A swarm of locusts on the move. Insect migrations seem to be much more haphazard than those of birds, and the direction of the wind plays an important part in determining where they go.

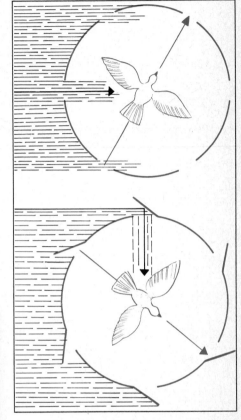

Caged and in direct sunlight, migrating starlings turn to the south. The birds can be made to turn westwards by diverting the sunlight through 90 degrees using a mirror system.

animals of either kind, however, it seems likely that some or all of the senses given to Man, and by which he himself finds his way about, are used. These are the senses of sight, hearing, taste, touch and smell – backed up by memory. Yet these senses are often employed by animals in different degrees and different ways.

The sense of smell is very poorly developed in Man, but is a great deal keener in the dog. To some insects it is as important as sight, and in the blind varieties takes the place of the missing faculty altogether.

Ant navigation

Some ants can see and some cannot, but all have highly developed senses of smell and of taste. They are needed for navigation within the darkness of the nest, needed to find food sources, needed to make repeated journeys between these and the nest. Thus, the sighted ant on the hunt for food marches out from the nest and locates the food source with its sense of smell. On the way out it notes visually certain landmarks and by these it is able to retrace its steps and so tip off the colony. However, it is *not* able to pass on to the other ants its own memory of the route to be taken.

137

Nor are others able to smell the food themselves, it is too far away.

So on the way back the forager lays down a chemical trail. This comprises tiny drops of liquid which the ant squeezes from its abdomen from time to time as it hurries along. Like tooth-paste squeezed from a tube which is being moved over a horizontal surface, the ant's trail material is laid down along the line of its march. Each spot has an individual shape.

The next step in feeding the colony is that a column of worker ants back-tracks over the trail left by the food finder. And this is where the ants' sense of taste becomes important. They use tiny chemical-sensitive organs on their antennae to taste the trail material, moving from one drop to the next until they reach their goal. (It has been suggested, but not universally agreed, that they are also able to use their antennae like calipers and so discover the actual shape of the droplet left on the ground, and that this gives them even more directional information.)

As long as the food supply holds out, there is no chance that the trail will lose its chemical magic. For each worker ant, having filled its abdomen with food then heads back towards the nest laying its own trail along the line of the original. When the food source gives out, so does the trail maintenance, and after a couple of hours at most, the potency of the chemical is gone.

Not so the trails left by the army ants of Central America. These marauders are blind and nomadic, wandering at will about the countryside in a great column. They keep their formation by touching, tasting and smelling each other.

Every now and then they decide to bivouac and then a subsidiary column of voracious forager ants is sent out which almost soaks the ground it covers in marker chemical. As the workers at the head of the column pick up the food they have found and work back the way they came through the horde, their places are taken by fresh workers. By following the broad chemical trail which has been laid down, the food-laden worker returns to the main body of the column.

Underwater scents

Scent is also a potent direction finder for certain animals underwater. Some planarians – small, flat, carnivorous worms – live in streams. Searching for food, they progress in a straight line along the bottom. The food they seek will be diffusing its constituent juices into the water and when the planarian gets close enough, organs on its head scent certain chemicals contained in the juice and carried by the water.

At this point the animal begins to wave its head horizontally, thus sampling the water to either side of its path. Naturally, the amount of attractant chemical on the food side will be greater than on the other, so the worm begins to move slowly in that

The waggle dance performed by returning bees indicates sources of nectar to other bees in the hive. The bee's dance indicates the angle between the source and the sun's position.

138

1

direction. It continues testing as it goes, continually curving in the direction of the stronger chemical stimuli, until eventually it fastens on to the food.

This is a remarkably efficient homing process, but it is nowhere near as spectacular in its scope as that of the salmon. Salmon born in streams and rivers far inland then swim down to the sea to mature. There they feed and grow to full size. After four or five years they return to the fresh waterways of land to spawn so that the cycle of birth, migration and return can begin all over again.

If that was all there was to it, perhaps there would be no great cause for interest. But the fact is that many salmon actually return to the specific water course in which they themselves were hatched, fighting their way up cataracts, waterfalls and even man-made dams to get there.

Now, it is known with certainty that when young salmon descend their particular river to the sea, they do not remain in the vicinity of that river mouth. One

2

marked salmon, for instance, was caught as far as 115 miles from the Vancouver Island creek in which it was hatched; other wanderings on a similar scale have also been recorded. Yet just how these fish are able to navigate over such large distances to return to their birthplace is one of the great unanswered questions in marine biology – and for the time being must be left at that.

However, navigate they do, and we are on safer speculative ground once the salmon has reached the vicinity of its river mouth or stream outlet. Some experimentation with minnows has shown that these fish are capable of differentiating between water taken from two different streams. They will come to the surface of their tank to feed when water of one kind is introduced but shy away when the other is injected in, however subtly this is done.

Water from different sources has a dis-

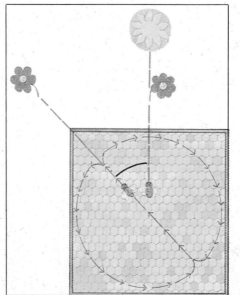

Migration habits of birds are studied by ornithologists through a world-wide correspondence network. Some of the stages in tracking migration routes are shown.

1 Sandmartins caught in a fine mist net. The mist net allows the capture of birds unharmed which can be recorded and released.

2 Weighing a willow-warbler after capture in Jordan. The weight is a rough guide to how far the bird has flown since it began migrating.

3 The metal ring being clamped round the leg of this lesser whitethroat records the place and date of its capture. If caught again, the bird can be identified and its route traced.

4 Measuring the wing of a lesser whitethroat. This gives some guide to the bird's age.

tinctive chemical signature due to the different organic substances which find their way into each waterway from the soil which it drains. The minnows were aware of this, and it seems likely also that salmon can find their home stream by the smell of the chemical or blend of chemicals peculiar to it.

Indeed, this theory has been put to the test in a small way: in one experiment the nostrils of a small batch of marked salmon were plugged. Subsequently, it was found that these rediscovered their home stream less easily than others in the sample batch which were left untouched.

Polarized light

While the senses of touch, taste, smell and so on are extremely important to some animals, sight is just as important to others. Bees are one such group and provide a splendid example of the way in which a sense shared by humans is used in a totally different way.

Bees are able to detect polarized light, a very important factor in their ability to navigate between hive and food. But before this is discussed, we should understand what polarized light is.

Ordinary light can be considered to consist of waves which vibrate randomly in relation to the line of travel; that is some are vertical, some are horizontal, the rest are inclined to the path at all angles in between.

Now when ordinary light emanating from the sun strikes the tiny particles which abound in the outer atmosphere of the Earth, some of it is reflected in a way which is said to be *plane polarized*. Simply, this means that only the waves which vibrate in one plane to the direction of the beam (the vertical, say) are reflected.

Not all the sunlight is polarized in this way. The percentage of polarization varies across the sky, as does the angle of the plane of polarization. (In other words, perhaps only the horizontal vibrations are reflected at some points.) The result is that a characteristic pattern of polarized light is beamed continuously down from the sky. It is constant in relation to the sun, and therefore, for eyes that can see it, provides a kind of map of the sky overhead. The bee's eye, and indeed that of a number of other animals and insects, is so constructed that it can detect polarized light. (Most humans cannot do this; a polaroid filter is necessary to do the job.) And such creatures are able to judge the position of the sun from the pattern – even on an overcast day, provided some part of the pattern of polarization is visible.

But before leaving bees entirely, it must also be said that they navigate over short distances by means of visual landmarks and home by means of scent and colour discrimination. Likewise, they apparently measure distances by the amount of effort necessary to cover them. They can also communicate information concerning the direction and distance of a required goal to others of their hive by means of a set of complicated dance routines.

Homing pigeons, for example, are natural navigators. They are trained for a particular event by being removed from the loft and then released at various points along a line between home and start, the distance between release and loft being increased day by day.

Now, like most birds, the homing pigeon has prodigiously developed powers of sight. And over the shorter training flights it is easily understandable that the bird is able to spot familiar landmarks from afar. However, in the later stages of training, the pigeon is moved over distances so great that from the height at which it customarily flies it is geometrically im-

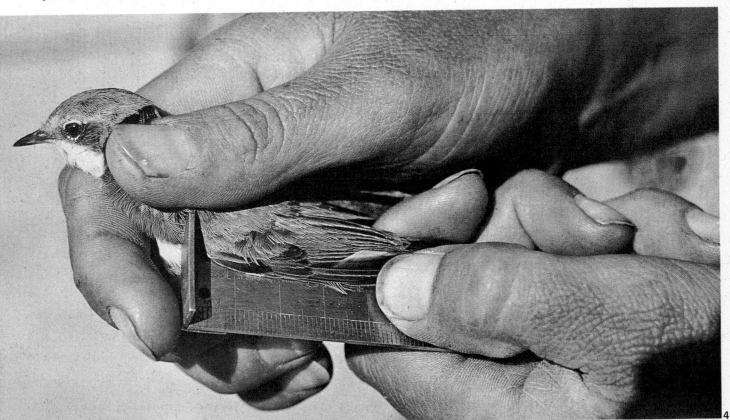

Autumn in Michigan. Swallows muster on telegraph wires for their migration, while a flock of
Canada geese is already winging its way to the
warmth of the south.

possible for it to see landmarks noted on
previous days. Obviously then, the birds
must navigate by some method of reckon-
ing, and this is where the sun-compass
theory comes in.

This is similar to the way in which the
sailor can use the sun to establish his
location and hence the course he needs to

take for home. To start with he requires
two basic facts: the position of the sun in
the sky above him; and the position of the
sun at the same time in relation to some
fixed point elsewhere on the face of the
Earth – say the Greenwich meridian. Now,
provided the sky above him is not clouded
he can easily obtain the first piece of
information – he can see it. But the human
navigator requires chronometers and
charts to obtain the second.

Homing pigeons and other birds seem
able to *remember* what the position of the

sun would be in their home territory at any
given time. And just like the sailor, they
then compare this with the position of the
sun as they see it. Needless to say, they
have no chronometer set to their home
time, but it seems likely that they do have
internal physiological systems which mark
time at a steady pace, irrespective of
conditions outside the body, and these
they use to clock the sun.

By using their internal clock and following the motion of the sun, the homing
pigeon, and its cousins, could know where
they are in relation to home territory and
therefore the direction they must fly in
to reach that destination. It is true, also
incidentally, that some birds migrate by
night, and for this situation similar systems have been postulated in which the
moon and the stars are used instead of
the sun.

Again, butterflies and locusts migrate
in great numbers, regularly, and over
considerable distances, but generally navigation here seems to be a much more
haphazard affair than with birds. Prevailing winds are known to play a great
part in the direction which the swarms
take, although over shorter distances sun
orientation and the use of visual landmarks may be concerned as well.

Natural radar

But finally, there is a sense which has yet
to be mentioned – that of hearing. An
extremely important factor for survival
with many animals, it is for one animal at
least a vital means of navigation.

Although bats are known to move over
long distances, little is known about the
way they achieve this. But the mechanisms of short-distance navigation are well
understood. What the bat possesses in
effect is a natural echo-location system, a
built-in radar set. While feeding or moving
about at night, it emits certain cries consisting of high-frequency waves – so high
in fact that they are outside the range of
the human ear – which bounce off objects
in the bat's path and are returned to its
own ear. In some way the animal is able
to judge the time the sound takes to go out
and back and relate this to the distance of
the object. In other words, the bat is able
to 'hear' distance, and it is also possible
that the bat can tell something of the
nature of the object it has located by modifications in the returning sound waves.

These then are the ways in which some
animals employ the various senses in
order to find their way from one point to
another. Not only does the usefulness of
these senses differ between different animals (including Man), but animals also
often use these senses in totally unexpected ways.

Much remains to be learned; and animal
navigation remains an area of considerable mystery. It is not surprising then that
it is one of the most fascinating areas of
study for zoologists and biologists alike.

Arctic Circle

Antarctic Circle

B   Breeding
M   Migration record
R   Recovery point
W   Winter

(Recovery points record birds ringed
as nestlings in North America)

Arctic terns breed in Canada, Greenland and
Norway and migrate to the South Atlantic to
spend the winter. Note how the tracks of their
migrations follow the coastline.

Habits and habitat

The way animals behave has a strong influence on their geographical distribution. Aggressive territorial behaviour keeps members of the same species apart, while social behaviour brings them closer together.

EVERY SPECIES of animal requires an environment suited to its own bodily requirements. Each has different traits of behaviour which have the effect of bringing it to the place where conditions are right for it. The total effect of all these many different behaviour traits is the distribution of animals across the globe.

Some animals need such special conditions in the place where they live that they are distributed in a very restricted way. The parasitic wasp, *Nemeritis canescens,* will only live naturally in one host, the moth, *Ephestia kuhniella.* Its behaviour is such that it responds only to the smell of that host, even when raised artificially in the laboratory on a different host species. At the other extreme the honey-bee is widely distributed and survives well in many environments from the subarctic regions through the temperate zones to the tropics. The behaviour of these animals helps them to find suitable areas to live in, and thus propagates the species as a whole.

This last point is important. It is no good having too many of the same species in one suitable environment if there is only a limited amount of food available for them. There must be some behaviour mechanisms causing the animals to spread out more and seek other similar places to live.

Darwin first pointed out that food resources are the 'ultimate' factor determining the upper limit of animal population density. Each habitat can support a certain number of animals. This number can vary with the season (the supply of food fluctuates). It can also vary over the years as the climate changes. The number of mouths to be fed is balanced as nearly as possible by the availability of food. As well as behaviour other things, such as the mortality rate, and certain physiological changes, can assist this balance.

Very few complete patterns of behaviour in invertebrates have been analysed properly. Those that have show the complex nature of the stimuli to which the animal reacts. *Lepidiochitona cinera* lives in the upper part of the tidal zone on the sea shore among rocks. When the tide is out the chitons can be found beneath stones, but when the tide comes in and the stones are covered by water the chitons move to the upper surfaces of their stones.

Gravity and light

These movements are governed by responses to gravity and to light. When the stones are uncovered the chitons react positively to gravity and move downwards. Their response to any light falling on them at this time is a change in speed; bright sunlight makes them move downwards more quickly than duller light. Once they reach the underside of their stones the light is cut off and the chitons stop. As the tide comes in their response to gravity changes and when covered with

1 Roosting starlings on a television aerial. The birds space themselves along the wire so that they are not quite near enough to peck one another – a tiny version of territorial behaviour.
2 An ichneumon fly lays its eggs inside its caterpillar host. Because of its specialized egg-laying habits, each ichneumon fly species is restricted by the hosts' distribution.
3 Black rats fighting. Like many other animals, rats will fight in defence of territory. Intruders are challenged by the 'home' rats, and are generally fought to the death.

water the chitons move upwards. The sun's light is more constant underwater and the chitons can move about more freely without having to stop in dark places. In this way simple reactions to stimuli interact to give a much more complicated behaviour pattern. The end result is that the animal's distribution changes with the tides.

Barnacles congregate in places which are suitable for their mode of life by means of an ingenious mechanism. The barnacle larvae have antennules which feel around on hard surfaces for a good place to settle, in order to metamorphose into adult barnacles. They react positively to the presence of other barnacles of their own species, or to the traces of cement left on a rock by other barnacles. These 'clues' are a good enough indication to the larva that its detective work is over – if a spot was good enough for other barnacles it is good enough for a new batch.

There are exceptions to this; barnacle larvae will not settle on glass, even if other barnacles are fixed to it. They prefer a rough surface if one is available nearby. Thus the distribution mechanism seems to be a combination of response to the texture of a surface and a more specialized response to the clues left by other barnacles. The total effect is to keep barnacle colonies only in those areas where conditions for development are good.

Many winged insects are distributed over wide areas by a behaviour pattern which acts on them just after they have emerged from metamorphosis. At once they are impelled by some inner mechanism to fly upwards, or in some particular direction which may be determined by the angle of the light at the moment of departure. In some insects, especially aphids and locusts, this migration is a highly developed dispersal mechanism, and enormous numbers of newly emerged insects swarm in the air. Both of these insects fly upwards and become caught in rising air currents which sweep them away, high into the sky.

Pilots of planes flying at 1,000 to 5,000 feet tell of the masses of insects floating there on a warm day. But in the evening the air cools, and the sky becomes clear

again. The insects fall slowly to more normal levels, and there the aphids are attracted by green leaves. They land, and if the leaves are a suitable breeding ground they stay there living out the rest of their lives in a much less exciting way. The drives which make different types of insects fly upwards are varied. Aphids are attracted by the sun's ultra-violet light, and the Scolytid bark-beetle is attracted by the brightness of the sky. But whatever the drive, there is a brief period after emergence when it overcomes all other drives, including sex and feeding drives. In the case of the aphids, the drive is soon replaced by the drive to find green foliage, but the bark-beetle responds to height in a different way. On the way up it swallows air, and the size of the air-bubble in its stomach seems to signal a change in

response – it turns from the light, and heads towards pine trunks, which is its breeding grounds.

Behaviour patterns involved in the distribution of the higher animals are usually more varied. The most obvious patterns which govern the number of animals in an area, preventing their numbers from exceeding the limits set by food supplies, are those which cause simple spacing out. Many animals use territories, each territory being held by a single animal, a pair, or a social group. Entry into foreign areas causes fighting, and thus the animals are forced to spread out. As long as each animal can hold on to his own territory, then the total number of animals which can live in a larger area is limited. If there are not enough territories for all the animals in the area, then surplus

1 Threatening behaviour among fiddler crabs. These males displaying their claws are taking part in a form of aggressive display, which has the effect of maintaining territorial separation.

2 A swarm of honey-bees on a comb built in the open air. Such combs are very rare. Swarming in social insects is a way of reducing population pressure by expanding to new areas.

3 Territorial behaviour in the robin. A stuffed robin placed on the territory of a live male provokes a strong reaction. The male displays his red breast in an aggressive way.

4 Hibernation provides a means of extending the range of mammals into cold regions. This fat dormouse curls up and sleeps through the winter, emerging in the spring.

5 Masses of aphids find new feeding grounds by flying upwards on warm currents of air during the day, and falling to the ground as the air cools at night. They may reach 5,000 feet.

6 The chiton, or coat of mail shell, migrates as the tides comes in from under its stone to the top of a rock. Its movements are a response to gravity and light.

animals may be expelled from the area, or may even be allowed to stay on as non-breeders.

There are many kinds of territory-holding in the animal world. In more gregarious animals a personal hierarchy often develops. The dominant animals of a group have the first choice on every occasion. This cuts off the lowest members of the hierarchy from their food, and thus again limits the total population. Ordinary hens exhibit this type of hierarchy: the *pecking order;* each hen knows where all the others lie in the hierarchy and thus it knows whether to expect submission from another hen, or whether it ought to submit.

Sometimes, when there are large groups of animals, such as in a dancing swarm of gnats, or flock of seagulls, such in-equalities in status may show up only in adverse conditions, when total numbers must be restricted.

Aggression plays an important part in spacing out animals of a species. It is, in effect, the opposite of herd attraction. Very aggressive animals are not able to live in herds, but moderately aggressive animals can do so as long as they keep a certain distance between each animal. A line of starlings sitting on a telegraph wire are spaced along it so that each bird cannot quite reach out to peck at the next. This space, which each animal needs around it, is, in fact, a tiny version of a territory.

Aggressive displays

Fighting can be a means of spacing, but it may lead to damage being inflicted on other members of the same species. Because of this, aggressive displays evolved which have the same effect as fighting but none of the dangers. Aggressive displays are usually so effective that they do not end in contact fighting. Many species have even evolved methods of reducing the frequency of aggressive displays in certain social relationships so that they can live together more closely than would otherwise be possible.

Birthrate is clearly a very important factor in controlling the number of animals of one species in an area. Where there is a high density of animals the reproductive rate may drop. But this is a physiological effect. Often, under crowded conditions, adults tend to move elsewhere to reproduce. The main effect of high density is thus to promote movement.

Specialized animals have special problems of distribution. Cryptic moths (which mimic some part of their environment in an attempt not to be seen) need a low population density. If there are too many moths close together this increases the chance that many of them will be eaten by predators at one go, but if they are well spread out this threat is reduced. To help this the adults lay their eggs singly, and scatter them widely.

Migration is a common phenomenon which has evolved where it results in a higher reproductive rate, or a lower death rate, than a static existence would allow. Migration is more common in areas with marked seasonal changes, for example, extremes of heat and cold. These regular seasonal journeys from one area to another and back again are undertaken by many birds, whales, seals, bats, fish and some

4

5

6

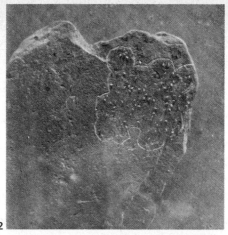

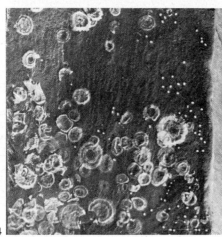

1 A patch of adult barnacles outlined by a deeply scratched groove. **2** After removal of the adults, barnacle larvae settle in the grooved area, though the whole stone is available to them.

3 Two species of barnacle (*Balanus crenatus*, smooth margins; *B. balanoides*, indented margins). **4** After removal of the adults, *balanoides* larvae will not settle on old *crenatus* bases.

lemming population of an area becomes excessive and the lemmings are overcrowded, the animals become very excited. They begin to travel, and sometimes cover great distances, even swimming across fjords. Their aim is to find new habitats suitable for the propagation of a colony. The lemmings just carry on until they find somewhere; those that are unlucky enough to find the sea first are the best known casualties. Not all the lemmings of a colony depart – some are left behind to continue the existing colony.

Perhaps the best known animal which erupts under overcrowding is the locust. It has been shown in the laboratory that crowding will change the locust from a solitary into a highly gregarious insect, and that its structure also changes.

Swarming of bees is a more common type of this eruption. When a colony of bees has grown too big for its hive or nest space, then swarming is likely to occur. In such overcrowded conditions the queen bee is fed less by the workers, and has little space for her eggs, so she lays less. The workers thus have less to do in foraging for food as they have a smaller brood to bring up. This compounds the difficulties; the workers stay in the hive more, and tend to live longer, thus increasing the population in the hive and setting up the swarming mechanisms.

When the colony swarms to relieve this congestion, one or more queens leave the hive, accompanied by workers, and settle in a new home. New queens usually go to the new hive, but honey-bees send the old queen away and the new queens stay and occupy the old hive.

Battles for food and space

The interaction between different species in an area makes the question of distribution even more complex. If a new animal moves into an area it may easily upset the balance of the original population; animals compete with each other for food and space, prey on each other, and are parasitic on each other. The fox has moved into Australia, and there is a great danger that it will destroy many of the older population. In England the red squirrel was largely ousted by the American grey squirrel, mainly because their requirements in the way of food and shelter were far too similar. One species had to give way.

All these examples, of behaviour which distributes animals, have arisen as a result of natural selection. The species must be propagated, but not so well that it is overcrowded and starved out of existence. Behaviour patterns have thus developed to temper the propagation, by forcing the species to spread out and find other suitable places to live. Only in a completely constant environment populated by animals that breed evenly all the year round can a perfect balance be indefinitely maintained. This static balance may possibly be achieved in some marine habitats, but elsewhere the rough and tumble of natural selection forces animals to develop their specialized safety-valve behaviour patterns which ensure the best possible distribution of the species.

insects. The longest known migratory journey is that of the Arctic tern which travels some 10,000 miles to its breeding ground, and the same distance back. Sometimes each individual travels each way only once in its life. Eels breed south of Bermuda, and the young larvae journey to Europe where they spend about 20 years maturing. They then swim back to the tropical breeding grounds. In some animals only one such journey is performed, the return trip being made by the next generation.

Migration is a recurring phenomenon occurring in only certain animals. Mass movements can occur which are not at all

Chickens have a rigid social hierarchy, the pecking order. Chickens low in the pecking order submit to pecking from superior birds, and are able to peck birds lower in the scale.

regular. The number of animals in a given habitat becomes so excessive that something drastic has to happen. Here again the vital factor is food shortage. The suicide pact of the Norwegian lemming, when thousands of animals race westwards, not stopping even for the sea, where most of them drown, is a good example of this. This mass emigration used to be thought senseless, but it is now known that this is not the case. When the

Instincts in action

Animal behaviour is often explained by zoologists on the basis of built-in 'drives' — the sex-drive, hunger, thirst and maternal instinct. What are these powerful forces and how do they operate?

WHY DOES a bird suddenly begin to make a nest when during the winter it has shown no sign of nest-building? Why does an animal begin to look for food when it has shown no interest in it for some hours? What is it that makes an animal behave in a particular way, often ceasing to do one thing and beginning to do something quite different? What the animal sees or hears will, of course, affect what it is doing but an animal which ignores food when it is well-fed will eagerly eat the same food when it is hungry. What has made it change its responses?

Watching a hungry animal seeking food gives the impression that it is being forced to look for it, ignoring everything else. It looks as if the animal is being 'driven'. This gives rise to the idea of *drive,* of something within the animal which orders its behaviour. When looking for food the animal is under the influence of a feeding drive, when looking for a mate, a mating drive and so forth. The drives must all be present in the animal but remain latent until they are aroused.

The strength of a drive can be measured by seeing what obstruction the animal will overcome to pursue the behaviour. For example, a rat can be confined in a box which connects by a corridor with another box. On the floor of the corridor is a metal grid through which a small electric current can be passed. If the rat is hungry, it may be tested by putting food into the other box. Then it is a question of finding out what strength of current will deter the rat from going down the corridor to the food. It will be a stronger current for a hungry rat than for a rat which has fed recently. In fact the strength of the drive increases steadily with the time from the rat's last meal, and reaches its maximum after four days of starvation. But thirst makes its maximum effect earlier, for it reaches a peak at the end of one day without water.

Exploration

An interesting discovery in this type of experiment is that a rat will try to run along the corridor even if the box at the other end is empty. There seems, in other words, to be a drive to *explore.* This of course would be useful in nature for it would cause the animal to find new food or nesting places during its searching.

It is easy enough to put forward the idea of drive and it 'explains' the observations, but what is it we are calling 'drive'? Like so much that goes on inside an animal, scientists at present can only get clues about its nature. We can certainly point to changes in an animal's physiology which could account at least in part for the change in behaviour.

An active animal is using up blood

sugar to provide energy for its muscular movements and so forth. This blood sugar comes from stores in its liver and directly from the food in its gut. If it has gone unfed for a time, the level of the blood sugar will have dropped, and indeed the reduced level will affect areas in the brain. These are stimulated to produce the

1 The Friesian bull gauges the cow's readiness for mating by resting his chin on her rump. If the cow does not move away, the bull mounts and mates with her.
2 A rabbit's nest is lined with fur plucked from her own body. Sex hormones released during pregnancy loosen the hairs on her chest, making it easier for her to pull them out.

activity which we see as a search for food. If the animal is successful in its search it takes more food into its gut, the blood-sugar level rises once again and the searching behaviour ceases. Incidentally, when the blood sugar is low, nerve impulses pass from the brain to the stomach which contracts in a way which makes itself felt as hunger pangs.

Hormones – the chemical messenger substances produced by ductless glands – play a large part in determining the behaviour of vertebrates; their role in insects and other invertebrates is also beginning to become clear.

The cycle of changes which go on in a female mammal as she comes into season brings about changes in her behaviour. She becomes sexually receptive and accepts the advances of a male which at other times she rejects. This period is known as *oestrus*. Ultimately this leads to mating and, with a fertilized egg in the uterus, further changes take place as she becomes 'maternal'. The end result of

these changes is that when the young are born, she is capable of nursing, and nest-building. Her behaviour cycle is controlled by hormones from the ovaries and other glands. She cannot be in oestrus while she is pregnant nor, usually, for a time after birth when she is suckling her young. During these times the particular hormones responsible for sexual behaviour are not being secreted by her glands.

A cow will refuse to let a bull mate with her except when she is in oestrus which occurs for only a few hours every few weeks. The bull can detect a cow that is soon to come into condition, perhaps by her scent or by something in her behaviour that is not obvious to us. At this time he guards her, remaining near and standing parallel to her, nose to tail. When she is in full oestrus the bull becomes greatly excited. He may paw the ground or dig it with his horns, tossing dirt over his back. Then he moves behind the cow and places his chin and throat on her rump. Then if the cow permits he

1 Hedgehogs emerge at dusk and begin foraging for food. Like many other animals, their activities are closely governed by cycles, some due to external and some to internal influences.

2 Pigs breaking through ice on a pond to drink. The drives released by thirst are often even more insistent than those due to hunger, and take far less time to come into operation.

3 A herd of wildebeeste (better known as gnus) on the march near Lake Manyara, Tanzania. Many animals follow regular routes from waterhole to waterhole or from breeding ground to pasture.

mounts and mates with her.

A female rabbit makes a nest which she lines with fur plucked from her own body. One of the effects of the sex hormones circulating in the blood is to loosen the hairs on her chest, so that they can easily be pulled out. When the young are in the nest, she suckles them, and protects and cleans them. The nest-building is stimulated by the circulating hormones, and not by the presence of embryos, for removal of the embryos (and even of the ovaries) during pregnancy does not stop the nesting behaviour. Indeed, the injection of stilbestrol, progesterone and prolactin (from the pituitary) will bring about nest-building in some rabbits even when they are not pregnant. A rabbit is not very good at nursing on her first pregnancy. She improves during subsequent ones so that

4 A young dove thrusts its beak into its mother's mouth to drink the 'milk' produced in her crop. The crop begins to secrete 'milk' under the stimulus of the sex hormone prolactin.

5 Swans grubbing for food on the river bottom. Much of their time is spent compulsively exploring the river bottom for the larvae and small animals that make up their food.

she builds a better nest rather earlier each time, suckles a greater percentage of the live-born animals, scatters them about less and is less likely to eat her own offspring. So though hormones produce the behaviour, experience shapes it into a more efficient pattern with time.

Doves, though they are birds, feed their young with 'milk', produced not in mammary glands like mammals, but by the walls of the crop. This crop milk is regurgitated into the beaks of the squabs (as the young are called). The crop-milk production is brought about by prolactin, and injection of this hormone into the female doves which are not incubating eggs causes the walls of their crops to thicken ready for crop milk to be secreted. If the injected birds have previously brought up young they will feed a hungry seven-day-

old squab as if it were one of their own young ones.

The increase of bird song in spring is so noticeable that it has been recognized as a sign of the change from winter to summer for hundreds of years. It stresses the fact that birds, like a number of other animals, do not breed just at any time of the year; they begin when the temperature is increasing, bringing plants into flower and insects out from their winter hiding places, in other words when food with which to feed the young is beginning to be abundant. Breeding time seems to be brought on by the increase of the hours of daylight which shows itself in early spring and continues steadily until midsummer. It is possible to bring birds into breeding conditions earlier than usual by providing them with increasing periods of artificial

light each day during the early part of the year. The greater length of day gives birds a longer time in which to find food for their young, so that spring is the appropriate time for mating to take place.

In both males and females hormones are responsible for the sex drive that brings about courtship. Longer daylight hours are perceived through the eyes; this in turn affects the pituitary at the base of the brain which through its hormones causes the sex glands to increase in size, the eggs to ripen in females, and sperm to be formed in great numbers of males. In tropical countries many species of birds are brought into breeding conditions not by lengthening days but by the rains which waken plant life into greenness, supplying abundant food and pliable nesting materials.

Marking out territory

The first signs in the male of the change in hormone levels come earlier than the actual nest-building. The flocks which many birds, like reed warblers, form during the winter break up, for the males become aggressive to each other. Instead of feeding with the other birds, each male begins to mark out his territory, taking over a tall tree as a song post from which he sings, loudly advertising his ownership of the area. This song also serves to attract the female to the area; while the territory owner scares off male intruders of his own species, he admits the female. Then courtship can begin.

When hormones were discovered in insects, it was their effect in controlling growth and metamorphosis which attracted attention. Nowadays a great deal is known about the actions of insect hormones in that way but far less is known about their effects on behaviour. There is no doubt that they will prove to have as great an effect as those of a bird or a mammal, but for the moment we have to do with scraps of evidence. One of these pieces is the effect of removing one of the glands, the *corpora allata*, from a female grasshopper, *Gomphocerus rufus*. After

on bird behaviour, acting through hormones, is an example of external events bringing about behaviour. In this way, the reproductive drive is set going in spring and the migratory drive in the autumn. We can explain a great deal of behaviour in this way, but there are some pieces of behaviour which appear not to be connected with what is going on outside the animal, but seem to be initiated from within. This is particularly true of some rhythmic behaviour, when an animal does something repeatedly but at set intervals of time.

If you want to see some animals you have to go out at night. Badgers, for example, come out only in darkness. Other animals can be seen only by day. They have a rhythm of activity on a 24-hour basis. It may be the result of the change from light to dark but sometimes the cycle goes on even if the animal is kept in continuous light or in permanent darkness. Cockroaches begin to be active just before dusk and their activity increases to a peak in the early part of the night. After this they move about less and less, and remain relatively inactive through the remainder of the night and the next day until dusk comes. But if the insects are kept in cages which are lit throughout 24 hours they show peaks of activity which fall at approximately 24-hourly intervals. Under these conditions, of course, there is no dawn and no dusk to trigger off activity. The behaviour is controlled from within the animal.

The cockroaches' behaviour is in fact controlled by the cyclic secretion of hormones from cells in the sub-oesophageal ganglia, the part of the nervous system which lies beneath the insect's gullet. But what makes the glands secrete at these fixed intervals is still a mystery.

Tidal cycles

Other animals have cycles of different lengths. Many animals on the sea-shore, for instance, follow the tidal cycle. They will continue to show the rhythm in a tank in the laboratory where there is no rise and fall of the tide to stimulate them into activity. Yet others follow a lunar cycle. The Palolo worms of the Pacific swarm in October and November at the third quarter of the moon. The worms break off the ends of their bodies which are by then stuffed with reproductive products. The ends wriggle their way to the surface to discharge the eggs and sperms in clouds, turning the sea milky.

Longer cycles can be detected in birds, for there appears to be an internal cycle of one year which brings the birds into readiness to react to the changes in day length at the beginning of the year. These long cycles are far more difficult to detect than the shorter ones but they are probably equally as free from the environment as the daily cycles.

The word 'drive' is a convenient shorthand, but when it is necessary to explain just what a drive is we are forced to look deeply into the physiology of animals to discover reasons why animals behave one way one minute and another way the next.

1 A vast herd of gnus driven by the heat to seek water. When water is scarce, many different species congregate at waterholes and river banks and elaborate behaviour rituals take place.
2 Mating among weaver birds involves the drive to build carefully fashioned nests by sewing together two or three leaves and filling the resulting tube with down and fluff.
3 A young cuckoo, having ousted a reed-warblers' brood, already dwarfs its foster-mother. The warbler's instinctive drives give her no rest as she feeds the voracious young monster.

the operation she will not sing in the usual way, nor will she copulate with singing males. However, her normal responses are restored within seven days after the corpora allata from another sexually mature female have been implanted in her.

At the end of the summer, as the days shorten in the autumn, some species of birds begin to gather in flocks which wheel restlessly in the sky. These are species which migrate to spend their winter further south than their breeding places. They and other migratory birds build up considerable stores of fat in their bodies. This will supply the food they require for their journeys. Their restlessness heralds their actual departure. But what brings about this change in behaviour and the accumulation of the fat? There seems little doubt that for birds in the northern hemisphere the cause is the same – activity of the pituitary gland. Unlike the spring burst of secretion this one is brought about by decreasing day length. Experiments by Rowan in the 1920s showed that temperature had no effect and that light was important. He kept juncos in cages in their breeding areas in Canada. Some were kept under normal lighting conditions, others were lit by artificial light which gave them longer and longer days though the autumn real day was decreasing, while others had artificial days which shortened more rapidly than the real day. The ovaries and testes in the birds in the last group regressed faster than the ones under normal conditions, while the longer day-length birds' ovaries and testes increased as they would do in spring. When he released the birds he found that the birds with the reduced gonads migrated south as did the controls a little later, but the other birds hung about. The temperature had been the same for all, so it was the light regime which was controlling the behaviour.

The effect of the change of day length

Hives of industry

'Go to the ant, thou sluggard; consider her ways, and be wise.' While King Solomon's advice may not cure idleness, it shows how old is Man's fascination with the busy lives of social insects.

AN INSECT SOCIETY conjures up a ruthlessly efficient organization with all the individuals bent more or less without exception upon some task for the common good. It is a kind of 'brave new world' where the individuals are totally subservient to the state as well as being born to their role in life. A queen bee passes her few years of life laying thousands upon thousands of eggs to keep the hive populated. The worker bees, incapable of reproducing under normal circumstances, keep the hive in order and replenished with food by their tireless and selfless activity. The insect society seems to us, bedevilled as we are by disorder, a paragon of faultless organization, whereas our societies appear to pass through one cycle after another, first of flourishing growth, then of ageing and crumbling decay, the insect society seems to maintain itself over the years, efficient, active and unchanging.

Evolution

But insect societies, like our own, have had to evolve and, in all instances, their most complex organizations, as for example, the hive of a honey-bee, have had to spring from a far simpler form and way of life. In fact, if we went back far enough in time we should find the ancestor of the honey-bee living a virtually solitary existence, except perhaps for a short period after fertilization and reproduction, when it might care for the helpless growing larvae by providing them with food.

How has the evolution of the multi-individual insect society come about, and what advantages does it bring? As is so often the case in studying the way a species has evolved and the way it has adapted to living, it is necessary to look among the existing species of social insects, especially the ones with primitive societies, for any clues that may indicate evolutionary trends. We must, therefore, take a look at some of the solitary wasps and bees living for inklings of social behaviour and co-operation.

Some of the most successful wasps are the ichneumon flies; these are tiny creatures with a delicate hovering flight, and the females bear a long proboscis-like projection from their tails which is, in fact, a needle-sharp ovipositor. The ichneumon flies parasitize large juicy caterpillars, laying their eggs deep in the caterpillar's tissues by means of their ovipositor. Only one egg is laid in each caterpillar and the female ichneumon flies are somehow able to sense, by smell, whether or not a caterpillar has already been parasitized. The young wasp larva then hatches from the egg and starts living on the tissues of the caterpillar, which it in time kills, but not until it is mature and ready to leave its host.

1 A honey-bee removing the dead body of one of its comrades from the hive. Keeping the hive clean is one of the first tasks carried out by newly hatched worker bees.

2 The carpenter ant builds its colonies inside dead trees: the ants' powerful jaws allow them to cut out tunnels through the wood, in which they rear their young.

Apart from finding precisely the right environment for its developing young to grow in, there is nothing particularly social about the ichneumon fly's behaviour. But the digger wasp, *Ammophila adriaansei* takes the care of its young one stage further. This wasp digs a hole in the ground for its young and then, having carefully covered the opening with small stones or pieces of earth, goes off to seek food. Once again the food is a caterpillar, but this time the wasp paralyses the caterpillar completely with a nerve poison that it injects into the tissues of the prey. The wasp now drags the paralysed caterpillar to the nest, removes the stones and hauls the caterpillar in after it. It lays an egg on the caterpillar, climbs out of the nest and replaces the stones to close the entrance. The caterpillar makes ideal food, for by being paralysed and not killed it remains wholesome and does not putrefy. Some species of digger wasp have several nests on the go at once. The female must, therefore, remember exactly where each nest is and, before leaving a nest, she can be seen making an orientation flight in which she looks for special landmarks, like a stone on the ground next to a tree, or a fallen pine cone. Having remembered where each of her nests is, she also seems to know intuitively how much of the food supply is left, and she will keep on replenishing the nests until the larvae are fully grown and about to pupate. The female wasp has now done her duty and she does not survive much longer. After a time the pupae emerge as adult wasps and the cycle is recharged for another season.

Some species of Halictine bee, *Augochloroposis sparsilis,* have developed their society a little more. About ten per cent of the females that emerge in the summer months are, for some inexplicable reason, not disposed to mating. These unmated females become industrious workers, confining their activities to nest-building and foraging for food.

Bumble-bees

In bumble-bees for the first time we find that division of labour is absolutely essential for the survival of the species. There is now one predominant female, the queen, and she, having been fertilized the season before, passes the winter sheltering in the earth. In the spring she goes off to found a colony of her own, selecting a suitable hole such as a mouse hole for her first brood to develop. She builds a few rounded waxen cells for these and occasionally opens the cells to replenish the food store. The first larvae all develop into females. They are quite distinct from the queen, being much smaller and having underdeveloped ovaries so that they are in fact sterile. From that moment the queen no longer has time for any duties other than laying eggs, and she relies on the first brood of emerged females to do all the other work. They build new cells, fly out to gather food and feed both the queen and her offspring. As in the social wasps, *Vespa,* and the hornets, the bumble-bee society comes to an end in the autumn. Instead of sterile workers emerging from the cells, the newcomers are sexually mature and some of them are now, for the first time that year, males. These sexually mature adults now mate and the large family disintegrates. All except the newly fertilized females die. These, the prospective queens, seek a place to hibernate, and so the cycle is complete.

All societies of insects can be considered as overgrown families, for they have all originated from the egg-laying of one female. Some experts have even called these families 'super-organisms' for in one sense they are like an organism which needs all its parts to survive healthily.

Of these overgrown families the honey-bee community is undoubtedly the best known to Man. It is a staggering thought that the 60,000 to 80,000 worker bees in a flourishing hive are all the offspring of a single female. In the honey-bee the division

1 Wasp colonies last only one season, as the insects make no provision for the winter. Only the young queen wasps survive the rigours of the winter to produce a new spring brood.
2 A large termitarium in central Africa. Termites are the architects of the insect world, and their colonies often rise to considerable heights above the African plain.
3 Worker bees lick the 'queen substance' — a pheromone — from their queen's body and circulate it from mouth to mouth. The flow of the pheromone prevents production of new queens.
4 A bumble-bee nest. The irregular cells on which the insects are standing are used for storing honey and pollen. The worker bumble-bees are all sterile females, smaller than the queen.
5 An ant queen outside the entrance to her nest. Once she has established a suitable site, the queen is rarely seen again, as she proceeds to full-time reproduction.

of labour is carried to an extreme, and the hive may remain in existence for year after year. The queen lives for several seasons, but the males and the remainder of the females, the infertile workers, are relatively short-lived. From time to time new queens are reared and the old queen is forced to leave. She takes with her a large contingent of workers as a swarm and sets out to establish a new hive community. The new queen, a lone dictator so to speak, now embarks on her nuptial flight where she is fertilized by a male

drone bee. This one act of fertilization lasts her for the remainder of her life, and the drones having fulfilled their function in life are driven from the hive by the worker bees and destroyed by being stung to death. The sting of the worker bee is a modified ovipositor.

As in bumble-bees, the worker honey-bees have a variety of tasks in the community. Some of them collect nectar from flowers, others pollen. Others again do nothing except build new combs, or specialize in looking after the developing larvae, either by cleaning out their cells or feeding them on special secretions that they regurgitate from their mouth parts. In the

honey-bee the exact task of a bee depends largely on its age, although there is a certain built-in flexibility depending on the requirements of the hive.

After emerging from its cell, a worker bee's first task is real drudgery – to clean and sweep the cells from which other workers have recently emerged, in preparation for the cells to be re-used by the queen for laying eggs.

After about three days, the worker matures to feeding the larvae, in particular the older ones, and she gathers pollen and honey from the stores. Her next task, a few days later, is to feed the younger larvae and this she does by giving them, in addition to pollen and honey, a kind of milky food secreted from special glands in her head. Bees of this age also begin to brave the open for the first time and they make short reconnaissance flights. When it is ten days old the worker bee no longer concerns itself with the brood and it takes on jobs like packing pollen into cells, feeding the foraging bees with honey and building new cells. For this it secretes wax

from glands in the abdomen. On about its twentieth day the bee takes on guard duties. Every bee that enters the hive has to be inspected, and if the incoming bee does not have the distinct smell of the hive about it, it is immediately recognized as a foreigner and attacked. Finally the bee is mature enough to forage for food in the surrounding countryside.

Bees' foraging behaviour has been the subject of exciting research particularly by Professor von Frisch of Vienna. He discovered some years ago that the bees

The grotesquely distended body of the queen termite is esteemed as a delicacy by African tribesmen. The tiny head and thorax is tacked on to the enormous abdomen.

A flying digger wasp bears a paralysed caterpillar to its solitary nest. The wasp lays its egg on the caterpillar, thus ensuring a supply of fresh, live food for the larvae when they emerge.

are able to convey precise information to each other as to the whereabouts of sources of food, whether nectar or pollen. The bees communicate this information by means of a special dance enacted in the hive. There are two sorts of dance – the *round dance,* which is only used when the source is relatively close to the hive; and the *waggle dance* which is used for longer distances.

The dance on its own is not enough to stimulate foraging bees to activity; they also need to get a taste of the food source. Smell and taste are in fact extremely important to social insects as methods of communication. All the many thousands of bees in a hive, know whether their queen is alive. This comes about because the queen secretes a special *pheromone* substance – oxodecenoic acid – from her mandibular glands. This substance is transmitted from one bee of the hive to the next and prevents any of the worker bees from taking action to raise another queen. Should the queen disappear or die, the worker bees – lacking the queen pheromone – start building large 'queen cells'. At the same time the ovaries of some of the workers begin to ripen, and in time these bees lay eggs in the new cells. The developing larva is fed more or less exclusively on the worker-bee secretion, 'royal jelly', rather than on pollen and honey, and this food seems to possess some factor which stimulates the young larva to develop into a queen rather than another worker.

Two other groups of insect society, the ants and the termites, also depend largely on the exchange of foods and secretions for the integrity of their communities. In termites, all the eggs laid by the queen termite have the genetic potential for developing into any one of a number of castes. There are worker termites, soldier termites with large aggressive-looking mandibles and supplementary reproductives, as well as the primary reproductives – the queen and her mate. In

A single guard at the entrance to a hornet colony. Hornets make their nests of paper by chewing up wood and plant fibres. Usually they nest only for one season, and then move on.

between all these forms is a general factotum termite – the *pseudergate* – and this caste is an intermediate larval form, which unlike the larvae of the *hymenopteran* insects, the bees, wasps and ants, looks more or less like an adult termite. Which caste of termite develops depends, it seems, on these *ectohormonal* substances – the pheromones – which act by controlling which of the genetic blueprints of the cell are going to be switched on and used during the development of the termite.

Termites

The termite mound is an extraordinary structure, sometimes rising to a height of ten feet or more and containing millions of termites. The mound contains many chambers and passages including a chamber for housing the royal couple and other chambers for growing fungus, on which the colony feeds. Because of the sheer numbers of insects, the oxygen requirements are very high, and the mound has

an elaborate system of ventilation built in.

At certain times the pseudergates develop wings and fly away from the colony in huge swarms. There are males and females among the swarm and these settle on the ground in pairs. The paired male and female now lose their wings and start burrowing. They then copulate, the female lays eggs and a new termite colony is in the making.

Although from an entirely different order of insects, the ants show some remarkable similarities to the termites. The ants, too, have a winged sexual pair which loses its wings after settling on the ground to start a new nest. They, too, have castes made up of worker ants and soldiers.

Pheromones play an important part in an ant's life. One type of pheromone, secreted from the underside of the abdomen, is left as a trail by foraging worker ants when they return to the nest laden with food. This pheromone trail attracts other ants from the nest and they find their way to the food. When these ants have also gathered food they leave more trails and the composite trail attracts more and more ants until the food source is drained. Some ants have developed a method of milking aphids of some of the sap sucked from plants via the aphid's sharp stylets. This milking behaviour shows an extraordinary relationship between two species of insect.

Despite its complexity, a social insect's behaviour is based entirely on instinct. Nonetheless insect communities are remarkably flexible in the face of a crisis. Honey-bees, for example, should the hive be running short of water, will all rally round in search of supplies, or should the hive be getting too airless and hot, will begin beating their wings in the hive to generate a current of air. Such a response, however intelligent and reasoned it may seem to the human onlooker, depends on a swift instinctual communication of mood between one bee and another. The result is a highly adaptable and efficient organization.

Living in communities

The social life of animals involves a constant tension between individual aggression and the need to associate with others. This conflict underlies the dynamism of all communal life.

FOR A SPECIES TO SURVIVE it must breed enough young to take the place of its adults when they become aged and die. Broadly speaking, in striving to reproduce, animals can either blanket the environment in a mass of young, in the hope that sufficient numbers will get through the hazards of development; or they can guarantee that most of their progeny survive by carefully nurturing and protecting a small number of young. These two types of sexual reproduction – the profligate and the highly economic – can occur only if there is some sort of co-operation between males and females.

In fish and amphibia the beginnings of social co-operation between the two sexes can often be seen. Mature males seek out females that are about to spawn, and although there may be no physical contact, the male is ready to ejaculate sperm as soon as the female has unloaded her swollen belly of eggs. The female frog has to be physically stimulated by the male, and for this he rides on her back; clinging on tightly with special pads that develop on his front feet during the breeding season.

Profligate and economic

This is the *profligate* type of reproduction, while in the *economic* type, with its associated 'care of young', there are some extremely complicated behavioural interactions between individuals. During the breeding season some species of animals become territorial, with the result that all sorts of new patterns of behaviour appear; such as aggression against intruders, and the feeding and defence of the young. Very often both male and female parents co-operate closely in defending the territory and young.

Herring gulls behave quite differently at different seasons of the year. In the autumn and winter they live together in flocks, which consist of a homogeneous mass of birds that feed, sleep and fly together. During this period the herring gull does not recognize any individual in the flock, but responds to group behaviour. Thus one gull of the flock may be disturbed while eating and start uttering the rhythmic alarm call – a 'ga-ga-ga'. The other birds all stop to listen and, should the alarmed bird take off, the rest without being at all aware of the cause of danger, will immediately follow.

Then, in the spring, the flock makes for the sand dunes, which are its breeding grounds. There, many of the birds settle on the ground in pairs of opposite sexes and take possession of patches of ground, that they will defend as their territories. At first not all birds have territories and any unmated female has to entice a male. She does this by approaching a

An eagle – a foreigner and a predator – is driven from their territory by 'dive-bombing' crows. The mobbing eventually induced the eagle to move away from the crows' nests.

Grooming plays an important part in the social lives of baboons: it reflects the relative social standing of groomer and groomed. The groomer is always lower in the social scale.

lone male in a very special 'appeasing attitude'; for he at this time, in anticipation of having a territory of his own, is becoming quite aggressive. She approaches him with her neck withdrawn, her bill forward and upward and her body held horizontally. This attitude contrasts absolutely with the herring gull's upright threat posture. Should he accept the female's submissive approach, he may either strut around and threaten any males in the vicinity, or he may utter a long-drawn cry and make off with the female. Very often the female then confirms her willingness by begging for food with a curious tossing of her head, to which the male responds by regurgitating a morsel of something.

All this courtship serves to acquaint the two birds with each other and strengthens the bond between them. Once the pair have established themselves they leave the 'unmateds' and select a territory somewhere in the colony. After they have established their territory they become intolerant of any trespasser. Actual attacks on intruders are rare as threatening gestures are generally sufficient to send the stranger away. The mildest form of threat is, as described by Professor Niko Tinbergen, the 'upright threat posture': the male stretches its neck upwards, points its bill down and sometimes raises its wings. If this threat fails to drive the intruder away, the male may resort to 'grass-pulling'. He approaches close to the other gull and all at once bends down and starts pulling up with his bill bits of grass or moss – this movement is an *intention movement*, as if to say 'if you don't go, this is what I will do to you'. Sometimes both the male and female join together in driving strangers away; with their legs bent, their breasts close to the ground, and their beaks lowered, they make a series of incomplete pecking movements at the ground, at the same time emitting a hoarse sort of cooing sound. After copulation and nest-building, the female lays her eggs and both birds begin their long vigil of incubating the eggs and, once the young have hatched, of protecting and feeding them.

This utter transformation of a bird's behaviour from being a homogeneous part of the flock to becoming territorial, having a mate and then caring for the young, depends on entirely new patterns of nervous activity being unleashed in the brain. A sense of the season of the year plays a major part in triggering off this new mode of behaviour, and it seems that the message of the change in the season is carried from the sense organs to other parts of the brain by special hormones. Certainly in birds and mammals the hormone, prolactin, which is secreted in the pituitary gland, plays a major part in bringing out the parents' instinctive reactions to build nests and then care for the young.

Often there is some form of conflict involved. For example, a bird which is territorial during the breeding season will make aggressive threats to any intruders, and yet will protect and care for its young. The young must, therefore, not arouse any aggressive instincts in its parents, and for this reason the young are very often marked in a nondescript, unaggressive way. Furthermore, when the adult birds see the open beaks of the young clamouring for food, they respond by regurgitating a morsel and passing it on to the young. In their turn the young only expose themselves when the parents are present. The herring gull has a red patch on the end of its bill, and only when the young see this do they become active and beg for food. This behavioural response serves to protect the young from the danger of exposing themselves at the wrong time, perhaps when a predator is lurking somewhere in the vicinity. There are innumerable examples of parent-young response in birds, and they all indicate how complicated social life is even at the level of the care of young.

As an animal's life becomes more concerned with other individuals of its species, the more it seems that aggression comes to play an important part. At one level, in, say, the flock behaviour of birds

like the house-sparrow, the wagtail or the jackdaw, we can see a sudden communal attack on a predator such as a sparrow-hawk, an owl or a prowling cat. Such an attack usually takes the form of the entire flock 'dive-bombing' the unsuspecting 'foreigner' so that it is forced to flee or take cover. But, as soon as animals exhibit any form of territorial behaviour in combination with social behaviour, aggression becomes more and more prominent. Aggression can be seen in the social insects like the honey-bee which set up their territories in the form of the hive. The honey-bees have bees on 'guard duty' at the hive entrance to prevent any intruders, including bees from other hives, from entering. In fact, the bees of any one hive have a distinctive smell which the guards recognize, and should a foreigner

come with a different smell he is immediately set upon and if possible put summarily to death. The situation is analogous to the frontier guards, or the immigration authorities who check passports before they will allow anyone to enter their country. When social animals live in territories their aggression against members of their species serves a very valid purpose; it causes the species to spread out over a much larger area of

1 A pair of guard bees at the entrance to their hive. The guards distinguish 'alien' bees by their scent and drive them away, or put them to death with their stings.
2 A crèche of Adélie penguins on Anvos Island, off the coast of Antarctica. The birds have spaced themselves out over the area so that each has its own small patch of ground.

land than it would perhaps if fraternizing among all members of a species were tolerated. Such aggression rarely harms any of the species through fighting and squabbles; threatening behaviour by the defender of the territory is usually enough to drive away the intruders.

For the most part, animals which set up territories in the breeding season and spend the rest of the year in homogeneous flocks behave instinctively – responding to a way of life that is entirely inborn. There are animals, however, of which human beings are of course a superb example, that depend very much on experience in their behaviour. It is to such animals' advantage to live in complex social groups where the animals all know each other and can learn from each others' experience. In such societies we see the origins of what is called the *peck-order*, or *social status*, or again, the *hierarchy*. And because wisdom and experience is equated with age it is very often the older animals that become the leaders of the group.

Bird societies

Among birds, members of the *Corvidae* family, such as the jackdaws, live in social groups, and there is always a well-established peck-order. Jackdaws do not instinctively know what their predators are, and it is experience handed on from generation to generation that dictates how the birds react at any given moment. A younger bird, lacking experience, may sometimes show alarm and try to rouse the rest of the social group to activity, but unless the older, supposedly wiser bird, makes a move, the group will remain quiet. Again it is the older birds that keep the social group in order and prevent it drifting into anarchy; birds of high rank will protect birds of low rank from birds of intermediate rank. Konrad Lorenz supposes that a bird of low rank elicits less of an aggressive response in the birds of high rank than do the birds of intermediate rank; the high-ranking birds therefore come out on the side of the 'underdogs' – and peace returns to the group. An interesting situation develops when an unpaired female jackdaw, who automatically ranks low because of her status, gets paired off at some later date to a male of high rank. She now acquires

1 Herring gulls courting. The female, her beak pointing upwards, is soliciting scraps of food from the male. This odd behaviour is part of the ritual which overcomes both birds' aggression.
2 Threat behaviour among stags. The stag on the left has intruded on the other's territory. His opponent has lowered his antlers in a threatening gesture to show him he is unwelcome.
3 Different species can sometimes live cheek-by-jowl without friction. Here a goliath heron has built its nest just above that of a long-tailed cormorant.

1 Animals living in a social group observe a strict social order. About to be attacked, the bank vole, on the right, adopts a submissive attitude to a dominant vole.

2 An old bull sea-lion faces inland over the bodies of his populous harem. Frequent fights during the spring months decide which males will acquire harems.

based on stable relationships between the males. Two rats encountering each other will, if there is any doubt as to the status of one or the other, sway back and forth between offensive and defensive postures until the one conceding will roll on its back. The other rat now straddles over the submissive rat and somehow this very act is enough to establish dominance. On the next encounter the two rats may act in just the same way, but in time they both get used to each other and the dominance of one is tacitly respected by the other without there being any need for a submissive posture. Mice on the other hand, have no built-in submissive posture and it is significant that, given space, they do not set up large communities.

In their natural surroundings, primates like baboons and rhesus monkeys form well-organized social groups in which the leaders co-operate to protect the females and young from any outside dangers. Not only do the leaders take the group from one feeding ground to the next, but they guard the group and maintain a constant look-out for predators whenever the group stops to feed or rest. Here again there is a new component in the animals' behaviour; for instead of fleeing or trying to avoid a dominant animal, the lower-ranking individual will very often seek out an animal of higher rank. Possibly it feels some kind of protection in the presence of the dominant animal, and it has been pointed out that this turning towards the dominant animal may be based on the young monkey's relationship with its mother. Whenever afraid it flees towards its mother. Then as it grows up it retains this element of infantile behaviour and when afraid projects itself on ever higher-ranking individuals. In this way the threatened animal tends to go towards the centre of society, and when adult to congregate in the region of the dominant males. In the primates the bond uniting the society appears to be the complete suppression of the escape or avoidance reactions. Obviously such a situation is never absolutely easy for the weaker individual and there will be some conflict as to whether to stay or go. One way he has resolved this conflict is by showing his intention to appease the dominant animal. In monkeys the act of grooming is an act of appeasement, and a dominant male will often solicit grooming from a submissive female.

There are few open aggressive attacks in monkey societies in the wild but as soon as monkeys, like the Hamadryas baboon, are held in captivity in their social groups the organization breaks down entirely. Instead of co-operating with each other to protect the group against natural enemies, terrible squabbles develop between the animals, and the dominant males, instead of leading the group, become tyrants that attack and maim or kill the females and infants as well as submissive males. The whole structure of the society in captivity becomes violent and destructive. How relevant this type of behaviour is to our situation of overcrowding and lack of freedom is a matter of conjecture.

the status commensurate with being paired off with a high-ranking male and can 'lord' it over females that before had been of higher rank. Apart from occurring in jackdaws such behaviour can be seen in primates like the baboon or ourselves, where despite great jealousy, a female of low social standing can, by marrying above her, acquire the higher status that is in keeping with her new role.

In animals which live their entire lives in the social group there are all sorts of behavioural mechanisms to prevent animals of high status attacking and severely wounding animals of low status. We have already seen the appeasement behaviour of the unpaired female herring gull as she solicits an unpaired male who is at that time potentially aggressive.

Although the 'threat' is enough to drive off intruders, in the social group the animals must live in harmony and yet be aware of their status, albeit unconsciously. A new element of behaviour then

enters the scene – the *submissive response*. Whenever an animal feels itself about to be attacked by a dominant animal it throws itself into a posture of submission and remains inviolable while it is in that posture. Two dogs, for example, meeting each other on one or the other's territory may well attack each other. Usually one feels its position to be weaker and less tenable and so take up a submissive posture. It stands sideways, cringing to the dominant animal with its head turned away and its neck exposed. The aggressor could very easily grab the submissive dog by the throat and kill him, but some built-in instinctive code of honour prevents this. Then, having assured his dominance he walks off proudly, leaving the other dog to slink off as honourably as he can.

How important the submissive response is to animals living in complicated social groups can be seen from the behaviour of rats living in their large communities

Animal languages

The smile of the chimpanzee, the grasshopper's song and the bright colours of an insect all involve communication. These simple 'languages' are specially adapted to the animal's way of life.

IN THESE DAYS of artificial satellites, very high frequency radio and messages sent by light beams, the word 'communication' conjures up all these advances in the speed and accuracy with which human beings can pass information to each other. Human beings have an elaborate language with which to communicate with other members of their species. So elaborate is the structure of this language that present men can not only tell one another about past and future events, but they can also discuss abstract concepts. Communication in this complex form may not be found among animals but communication itself is not unique to human beings – animals also pass information to each other.

Few, if any, animals exist without contact with fellow members of their species. At some time in the lives of the great majority of animals, the sexual products of the male must find those of the female for reproduction to take place. It is therefore no surprise to find that under these conditions animals of opposite sexes must behave in such a way that the behaviour of the other animal is altered. The special behaviour which is produced is mating. Even relatively inactive animals in the sea, like sea-urchins, are influenced by others; the discharge of sexual products into the water by one stimulates other animals to release their eggs or sperm likewise. This is communication by

1 Grasshoppers signal one another by rubbing their hind legs across their wings. Variations in volume give the grasshopper a vocabulary of about 13 different sounds.
2 The Japanese sika deer, now found in America and Europe as well as Japan, displays the white patch on its rump as a reaction to danger, thus warning the other members of the herd.

chemicals.

Courtship shows clearly the kind of information which may be transmitted from one animal to another. The species must first be identified so the signal must preferably be one which is unique to that species; secondly, the sex of the animal has to be signalled. Thirdly, the physiological state of the animal – in this case, its readiness to mate – must be conveyed, and finally, its position given, for if it is to be located by the other animal it needs to indicate where it is. This is a good example of the range of information which can be conveyed by a relatively simple piece of behaviour.

Mutual behaviour

All kinds of mutual behaviour can be viewed as examples of communication, for in them one animal influences the behaviour of another. The behaviour of the animal which we can call *the sender* is a reflection of its physiological state. If, for example, a male stickleback threatens another male intruding on its territory, its behaviour reflects the aggressive internal state of the fish. Such a posture seen by an intruding fish, one which is off its own territory, causes it to retreat. No consciousness occurs in either fish; both the behaviour of the territory owner and that of the intruder can be considered to be inborn and automatic.

The essence of communication is a signal which bears information. It is sent by a sender and received by a receiver. The signal can be in any form which the receiver can sense. It is not unexpected, therefore, to find that animal signals can be visual, auditory, touch and chemical;

indeed, any kind of stimulus that falls within the spectrum of action of the sense organs. But each of the kinds of signal have their own advantages and disadvantages making one suitable for one way of life and another adapted to some other habitat. It is best, therefore, to look at communication by considering the different kinds of signal.

The bright colours of some insects, fish and birds immediately suggest they have importance in the life of the animals bearing them. Some of them, like the black and yellow stripes of a wasp's abdomen, serve as warning signals marking out distasteful prey to possible predators; birds, for example, learn to avoid cinnabar moth caterpillars with their black and yellow rings round their bodies, after their first unpleasant encounter. Others camouflage the animal. But very many colours are used as parts of displays which make an animal conspicuous to its species mates. The brilliant bluish colours to which a male Siamese fighting fish turns on sighting a rival is a simple example. Among birds, coloured tufts and patches of feathers are displayed in the movements of courtship.

Birds of paradise

Perhaps some of the most amazing are the feathers and plumes of birds of paradise. The riflebird, for example, throws its head back at one point in its display to show an iridescent blue and purple chest patch; while the ribbon-tailed bird of paradise trails a pair of two-foot long white feathers, tipped with black, from its tail.

But splendid colours and patterns are not the only visual signs which may be employed. The pattern of movement of some part of the body may be important. Different species of fiddler-crab, for instance, can be distinguished by the way in which their enlarged claw is raised and brought down again. In general the path followed is from flexed in front of the eyes – extended out horizontally sideways – flexed vertically upwards – brought down to the starting position. The various parts of the movement may be made quickly or slowly, the downward movement may be jerky or smooth and so forth. These are the gestures of male crabs attempting to lure a female to join them as they stand beside their burrows. So distinctive are the signals that as many as five species of these crabs can live side by side on the same beach apparently without confusion between the species.

Another kind of visual signal is the light flash of fireflies. The light is produced at special places on their abdomens. The males of one common species flash their lights in a short series of 'Morse' dots, and the female responds by showing her light exactly two seconds after the end of the male's signal. He will respond by heading towards the female, but he will only move to lights which show at exactly the right time interval after the end of his. In this way he is attracted only by females of his own species.

Facial expressions play a great part in human communication, for by a look at a person's face we can get some idea at least of whether he is angry, sad and so forth. In monkeys and apes whether a smile is given with the teeth exposed or with them covered by the lips makes a great deal of difference in the information conveyed.

Visual signals are therefore varied. But they all require that the sender and receiver should be in view of each other – which rules out the use of these signals among the leaves and branches of a tropical forest. Furthermore, the sender will be conspicuous as he has to get his message across; he therefore exposes himself to danger from watchful predators. The advantage of visual signals is that they may be visible over a great distance;

1 The splendid plumage of New Guinea's birds of paradise has a purpose: it is used in courtship to win the interest of the mate.
2 Male fiddler-crabs have an elaborate signalling 'language' involving the display of their prominent claws. Some displays attract a mate, while others are for threatening intruders.
3 Its feathery antennae enable the male emperor moth to detect minute amounts of sex attractants released on to the wind by females. Males follow the sex attractant to its source.
4 The flickering light of the firefly also has a part to play in courtship. Different species have their own 'codes' of lighting to avoid confusion during courtship.
5 Chemical communication brings these barnacles together on the same rock. Larvae which are about to settle down are attracted to other barnacles by chemicals they emit.

1

2

when they are employed we can guess that their possible disadvantages have been weighed, by natural selection, against the advantages and found wanting.

Sound, however, can be used for communication even among the roots of grass or in the thickest bush. Also sender and receiver can remain hidden from view. The range over which sound will travel is often restricted, so that this kind of signalling is usually over a shorter range than visual signalling.

No animal has as complicated a language as a human being; the vocabulary of a grasshopper, for example, may consist of only 13 different sounds. These insects make the sound by rubbing their hind legs across their wings which are folded along their bodies. On the inside of their legs there is often a row of pegs each of which strikes the wing in turn. This sets the wing into vibration, at the natural vibration frequency of the wing material. In a sense this is like the movement of the violinist's bow across the strings – the bow plucks at the strings, setting them into vibrations which produce the sound. Such a sound from a grasshopper does not vary in note, for the sound has the frequency of the natural vibration of the wing. But each time a peg hits the wing the vibration is increased in intensity, for the *amplitude* of vibration is increased. Thus the song of a grasshopper is *amplitude modulated*. It is the pattern of these modulations which renders the song of one species unique. And this pattern can be altered by a change in the rate at which pegs strike the wing. So different species have different pat-

he may have a 'triumph' song, a special song made during mating, a rivalry song and a number of others. But the range of possible songs is rather limited as they depend for their variety on amplitude modulation alone.

When frequency changes are introduced songs become far more variable. One only has to compare the songs of birds with those of grasshoppers. Making their songs by the effect of air moving over vocal chords with a range of cavities in the head acting as resonators, birds produce notes joined into distinctive phrases. Even to our ears, bird and grasshopper species can be identified by the noises they make.

The best known bird song is that of the

piece of communication behaviour among animals. This is the honeybee's dance by which a successful forager informs her hivemates of the place where she has found food. On her return from a nectar-gathering expedition to flowers within about 80 metres from the hive she dances in a circular pattern on the vertical face of the comb within the hive. This gives much less information than the figure-of-eight dance she will perform after finding food at a more distant place. This dance conveys both direction and distance of the food source. If the line of the middle part of the dance is straight up the comb, the food is in the direction of the sun; if vertically down the food is in the opposite direction to the sun. Thus the direction of the sun is indicated as vertically upwards and a line of dance at an angle to the vertical shows food at the same angle from the sun's direction.

During the dance, the bee makes low-frequency sounds in a series of bursts. The rate at which these bursts are produced seems to bear a relationship to the distance that she has flown and thus indicates the distance of the food. It is difficult to know precisely what information another worker gets from the dance and it may be that the speed with which the dance is performed is also very important in 'describing' the distance of the food. The bees which follow a dancing forager cannot see her movements as we do, from above, as they are in the dark, moving with their antennae lightly touch-

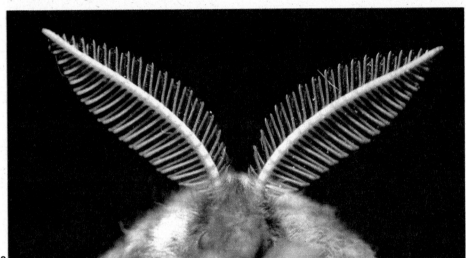

3

4

5

terns of pegs or move their legs at different speeds from others.

The sound signals of grasshoppers are particularly important in courtship. The males, for example, have one song which they sing together, duetting with each other. This makes a group of males conspicuous and attracts females to them. When a male sees an approaching female, he literally changes his tune, to a courtship song. In addition to these two songs

male advertising his presence from a tall tree in his territory. The songs of blackbird, thrush or robin are examples of this advertisement song. It conveys the singer's species, his sex, that he is in reproductive condition, that he wishes to attract a female to his territory and that he defies another male to attempt to enter the territory.

Sound is now known to play a part in what is probably the most remarkable

ing her body. They must pick up the pattern of the dance in this way.

When animals have acute powers of smell, they may communicate by scent. Moth collectors know that males of a number of species will congregate around a female of their own species, coming to her from thousands of yards away. They will even be attracted by an empty box in which she has been. This is the result of sex-attractant substances produced in the glands on the female moth's body. At least one of these has been isolated and synthesized in the laboratory. Under the name of Gyplure it is used to attract male gipsy moths to insecticides. The scent is picked up by the feathery antennae of the male insects.

In social insects chemicals play a very considerable part in organizing the activities of the thousands of insects which often make up colonies of bees, ants, wasps and termites. The queen honeybee advertises her presence to the hive by the 'queen substance' she produces from glands in her head and which she spreads on her body. The 'queen substance' is licked off her by the workers attending her and passed round the hive as they exchange food with each other. So long as this substance is circling through the hive no queen cells are produced on the comb – without these no larvae will be raised to give queens. But should the queen be removed, or should she fail to produce the substance in sufficient quantity, workers in more distant parts of the hive begin to construct the larger cells in which new queens will be reared.

Ants use chemicals to mark the paths they make back to the nest after finding

1 Angry wolves circle one another, making threatening gestures. The bared fangs and the raised mane are both part of an attempt to intimidate the opponent and indicate anger.
2 Smiling – baring the teeth to indicate pleasure and greeting – is universal among the primates. Monkeys can interpret human facial expressions, just as we can this chimpanzee's.

food. The marks remain attractive for a short time only and new marks are laid only if the food supply is a good one. An unreinforced trail rapidly loses its attraction so that workers are not drawn off along paths which lead to an exhausted source.

Scent marking of territory is common among mammals. Dogs use their urine to mark areas and the urine of a bitch in heat is particularly recognizable, advertising her presence to the dogs of the neighbourhood. Many of the ungulates on the African plains mark the bounds of their territory. Some smear the ends of twigs with material from a gland on their faces, others have glands in their split hooves.

The specificity of scent depends upon the chemical structure of the substances which are used. These are many and are sufficient for a large 'vocabulary', but cannot be patterned like a sound or like the pattern of light from a butterfly's wing. If scent is produced in puffs, like the bursts of a grasshopper's song, the pattern is soon lost as small wind movements mix up the odour. Nevertheless, scent has shown itself to be an efficient means of communication.

Human language has a quality that is absent from all the methods of communication used by animals. It is able to convey abstract thought, concepts derived from the development of human society, mathematical expressions, humour, justice, truth. It has what biologists call predictive value, because it can convey not only the present moods and desires of the person involved, but his future intentions. Animal communication, on the other hand, lacks the abstract quality of human speech. The various signals that animals make between themselves are, in many cases, sophisticated but lack this feature.

The distinctive difference in all these signals from those used in human language is that they reflect the animal's present physiological state. Only in that a mammal, for example, which is aggressive and whose fur is standing erect may well attack have these signals the predictive value of human language. But all animal language, simple though it may be, is highly adapted to the life which the animal leads.

Learning by experience

Most animals learn something in the course of their lives, though not all learn in the same way. The study of animal learning is still in its infancy, but it may give vital clues to human learning.

TO SURVIVE, animals need information about their environment. The hydra feeds by stretching its tentacles towards protein-like molecules exuded by the tiny pond creatures on which it feeds. This method of feeding implies that the hydra 'knows' that the protein-like molecules floating past it indicate the presence of potential food. Again a mouse might avoid the marauding owl through its ability to dash back to its hole by the quickest possible route – an ability that depends on the mouse's 'knowledge' of the layout of its immediate environment.

These two examples illustrate the two fundamentally different ways in which animals acquire and store information. The information that nitrogen-containing molecules are exuded by potential prey animals is encoded in the hydra's genes; it stretches towards such molecules because it has inherited the behavioural mechanism that makes it do so. Its knowledge and activity are purely 'instinctive'. But the mouse cannot be born with knowledge of the exact position of its burrow and the objects around it. It acquires this knowledge through the agency of its senses – particularly its eyes and nose – and stores it in its brain. The process of acquiring knowledge in this way, through the agency of the nervous system, is known as learning.

Professor W. H. Thorpe, whose *Learning and Instinct in Animals* is the classic text on this subject, defines learning as '... that process which manifests itself by adaptive

changes in individual behaviour as a result of experiences'. The key word in this definition is 'adaptive': the essential point is not merely that the animal's behaviour changes as a result of experience (for example, an animal's behaviour would change following the experience of having half its brain blown away; but this change could hardly be considered the result of learning), but that the animal's behaviour following an experience becomes more appropriate, more apt, more likely to increase the animal's chances of survival.

To analyse the behaviour of the more intelligent animals in the wild is extremely difficult, because their activities are very complicated and subject to changes of

Young lions graduate from playful fighting among themselves to making their first kill. These lions, co-operating to bring down a buffalo, are learning skills they will use as adults.

mood, just as ours are. But by studying animals under controlled laboratory conditions, and by concentrating a great deal on simple animals whose behaviour tends to be more rigid, experimental psychologists have demonstrated many recognizable systems or patterns of behaviour among animals. Thus they have defined several different kinds of learning, which Professor Thorpe has tentatively classified into six types: habituation; classical conditioning (which depends on the conditioned reflex); instrumental conditioning, otherwise known as trial-and-error learning; latent learning; insight learning; and imprinting. It could be that these are false classifications. Perhaps, for example, imprinting might turn out to be a special case of classical conditioning. Nonetheless, some kind of classification is always needed in science if only to give scientists definable problems to work on, and it is worth examining what each of these terms means.

Habituation is in some ways the simplest manifestation of learning and it is possibly the most primitive. As Aubrey Manning points out in his excellent *Introduction to Animal Behaviour,* habituation involves not the acquisition of new responses, but the loss of old ones. Manning quotes as an example the case of a snail crawling over a sheet of glass. If you tap the glass, the snail instinctively and immediately retracts into its shell. There it stays for a little while and then re-emerges and carries on its way. If you tap the glass

Play has an important role in learning. These otter cubs rapidly overcome their initial clumsiness through playing together and develop control over their body movements.

Apes are able to tackle problems requiring some degree of insight or reasoning power. This chimpanzee displays obvious concentration in his efforts to darn a sock.

again it will again retract; but this time it stays in its shell for a shorter time before re-emerging. After a few more taps the snail hardly 'bothers' to retract at all and, eventually, it 'ignores' the taps completely. It has, in fact, learnt to ignore a stimulus to which, if untrained, it would instinctively react.

The second form of learning, classical conditioning, is the most elementary example of 'associative learning'. It depends on the conditioned reflex.

Reflex learning

At the beginning of this century the great English physiologist C.S. Sherrington studied what are now called simple reflexes in so-called spinal animals – that is, animals in which the brain has been removed and only the spinal cord remains. He showed, among other things, that if an electric shock was applied to the foot of a 'spinal' cat then the animal immediately withdraws its foot, even though there is no brain to tell the animal to move. In this experiment the electric shock is called the stimulus and the withdrawal of the foot is called the response; the whole action – the 'automatic' retreat from the noxious stimulus – is called a reflex action.

At about the same time the Russian physiologist I.P. Pavlov was studying reflexes of a slightly different kind in whole animals, with intact brains. It was known that if meat is placed in a dog's mouth, then the dog salivates; this is a reflex response, though it is slightly more complicated than the ones studied by Sherrington. Pavlov found that he could measure the strength of the response by making the ducts from the dog's salivary glands run to the outside of the animal's cheek, instead of the inside of the mouth. Then, after introducing meat to the animal, he could simply count the drips of saliva running out.

In one series of experiments, just before giving the meat, he would sound a bell, or set a metronome ticking. At first, the dogs 1

would ignore this sound; after a time, if the sound *always* preceded the presentation of the meat, the dogs would salivate when sound was made – that is, before the meat was given. The animals had learnt to associate the sound with the meat. In this experiment the meat is known as the unconditioned stimulus and the sound of the bell is called the conditioned stimulus. The point is that the unconditioned stimulus always produces the reflex response, such as salivation; but the conditioned stimulus produces the response only after the animal has been 'conditioned', or trained, to associate the bell sound with the meat. Eventually, conditioned animals would produce as much saliva when they heard a bell as when they were presented with meat; and finally,

they would salivate at the sound even if no meat was given. After a time, however, if the experimenter repeatedly sounded the bell without then giving meat, the dogs ceased to salivate at the sound of the bell. In other words, the conditioned reflex was lost, or, as psychologists say, it was 'extinguished'.

The possibilities of learning by conditioned reflexes are limited; all an animal can do through this method is to respond in a very stereotyped way to some new stimulus which it associates with a stimulus to which it would normally respond instinctively. And we know that animals learn things that would be very difficult to explain in terms of this simple conditioning process. For example, the American physiologist B.F. Skinner ob-

1 Pavlov's set-up for his famous conditioning experiments. The duct from the dog's salivary gland is diverted to the cheek so that salivary output can be measured.
2 The Indian elephant *(Elephas maximus)* can be trained to carry out heavy work like logging, and is widely used for this and similar purposes throughout South East Asia.

served pigeons which he kept in a special cage of the kind that has become known as a 'Skinner box'. The pigeons wandered around pecking at this and that, in purely random fashion, and quite spontaneously, without any encouragement from the experimenter. But the cage was so designed that if they happened to peck at a particular bar, a small amount of food was released. Eventually the pigeons stopped pecking at random and pecked only at the bar that caused the release of food. Skinner proposed that animals could learn to perform particular actions if that action (called a response, though strictly speaking it is not a response since it can be a piece of spontaneous activity) is immediately rewarded.

1 The squirrel's characteristic posture for nibbling a nut is arrived at by instrumental or trial-and-error learning. Young squirrels rapidly become able to hold nuts and nibble them.

2 Sheepdogs, like these animals herding a flock in southern Germany, have to be trained by a combination of instrumental learning and classical conditioning.

3 Dolphins are highly intelligent animals and can be trained with very little difficulty to carry out a wide repertoire of tasks. They undoubtedly possess some ability to reason.

Skinner called this kind of learning 'operant conditioning', and it is also known as 'instrumental conditioning', or sometimes, more simply, as 'trial-and-error learning'.

Many activities of wild animals can be explained in terms of instrumental learning. When kittens or baby otters, for example, play they make all sorts of peculiar and comic movements that achieve nothing more than making the young animal look a fool. But some of the animal's random movements achieve a particular effect; for example, a cuff to the side of a playmate's head will send it spinning. Soon the animal learns which of its movements will achieve a reward (such as tumbling an opponent) and which will merely serve to trip itself up. Very quickly its gambollings become less random and much more streamlined and directional. And this improvement can be explained in terms of instrumental conditioning: the 'good' movements are rewarded and become established; the 'poor' ones are not and are eliminated.

Instrumental learning, like classical conditioning, is an example of associative learning. The third and final type of associative learning, which is much more difficult to explain than the other two, is known as latent learning. Professor Thorpe defines this as '.... the association of indifferent stimuli or situations without patent reward'.

Exploration

If a bird or a mammal is put into a strange cage the first thing it does, after it has got over its fright, is to explore. And soon it becomes evident that it knows every inch of that cage. Obviously animals in the wild know a great deal about the terrain they inhabit; we already cited the mouse which, in the dark of night, can make an instant dash back from any part of its territory to its hole. Many insects make special 'orientation flights' in which they learn enough of their environment to be able to move around freely in it. They learn a few fixed points in the terrain and the position of those landmarks relative to the position of the sun.

But a conditioned reflex in a dog can be induced only if it is taught to associate an otherwise meaningless stimulus (like a bell sound) with a rewarding stimulus (like the bit of meat). And animals only learn instrumentally if particular actions (like pressing a bar) are followed by rewards (like receiving some food). But what reward does the animal get from learning something about its territory? How can it learn to associate a particular tree with a particular part of its territory when this association is not consolidated (or reinforced as the psychologists say) by any immediate reward?

Followers of the American psychologist C.L. Hull have produced one answer. They argue that all activities by animals are motivated by some kind of 'drive' – a hunger drive, a thirst drive and a sex drive. And, they say, an activity is 'rewarded' when the drive is reduced; thus food rewards foraging activity because it reduces the drive (hunger) that first induced the foraging. And the Hullians propose that animals have an 'exploratory drive', which makes them explore and that this drive is reduced – rewarded – as the animal becomes familiar with its territory. But although it is true that an animal explores less as it becomes more familiar with the terrain, just as an animal forages less when it becomes less hungry, it is not true that an animal can be sated by exploration as it can be by excess of food. If an animal is taken from a cage that it has been vigorously exploring and then put into another cage, it will explore the second cage no less vigorously than the first; it has not become 'tired' of exploring. Thus the analogy between 'exploration drive' and 'hunger drive' does not seem all that helpful and the process of latent learning, whereby an animal learns something that may or may not be useful at a

1 Performing animals in circuses are now trained by rewarding the successful performance of tricks. The reward reinforces the behaviour the trainer wishes to develop.

2 Young geese become imprinted with the first object they see at birth. Professor Konrad Lorenz here demonstrates how a young goose will follow with a dogged fixation the first object it sees.

1

2

future date, and may or may not be rewarded, remains a mystery.

Yet another form of learning that is difficult to explain is illustrated by the famous Kohler's apes. In one experiment Kohler placed chimpanzees in cages and put bananas outside the cage, well out of reach. Inside the cage were a number of sticks, which the chimps could join together to make one long stick. The animals learned to attach the sticks together so as to reach the bananas, which they could not reach with their hands or with the aid of only one stick. It appeared that the animal had sat down and arrived at a solution to the problem, just as a human being might. To perform several quite complicated acts in order to achieve a particular end seemed to require an insight into the problem that went beyond any of the mechanisms of learning that have so far been discussed. Insight implies reasoning power: we cannot doubt that apes do reason and it is very possible that other intelligent animals, like dolphins or dogs, can do so as well.

Finally, some animals learn at a particular time of their lives to attach themselves to particular objects and they never lose that sense of attachment. This form of learning, so brilliantly described by Konrad Lorenz, is known as 'imprinting'. This phenomenon is seen most clearly in many birds. Generally, when they hatch, the first thing the young birds see is their mother and from then on they follow the mother around everywhere, with a dogged fixation. This has obvious survival value since it means the young birds are unlikely to get lost. But if the mother is missing and the young birds spot some other object instead, then they will follow that object around as if it was their mother. If young goslings, for example, are reared by hand they will follow a human being. They are particularly impressionable during this period and what they see may affect them for the rest of their lives.

Courted by a jackdaw

Lorenz relates how a young jackdaw which he reared was convinced that Lorenz was another of his own species, since Lorenz was the first object the jackdaw saw. When the jackdaw grew up, it tried to court Lorenz as a mate. Jackdaws, when courting, perform ritual feeding – the male suitor presents the female with tit-bits. Lorenz's jackdaw, in the mating season, would attempt to thrust chewed-up worms into his ear. The idea that Lorenz was a jackdaw was 'imprinted' in the bird's 'mind'.

The behaviour of animals is the most complicated of their attributes and the most difficult to understand. The classifications of learning described here are no more than crude gropings, the very early beginnings of Man's attempt to comprehend his own behaviour and that of his fellow creatures. But as an intellectual exercise it is interesting to try to classify the behaviour of yourself and friends. Next time you pull on your socks ask yourself whether this is a conditioned reflex or the result of instrumental learning, or a masterly piece of insight.

Animal courtship

The strange, often colourful, rituals and fierce fights for territory are closely connected; they are vital to the successful mating of animals which preserves the balance and continuity of species.

A pair of garden snails embrace. After circling round one another, getting closer and closer, each fires a 'love dart' at the other. A dart can be seen in the neck of the left-hand snail.

Two male ruffs fight for supremacy while two reeves (females) wait unconcernedly for the outcome of the contest. Note the finer plumage of the male birds.

Hanging from a branch on a thread of mucus, two slugs lock their sex organs together. At this point in copulation, sperm liquid is transferred from one animal to the other.

THE GREAT MAJORITY of animals reproduce sexually, a method which requires two separate sexes. By bringing together the genes from two distinct hereditary lines, this system of reproduction at least ensures that the offspring of a species will differ to some extent from its parents. Since we equate 'variety' in a species with a more flexible approach to survival in the struggle for existence, we have come to think of sexual reproduction as being one of the means whereby the species can best adapt to a changing environment.

But, unless they interact in some way, males and females are incapable of reproducing. There must be some means by which sperm and eggs are brought together when both are ripe, and this event must also be synchronized with other factors, like, for instance, the season of the year; for fertilization that led to the birth of young in the depths of the winter would hardly benefit the future survival of any species.

Some animals, such as the oyster or the sea-anemone, do not come into close physical contact with each other to mate. Nonetheless, when they release their sperm and eggs into the water, it is not a random event taking place at a random time of year in a random place. Instead the eggs and sperm are released more or less simultaneously in established breeding grounds and fertilization can therefore take place readily.

Animals are generally able to respond to set conditions of the environment, such as the length of day or temperature, and for this purpose they have built-in physiological mechanisms linked to a hormonal control system. Strangely enough, it is the moon that influences the oyster, and

several other species, like the Palolo worm of the Pacific. The oyster spawns two days after a full or new moon, particularly between 26 June and 10 July. In reality, the oyster is not observing the fullness of the moon, but is responding to movements of the sea as it ebbs and flows more strongly than usual with the tides of that season – the spring tides. Dutch oyster breeders use this response to increase their yield of oysters. The larvae swim in the upper waters ten days after the spring tide and then sink to the bottom where they settle. They flourish much better on a clean, hard sea bed and so the breeders put down roof tiles. The tiles, however, must only be put down at the last moment, otherwise they get cov-

ered with other organisms. The breeders can calculate more or less to the day when to put the tiles down.

Nature is always striving for economy, and the shedding of sperm and eggs indiscriminately into the environment, however synchronized, leads to much wastage. If instead males can be induced to stand over females while they spawn, at least the sperm should have more chance of finding the eggs. In fact, the two sexes of many fish, including the salmon, come together in close proximity during spawning, and the male frog goes so far as to mount the female. She may take many hours before she spawns – which she will only do if a male is on her – and the male develops special breeding pads on his front legs which enable him to cling on safely. As soon as the eggs are out of the female he liberates a generous volume of sperm. But the male must first attract a mature female and this he does by croaking in competition with all the rival male frogs. Each species of frog has its own characteristic croak, and a female is only attracted by a male of her own kind.

As nature has devised more intricate methods of mating, including insemination actually inside the female, the relationship between the two sexes becomes more elaborate and difficult. Imagine the problem: two animals which have never seen, let alone encountered each other, have to come together into close, harmonious physical contact. How can the animals recognize each other as being of the same species, and at the same time of the opposite sex, and how can they know that having encountered each other, both are going to be ready and ripe for mating? Each species has developed an

The distended air sac of this male tree frog is a secondary sexual characteristic. It acts as a sounding box for its booming cry, calling the female at night.

extraordinary mode of behaviour that is only put in action during the breeding season. This behaviour, 'courtship', may prelude and release a whole new pattern of behaviour that serves for the care of the young. This then is the final economy: insemination inside the female, the development of the embryo within the female, giving rise to *viviparity*, and then the care of young.

The essence of courtship is therefore to bring males and females together. It is not confined to vertebrates and we can see beautiful examples of it in certain insects, like the Grayling butterfly, and in the molluscs, including the common garden snail and its more sophisticated relative, the squid. Outside the breeding season the Grayling butterfly is not a social animal, and although several butterflies may be seen together in one habitat, this gathering is purely a response to abundant food. Nevertheless, sometime after emerging from their cocoons at the beginning of July, the butterflies develop their reproductive behaviour. The males stop feeding and take up position on the ground, or on the bark of trees. When another butterfly flutters by, the male takes off and pursues it. Should it be a receptive female Grayling butterfly, she reacts to the male's approach by alighting on the ground. The male walks round her until he is in front, facing her. If then she keeps motionless he begins his stately courtship.

A ritual courtship

First he jerks his wings upward and forward a few times, then keeping them slightly raised to show off the beautiful white-centred spots on his forewings he opens and closes the front part of his wings rhythmically, then comes the most elegant part of the ritual: he raises his forewings and opens them widely with a quivering motion so that it seems he is executing a low bow to the female. Still in this posture, he folds the two forewings together and clasps the female's antennae between them. Now the actual mating takes place. He walks quickly behind the female and placing his abdomen with its copulatory organs against the female's, he remains facing away from her for some 30 to 40 minutes, while he passes sperm. The two animals then break contact and never see each other again. The 'bow' is more than just an elegant behavioural quirk. The male has a number of scent scales on his forewings in a narrow strip at the front, and when he clasps the female's antennae within his wings he is essentially bringing her smell receptors into contact with his scent. Once she has sensed his particular scent, she is ready to copulate.

Male scorpions fighting. The darker male has just torn off one of the other's claws, and its opponent is lying on his back, struggling to right himself.

Many insects rely on scents to bring about mating. Some insects, like the male silkmoths, can attract the females from more than a mile away should the wind be in the right direction. Then again, the female cockroach, when she is ready to mate, releases a particular scent, and this brings the males scurrying to her. A scent of this sort, which influences the behaviour of other members of the species, is known as a *pheromone*.

The garden snail is hermaphrodite; nonetheless for sexual reproduction to occur a mate must be found, and then a sort of cross-fertilization takes place with the sperm from each snail fertilizing the ova of the other. When two reproductively mature snails have found each other, they circle around, coming closer and closer. At the climax each snail fires a calcareous 'love' dart at the other from a special organ peculiar to the species. This 'Cupid's' dart embeds in the tissues of the other snail and is the prelude to copulation.

The final act of the elaborate courtship of the six-spot Burnet moth. Male and female can remain linked together, abdomen to abdomen for an hour or more.

The magnificent plumage of the turkey-cock rivals that of the peacock in splendour. The cock struts and preens during courtship, displaying his finery to his dowdy mate.

A great many species of animals, the majority of birds for example, as well as fish like the stickleback, take to living in territories during the breeding season. These species for the remainder of the year, comprising mainly the autumn and winter, live in flocks (or, in the case of fish, schools) and these flocks consist of an anonymous group of animals that do not recognize each other individually. When the animals become territorial, their behaviour changes drastically. Instead of living in harmony with each other, the animals, in general the males, go off and find territories which they then defend against any intruders. This territorial behaviour serves several purposes. It promotes mating; it provides an area where the young can be cared for and protected against possible predators; it prevents overcrowding and therefore safeguards an adequate supply of food; and finally it effects at least for a season the dispersal of the species.

To defend their territories animals have to become aggressive. This does not mean that any intruders are fought with to the death; instead by a series of stereotyped threats the defender of the territory can make his claims known and clear to any possible rival. The further inside his territory the more intense the defender's

Great crested grebes exchange gifts during courtship and nesting. These conciliatory gestures play an important part in maintaining the family unit during the breeding season.

snout into the ground. This strange display usually drives the intruding stickleback away.

While not concerned with defending his territory, the male stickleback makes a nest. He hollows a pit out of the river bottom and presses pieces of nest material, usually threads of algae, into it, binding these all together with a glue substance secreted from his kidneys. Then, when this part of the work is completed he bores a tunnel by wriggling his body through.

But, now he has to attract a female, and for this to occur he must overcome his innate aggression. The females which have become swollen with eggs, are parading over the territory while still swimming with the school. Being a drab colour they do not elicit much aggression from the male, whose colours are now even more glittering: his back now being a brilliant shiny blue and his belly dark red. The male approaches the stickleback school in a peculiar zig-zag dance. First he swims towards the females with his

aggressive intentions, and the closer to the boundaries of his territory, the less sure he becomes of himself. This doubt can lead to an amusing ding-dong battle. First one male chases the other, but in his enthusiasm he may get carried too far into the other's territory. This latter, finding himself on home ground, swiftly turns and now becomes the aggressor, forcing the original aggressor to flee. Finally, both animals having determined to their own satisfaction where the boundaries lie, leave each other in peace.

The male stickleback first shows this aggressive behaviour when he leaves the schools of fish and goes off to select a territory. Concurrently with his changing behaviour, he assumes brilliant nuptial

colours. The eye changes to a shining blue, the back from a dull brownish becomes greenish, the underparts red. If another fish, particularly a male, should enter the territory, the defendant darts towards the opponent with raised dorsal spines and open mouth, looking as if it were just about to bite. If the newcomer does not flee, instead of gripping it with its teeth, the attacking stickleback points its head down and standing vertically in the water makes a series of jerky movements as if it were about to bore its

A male three-spined stickleback takes up his aggressive display posture, nosing the bed of the river. This territorial defence position also plays a part in courtship.

mouth open then turns and swims away again. The 'zig' part of the dance has the elements of aggression in it, and most, if not all, the females are frightened away. One female, however, may be ready to spawn and she turns towards the male, adopting an upright attitude of appeasement. In the soliciting 'zag' part of the dance, the male swims to the nest and thrusts his snout inside, while turning over on his side. The female now enters the nest, and, because of her swollen abdomen, gets stuck half-way, with her head and tail protruding at either end. The male next prods the base of her tail with his snout and persuades her to spawn. This done, she leaves the nest and he enters and fertilizes the eggs. While his mating urge is on the male may collect eggs in this fashion from other females. After a time his behaviour changes and he spends long periods just outside the nest, fanning it with broad sweeps of his pectoral fins. This motion keeps a steady flow of aerated water over the eggs and is essential for their healthy development. Once the young have hatched – until they are big enough to escape his attentions – the male guards them against all intruders and possible danger.

Displacement activity

Professor Niko Tinbergen points out that there are some fundamental elements in the stickleback's behaviour that can be applied generally to animal behaviour, particularly courtship and aggression. The whole course of events can only unfold if both animals of the partnership respond precisely to the other's intentions. The zig-zag dance serves to entice only those females that are absolutely ready to mate, the remainder flee; while the male must show the female the nest entrance she must enter before he will prod her with his snout and entice her to spawn; then only after she has left, will he enter and fertilize the eggs. His colour is also very important, especially his red belly, and a model hardly resembling a male stickleback at all, except for a dark red underside, can be used to attract a female to a stickleback's nest, so long as the motions of the model are sufficiently imitative of the male's movements. The female can then be made to spawn by prodding the base of her spine with a rod, just as if it were the snout of a proper male.

The upright threat position of the stickleback has some characteristics in common with its nest-making activities, when it actually buries its snout in the sand to make a depression. Such displacement activities have become highly meaningful signals for other members of the same species, and are a communication of mood. By instantly understanding the intentions of the other animal, a member of the same species will respond correctly. If the movement is one of threat, then bloodshed is averted when the intruder either goes away, or makes some appeasing movement.

Complex rituals like those found in stickleback courtship may appear to be absurd but they are vitally important to the successful mating of the species.

1

2

1 Love-play of the giraffe. These huge animals go through elaborate and touching courtship preliminaries, caressing one another with their long necks and rubbing flanks.
2 The male lyrebird of Australia dances on a mound during courtship, displaying his superb plumage to his mate. The lyrebird's long tail feathers are brilliantly coloured.
3 Aggressive behaviour in insects. Two male stag beetles lock mandibles together as they fight. Aggression is not uncommon among insects as well as among higher animals.

3

Almost human

Despite obvious differences, many features of human behaviour can be found in animals. In fact, human beings bear comparison in some aspects of their lives even with lowly shellfish and ants.

1

GO TO any big natural history museum and compare your arm with, for example, a bat's wing and a seal's flipper. Outwardly, they are as different from one another as the functions they perform. But the bones of these 'limbs' reveal such an essential similarity of design as to suggest that Man, the bat and the seal evolved in the course of millions of years from a common ancestor. The similarity of animal skeletons, including that of Man, demonstrates that a basic skeletal structure persists throughout geological time in spite of widely diverging functions of its components.

And just as the skeletons of Man and animals reveal a common origin, so does the behaviour of Man and animals show a close relationship. Indeed, the consensus of scientific opinion is that behind all the many variations in the behaviour of Man and the animals there is a fundamental structure of inherited behaviour common to all. When we remember that other animals inhabited the Earth for millions of years before Man, it is not too fanciful to suggest that Man has inherited his pattern of behaviour from animals.

As Man slowly learned the art of personal adornment it was the male who decorated himself the most fancifully. Indeed, clothes were originally not so much a matter of keeping warm or symbolizing modesty but much more a form of decoration. And when it came to personal adornment, the man invariably outshone the woman. Just as the peacock's magnificent plumage and display dazzles the drably feathered peahen, and the lion's mane distinguishes the male from the lioness, so early Man far outdid the woman in self-decoration. Apart from the effects of human hunting and the taking of grazing lands for agriculture, most animals maintain a remarkably steady population level, decade after decade, and even century after century. It would, therefore, seem that non-human animal population is

2

1 Like many human beings, animals show aggression. This whooper swan, angered by the intrusion of a photographer, speeds aggressively across the water's surface.
2 Play is another aspect of behaviour young animals have in common with young human beings. Here, two otters frolic playfully in a rough and tumble which teaches them co-ordination.

regulated by some system that keeps it within fairly narrow limits of a set average density.

Ecologists were for long of the opinion that increase or decrease in population of any particular animal was the result of natural factors over which the species had no control. The chief of these factors were predators on the particular species, accidents, starvation, and infestation by parasites causing disease.

Animal populations

The idea that disease or predators are essential controllers of animal population has little real scientific basis. There are several animal species that are not readily liable to parasite diseases and seldom fall prey to predators. The lion and the eagle, for example, are remarkably free of disease

and have no predators, yet they have a very stable population level.

Shortage of food is not the all-important factor once considered chiefly responsible for limiting animal population. Careful study and observation reveal that starvation is comparatively rare in animal communities. It is very unusual for all the members of a species living in an area not to get enough food to survive. Sometimes severe cold or drought starves animals out, but this is a meteorological 'accident' that does not arise from population density.

One way in which animals artificially restrict their population density is related to their food supply. The practice of certain birds staking out a territory for nesting and hatching and rearing a family is an example. During the breeding season, each cock bird lays claim to an area of a minimum size and drives out all other cocks of his species. By this means a group of cock birds will divide up the available ground as their individual territories and so limit over-population by adjusting itself to the food sources available. Instead of fighting furiously in competition for the food, the members of the group each competes for a piece of ground which becomes the exclusive food preserve of itself and its family. Any cock bird unable to win and hold a feeding territory is obviously a weakling, and without a territory it cannot win a mate and feed a family.

With certain species of mammals, biological reaction keeps animal population at a fairly steady level. At certain times the rate of ovulation in the females is reduced by changes in the output of hormones. Rabbits, foxes and deer will reabsorb embryos in the uterus during times of stress.

The human male is by nature a family man. He prides himself on being the head and protector of a family, and this trait in human behaviour has its counterpart in

1 Some ants, like these red wood ants, carry on a primitive form of 'agriculture'. The ants live together with colonies of aphids, which they 'milk' for their nectar.
2 Curiosity is a feline characteristic shared with human beings. Here, a cat explores the inside and outside of a glass-sided box. The exploring instinct is strong in many animals.
3 Biological rhythms, many of them tied to natural cycles like day and night, the tides, and the seasons, play a part in the life of most animals. Human beings are often governed by internal 'clocks' as are these scallops, which open at a predetermined time each day.
4 A tool-using finch photographed on the Galapagos Islands. Apart from Man, very few animals use tools.
5 Another bird which uses tools is the Egyptian vulture. It holds sharp stones in its beak and breaks open eggs with them.

Life's history in stone

Forms of life many millions of years old lie locked in the layers of the Earth's crust. This vast specimen case of petrified remains shows how life developed in the aeons before Man.

PALAEONTOLOGISTS ARE SCIENTISTS who study the living things that dwelt on this planet in its distant youth. And, from a few fragmentary remains they have been able to piece together the crowded story of living things on Earth and their evolution. Most of these remains take the form of fossils, and to be able to date them and place them on the evolutionary tree of life, we must know something about the rocks in which they are found. For instance, layers of *sedimentary* rocks laid down under the sea contain characteristic groups of fossils which differ in some respects from those found in layers of older rocks below, and in more recent layers above.

The major rock groups or *systems* distinguished by the fossils they contain, and the time intervals or *periods* during which they were laid down, are generally illustrated by a diagram called the *Geological Column.* Palaeontology also has a second equally vital role. Study of the fossils of plants and animals in rocks shows that some groups increase in number and variety in the layers of younger rocks above, whereas others die out. Some forms became extinct in rocks millions of years old, while in the case of others, the line along which they have evolved can be traced right through to their modern descendants.

Carbon dating of rocks

Today, scientists have available improved techniques for measuring the ages of rocks. Some rocks contain radioactive elements which gradually decay as atoms lose electrons and particles from their nuclei. In the decay process, some of the original 'parent' material is lost, leaving a new 'daughter' substance. The rates at which these changes take place follow a known physical law and are characteristic for a given radioactive element. As a result, from a knowledge of the proportions of parent and daughter elements in a sample of rock, scientists can calculate its age. Fossils themselves can also be dated by similar methods. We can now therefore view evolution in terms of actual numbers of years.

How life began still remains much of a mystery. Experiments have shown that electric sparks passed through a mixture of gases such as methane, ammonia and water vapour – the same gases as are thought to have existed in the Earth's early 'atmosphere' – produce several kinds of amino acids. These are the 'building bricks' from which proteins are constructed. Lightning flashes passing through this mixture may have produced the earliest organic compounds which, aided by clay minerals acting as catalysts in the mud of a primeval shore, became the first living things. Another theory is that

1 Fossilized graptolite colonies, occurring in many parts of the world, provide a means of correlating the age of rocks in different geographical locations.
2 Trilobites possessed a pair of compound eyes and had the ability to roll themselves into a ball to conserve moisture. They were the dominant form of life for more than 100 million years.
3 This fossil of *Portheus molossus* shows another fish in its stomach. Apparently the predator died before digestion was complete.

the change from inorganic to living matter was brought about by radiation from space penetrating a less protective atmosphere than that of today.

Among the earliest organisms were probably simple single-celled plants living in water without needing free oxygen but producing it through their life processes. The development of photosynthesis by plants could have produced the oxygen in the atmosphere necessary for the development of animal life, and experiments have shown that substances resembling chlorophyll – necessary for photosynthesis – can be formed from simple starting materials.

The point at which life originated may never be known, but evidence from Pre-Cambrian rocks, such as limestone from Rhodesia over 2,800 million years old, indicates that simple organisms existed in very early times. This Rhodesian limestone and other ancient limestones contain lumpy structures known as *stromatolites,* which are made up of thin layers of calcium carbonate similar to those secreted today by blue-green algae. Almost

certainly stromatolites are also traces of similar marine plants. In Ontario a rock known as *chert,* some 2,000 million years old, has yielded fossils of primitive fungi, algae and bacteria.

The record of life from these very early times until the beginning of the Cambrian period 570 million years ago is obscure. Cambrian animal fossils are plentiful and varied, with life forms so complex that highly organized ancestors must have existed well back into the Pre-Cambrian era.

Fossils of soft organisms

Fossil remains are lacking because these creatures were soft bodied, and so left few traces. In recent years, however, geologists in South Australia have found the impressions in sandstone of a group of late Pre-Cambrian fossils. These resemble jelly-fish, annelid worms, and frond-like objects, possibly sea-pens. Frond- and disc-like impressions also occur in rocks aged about 1,000 million years from the Charnwood Forest area of Leicestershire. All Pre-Cambrian fossils found so far have been in rocks laid down in shallow water.

When the Cambrian period began, almost seven-eighths of Earth's existence (up to the present) had already elapsed. Suddenly the record of life was transformed. Within the deposits from Cambrian sea-floors, fossils of nearly all the invertebrate phyla have been found. The reason for this transformation appears to be that animals began to develop hard parts, usually of calcium carbonate (chalk), but sometimes of horny chitin. The chances of fossilization were thus greatly increased. Most highly organized and certainly the most striking in appearance of the Cambrian animals were the *trilobites.* Crawling over the sea-floor, burrowing into the mud, or swimming near the bottom, these creatures were the dominant life forms for at least 100 million years. Their importance continued through the succeeding Ordovician and Silurian periods, and their final extinction was not until Permian times, less than 280 million years ago.

Brachiopods, mostly with horny shells, were fairly common, but although bivalves (two-shelled animals resembling cockles) and gastropods (single-shelled animals resembling snails) existed, they were rather rare. Early forms of corals and *graptolites* (colonial animals similar to coral) were already in existence.

Existing through 90 million years of Ordovician and Silurian times, the graptolites provide the most useful fossils for geologists. These were tiny individual creatures inhabiting branching colonies resembling fretsaw blades which drifted at the mercy of waves and currents over deep oceans and shallow seas. New shapes with different arrangements of branches rapidly evolved and their remains, entombed in the bottom sediments, enable detailed correlations to be made between rocks in widely separated parts of the world.

Jamoytius – a primitive fish-like creature with a skeleton of cartilage, found in Silurian shales – may perhaps illustrate the form taken by the earliest chordates.

Coal forests developed during the Carboniferous period. These were mainly giant club mosses, up to 100 feet high, in an undergrowth of horsetail trees and seed ferns.

The date at which the earliest vertebrate animals branched from the same stock as the echinoderms is still unknown, but must have been much earlier. The teeming life of the warm shallow Silurian seas is wonderfully illustrated after 410 million years on weathered slabs of Wenlock limestone crowded with fossils such as bryozoa, crinoids, brachiopods and trilobites.

The Earth dries out

Late Silurian and early Devonian times – about 400 million years ago – were

Sedimentary rocks were laid down in the sea or in a lake, and show distinct stratification. The strata, or layers, are particularly noticeable in sea cliffs such as this.

periods of dramatic advance in the story of life. Plants with well-developed sap-conducting systems and spores dispersed by the wind began to spread on to the land, and the first air-breathing insects and spiders appeared. In lakes, rivers and estuaries, heavily armoured, jawless fish – the *ostracoderms* – became abundant while true fish of many varieties soon followed.

Dry conditions were widespread during the Devonian period and some fishes developed lungs and limb-like pairs of fins and were able to crawl from drying pools to more permanent water. These were the ancestors of the amphibians which came into existence by the early Carboniferous period, which began 345 million years ago.

Carboniferous times began with the British area largely submerged by shallow tropical seas, abounding with corals, crinoids, brachiopods and some coiled cephalopods – squid-like creatures called *goniatites.* River deltas were built up, converting the seas into swamps on which the coal forests grew in the steamy heat. Giant club mosses growing up to 100 feet tall towered above the profuse smaller growth of horsetail trees, seed ferns and primitive gymnosperms. Thin-shelled freshwater mussels flourished in delta channels and estuaries. Fishes were common and salamander-like amphibians – the *labyrinthodonts* – sprawled on the mud-flats.

At this time Europe, North America and much of Asia formed a single continent lying far to the south of their present latitudes – a fact which explains the tropical nature of the vegetation. Africa, Australia, South America and Antarctica, together with much of India, comprised a continent called Gondwana centred close to the South Pole and suffering repeated glaciation. From Permian times onwards, as the ancient land masses were split and shifted to their present positions by the processes of continental drift, climatic changes, together with the isolation of some areas in the southern hemisphere, had a profound effect on the development

	Evolutionary Time Scale	Geological Time Scale	Biological Time Scale
Cryptozoic	**Pre-Cambrian** — Primitive life — algae, fungi, soft-bodied marine animals — appears on earth.	**4,550,000,000 years ago** — Formation of the earth's crust, and the appearance of the seas and continental land masses.	
Palaeozoic	**Cambrian** — Appearance of primitive arthropods, plus a few molluscs, worms and sponges.	**570,000,000 years ago** — Large areas of Europe covered by shallow seas. Sinking of Norway and parts of England.	
	Ordovician — Clams, starfish, coral and other marine invertebrates join arthropods in sea. First fish appear.	**500,000,000 years ago** — North-west European troughs built up from the Caledonian Mountains.	
	Silurian — Beginning of plant and animal life on land.	**440,000,000 years ago** — Formation of the Caledonian Mountains from the old red North Continent.	
	Devonian — First appearance of large, tree-like plants on land. Rise of the amphibians.	**395,000,000 years ago** — Elevation of the Varistic Mountains. Shallow seas of Scandinavia displaced by elevations.	
	Carboniferous — Fish abound in seas. Appearance of first reptiles. Giant insects dominate forests.	**345,000,000 years ago** — Filling up of Central Europe by Varistic Mountains. Swamps and forest which become coal.	
	Permian — Rise of modern insects and increased expansion of vertebrates, i.e. amphibians and reptiles.	**280,000,000 years ago** — Varistic Mountains buried under own debris. Period marked by violent volcanic activity.	
Mesozoic	**Triassic** — Rise of the dinosaurs. Vertebrates begin replacing invertebrates as dominant life form.	**225,000,000 years ago** — Continued levelling of the earth.	
	Jurassic — First appearance of mammals and birds. Dinosaurs reach their peak.	**195,000,000 years ago** — Spreading of the seas over extensive areas of Europe and Asia. Gentle warping of the earth.	
	Cretaceous — Extinction of the dinosaurs. Sharp increase in mammals. Modern trees appear.	**136,000,000 years ago** — Mild climates nearly everywhere. Further expansion of the seas.	
Cenozoic	**Tertiary** — Mammals dominate the earth and bony fish dominate the seas.	**65,000,000 years ago** — Violent volcanic activity. Rising of large fold-mountains of Pyrenees, Alps and Carpathians.	
	Quaternary — Mammal dominance continues. Man appears.	**1,500,000 years ago** — Movement of glaciers from Scandinavia into German uplands and Alpine glaciers into foreland.	

Biological Time Scale (bar labels): Seaweed and invertebrates, Fish, Land plants, Amphibians, Reptiles, Mammals, Birds, Man

The relation between the geological and biological time scales is clearly shown in this diagram. Carbon dating plays a large part in determining the ages of fossils and rocks.

of plant and animal life.

Earth movements, beginning in the late Carboniferous period, produced high mountain chains. Large areas of the northern hemisphere, formerly clothed by the coal forests, became deserts. Ice Ages continued to afflict the Southern Continent. The disappearance of the last trilobites typified the dying out of many forms of life that had existed since the Cambrian period. The Palaeozoic era ('the time of early life') was over, but new groups of animals and plants that were to dominate the Mesozoic era ('the time of middle life') began to emerge. Early reptiles which had evolved from the Carboniferous amphibians increased in variety and number. Ammonites and belemnites appeared in the seas, while land vegetation included the first conifers.

The 165 million years of the Triassic, Jurassic and Cretaceous periods have been called the 'Age of Reptiles'. This develop-ing group, unlike the amphibians, was not confined to water for breeding, and varieties such as the dinosaurs which appeared in the Triassic period rapidly spread over the land, even to hostile desert areas. The streamlined ichthyosaurs and plesiosaurs were adapted to life in the open sea, while by the Jurassic period the light-boned pterosaurs had taken to the air. The ancestors of the dinosaurs were the small and agile Triassic thecodonts, from whom many different varieties descended. The 80-foot-long, four-legged Diplodocus waded through the Jurassic

1 The fossil of a sea lily, which is a relative of the starfishes, was found in Wenlock limestone, and is about 430 million years old. Each 'head' is about 4½ inches long.

2 This model of a jawless fish was reconstructed from a fossil about 410 million years old. The creature, known as *Cephalaspis,* was well protected by heavy armour plating.

changes in the Earth's magnetic field may have reduced protection from radiation from space, which might have accelerated genetic changes.

Although subdivided into seven epochs – the Palaeocene, Eocene, Oligocene, Miocene, Pliocene, Pleistocene, and Holocene – the entire Cenozoic era covers only 70 million years. By Eocene times vegetation had a generally modern appearance. Deciduous trees and other flowering plants were more important than conifers and ferns. Grasses, developing later in the Oligocene period, spread widely in drier areas. Generally warmer climates in the earlier part of the Cenozoic era accounted for tropical flora as far north as Britain and temperate plants in the Arctic.

Ultimately dependent on the new vegetation, the mammals rapidly increased in early Tertiary times to dominate life on land. Despite the incoming of snakes, reptiles and amphibians were of relatively minor importance. Among the new animals were the creodonts, ancestors of the carnivores, and condylarths, predecessors of the hoofed herbivores. Other strange forms now extinct include the lumbering Uintatherium with six bony projections on its head, and Baluchitherium, a rhinoceros 18 feet high at the shoulder.

The ascendancy of the mammals

Mammals as a group probably reached their acme in the Miocene period, for although most families alive at that time have persisted to the present day, some of the larger forms, including Moropus 'the clawed horse' have become extinct.

A trend towards cooler, drier climates continuing through the Pliocene period was accompanied by the extension of grasslands and shrinking of forests, thus favouring fast-running hoofed animals such as the horse, antelope and gazelle. These were the prey of carnivores like the sabre-toothed cat. Cenozoic marine life was similar in many respects to that of today. Gastropods and bivalves were abundant. Early whales had developed in the Eocene period and the teeth of 60-foot-long sharks are found in Pliocene marine rocks. As on land, the distribution of marine life changed with climatic conditions.

Since the Miocene period, apes had become abundant and the fossils of some showing certain man-like characteristics have been found in the Pliocene rocks of Africa. Almost three million years ago in Kenya, Australopithecus chipped stones to form the first edged tools. Modern man has evolved against the fluctuating climatic background of the Pleistocene Ice Age. Today, three million years after the earliest stone axes, he operates the mass spectrometer to probe the history of the Earth.

And it is with such advanced scientific tools as the mass spectrometer that biologists are able to read and understand the story of the fossils, which form an exact and detailed calendar of the Earth and the plant and animal life which grew, flourished and died in its forests and seas.

swamps, a contemporary of the ten-ton Stegosaurus with its three-ounce brain; both were harmless herbivores. By contrast Tyrannosaurus (20 feet in height and living in the Cretaceous period) was probably the most formidable predator ever to walk the Earth's surface. The ankylosaurs developed heavy defensive armour whilst Triceratops, with its three horns and head armour, typified another prominent group. Small light dinosaurs, including the ostrich-like Struthiomimus, relied on their speed for safety.

Fossil teeth and jaws about the size of a shrew's found in Triassic debris filling cracks in older rock are the earliest evidence of the mammals. Through most of Mesozoic time these were insignificant creatures inconspicuously coexisting with the dinosaurs.

Archaeopteryx, the first known bird, still possessing teeth and many reptilian features, was excavated from fine-grained Jurassic limestone in southern Germany. The Mesozoic seas swarmed with ammonites. Hundreds of species with subtle differences in their coiled shells rapidly evolved and spread far and wide. These fossils are of the greatest value in correlating Jurassic and Cretaceous rocks throughout the world. Among the other marine invertebrates belemnites, bivalves, gastropods, echinoids and corals also flourished.

From the character of the plant life, the Triassic and Jurassic periods have been termed the 'Age of Gymnosperms'. Conifers and their more primitive allies, the cycads, together with ferns, dominated the vegetation. In the Cretaceous period, however, flowering plants – the angiosperms – appeared, and increasingly trees familiar in the modern world entered the scene.

One of geology's greatest mysteries is the wholesale extinction, at the close of the Mesozoic era, of flourishing groups of animals and the drastic reduction in the importance of others. The dinosaurs, ichthyosaurs, plesiosaurs, flying reptiles, ammonites and belemnites disappeared before the earliest Cenozoic ('the time of recent life') rocks were laid down. Some forms had become so specialized that they failed to adapt to geographic and climatic changes. A recent attractive theory suggests that

The evolution story 1

Did all living organisms develop from common ancestors? The case is still not proved, but Darwin showed how they could have done, and presented a mass of evidence in support of the theory.

FOR HUNDREDS OF YEARS thinking men have been asking the question, 'How did life as we see it today, in all its diversity and complexity, come to be present on Earth?' There have been many attempts to answer this question, perhaps the earliest being the Theory of Special Creation.

The Theory of Special Creation is fundamental to many religions because it says that at some time in the past some 'outside force' (God) created all forms of life, and since the 'time of creation', there have been no changes in the species.

Another theory, that of Spontaneous Generation, suggests that some forms of life suddenly appeared from non-living things, and are still doing so now. This theory was proposed to account for various observations, such as the appearance of maggots in cooked meat left on a plate, or even mice in a closed barn. The work of Louis Pasteur (1822–95) with micro-organisms led many men to believe that organisms do not arise except as offspring of pre-existing organisms. Maggots were found to be the offspring of flies. Mice and other rodents, of course, have a host of ways to appear where they are not wanted.

The Theory of Evolution

As a result, the theory of Spontaneous Generation was largely abandoned, but not completely. It survives, greatly modified, in the widely held Theory of Evolution, which states that non-living things (chemical compounds) gave rise to living things (simple one-celled organisms). However, the theory further suggests that spontaneous generation occurred only once. Then these single-celled organisms gave rise to the many-celled organisms up to and including Man.

Evolutionary views had in fact been held by a number of people long before that time, even before rival theories were discredited, but they did not gain general acceptance because there was no satisfactory explanation of how the changes necessary to create one species from another could have occurred. This lack was filled by the British naturalist Charles Darwin (1809–82) when he put forward his views, together with those of another great nineteenth-century naturalist Alfred Russell Wallace (1823–1913), in the book *Origin of Species*. This book contained Darwin's *Theory of Natural Selection*. Darwin became greatly interested in Nature while a student at Cambridge University, and so when H.M.S. *Beagle* left Devonport in December 1831, the young unpaid naturalist was aboard. During his voyage on the *Beagle* between 1831 and 1836, he had noticed how the geo-

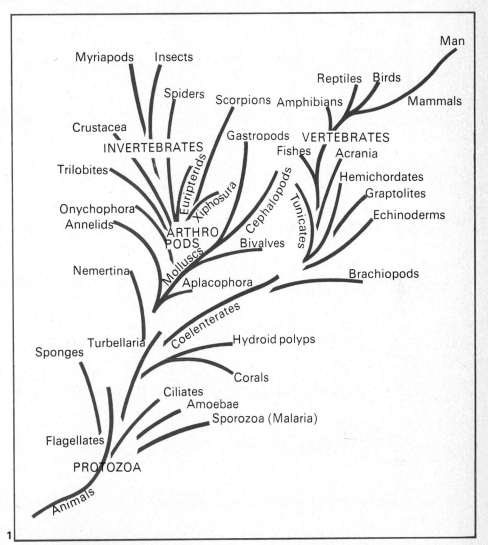

1 Relationships between the organisms occurring in the animal kingdom are clearly shown in this diagram. The development of any species can be traced back through its intermediate stages.
2 Much of the evidence for evolution comes from fossil remains. In the case of soft-bodied animals or plants such as this fern, the organism rots away leaving behind an imprint in the rock.

graphical distribution and variation of species could be explained by assuming that related species have evolved from a common stock. In 1854, he wrote of the finches on the Galapagos Islands (in the Pacific), 'seeing this gradation and diversity of structure in one small, intimately related group of birds, one might really fancy that . . . one species had been taken and modified for different ends'.

Darwin was also greatly influenced by the social and economic conditions of his times, and by the writing of Malthus, who in 1802 wrote an *Essay on Population*. Referring to human populations, Malthus stated that the population is capable of increasing indefinitely in geometric progression, and must therefore be held stable by limiting the amounts of food available. For this last part, that food supply could limit the population, there is no proof, and herein lies one of the greatest problems confronting the human race – how to provide enough food for an exploding population.

Darwin also noticed that many animals and plants produced more offspring than ever survived, and that there must be some factor, such as shortage of food, which kept the populations at a stable level. There was, therefore, a 'struggle for existence' in the natural environment. He also observed that any variation which better suited the individual to its particular habitat would have two effects: to give the individual a better chance of survival, and, if offspring could inherit this characteristic, they, too, would have a better chance of survival.

In 1859, Darwin's *Origin of Species* was published, which provided a coherent theory for the evolution of life. It included three major points. Firstly, there exists in Nature a struggle for existence, such that not all the progeny of a species will survive. Secondly, the individuals within a population differ from each other in small details (the concept of continuous variation) so that those animals and plants best adapted to survive have an advantage. This corresponds to 'the survival of the fittest'. Finally, an individual which has the advantageous characteristics is more able to live and reproduce, and so the characteristics will be passed on to the offspring by the phenomenon of heredity.

There were a number of weaknesses in Darwin's theory, due mainly to the ignorance during his times of the concepts of mutation and genetic (sex cell) inheritance. The theory lacked a convincing account of the origins of variations and inheritance. In fact, Darwin accepted

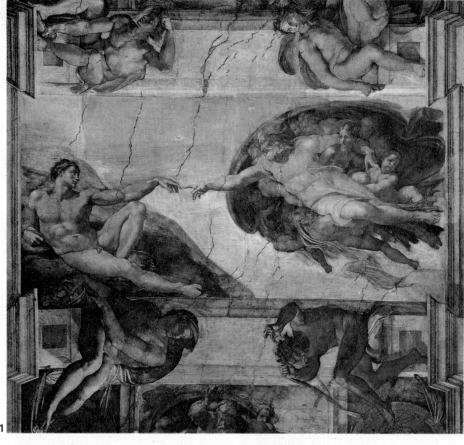
1

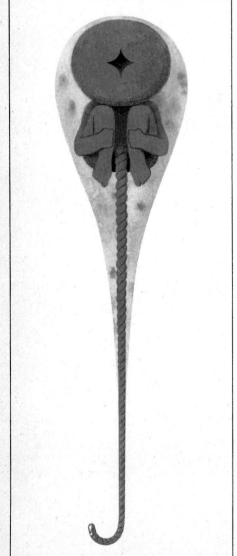

2

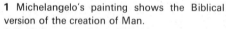
3

1 Michelangelo's painting shows the Biblical version of the creation of Man.
2 Early drawings showed 'little men' in human sperm cells, an idea in flat contradiction to evolutionary theories.
3 Even after the publication of Darwin's work, many people still preferred the traditional view, as shown by this *Punch* cartoon of 1882.
4 Fossils such as this ammonite shell provided evidence of links in the evolutionary chain.

two ideas that today are not acceptable, that inheritance took place via the blood (and so characters were a kind of alloy of all previous ancestry), and that the variations induced in an organism by the environment could be passed on to the next generation. This latter idea was due to the French naturalist Jean-Baptiste Lamarck (1744–1829) who tried to suggest a way in which an animal can change according to its needs (the Law of Use and Disuse and the Transmission of Acquired Character). This idea can best be explained by the well-known example of the giraffe. Lamarck believed that because the animal was constantly stretch-ing its neck to reach food high in the trees, its neck had become increased in length, and the increase could be passed on to the next generation. In the same way, the fact that some birds found it unnecessary to use their wings led by the Law of Disuse to the evolution of the 'flightless birds' (ostriches, emus, rheas, and so on). However, although later work on genetics showed that such characters could not be produced in this way, Lamarck had grasped the importance of the environment in producing changes, which was so strongly stressed by Darwin.

The Dutch biologist Hugo de Vries

Certhidea olivacea
ALBEMARLE ISLAND

Geospiza fuliginosa
BARRINGTON ISLAND

Catamblyrhynchus diadema
EAST ECUADOR (Mainland)

Geospiza magnirostris
CHATHAM ISLAND

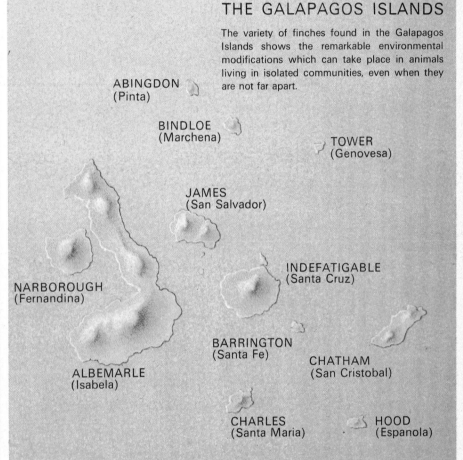

THE GALAPAGOS ISLANDS

The variety of finches found in the Galapagos Islands shows the remarkable environmental modifications which can take place in animals living in isolated communities, even when they are not far apart.

ABINGDON (Pinta)

BINDLOE (Marchena)

TOWER (Genovesa)

JAMES (San Salvador)

NARBOROUGH (Fernandina)

INDEFATIGABLE (Santa Cruz)

BARRINGTON (Santa Fe)

ALBEMARLE (Isabela)

CHATHAM (San Cristobal)

CHARLES (Santa Maria)

HOOD (Espanola)

Geospiza fortis
INDEFATIGABLE ISLAND

(1848–1935) showed that chance occurrences (induced by radiation or other means) can produce marked changes in the genetic make-up of an individual, and that these changes are inheritable. So if an individual is born with exceptionally good eyesight because of a genetic mutation, his children will probably have exceptionally good eyesight, because this characteristic is carried by the sex cells from one generation to the next. (Genes are chemical units strung together on chromosomes, which determine the characteristics of an individual when born.)

Darwin's theory of natural selection (survival of the fittest) could account for small changes within a species, but mutations were needed to explain how the large changes leading to the establishment of new groups of animals could occur. So in the 1930s, the modern theory of evolution (often called the Synthetic

Theory) was proposed. This theory is based upon the theory of natural selection, but includes the concepts of mutation and genetic inheritance.

Fundamentally, this theory suggests that when a spontaneous gene mutation is such that it provides the offspring of the animal with a characteristic favourable for survival, i.e. makes them better equipped to compete for the available food or to withstand the stresses of a changing climate, the animals carrying this gene will become more and more numerous. Thus, the new gene will become 'established' and the species will acquire a new characteristic.

Having considered the theory of evolution, we must now deal in more detail with how new species are created. Although Darwin did not believe in the existence of the species as a separate entity (in his own words, 'I look at the

term *species* as one arbitrarily given for the sake of convenience to a set of individuals closely resembling each other'), it is generally accepted today that a species is in fact a unit. Ignoring one or two exceptions, we may say that a species is considered as a group of individuals which are able to breed amongst themselves, but not with individuals of another group (for example, a bear does not mate with a monkey). Therefore, a species forms a reproductively isolated group.

Over very long periods of time, species can begin to change into new forms when two or more groups of one species are separated in such a way that they are unable to interbreed. This allows them to change (i.e. to evolve) in isolation from each other until a stage is reached where they cannot, even if they are brought together, mate and produce viable offspring (hybrids capable of living and reproducing). By this time, the differences may be obvious, for example as they now are between a lion (*Felis leo*) and a tiger (*Felis tigris*), but this is not always the case. The differences between the various species of the fruit fly (*Drosophila*), for instance, are often so minute that they are virtually indistinguishable except to an expert.

The most important way in which populations may become isolated is by being separated by geographical features, such as an expanse of ocean, a large river, or a mountain range. A classical example of the effects of geographical isolation is to be seen on the Galapagos Islands, where each island tends to have its own particular species of giant tortoise. These species have resulted from the tortoises being unable to cross the stretches of sea between the individual islands.

Once isolated, two such populations will be acted upon in a number of ways which will result in their having different genetic make-ups (*genotypes*), such as natural selection and gene mutation. When the genotype of local populations are such that they cannot interbreed with those of other local populations, they are then usually considered as separate species.

Preserved in rock

The evidence that such changes are occurring or have occurred in the past comes from a number of sources, including classification, effects of physical influences, the natural appearance of new species and races, comparative morphology and anatomy, embryology, geographical distribution, comparative physiology, genetics and palaeontology. Man-made variations through artificial selection (animal and plant breeding) show that these changes can be made to occur, but do not necessarily prove that such changes have occurred in nature.

Even the study of fossils (*palaeontology*) does not prove evolution, but it certainly

1 Comparison of this Galapagos turtle with other members of the species on other islands led Darwin to conclude that geographical location could produce adaptive changes in organisms.

2 H.M.S. *Beagle* was the ship in which Darwin sailed round the world. Data collected on this trip provided evidence for the theories of evolutionary development and adaptive changes in organisms.

provides strong evidence that evolution has occurred in the past, and enables scientists to build up a picture of the past history of animal and plant groups. A fossil is the remains of an organism, or direct evidence of its previous existence, preserved within rocks. There are three main types of fossils. There are the *trace fossils,* for example worm-holes or footprints, which obviously do not involve the death of the organism. Then there are the two types of *body fossils*: one which is a whole organism or part of it (such as the skeletal remains of an extinct dinosaur); the other, which like trace fossils does not involve the death of the organism, occurs when for instance an insect moults and leaves its cast skin for preservation.

Fossils are produced only when remains are situated in such a position that they quickly become covered with sediment. This can occur when an animal or plant drops into a peat bog and quickly sinks down beneath the surface, or when a landslip, or volcanic ash and lava cover it up. However, such instances are comparatively rare, and by far the most

common place for fossils to be formed is in the sea or in large lakes where sediment is constantly being deposited at the bottom. Apart from being quickly covered, in the case of body fossils, there must also be present some hard skeletal parts (such as bones or shells) as the soft parts soon decay and are lost. For this reason, 'soft' organisms such as jelly-fish are seldom found as fossils.

Once the remains have been covered by sediments, they are acted upon in a number of ways before we come to dig them out of the rocks. Only rarely is an organism found unaltered, as for example in the rare finds of whole mammoths, extinct relatives of elephants, preserved intact in frozen mud and ice in Siberia (their meat was still edible), or insects encased in fossilized resin (called amber) found on the shores of the Baltic Sea. Usually the remains are altered, the hard parts being converted to rock such as calcite or silica, or they may be leached (dissolved) away, leaving a space which is filled with minerals resulting in the formation of an internal mould or replica.

The fossil record

Although there are gaps in the fossil record enough fossils exist to suggest strongly that most groups of animals and plants have undergone a gradual series of modifications from prehistoric times to the present. For example, by examining the fossil ancestors of the horse, a number of trends can be identified, culminating in the modern horse (*Equus*). Modern horses are considerably larger than their Eocene ancestor, *Hyracotherium,* and their legs are longer and thinner with reduced skeletal elements (early horses having feet somewhat similar to those of a dog).

Evolution is not complete; it continues at the present time. If climatic conditions on the Earth undergo dramatic changes during the next million years (as they have in the previous million years), then new species will evolve from those existing today. Man may still be master of all he surveys, but he will be a creature very different from the one which bears that name today.

3 Charles Darwin (1809–82), the British naturalist, whose Theory of Natural Selection suggested how changes could have taken place in an organism to give entirely new species.

4 Jean-Baptiste Lamarck (1744–1829) was the first biologist to grasp the importance of environment in producing adaptations, a point which was strongly emphasized by Darwin.

The evolution story 2

Darwin expounded the what and why of evolution. Modern biological research goes a long way towards explaining the how — the mechanism of evolutionary change which may lead to new species.

EVOLUTION IS such an extremely slow process that it is almost impossible to observe significant changes in the structure of a creature over a short period of time. For this reason many people find evolution is a rather difficult idea to understand. When zoologists first began to study the great variety of animal life on Earth, they began noticing marked similarities among various species. For instance, the group of animals called the *Amphibians* – comprising frogs, toads, newts, and the like – all have moist skins for 'breathing', all have rudimentary lungs, all have similar skull structures, and so on.

Classifying the animals by their physical characteristics gives support to the theory of evolution, because there seems to be a logical progression of structures from simple to more complex. It is by examining the physical structure of an animal that its place on the evolutionary ladder may be found.

It is possible to study the physical features of extinct species, which may have vanished from the Earth millions of years ago, by their fossil remains. The vertebrates (animals with backbones) are easier to study than invertebrates (animals without backbones) because the vertebrates' bony structures have provided a good collection of fossils, whereas the invertebrates' soft structures are nearly always lost without a trace in fossilization.

Fish out of water

Fossil remains show that *Crossopterygian* fishes, believed to be the evolutionary ancestors of modern amphibians, had what are called lobed fins. Part of the body extended into the fin, giving it extra support. The fleshy lobe was supported by bony structures. Similar bones are also present in the limbs of amphibians, although they may be enlarged and differ a little in shape. It is therefore reasonable to assume that when these fish were stranded by drought on the beds of the lakes and streams in which they used to live, they used their fins to move from one pool to another. Thousands of years later, perhaps owing to climatic change or a mutation enabling a few individuals to possess better developed 'limbs', the fish evolved into walking amphibians able to lead both an aquatic and a terrestrial life.

Throughout the vertebrates, it can be seen that many of the bone formations are similar. It is easy to find bones present in an amphibian's fore-limb also present in, say, a reptile's or a mammal's. The difference may be only in size, or the structure may be slightly modified to fit the new function. The best example of this can be seen in the pelvic girdle

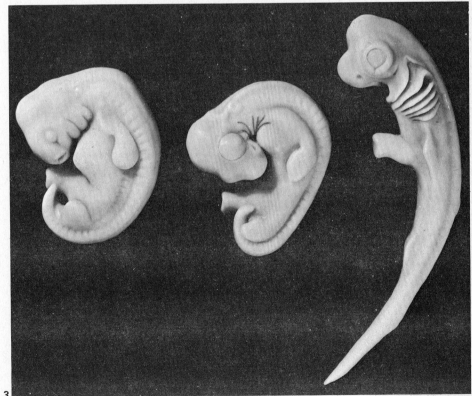

1 Fossil remains of a coelacanth. Until about 20 years ago, this unusual fish was thought to be extinct.

2 Discovery of this modern coelacanth enabled biologists to establish that it has not changed from its fossilized predecessor.

3 Embryos of a man, a chicken and a dogfish, showing the remarkable similarity between them. The gills of the dogfish and its elongated tail distinguish it as a marine creature.

1

2

3

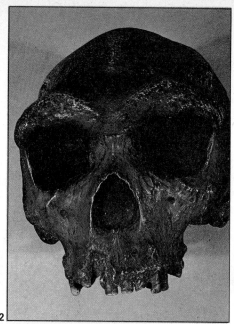

4

5

1 Drawing of Rhodesian Man (*Homo rhodesiensis*) showing the probable appearance of this early cave-dweller.
2 Cranial remains on which drawing of Rhodesian Man was based. Note the low receding forehead.
3 Skull of *Zinjanthropus biosei*, with reconstructed jaw. The ridge of bone on the crown of the head provided additional area for the *temporalis* muscle.
4 Resemblances between anthropoid apes and Man lend credence to the evolutionists' arguments.
5 Woodpeckers have adapted to their environment in a number of ways. Their beaks are hard and bony, a rigid tail gives support, and grubs are taken from the tree by the long tongue.

Reptiles evolved from amphibians and eventually superseded them as the 'ruling' animals. Some remained on the land and evolved more powerful limbs. With the reptiles also came the first two-legged creatures, so that the pelvic girdle had accordingly to be further modified. Some reptiles returned to the water and as a result underwent a reduction of their supporting skeleton. The girdles slowly dwindled to rudiments and dissociated themselves once more from the vertebral column.

The extinct *Plesiosaurs* were such reptiles which returned to the water. The neck was elongated and the limbs became flippers for paddling. The girdles were still attached to the vertebral column. The *Ichthyosaurs* were also secondary aquatic forms. They became streamlined and fish-like, even reverting to the old method of locomotion, that is by using the entire posterior trunk region as a paddle.

All shapes of limbs

Other members of the reptiles took to the air – a feat demanding different modifications altogether. In this case the backbone was made rigid by fusion of the vertebrae, and the pelvic girdle was enlarged so that it could support the animal in the standing position. The girdle was fused to the backbone as in the terrestrial forms. These flying reptiles were called *pterodactyls*.

Among the modern mammals as a group there are also good examples of *homologous* organs, which are basically the same organ but have been modified during evolution in different ways to suit their different functions. One of the most noticeable examples, perhaps, is the difference between a man's arm, a bat's wing and a whale's flipper. A man's forearm is adapted for doing a variety of jobs. The upper arm consists of one bone, the *humerus*. The lower arm has two, the *radius* and *ulna*. The wrist is made up of nine *carpals* and the hand of three *metacarpals*, the digits being made up of 14 *phalanges*. This arrangement is modified in the bat where the radius and ulna are partly fused to increase the strength (although decreasing adaptability). The wrist bones are reduced and the metacarpals and ph langes are elongated to support the wing-tip surface.

The whale, also a mammal, has become adapted for life in the ocean once more. The fore-limbs are now modified as rudders

bone (corresponding to the hip bones in Man) during the change from the aquatic life of fish to that of land amphibians – and sometimes back to the watery life again.

A fish has a very small and rudimentary pelvic girdle which is not attached to the vertebral column. Locomotion is achieved using muscles running along the trunk and tail. The pelvic (hind) and pectoral (fore) fins are not used for locomotion at all but for maintaining or altering the fish's position in the water. However, when fish had moved on to land, locomotion by means of the tail was exceedingly clumsy and energy consuming, requiring extra food. As a result, the fins became enlarged into limbs to 'lift' the body from the ground. Simultaneously the limb girdles grew in order to support the extra weight and fused to the backbone to distribute it throughout the body. (In the water, the fish did not have to worry about this problem because most of their weight was carried by the surrounding water.) Of course, all these evolutionary changes required thousands of years to take place.

for 'steering' the animal. The power for movement comes from the trunk on which a large tail-fin has developed. This beats up and down, propelling the animal forward. The fore-limb is much reduced in the region nearest to the body. The humerus, radius and ulna are short, the carpals are small and insignificant and embedded in cartilage. It is only digits two and three which are elongated, with an increased number of phalanges.

The whale also shows how, as a result of evolution, some organs can become *vestigial* (no longer have a useful task to perform, and so become reduced in size and efficiency). It is believed that the whale evolved from a creature which was once terrestrial and had two pairs of limbs. Since it has returned to the sea and swims instead of walking, the hind limbs have become very reduced and are not visible from the outside. In fact, all that remains are the vestiges of the pelvic girdle, femur and tibia – not attached to the backbone but 'floating' inside the body wall.

It is believed that flightless birds, such as the kiwi, emu, rhea and ostrich once possessed the power of flight. They are descended from other birds, but since they lived originally in parts of the world where it was not necessary to escape from predators, the wings slowly degenerated over hundreds of generations into small vestigial stubs not capable of flight. Instead, the hind limbs have become enlarged and strengthened to support their large body weights. These birds are also specially adapted in several ways to compensate for their inability to fly. Thus, for example, they are all very swift runners, enabling them to travel almost as quickly as birds equipped to fly.

Man also has vestigial organs. The muscles of the ear are a good example. Whereas dogs, cats and most other mammals can turn their external ears towards the source of sound, most humans cannot, probably because Man is two-legged and walks upright. This fact enables him to move only his head to face towards a sound, instead of his whole body as he would have to do if he walked on all fours.

Convergent evolutions

In the early days of zoology, it was sometimes wrongly supposed that two animals were somewhat related because they lived in the same habitat or looked very similar. For example, in the sea, all the vertebrates are equipped with a similar method of locomotion. They all have a powerful tail for propulsion and have fins or flippers. The body shape is streamlined so that it passes through the water easily. It might be tempting to say that if two animals possess all these characteristics, they have evolved along the same path and are consequently closely related to each other. It is here that anatomical examination of the organisms is necessary to determine whether or not the two types with common features are closely related.

For instance, the porpoise and the shark are both marine, streamlined and eat fish; perhaps they are related? Closer examination shows that they are not, for several reasons, the most important being that the shark is covered in scales whereas the porpoise is not; and the shark breathes by means of gills whereas the porpoise must surface to use its lungs. The two animals have in fact undergone *convergent evolutions* (evolved side by side, influenced by the same environmental factors). In other words, both animals have evolved a basically similar design to cope with similar environments. At the same time, one remains a mammal and the other a fish.

Towards the end of the nineteenth century, scientists began to study the development of animals from the egg. This new science, called *embryology,* contributed to our knowledge of evolution. The problem at this time was to find out how the many-celled (*metazoan*) animals have evolved from the primitive one-celled (*protozoan*) animals. This investigation of the developing embryos has yielded many clues to the way in which organisms evolve.

From a study of the larval forms of invertebrate animals, it was revealed that many are alike in many ways. This could be due either to convergent evolution or to a common origin (that is, the groups concerned may have evolved from a common ancestor). In 1870, the German biologist Ernst Haeckel (1834–1919) established his *Law of Recapitulation,* based on the evolution of the metazoans but applicable to all other groups.

Haeckel thought that the original 'stem' metazoan was a *Blastaea,* a hollow ball of flagellated cells (cells with hair-like tails) which could easily have been formed from protozoans aggregating and forming a colony. He suggested that it moved through the water in one direction, and so caused a vortex at the back where food particles would collect. As a result, the colony got food more easily than could an individual. He said that the cells in the rear region would become adapted to absorb these food particles and would eventually

Darwin's experience in the breeding of domestic pigeons led him to the conclusion that there is much more variation in domesticated plants or animals than there is with organisms in the wild state. He found that he could breed desirable characteristics into his birds by careful selection. The varieties of pigeon in the illustration show how different in appearance these birds can be. However, there is still a basic similarity, showing their common ancestry.

ROCK DOVE

POUTER　　　　TRUMPETER　　　　JACOBIN　　　　CARRIER

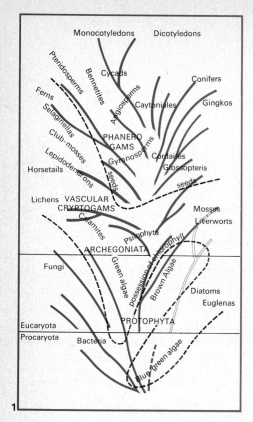

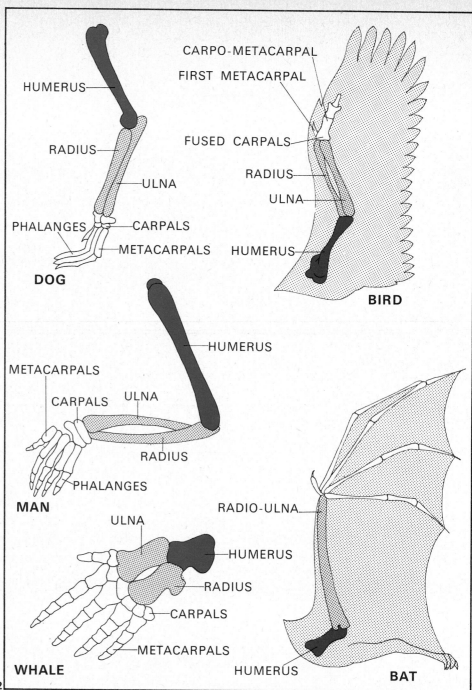

1 An attempt to show the main lines of evolution. The original organisms gave rise to bacteria, blue-green algae and plants. Further development eventually gave rise to seed-plants. As indicated in the diagram, the origin of fungi is obscure.
2 Modifications of the skeletal structure of the limb are clearly demonstrated in this picture. Structures are modified to suit the needs of the animals' environments, although the individual bones retain some common characteristics.

form an inward-facing cavity with a primitive mouth and gut. This stage was called a *Gastrea.*

Evolution in miniature

Haeckel's hypothesis was largely accepted. His Law of Recapitulation stated in effect that the stages in the development of an individual (called *ontogeny*) are a short recapitulation or summary of the stages in the history of the development of the whole group of animals to which it belonged (called *phylogeny*). This hypothesis means that some stage in the development of an advanced animal would closely resemble a more primitive animal, and that phylogeny is the cause of ontogeny. For instance, supporters of the theory would see a close resemblance between the early foetal stages of a human baby and the adult forms of some amphibians.

Then in 1922, the modern theory of evolution was put forward. Haeckel's original law was re-stated and it is now thought that the evolutionary history (phylogeny) of adults is the product of a succession of complete developments (ontogenies) – ontogeny does not recapitulate phylogeny but *causes* it. In other words, each life history of an individual producing offspring will slowly change the structure of the animal, so causing evolution.

For a long time after the theory of evolution was first formulated, there remained the grave problem of explaining how variations occur in the first place. Darwin proposed his theory of natural selection without any knowledge of genes, genetic mutation and heredity. The laws of heredity had, in fact, been worked out by an Austrian monk, Gregor Johann Mendel (1822–84), whose work went unrecognized until long after his death. Then, in 1900, Hugo de Vries and two other scientists unearthed Mendel's original papers.

But de Vries made one big mistake when he formulated the laws of heredity. He stated that mutation (a change in a gene, the fundamental unit of heredity) was the main cause of evolution. In fact natural selection – the moulding of an animal by its environment – is the *force* for change, and mutation provides the *opportunity.* Mutation and natural selection work in conjunction. Mutant genes create the possibility of a new species arising; natural selection can make this possibility a reality.

As its name suggests, natural selection takes place without any interference from an outside agency, such as Man. But good confirmatory evidence for the correctness of the theory of evolution comes from *artificial selection.* For instance, numerous varieties of pigeons have been created by controlled breeding. 'Man-made evolution' has also given rise to 110 separate recognized breeds of dogs (all belonging to the same species), as well as dozens of breeds of cats, cattle, horses, sheep and chickens. The fact that Man has caused evolution does not *prove* the theory of evolution. But until evidence to the contrary turns up, most scientists will continue to accept that over millions of years, what Man has done by intent, Nature has done by natural selection to give rise to the thousands upon thousands of life forms existing in the world today. Future forms of life in the ages to come will inevitably be moulded by these same forces.

The continuing struggle

The concept of natural selection is basic to modern biology. It explains how different species of animals and plants developed and how it is that living organisms 'fit into' their surroundings.

THE WHOLE EDIFICE of modern biology rests on the discoveries of the great biologists of the nineteenth century. The greatest of these discoveries, and the one which opened up the whole subject of biological evolution to scientific investigation, was the theory of natural selection put forward by Charles Darwin in 1859. His book, the *Origin of Species,* is probably the most important single biological work ever published: it revealed clearly for the first time that the development of animals and plants could be explained not on mystical or biblical grounds but on the basis of a continuous struggle between the make-up of organisms and their environment.

The discoveries of scientific geology made at the beginning of the nineteenth century showed that many of the forms of life in past ages were related to present-day animals. How could this be explained? Darwin's great achievement was to provide an over-all theory which has stood the test of time.

Darwin's finches

As a young man, Darwin spent some years voyaging round the world on H.M.S. *Beagle.* During the voyage he landed at the Galapagos Islands and there he noticed that some of the animals on the islands had diversified into a remarkable variety of related, but different, forms. Thus, birds of the finch family on the islands had become specialized to live in every type of habitat and eat every type of food: some to live on seeds, others on insects or berries. He surmised that all these different varieties had sprung from a single form which probably came to the islands from South America in an earlier period.

1 The ancestor of the modern domestic pig, the wild boar. This ferocious forest animal is still found in some parts of Europe.

How could this variety of forms have come about? Darwin's analysis of this problem led him to formulate his theory of natural selection.

Reproduction is one of the fundamental characteristics of living matter. The offspring have most of the characteristics of the parents. But at the same time they are subtly different. Animals and plants produce far more offspring than will survive to propagate the species; for example, fish like the stickleback lay thousands of eggs though only a small proportion of these eggs ever become adult. This profligacy on the part of Nature seems merely a waste but in fact it has an important purpose. Although each offspring is very similar to the parents, each differs from the parents in various ways. For one thing, no offspring inherits the exact genetic make-up of its parents. Secondly, the genes that are handed down from generation to generation in this way are subject to slow but continuous change. This change, which biologists call mutation, is horrifically demonstrated by the

2 The boar's domesticated descendants would not last long in the wild. Selected by breeders for their meat yield, pigs are sluggish animals.

effects of radiation on animal and plant life after the explosion of atomic weapons. But mutation is in fact going on constantly in nature. Most of these mutations are harmful. They are random changes in the chromosomes which are handed down from parent to offspring and determine in detail the characteristics of the organism.

Although the vast majority of mutations are harmful, a few are actively advantageous to the animal or plant and enable it to do things that its parents were not capable of. Animals that inherit these favourable mutations have an advantage over others competing for food or for living space. Unfavourable mutations tend to be rapidly eliminated.

Of course, some mutations are favourable in one place and unfavourable in another. One mutant of the tobacco plant, for example, was found to be unsuitable for life in its native Virginia, but was more suited than the parent strain for life in more southerly regions. In the absence of conditions which would destroy potentially harmful mutations, of course they survive.

3 During the breeding season, red deer stags fight over the does. Only the fittest and strongest of the herd mate with the females.

This has happened to many species of cave fish. These animals live the whole of their lives in darkness and there is thus no advantage in efficient vision. In most of these fish, the eyes have totally degenerated, and in some they have disappeared.

By constant small changes in the genetic material combined with a struggle for survival in which no more than a small proportion of offspring can survive, Nature has provided a very delicate mechanism for 'fitting' species to their environment. It is this process that Darwin dubbed the 'survival of the fittest'. He wrote in the *Origin of Species* that 'the ultimate result of natural selection is that each creature tends to become more and more improved in relation to its conditions. This improvement inevitably leads to the gradual advancement of the organization of the greater number of living beings.'

Order out of chaos

The efficiency of this natural process led many biologists before Darwin to postulate the existence of a creator, others attributed biological development to the workings of 'life force' or to some similar mystical conception. It was Darwin who saw that random processes *do* produce order. Not only does natural selection provide a unifying concept for the evolution that has taken place in the past, but it can be observed in operation at the present day, a startling example being industrial melanism.

Natural selection can also be observed to operate among bacteria. The bacterium *Escherichia coli*, for example, is normally killed by the drug *streptomycin*. But when the bacterium is grown in a medium containing streptomycin it is found that the few survivors rapidly become resistant to the action of the drug. Studies of this process have shown that this is not

1

2

3

4

1 Practically blind, and with its forelimbs adapted for digging, the mole has been refined by selection for its life underground.
2 A crab spider waits to catch flies inside the flower of an arum lily. This seemingly 'intelligent' behaviour is a product of selection.

3 These Characins, found in underground pools, are blind. Their eyes have degenerated because vision confers no advantage in the dark.
4 The red underwing moth has camouflaged forewings. A second line of defence is the threatening colour of its hindwings.

due to all the individuals in the bacterial colony becoming more resistant to the drug but to the fact that in every colony there are always a few individuals which have, quite accidentally, mutated so that they are resistant to streptomycin. The drug weeded out all those individuals not resistant to it, and left only those that could withstand its action.

This is the explanation for the finding of 'hospital strains' of common bacteria: these strains are frequently exposed to the action of bactericidal drugs and there is thus a strong selection pressure favouring the resistant mutants. These come to make up the majority of the population. Similar changes have been found in insect popula-tions exposed to the action of insecticides. The selection of resistant strains of malarial mosquitoes has created diffi-culties for malaria control programmes in many parts of the world. The first effect of the insecticide is to kill most of the insects, so that the problem appears to have been beaten. But later, the mutant survivors of the insecticide multiply and give rise to a more intractable problem.

Another example of selection in action is the way in which mutant strains of insects are selected back towards nor-mality. This phenomenon was first found in the fruit fly *Drosophila melanogaster*. This insect has been much used to study mutation, as it reproduces very rapidly and the geneticist can follow develop-ments through many generations. One of the mutants found in the fruit fly is the so-called 'eye-less' strain. This mutant is rare in the wild because the effects of the mutation are harmful. It can, however, be bred as a pure strain in the laboratory, where the fly can be cushioned against the harmful effects of mutation. Such a strain has been bred. But it was found that when the 'eye-less' strain was bred for a number of generations the characteristics of the population became more and more like those of normal flies. In fact, what was happening was that the odd normal mutants occurring in the population were at an advantage compared with the rest

1 The wasp beetle protects itself from predators by 'mimicking' the coloration of a wasp. Mimicry of this type is common among insects.

2 The pine hawk moth, by contrast, conceals itself against the bark of the pine tree by blending into its surroundings.

3 Most of this brood of ring-neck pheasants will die young. The survivors will be those best able to cope with their environment.

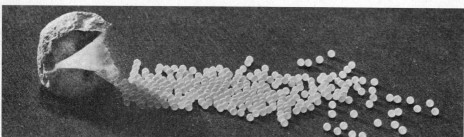

1 The large family of this black bullhead (a form of catfish) are a guarantee against the wiping out of the species by predators.
2 Palaeontologists are able to reconstruct ancient life forms from their fossil remains. The animals shown in the diagram lived 600 million years ago.
3 Eggs of the black widow spider. Like many other animals, the spider produces many eggs but only a few of them reach maturity.

of the flies. Natural selection comes into operation to produce a more and more normal population. In fact, after about ten generations, the 'eye-less' strain was very little different from normal populations of fruit flies.

But how can the development of diverse animals and plants, the rise and fall of species and the development of entirely new types of animals with very widely differing modes of life, be explained on the basis of random mutation picked out by the struggle for survival? Many people confronted with the evidence for natural selection or with the concept of evolution find it hard to believe. It seems to violate some deeply held preconceptions. There is no doubt, however, that this theory provides the only rational explanation for the development of life. The all-important element that many people forget is time.

High degree of improbability

Natural selection has been described as 'a mechanism for generating a very high degree of improbability'. What this means is that if the changes in living matter had been left entirely to chance, without the intervention of any form of selection, that is, if living matter had developed so to speak in a vacuum, it would be very unlikely to look as it does today. It has been estimated that the probability of producing a racehorse in this way is something like ten to the power of 1,000,000,000!

The fundamental weakness in earlier theories of the development of life was that they considered living matter to be fixed and unchanging, whereas in fact it is capable of being moulded into very different shapes and types. Mutation is, of course, in one sense a rare and abnormal

event. Perhaps only one in 1,000 mutations is favourable, while most of the remainder will be unfavourable. Again, the frequency of mutation itself is low. For some genes it may rise to as much as one in 50,000 but the average frequency is more likely to be of the order of one in 100,000. Once a favourable mutation has emerged, it may take anything up to 50 or more generations to become widespread in the population. But in the time-scale of evolution, 50 generations is not very long.

Evolution has been studied in action through careful examination of fossil remains. These provide a means of comparing the theory with reality. The work of examining fossils in this light is highly skilled and requires a detailed knowledge of the changes not only in the fossils but in the environment. The classic work in this sphere was carried out on fossils of horses. These are relatively numerous, and it has been possible to build up a fairly complete model of the evolution of the horse. These studies exploded a number of old myths. The most notable exploded myth was that evolution has proceeded in a straight line. The studies showed that this was seriously in error. Dr G. G. Simpson points out in his book *Horses* that there is not one line of evolution of horses, but a whole number of lines, branches and splits, most of which can be correlated with changes in the horses' environment. Many of the lines of evolution reached dead ends and died out after longer or shorter periods. The most marked split is between two types of horse, one group of which became specialized for grazing on grass and the other which became adapted for eating the soft foliage of trees and shrubs.

The early horses were relatively unspecialized, smaller than the present-day

examples of the species. Their brains were less developed than those of present-day horses. Interestingly, the development of the horse brain appears to be tied to the developments in the way of life of the horse: the parts of the brain that became developed were those concerned with speed and the detection of predators. Once these aspects of brain function had become fairly fully developed, the rate of brain evolution, as shown by the size of the brain-cavity in the skulls of fossils, slowed down markedly.

Climatic changes

Again, the sharp changes in the course of horse evolution can be shown to correlate with changes in the environment. For example, during the Miocene period (25–12 million years ago) the climate became drier and led to the formation of savanna-type country where previously there had been large forests. This development favoured the grazing type of horse. The sharp change in the climate is mirrored in a marked stepping up of the rate of evolution. This has been studied particularly in relation to the teeth. These became progressively more specialized to take account of the grinding processes needed to digest foliage and particularly grass. During the sharp environmental changes of the Miocene period, the teeth became relatively rapidly higher and flatter, and then later the rate of evolution slowed down as the teeth became more perfectly suited to the horses' way of eating.

The basic mechanism of selection seems to underlie the whole development of life on Earth and provides a means by which the blind chance of mutation can be harnessed to the struggle of living matter to survive.

Art of survival

For animals and plants, variety of colour and form is a matter of life and death. Only through its variedness can a species adapt to the stringent conditions imposed by its own environment.

IN THE YEARS spent sailing around the world in the *Beagle*, Charles Darwin collected thousands of different species of plants and animals and made painstaking observations of them and of the habitat from which they came. Without this voyage and his encounter with such a variety of life and its remarkable adaptations, Darwin would never have had the insight to create his theory that evolution occurs through the agency of natural selection.

But times have changed; many of those researching into the mechanism of evolution base their premises on experiments performed in the laboratory using animal or plant cultures kept under carefully controlled, often unchanging conditions. These modern geneticists very rarely go into the field to study the wild forms of the species they can culture so successfully in the laboratory; they believe that the results of their experiments can be related to conditions in the wild. Some of these 'armchair' theories have a certain plausibility; they often come to be accepted as true both for the laboratory and for the wild.

Field observation

Yet, there are biologists who continue to maintain that evolution can only really be understood by observing species living in their natural habitat. These biologists, known as ecologists, do not dispute that laboratory experiments are useful, nor that time spent thinking over ideas is essential, but if they are to provide an accurate analysis of evolution, they must be combined with meticulous observation in the field.

The difference between wild and cultured populations is often much greater than can ever be imagined. In 1935 an ecologist, C. Gordon, released 36,000 fruit flies into one locality in South Devon. The fruit fly was *Drosophila melanogaster,* a species that is commonly cultured in the laboratory. Gordon used a strain of this species that carried both the gene for *ebony* body colour and its dominant normal *wild type* gene. Although at the beginning of the experiment both these genes were present in equal amounts, after 120 days only 11 per cent of the ebony genes remained in the total population. It had, therefore, taken only five to six generations for the elimination of nearly all fruit flies that carried the ebony gene whether in a double or single dose. Yet in the laboratory ebony is one of the genes that, mixed with the wild type gene, confers greater viability and breeding success than does a double dose of the wild type.

Insects are excellent material for the ecologist. They breed rapidly and their external markings can be used to indicate

1 Some species of butterfly and moth, like this moth have vivid 'eye-spots' on their wings which, if mistaken for real eyes, make the animal look very large and fearsome.
2, 3 In contrast to normal red blood cells (left), sickle cells curl up (right) and cannot transport

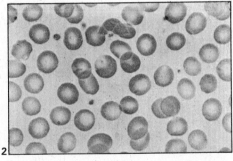
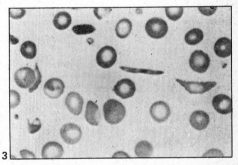

whether or not they are harbouring a certain gene. In *Drosophila,* for example, genes that have an effect upon the viability, the length of life or upon the fertility of the fly, may also have some other apparently trivial effect. Such genes may, therefore, be responsible for an associated change in eye colour, in the shape of the abdomen, or in the number and form of the bristles on the thorax. Genes with such multiple effects are very common – they are known as *polygenes.*

No one is more aware than the ecologist that external characteristics, like the markings on a butterfly's wings, can be tell-tale indications of some important, yet hidden, physiological adaptation of the animal to its environment. The British scarlet tiger moth, *Panaxia dominula,* for example, has almost tropical colours. The fore-wings are black with a green iridescence and have white spots, except for the two basal ones which are yellowish; the hind-wings are scarlet with black spots and markings. Dr H.B.D. Kettlewell, an

oxygen properly around the body. But they are more resistant than normal blood cells to malaria. Individuals who have half sickle and half normal red cells in their blood are, therefore, better adapted to survive in countries where malaria is endemic.

English ecologist, tried to breed a line of moths with the lightest possible markings on both wings. After ten years and, therefore, ten generations he had bred moths in which the white and yellowish-white spots had coalesced on the fore-wings, and in which a large amount of the black had been lost from the hind-wings. All who saw his moths after this long period of intensive breeding agreed that they bore little resemblance to the wild type.

In 1948, as he was leaving England for some time, Dr Kettlewell decided to found a colony of these moths in Hertfordshire. The first year after their release the moths produced very few offspring but, by 1951, the adults were fairly common. Ecologists, such as Dr. P. M. Sheppard, who saw these adults were astonished by the speed at which these cultured forms were returning to the ordinary wild English form of the moth. The next year thousands were flying – and the larvae were so numerous that most of them died of starvation. Dr Sheppard and his colleagues collected some of the survivors and bred them. The moths they produced had very nearly returned to the wild type. Dr Sheppard believed this return to the wild type in such a short time could only have happened because the powerful force of natural selection was acting on the hidden physiological effects of the same genes that controlled wing colour.

Ecologists are now realizing that natural selection is a more powerful force than they had first imagined. Instead of giving one gene or set of genes a 1 per cent advantage over another, it can on occasions give a 20 per cent or more advantage. Many evolutionary theorists have based their calculations on natural selection offering little more than a 1 per cent advantage at most. Some of these theorists, like Sewall Wright, have therefore thought up mechanisms of evolution, which according to many ecologists cannot under any circumstances fit the facts.

Population changes

Sewall Wright proposed the theory of *random genetic drift*. This theory, which some research workers still accept, concerns small populations of animals and plants. The idea is that should a population of a species become very small, a particular gene may show up in the next generation to a greater extent than could ever be expected on the basis of its selective advantage over other genes. This increase in the frequency of a gene, could, suggests Dr Wright, result from chance differences in fertilization and survival. Two opposing genes called *alleles,* present in equal amounts and conferring equal advantages should theoretically be passed on in exactly equal amounts to the next generation. But if in, say, a population of ten individuals, two more of one gene rather than of its opposing gene were passed on to the next generation because of random drift, then in the next generation there would be 12 of one gene and eight of the other – a difference of 20 per cent. Should the same happen again in the following generation, two-fifths of one gene would have vanished from the population – a very significant amount. On the other hand, in a large population such chance deviations would have an almost imperceptible effect and could therefore be discounted as a mechanism of evolution.

Sewall Wright calculated mathematically that evolution would occur most rapidly in a species that was abundant but divided into very small groups. It would be essential that these groups, though predominantly inbreeding, should have some contact, be it occasional, with several of the other groups; under these circumstances both random drift and natural selection would be operating. Thus there would be plenty of 'variety' for natural selection to operate on.

In small and completely isolated populations random drift would virtually operate alone, suggested Dr Sewall Wright, and in time whole sets of genes would be lost. Such a loss would cut down on the survivors' potential to throw up varieties and to adapt, and the population would probably be doomed to extinction. In large

1 By being coloured like a wasp some insects, such as this hoverfly, try to convince their predators that they, too, have an unpleasant sting. in fact they are quite harmless.

2 The harmless wasp longicorn beetle tries to seek protection by mimicking a wasp. Some insects, however, come to resemble wasps because they, like it, are unpleasant to eat.

3 To ensure cross-fertilization plants like the primrose have two forms – pin and thrum. The bumble-bee carries pollen from one form to the other when it feeds on the nectar.

4 Because it looks like barley, wild rye often escapes the attention of the farmer and is not weeded out. This is an example of mimicry aimed especially at confusing Man.

5 The snail, *Cepaea nemoralis* uses combinations of colour and bands around its shell to camouflage it for different localities. Grass and woods, for example, require different camouflages.

6 Some forms of camouflage are very effective, as in this stick insect from Java. But, to be effective the insect must stay on bark or else it will be noticed immediately.

7 The night moth, *Griposa aprilina,* rests on the bark of trees during the day. If it had no camouflage it would soon be eaten by a bird, but, looking like lichen, it escapes attention.

populations and the effect of drift would be minimal and that of natural selection all important. Under such circumstances evolution could occur, but more slowly than in the small, but not totally isolated populations.

Despite its plausibility the theory of random drift does not seem to fit what actually happens to a small isolated population struggling to survive in the wild. More than 50 years ago Professor E.B. Ford and his father, H.D. Ford, investigated a colony of the marsh fritillary butterfly, *Mellitaea aurinia,* in Cumberland. Records of this colony dated back to 1881 when the butterfly was quite abundant. By 1894 the insect had become very common indeed and then, suddenly, it began to disappear from that site. From 1912 to 1920 the insect was very rare. But, as suddenly as its numbers decreased they began to increase again and by 1925 the numbers of the colony were back at a high, well-established level.

During the first period in the 1890s when the butterfly was abundant, and during the period of declining numbers, all the insects captured had very uniform physical characteristics. Yet from 1920 to 1924, the period of rapidly increasing numbers, Professor Ford and his father caught an extraordinary number of varieties. Some of these insects were so deformed that they could not even fly. Then, after 1924, the colony settled down again to a uniform type – but this uniform type was noticeably different from the uniform type of the first period of abundance.

Professor Ford interprets these findings as follows: when the population is abundant selection pressures are powerful and any butterflies that are the slightest bit deformed or unviable are exterminated in the struggle for survival. When the population is declining, selection pressures are still as great as before, if not greater, and there is no room for experimental varieties. When, however, the population has been drastically reduced and is just beginning to expand again, selection pressures are at their lowest, and varieties can flourish. But, as the colony grows the fight for existence becomes tougher and selection pressures clamp down again on any varieties that are not absolutely viable. When the population is again abundant, variants of the successful uniform type become very rare.

Small populations in isolation tend to isolate themselves further by preventing the interchange of any genetic material between them and other populations. Such isolation can arise through genes that are responsible for a group of interrelated characters binding together in a linear fashion along the chromosomes. Because these associated genes are together they get passed on to following generations as such and they are not split up and fragmented. This mechanism serves, for example, to keep all the genes that govern a set of enzyme reactions together and under one control. Such a unit is known as a *super gene*.

Sometimes a species evolves alternative super genes. When a population contains a balance of several such alternatives, the situation may arise in which the individual that carries two such alternatives—one of them necessarily dominant over the other—is more viable and successful than its fellows which have a double dose of just one of the alternatives. Such a situation gives rise to a *balanced polymorphism* (polymorphism means many forms).

For example, sickle-cell anaemia is an inherited blood disease of humans that is very often fatal. Those with the disease have a double dose of the sickle-cell gene, and their blood cells tend to curl up in the veins where the oxygen tension is low. Yet, those with both a single dose of the sickling gene and a single dose of the normal gene have recently been discovered to have some resistance to mal-aria, a resistance which those with a double dose of the normal gene do not have. Indeed, the ecologist finds sickle-cell anaemia in countries such as West Africa where malaria is endemic.

Balanced polymorphism can become complicated. The snail, *Cepaea nemoralis*, is adapted to living in a variety of habitats – beechwoods, oakwoods, mixed deciduous woods, hedgerows, rough grass and short grass. Birds, particularly thrushes, go for the snails and break open the shells on a stone, the thrush's anvil. The better hidden or camouflaged the snail, the better its chance of escaping its predators. But each of the different habitats demands a very different camouflage, and the snail has evolved a variety of colours – from a near white right through shades of grey to black and even to red. It also has a series of black bands around its shell. The colour and the number of these bands, up to five, come under supergene control. Some combinations suit one environment better than another.

Colour adaptation

According to Dr Sheppard the darker the woods and the more uniform the underlying vegetation, for example in beechwoods, the darker the shells and the less banded they are. On the other hand, in grass and hedgerows, a lighter, less uniform habitat, the more yellow the shells and the more banded they are. Snails with other less suited combinations of shell colour and bands will be found in any of these environments, but their numbers will be very small because of predation.

A balanced polymorphism in plants like the primrose, *Primula vulgaris,* promotes outbreeding. There are three forms – pin, thrum and homostyle. In the pin form, the *stigma* (the female part that traps pollen) lies at the top of the corolla-tube, while the anthers (the pollen producers) are half-way down. In the thrum form, the position is reversed and the anthers are at the top of the corolla-tube and the stigma half-way down. In the homostyle form the anthers and the stigma are at the same level, whether at the top of the corolla-tube or half-way down.

Insects such as *Coleoptera* (beetles) and *Lepidoptera* (butterflies and moths) pollinate the thrum and pin forms of the primrose – but the homostyle form is self-pollinating and therefore inbreeding. When the beetle or butterfly thrusts its head into the corolla-tube it comes up against the stigma in the pin form and the anthers in the thrum form. To reach the nectar the insect pushes its proboscis down the tube. The tip of this comes into contact with the anthers in the pin form and the stigma in the thrum. By visiting first one form and then the other the insect carried pollen from one to the other. Cross-fertilization is therefore ensured.

As a result of ecological studies balanced polymorphism is now seen to be far more common among animals and plants than had ever been imagined, even by its most ardent proponents. Many species of insect, for example, carry sets of genes which enable them to mimic other unrelated insects that are immune from predators because they are poisonous or distasteful. By mimicking the vivid colours, the shape and the movement of the unpleasant species, the unprotected species strive to warn any would-be predators that they had best leave them alone.

Of course, if the unprotected species become too abundant their predators will get used to the idea that a great many insects with that distinctive colouring and behaviour are not distasteful after all, and may perhaps start taking 'pot luck'. For this reason some species of insect have a number of different forms so that they can mimic several different unpleasant species. Each of these forms depends on its own set of genes.

1 Breaking the shells open on its stone 'anvil' the thrush is one of the main predators of the snail. The more the snail can resemble its background the better it is able to avoid predation.

2 The *Thyrous abbotti* caterpillar has a large false eye at the rear of its body. When a bird approaches the insect tries to frighten it off by swaying its rear to and fro in the air.

Protective colouring

The colours of animals and insects are not merely decorative. Sometimes they help to conceal the animal from its enemies, whereas in other cases they warn potential predators or frighten them away.

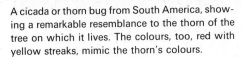

A cicada or thorn bug from South America, showing a remarkable resemblance to the thorn of the tree on which it lives. The colours, too, red with yellow streaks, mimic the thorn's colours.

The skunk's prominent stripes are warning coloration. With its foul-smelling secretions, the skunk has little need to worry about predators, and the colouring reminds them to keep away.

THE COLOURS of many animals help them to avoid unwelcome contact with others. This may be because they cannot easily be distinguished from their surroundings, or because they can give a warning signal that discourages others from approaching. These camouflage colours have been acquired because they are an advantage to their owners in the struggle for survival. It is useful for a predator to be able to conceal itself from the prey it wishes to catch, and of course it is also useful for hunted animals to be able to keep their enemies away, at least some of the time.

A great many predators blend with their natural surroundings so that they can stalk their prey unnoticed. The white coats of polar bears and other Arctic animals blend with the snow and ice, but many other animals that may seem conspicuous in the zoo are not at all easy to distinguish in their native surroundings. The stripes and spots of zebras, tigers, giraffes and leopards blend imperceptibly with the moving patterns of light and dark among the grassy plains and scattered trees of the tropical savanna that they inhabit.

These large animals have acquired their camouflage because it helps them to catch their food, but smaller animals, particularly invertebrates, including insects and small water creatures such as shrimps, are preyed upon by larger animals and need their colours to enable them to avoid capture as often as possible. The cater-pillars of many moths closely resemble the twigs of the trees on which they are to be found, and birds are unable to distinguish them. Other insects escape attention because they resemble objects that are not usually a source of food; the caterpillars of the swallow-tail butterfly, for example, have a black and white saddle on their backs and resemble bird-droppings. Birds would have to be very hungry before investigating these as a source of food.

Variable camouflage

Most insects that gain protection by blending with their background depend for their camouflage on their presence in very particular surroundings. But some animals are less confined because they can change colour to match a new background, sometimes quite spectacularly, as do chameleons. These reptiles can be green, yellow or cream or dark brown, often with darker or lighter spots, to blend with different backgrounds. This helps to conceal them from their snake and bird enemies.

The flounder is another well-known animal that can change colour. This fish will assume a speckled appearance against an unevenly coloured background, or a uniform colouring against a plain background. Many other sea creatures are adept at changing colour, and one of the most versatile is the octopus (*Octopus vulgaris*), which can change its colours and colour patterns to match practically any sort of background. This is possible because the pigments which give the animal its various colours are contained in many special organs called *chromatophores*, which vary in appearance accord-ing to their degree of expansion. The octopus has two sets of chromatophores, one varying from black to red-brown, and the other from red to pale orange-yellow. Below the chromatophores is a thin layer of special bodies called iridocytes that break up white light to give green and blue. Thus the octopus has a vast repertoire of colour patterns that it can adopt, to make itself inconspicuous on any sort of marine background.

The shrimp is another sea creature with a striking ability to change colour. At night its whole body becomes a beautiful translucent blue whatever the daytime colour may have been – green, brown or patterned. A crab known as *Uca* has a remarkably constant rhythm of colour change. It is pale at night and dark during the day and these changes are attuned to the tides. The organs which contain the coloured pigments are always at their largest and darkest just before low tide. This is the time when *Uca* is most actively foraging for food and so is also the time when it needs the most concealment.

Crabs in different localities have their own rhythms of colour change synchronized with the different times of low tide. *Uca* obviously has some kind of internal clock that maintains the rhythm of its colour changing, but like most biological clocks its mechanism is still a mystery.

The cuttlefish (*Sepia*) has an elaborate colour-change mechanism for deceiving its enemies. When it needs to make a rapid escape, the cuttlefish ejects the contents of its ink sac – many tiny granules of the dark-brown pigment, melanin. Immediately after sending out this 'smoke-screen' the animal becomes very pale and swims away at right angles to its previous direction. Predators are momentarily confused and attack the cloud of pigment while the cuttlefish makes its escape.

In other cases potential predators are frightened away by some special behaviour combined with the colouring of the animal they would have attacked. Some moths, butterflies and other insects have markings on their wings that closely resemble the eye of a large and much more fearsome animal. The 'eyes' are usually concealed when the animals are at rest but are displayed when they are disturbed, and have been observed to frighten away bird predators. Sometimes the 'eye' affords a different sort of protection. When a butterfly such as the grayling (*Eumenis semele*) comes to rest, predators tend to attack the conspicuous eyespot because the eye is usually on the head, the most vulnerable part of the body. If attacked in this way, however, the grayling will not lose its head but only a part of its wing. It can fly with a large part of its wing missing and so it is likely to survive the attack.

Eyespots are also found on the tails of some fish, where they serve the same purpose of directing attack to the least vulnerable part of the body. Some caterpillars, for example those of several swallowtail butterflies, have small eyespots which direct attention away from the unprotected abdomen towards a part of the body which has a special protection, such as a stinging mechanism. The attention of a predator is, therefore, drawn towards a part of the body which has properties that may well cause the attack to be broken off.

Warning colours

Another way of confusing observers is by a sudden change from bright colours to inconspicuousness, which is practised by insects such as the large yellow underwing (*Triphaena pronuba*). This is well concealed when at rest, but when it flies away its colours are conspicuous and give a flashing sensation. At the end of a flight the insect usually descends suddenly to the ground and immediately it has landed covers the bright parts of the body and remains very still thus confusing pursuing predators.

Some colour patterns do not actually deceive predators, but merely warn them not to attack animals that are distasteful or dangerous. Conspicuous, easily recognized colour patterns have evolved in many cases to advertise an unpleasant nature. This is an obvious advantage in saving the animal concerned from unnecessary attack. Birds soon learn to avoid the familiar yellow and black stripes of the wasp with its unpleasant sting, and the same goes for the black and orange caterpillars of the cinnabar moth (*Hypocrita jacobaeae*), which are very distasteful.

In summer these caterpillars can be seen in thousands feeding on ragwort, a sure indication that they must be dis-

tasteful, for otherwise they would surely be eaten up by birds which tend to concentrate on a particular food while it is available. Because of this tendency, most larvae that live in large groups need to be protected from attack; many of them are hairy and cause irritation when touched. The small tortoiseshell caterpillars (*Aglais urticae*) which gather in large groups are black and yellow, and the caterpillar of the peacock butterfly, which behaves in an equally conspicuous way, is black. Yellow and black are both warning colours and very few birds will eat these caterpillars.

Although the best known cases of warn-

1 The male orange tip butterfly *Euchloë cardamines* is well concealed at rest on orange blossom. The outer covering of the wings blends closely with the blossom, camouflaging the butterfly.
2 The caterpillar of the giant *Papilio* butterfly looks like a bird-dropping. This makes it unattractive to birds, and ensures the insect's immunity from predators.
3 The larva of the spice-bush swallowtail butterfly has a large false 'face'. Its ferocious appearance tends to frighten away enemies which might otherwise attack and eat it.
4 A hen pheasant concealed in brush. The plumage is broken up into areas of markings, breaking down the bird's outline and making it more difficult for predators to see it.

ing coloration are among the insects, there are many larger examples, such as the American skunks with their conspicuous stripes advertising the evil-smelling and pervading fluid they can squirt at their enemies. And there is a toad which has glands in its skin that secrete an unpleasant substance, while its underside is bright scarlet. When a potential predator, perhaps a stork, flies over a group of these toads the animals flop on their backs exposing their scarlet bodies. The birds associate the bright red colour with the unpleasant taste and do not try to eat the toads.

Some animals that have no special

means of protection against attack, such as stings or glands, gain protection by closely resembling and mimicking others that are distasteful or in some other way make life unpleasant for their attackers. Predators learn that it is as well to avoid eating anything with the particular colour pattern of the distasteful species. But in avoiding these colour patterns they must avoid the mimics as well as the unpleasant genuine models, without knowing that some of the animals they are avoiding would be quite harmless to eat and even enjoyable. Very familiar examples in temperate countries are flies that have striped bodies and look just like bees or wasps.

The advantage to an edible animal in resembling outwardly a much less edible animal, to which it may not be at all closely related, was first recognized in 1862 by H. W. Bates, and became known as Batesian mimicry.

There will, of course, only be an advantage to the mimic if there are many more models than mimics, so that young predators unused to the warning colours are more likely to try to attack the inedible models than the mimics. If there were more mimics, the predators might soon learn to associate a particular coloration with edibility and attack every time they saw it.

There are many examples of Batesian mimicry in the tropics. Among birds the distasteful and aggressive drongo (*Dicrurus adsimilis*) lives in savanna areas and is often found in company with the very similar black fly-catcher, *Melaenotnis pammalaina*; the second seems to be a mimic of the first. In Southeast Africa there are several types of friar bird which are noisy and aggressive. Their flocks are often accompanied by orioles, which are not close relatives, but always resemble the friar birds they are with. This again seems to be a case of Batesian mimicry, with the friar birds as the models.

More than one species may mimic the same model or models. In West Africa the colourful butterflies *Papilio dardanus* and *Hypolimnas dubius* have three models in common, showing how closely many species have come to resemble each other. Only the females of *Papilio dardanus* are ever mimics, but there are a great many different forms within the species, mimicking various models.

In 1879, F. Muller pointed out a different sort of mimicry. He argued that while young predators are learning to avoid distasteful species, a certain number of animals with warning colours are bound to be killed. But if two species, equally distasteful and warningly coloured, closely resembled each other, fewer of each species would be killed than if the predators had to learn to avoid two separate warning colour patterns. This idea has been proved experimentally, for the black and yellow markings on the caterpillars of the cinnabar moth have been found to save them from attack by a predator not familiar with them, provided that it has already tried to eat wasps. This is Mullerian mimicry, with all the species

1 The brightly coloured, unpleasant-tasting caterpillars of the cinnabar moth are often found on ragwort in hedgerows and on waste ground. Despite their bright colours, they are rarely attacked.
2 Like the chameleon, the octopus can vary its pigmentation to blend with the surroundings. It has several different types of pigment cell in its skin which respond to external colours.

concerned not only warningly coloured but also having some special means of protection from attack. Another difference from Batesian mimicry is that all the species involved, being equally distasteful, can be equally numerous.

In tropical Africa are two species of butterfly, *Heliconius melpomene* and *H. erato,* which are found in very many different forms with their own distinct colour patterns. In any one place, however, the patterns of the two species are very similar. Both are known to be extremely distasteful to birds, and provide a good example of Mullerian mimicry.

A further type of mimicry involves the eggs of birds such as cuckoos which are laid in the nests of other birds. These eggs closely resemble the eggs laid by the owners of the nest, who are deceived into brooding the eggs as their own and subsequently bringing up the young birds. This brood parasitism, practised by several groups of birds, is most highly developed among cuckoos. Parasitic species of the European cuckoo, *Cuculus canorus,* lay eggs that are rather smaller than those of their closest non-parasitic relatives – their eggs are about the same size as those of the usual foster parents, such as meadow pipits (*Anthus pratensis*), reed warblers (*Acrocephalus scirpaceus*) and redstarts (*Phoenicurus phoenicurus*). In some areas the cuckoo will lay several distinctly different types of eggs each mimicking the eggs of one species of the unwitting foster parent.

This rather extreme example is typical of animal camouflage in that one animal is deceived by another to the advantage of the deceiver. This does not mean that a camouflaged species will automatically survive while the species it is deceiving dies out. One might ask why the mimics and their distasteful models have not starved their predators out. But camouflage is a form of adaptation to the environment and all successful species, including the predators of mimics, are adapted to their environment or they would not be able to survive. Predators may have another source of food or perhaps, if very hungry, they will eat something relatively distasteful and warningly coloured.

Whatever the exact situation, camouflage is a very fine example of adaptation and shows just what elaborate systems have developed to fit animals to their various ways of life.

1 The brill, *Scophthalmus rhombus,* matches the sea-floor in an attempt to avoid detection. It is able to vary the pattern of pigmentation to merge with the sea-bed.
2 Though the stripes of the zebra make it very conspicuous in the zoo, they serve to camouflage it in its native savanna. The animal's outline is broken up against the scrub background.
3 The morepoke, an Australian bird, is camouflaged to look like a dead branch. The bird's plumage imitates the texture and colour of tree-bark and the head is camouflaged.

The conforming gene

Much animal, as well as human, behaviour is passed from parents to children through the genes. How are behaviour patterns inherited, and how are they affected by learning, trial-and-error, and reason?

WHEN STUDYING ANIMALS, it is not so much the differences between the individual members of a particular species that are striking but the broad, general similarities. With a good eye for detail and a microscope, an expert entomologist can distinguish between most of the million and more species of insects because he knows that certain external characteristics are typical of one species only. But another way of telling species apart, however closely they are related, is to study their behaviour. Once again, within certain limits and trends, there is remarkable conformity.

Such conformity is hardly surprising. In the struggle for existence the most successful animals are those best adapted to their environment. Everything counts; their shape, their physiology and their behaviour. With time, therefore, certain elements of behaviour are discarded, while other elements, more suitable and successful, are retained. A species is the sum of its evolution; a specific solution for coping with its environment.

Survival

Undoubtedly one single type of environment offers many different solutions, but a species cannot gamble on too many alternatives; it would soon be ousted by the other species because of its lack of specialization. An animal's behaviour must, therefore, be consistent and specialized. It must also be absolutely integrated with the animal's way of life. For example, the prehistoric reptiles discovered that by running fast on their hind legs and occasionally leaping into the air they were better able to escape their predators. By flapping their forelimbs they could go farther through the air, and the most successful were those with the broadest forelimbs. In time with this sort of behaviour, and through the agency of natural selection, the reptiles developed true wings. In birds, flying behaviour and body form have become absolutely integrated.

The inheritance of behaviour depends, like all inherited factors, on genes being transmitted from one generation to the next. While it may be comparatively easy to think of a gene controlling some specific trait, like the colour of the human eye or the number and form of the bristles on the abdomen of the fruit fly, *Drosophila*, it is almost impossible to understand how a gene, or a set of genes, can control anything as complicated as animal behaviour.

The stereotyped courtship behaviour of sticklebacks is known as a *fixed action pattern*, and it does not vary significantly from one to another. In studying the genetics of behaviour it is generally easier to look at such fixed action patterns

than at other forms of behaviour, like learning, which vary from situation to situation and are dependent to a large extent on the animal's previous experience.

Although it is to the species' advantage that its fixed action patterns should all be consistent, because only then can there be true co-operation between the members of the species, particularly with regards to mating, there are variations. It is these variations which are important in evolution for they provide the basic material for

natural selection. It is also these variations that give clues to the genetic control of behaviour, for they can be observed against the backcloth of the more uniform pattern of the fixed action pattern.

Drosophila is an extremely useful animal to study genetically because the chromosomes in its salivary glands are so enlarged that they are visible to the naked eye. Geneticists have been able to map these chromosomes by observing how certain features of the animal vary with

1 Bird-song, and particularly the mating call, is a highly specific characteristic. Stereotyped songs make it possible for birds to distinguish potential partners from non-mates.

2 The behaviour of ants has a rigid genetic basis. Every ant is born with a behaviour pattern which fits it neatly into one or other category in the ant community.

defective wing, when vibrated, fails to arouse the female sufficiently for her to copulate with the male. The reason why the mutant genes, *yellow* and *black* affect mating behaviour is less obvious. It has been suggested that perhaps the muscles operating the wings are slightly defective in some way, or the nerves to the muscles, and the wing vibration is sufficiently 'off-beat' to disturb the female.

An animal's behaviour and the genes operating it seem divorced from each other. Also, for any one behavioural

1 The greater part of its behaviour pattern is already fixed in the chromosomes of this baby American robin, though learning and reasoning play a part in its life.
2 This robin, removing a dropping from its nest, may be acting from learned considerations. But his scavenging behaviour has survival value and may be partly inherited.
3 An Australian frilled dragon lizard. Threat behaviour in lizards plays an important part in enabling members of one species to distinguish their own species from similar lizards.

changes in the appearance of small regions of the chromosomes. They have discovered that a mutant gene, which dramatically affects some morphological or physiological character of the fruit fly, very often affects the animal's behaviour. For example the gene called *Bar* reduces the number of facets in the compound eyes, *white* reduces pigmentation in the eyes, *forked* and *hairy* affect the number and structure of the bristles, *vestigial* and *dumpy* alter the shape of the wings, while *yellow* and *black* affect the general pigmentation of the body. These mutant genes also have other effects, which may be detected if tests are carried out on the animal's metabolism, and perhaps affect its span of life. Many of these mutations, even if made one at a time, have also been found to affect the fruit fly's mating behaviour, and males with such mutants are much less successful than normal males in stimulating females to mate with them.

Difficulties in mating

There are many different ways by which mating behaviour can be interfered with. Fruit flies with the genes affecting their eyes cannot see as well as normally, and they have difficulty in finding the females to mate with in the first place. Then, having found them, they miss some essential visual stimuli generated by the females. But, as well as vision, the tactile sense is also involved during mating, and males with *forked* or *hairy* genes have bristles which are defective as tactile sense organs. Then again, as in the stickleback, a courtship sequence always precedes mating, and should it be inadequately performed the partners fail to arrive at the stage of copulating. Fruit flies with *vestigial* and *dumpy* mutant genes have grossly malformed wings which cannot be vibrated properly.

During courtship the male *Drosophila* brings one of its wings out laterally and vibrates it in the horizontal plane. This action stimulates tactile sense organs at the base of the female's antenna. A

activity, even a fixed action pattern, a whole bank of genes is in operation. It is therefore very difficult to isolate any one gene as the operator of a particular action. Yet, a most exact piece of research has been done on honey bees by Dr W.C. Rothenbuhler. He studied the inheritance of certain characteristics which affect the bee's behaviour in cleaning out the inside of the hive.

Some strains of bee have been found to be 'unhygienic' and instead of, as is normal, cleaning out cells which contain dead larvae, they leave the cell dirty. Such behaviour has disadvantages; it can lead to disease and it prevents the queen bee from using all the available cells for laying eggs and thereby ensuring the continual emergence of worker bees. Rothenbuhler discovered that the hybrids between the unhygienic strain and a hygienic strain were all unhygienic, and therefore the abnormal gene must be dominant. He then crossed the hybrids to the recessive, hygienic strain with extraordinary results. From 29 back-cross

colonies he found: nine of the colonies took off the caps of the cells, but left the corpses untouched; six did not uncap the cells, but if the caps were taken off by hand, would remove the corpses; eight colonies were completely unhygienic and would neither uncap the cells nor remove dead larvae; and six colonies were hygienic and uncapped the cells and removed the larvae.

These findings suggest there must be two main genes involved. One gene is concerned with the uncapping of cells, and the other with the removing of the dead larvae. The hybrid colony had both the dominant genes – which supplement each other in making the colony unhygienic – and their recessive alleles. When back-crossing them to the pure-strain hygienic colonies, results conformed to classical genetic theory.

It could be assumed from these results that all the genes concerned with the complicated behaviour of cleaning the cells are absent in the doubly unhygienic strains and present in the hygienic strains. But Rothenbuhler points out that even unhygienic workers perform these activities to a small extent, though quite inadequately from the colony's point of view. It is therefore much more likely that

1 The ritual courtships of birds like these Indian cranes are chiefly designed to raise the sexual interest of both partners. Each stage of the routine triggers behaviour in the other.
2 Even the amorous activities of the walrus, which resemble a parody of human activity, have a large inherited component, though like most mammals, walruses have a variety of behaviour.

the factor which is missing from the unhygienic workers is a gene control mechanism, which in the normal worker bee switches into action this complicated social behaviour.

In the inheritance of complicated behavioural activities like these fixed action patterns, a means can be seen whereby the total gene action becomes modified by operator genes which switch on and off certain sections. Sometimes a distinct pattern of behaviour may be incorporated into an existing fixed action pattern, and the composite action needs to be modified. This change could be effected by such switch genes.

Gene control

It is also important for the organism that all the genes controlling a complete entity of behaviour should be as close together as possible. If not, there is every likelihood that when the chromosomes divide during reproduction the genes concerned with behaviour will become separated from each other, and the total form of the behaviour will be disrupted.

The courtship display of ducks consists of a series of patterns, most of which can be observed with slight modifications throughout the closely related family of species. The modifications spring from the operation of genes described above. Konrad Lorenz calls one such pattern the 'down-up'; in this, the drake dips his bill into the water and then suddenly raises his head and with it a plume of water. While many of their relatives possess this behaviour, both the yellow-billed teal and the pintail have lost it. When, however,

the two species are crossed, the hybrid is seen to have the 'down-up' pattern. The most likely explanation, says Lorenz, is that the block of genes necessary for generating this behaviour is present in both species, but cannot appear because of some inhibiting control. This control is lost in the hybrids.

Very closely related species are often widely separated from each other geographically. Although there is no contact between the species, the similarities between them may be striking. However, such species, because the natural geographical barriers between them, have broken down, may suddenly find themselves in close proximity. Because the courtship and mating behaviour are still very similar, the two species will mate as easily with each other as with their own kind. This is a danger because the hybrids are neither as viable as the distinct species nor as fertile.

Under these circumstances it is vital that the different species, through the agency of natural selection, develop modifications of their behaviour which will effectively isolate them from the other species. This happens in nature; for example, two related species of frog have a wide range in the southern United States; one tending to live more to the west and the other to the east. In the central regions the two species overlap somewhat. There the two species have developed quite distinct mating calls, which effectively keep the frogs of the two species apart. On the other hand, at the extremes of the country, where there is no overlap whatsoever, the mating calls of both species are remarkably similar.

In other species, as in the ducks with their elegant courtship display, rather than modify the details of such display, whole chunks of behaviour are blocked out, or incorporated. But there are other methods of modifying patterns of behaviour. Either the frequency with which a species can perform its display, or the emphasis placed on certain specific parts, can vary from species to species and make all the difference. Dr Aubrey Manning has selectively bred groups of the fruit fly *D. melanogaster,* to breed either faster than normal fruit flies of the same species, or much slower. Professor Niko Tinbergen has observed subtle differences in two species of gull, the common gull and herring gull, when making their 'long call'; a call equivalent to the territorial singing of passerine birds. Both birds stretch their necks forward at first, but then the herring gull jerks its head down more as the call is started.

In the next movement, when both birds throw their heads upwards, it is the common gull's turn to emphasize the movement more. The final horizontal movement is again practically the same in both birds. Another example is seen in lizards of the genus *Sceloporus* which show a curious rhythmic head-bobbing movement during courtship and also when they meet other lizards. The frequency of the bob immediately identifies the different species. Some species get three head bobs into the space of less than a second, while other species take practically three times as long and then add an extra inflection of the head. Such signals are rigidly interpreted by the species and only the right signal is recognized.

Inherited behaviour

Animal behaviour is much more than a sum total of stereotyped fixed action patterns. Learning, reasoning, trial-and-error movements all play some part in an animal's behavioural repertoire. The genetics of these aspects of behaviour are less easy to determine. It has to be assumed that the intricate pattern of the nerves and their relationships with one another are somehow laid down as a result of gene control. In such cases, it is the potential to behave in a certain way that is inherited. In some animals adaptation to the environment is best achieved when most of the behaviour is stereotyped; in other animals, learning and reasoning play a much more important part. In a changing environment, patterns of behaviour must be learned.

With regard to the control of the nervous system, certain differences in behaviour definitely arise from the state, or activity, of the nervous system. Rats can be selectively bred for their emotionality. Highly emotional rats placed under the glare of a bright light in an open arena become excessively frightened and, as well as defecating and urinating, remain crouched down in one spot.

On the other hand, the brazen, non-emotional rats, under the same circumstances, continue to move around and do not defecate. This emotionality also had other consequences; the highly emotional rats were much slower in learning how to avoid an electric shock than their 'cool' counterparts. In as far as Man also shows wide variations in his emotionality, it would be interesting to assess how his different powers of reasoning or learning vary under circumstances of stress.

1 Praying mantises locked in battle. Fighting behaviour can sometimes be as stylized as other aspects of behaviour, and for the same sort of reasons.

2 Ants co-operate in carrying away a matchstick. Some ants are born with the ability to act as part of a team, while related species — the solitary ants — are not.

1

2

All creatures great and small

Your favourite food is the leaves at the top of the tree. Do you grow a long neck to reach them, or agile limbs to climb to them? Nature tries many ways to fit bodily shapes to basic needs.

A KANGAROO is much bigger than a cat. Yet a new-born kangaroo is much smaller than a new-born kitten. Similarly, an acorn is much smaller than a tulip bulb, and yet a full-grown oak tree is hundreds of times larger than a full-grown tulip. What determines how large a living thing will grow, and how does it 'know' when it has reached that size?

The adult size of an animal is related to the most efficient way for it to survive in its natural environment. Since the young are much smaller than this size they obviously have to grow until they reach it.

Of course, not all animals achieve maturity simply by adding on weight and size to their infant body. A butterfly does not 'grow' at all, because when it emerges from its chrysalis, it is already an adult. Most of the butterfly's growth takes place while it is still a caterpillar grub, which eats almost continuously for several weeks until it is ready to transform itself into its adult form.

But whatever the path from infancy to adulthood, some fail and die before reaching maturity – they have to contend with predators, lack of food, drought and disease. Over a period of millions of years, this has meant that only creatures best suited to their environments – or which can adapt to changes in their environment – have continued to exist.

What is growth?

Growth, in the biological sense, is difficult to define and measure because it is not necessarily merely equal to an increase in size or weight. For example, when a dog breathes in, its chest expands but we do not say the animal grows. When an elephant drinks a gallon of water its weight immediately increases by ten pounds, but it does not 'grow'.

Biologists overcome these difficulties by defining growth as an increase in the *dry* weight of a plant or animal – that is, an increase in the weight of the tissues after all the water has been removed, generally by heating. Of course, to make such a measurement in practice the plant or animal must be killed and so true dry weight can be found only once. So for most purposes, measurements of live size and weight are used, inaccurate though they may be.

The important thing to remember is that when we say growth has occurred, we mean that the creature concerned has increased the amount of living material in its body. Using this definition, we find that there is nearly always a particular size at which growth ceases, although some fish and a few animals continue growing all their lives. Size varies from species to species, but generally corresponds to the size at which maturity is reached.

The genetic heritage of an animal sets the limits of growth. A cat is a cat, and nothing it can do will ever change the fact that it is a cat. Cats have a certain range of size within which they may develop. One would be very surprised to see a cat as small as a humming bird, or as big as a horse, because these sizes are out of the cat's range. But cats may vary within their normal range, depending on their environment.

All living cells rely on diffusion to get raw material into and out of them. The oxygen needed for respiration passes through the cells to the places where it is needed. Simple one-celled animals and some more complex ones carry on diffusion directly with their liquid surroundings.

Environment greatly affects size and bodily features. The flat face and pug nose of the Alaskan Eskimo may have evolved to minimize heat loss from the body in the frigid arctic climate.

In higher animals, special transport systems such as the blood and lymph systems carry gases and foods round the body, right up to the cells. But in the final stages, it is still diffusion that is the essential process.

This reliance on diffusion is one of the chief factors limiting the size of any cell. The extent of 'control' exerted by a nucleus on the cell depends on diffusion and so cells must be small. Of course, not all cells are exactly the same size – they cover a range relatively greater than the difference in size between a mouse and a whale – because cells live under different conditions and perform different functions in various parts of the same body.

Cells have an optimum size in a given situation when they function most efficiently, and so do whole organisms. The most efficient animals are obviously best fitted for survival and, in the long run, all animals evolve hereditary controls which stop the cell growth process when the optimum size is reached. Up to this point, animals generally grow as fast as their food supply allows.

After maturity, some of the food goes towards producing eggs or sperm which are needed for reproduction. So that although growth has stopped, the animal is still using food to build new tissues. These tissues are then released, as sperm, eggs or young animals, and so the building of these particular tissues does not constitute growth in the strict sense although there is no real difference in the cell processes involved.

The most efficient size at which to stop growth depends on many factors. And these are interwoven to such an extent that it is difficult to say which are the main reasons why a particular animal is the size it is. But we can consider some of these factors and see how they contribute to growth.

Many of these controlling factors are part of the natural environment. They include such things as climate, food supply and the medium in which an animal lives. An animal's surrounding medium can play a large part in determining its optimum size. For example, most birds which fly are small whereas those that have given up flying and run on the ground (such as ostriches and emus) can grow much larger and heavier. A similar trend in size is shown by various kinds of plant seeds. Those that are distributed by the wind (such as thistles, dandelions and maple trees) are small and light; those distributed on water (such as coconuts) are large and heavy.

On land and sea

Land animals are limited in size by the need to support their own bodies, particularly land animals which stand. The legs are on solid ground, but the soft parts of the body 'hang' from the skeleton, because they get little buoyant support from the air.

Animals that live in water grow much larger than their land-bound relatives because of the extra support they get from the water. For this reason, the massive dinosaurs of prehistoric times are believed to have spent much of their life in water. A whale is a modern example of such a creature: if it becomes stranded on a beach, the weight of its own soft parts can crush it to death in quite a short time.

Carnivorous animals (meat eaters) are generally most efficient as killers if they are about the same size as their prey – or even a little smaller and so more agile. Animals that eat plants or insects do not have to kill for food, but their food affects their size in other ways. Tall animals, such as the giraffe, can reach high into a

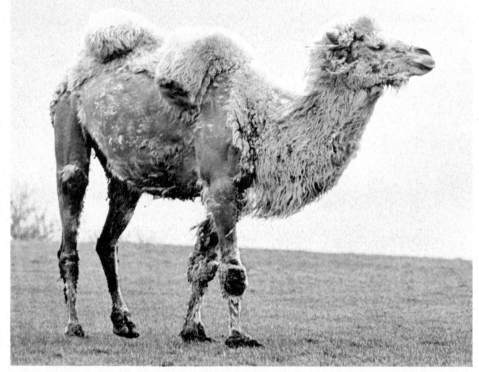

The fleet-footed ostrich, *top,* clearly demonstrates the compromises an animal must make in adapting its size and structure to meet the demands of its environment. The enormous bulk of its body has stripped the ostrich of the ability to fly. The large size of the camel, *above,* and its one-humped cousin, the dromedary, is made possible by storing water-holding fats inside their humps. Without this reserve, such a large animal would perish in the dry desert heat.

tree to eat the upper leaves – although treetop leaves can also be reached by small animals, such as koalas and some monkeys, climbing up the tree. Climbers cannot be too heavy or they could not cling to small branches, and so most climbing animals are fairly small. Eating plants growing at ground level seems to be one of the ways of feeding which favours large size, because such food is generally plentiful, and reaching it requires no special adaptation. Many of the large land animals feed in this way; for example, the rhinoceros and the bison.

There are also parasitic animals. In fact, there are more of this type than any others, ranging from microscopic protozoa to mosquitoes and ticks. Most kinds of free-living animals have several kinds of parasites which are, of course, much smaller than their hosts.

The temperature of an animal's environment also plays a part in limiting its size. Since heat is lost over an animal's surface, and since surface area increases more slowly than does volume (or weight), animals that live in colder regions tend to be larger than their relatives in more

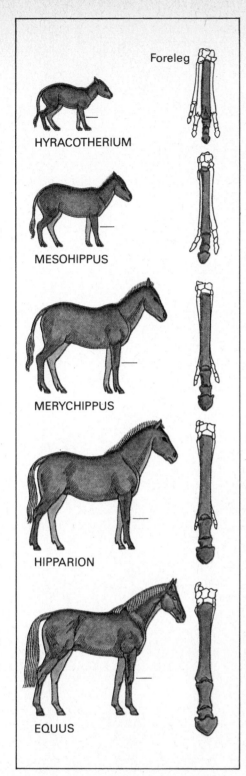

HYRACOTHERIUM

Foreleg

MESOHIPPUS

MERYCHIPPUS

HIPPARION

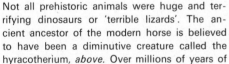

EQUUS

Not all prehistoric animals were huge and terrifying dinosaurs or 'terrible lizards'. The ancient ancestor of the modern horse is believed to have been a diminutive creature called the hyracotherium, *above*. Over millions of years of evolution, it continually altered its size and structure to adapt to its changing environment. 'Twiga', the Swahili word for the African giraffe, suggests its origins. One evolutionary theory states that the giraffe came from an animal with a much shorter neck, as an adaptation for reaching the twigs and leaves high up in trees, *top right*. The little koala bear, native to Australia, solves the problem of nourishment another way; it climbs up after it, *above right*.

temperate climates. For example, polar bears are much larger than the sun bears of Malaysia, because they lose proportionately less heat from their larger bodies. This fact was first noticed by the German zoologist Karl Bergmann more than 100 years ago. The rule named after him states that animals of colder climates are relatively larger and have relatively smaller extremities than do their cousins in warmer climates.

Bergmann's Rule may be used to separate the races of some kinds of birds. In the northern hemisphere, birds from the colder northern regions tend to be larger and have shorter wings and legs than do similar species in warmer regions further south, though there are exceptions, such as the ostrich. Warm-blooded animals that live in the sea also follow the rule. Elephant seals, which live in the polar seas, grow much larger than, say, the common grey seal of Europe.

The way an animal is 'built' also plays a part in limiting size. For example, the size of an insect's body is restricted by the way an insect breathes. The tracheal system used by insects is efficient only for a body up to about an inch across, because it relies on the relatively slow process of diffusion. In a body much larger than an inch, diffusion could not keep up with the demands of the insect's metabolism. Within this maximum limit, the size of insects varies according to the principles we have already described.

In a similar way, the heavy exoskeleton of crustaceans, such as crabs and lobsters, restricts their size – especially on land – because there is a limit to the weight their muscles can support. Even in water, there is a limit to the size and weight which the

Biologists believe that massive prehistoric animals such as the diplodocus, *top,* spent most of their lives in water, because their flesh was too heavy to be supported on land for long.

Some animals, such as the common lizard, can re-generate severed limbs and other parts. The new tail of this lizard, *above left,* looks peculiar because it contains cartilage rather than bone,

as in the original tail. The polar bear, which is generally larger than its cousins in warmer regions, illustrates 'Bergmann's Rule' that size is strongly influenced by temperature, *right.*

muscles of these animals can move.

Just as individual cells in a multi-celled animal's body are limited in size, so are the single-celled protozoan animals. When an amoeba grows to a certain size, it splits into two and each half continues to grow as a separate creature.

The actual process of growth is the addition of new living material to the body of an animal or plant. It is not, however, a haphazard form of addition. The various types of body tissue are built as they are required. Using the same basic food materials, an animal's body can repair a wound, produce eggs or sperm, grow hair, or, if it is a developing embryo, form an eye or a heart – all from the same sorts of cells and all from the single cell that was the egg.

Every cell in the body has its own nucleus, and every nucleus is an exact copy of that in the fertilized egg which gave rise to the body. For this reason, each nucleus contains enough information to develop any of the characteristics shown by the cells of the animal. But during the growth of the animal, this information is selectively inhibited so that, as development proceeds, certain cells develop into one kind of tissue while others become a different kind. All cells in a given kind of tissue still retain a faithful copy of the information needed to become any other kind of tissue cell, but this information is somehow 'switched off'. In some cells the switching off is permanent, and in others it is only temporary and cells can modify their function as necessary.

An interesting example of the late

growth of new tissues is the phenomenon of *regeneration,* in which an animal or plant grows a new part to replace one which has been lost. All animals can regenerate parts of their body to some extent, but some are much better at it than others. For instance, flatworms (*planarians*) can regenerate a completely new 'head' or 'body', and a starfish can complete its body even if only one arm is left. Crabs and lobsters can regenerate legs and claws when these are lost, and lizards can grow new tails. Higher animals have only feeble powers of regeneration which do not extend much beyond healing wounds, although structures such as tonsils are sometimes regenerated after removal.

Build up and break down

In some cases, especially with lower animals, the regenerated parts are identical with those replaced; but often they are only similar to them. This is because the conditions which allow a structure to develop the way it does in an embryo obviously cannot be reproduced in an adult. For example, a lizard's regenerated tail looks much the same as the original one but contains no true bone and no notochord tissue. This is because in the embryo, the bones of the back and tail develop around the notochord, which becomes obliterated in the adult. But in the regenerated tail, conditions are not right for the formation of a new notochord and so no true tail-bones can form. Instead, the new tail gets its stiffness from a rod of cartilage.

No matter how complex animals become,

the basic processes of life remain amazingly similar from animal to animal. In all animals, cell respiration oxidizes foodstuffs to liberate energy, and the same foodstuffs can be broken down into their basic constituents and used as the building blocks for growth processes. The break down of food for energy is *catabolism,* and the building-up of body tissues from food is *anabolism.* Together these processes make up *metabolism,* which is the total of all the chemical processes occurring in an animal's tissues. When anabolism (building-up) takes place faster than catabolism (breaking-down), growth occurs. When the two are equal, growth stops and there is a state called 'equivalent metabolic turnover'.

When one views growth in terms of the food supply, it soon becomes evident that an animal's social environment – what other animals it lives with – may be just as important as its physical environment. When sheep herders began moving their animals into the American West, cowboys were quick to recognize the danger. Sheep cropped the rangeland grass so close that there was little left for the cattle. In some cases, the sheep and their owners were driven out at gunpoint.

The general study of how an animal relates to its environment is called *ecology.* Since Man is the only creature that can consciously alter his environment, knowledge of ecology is very important. As history has shown, altering the environment without giving due consideration to the consequences can be a very costly business.

Change, modification and decay

Four-legged chickens and two-headed sheep are too common to be ignored. What is the mechanism that produces such freaks along with the many other variants which make up the variety of life?

ANYONE WHO LOOKS around him can see changes in the forms and colours of living things. Some changes come about during the course of normal growth and development: a caterpillar changes to a chrysalis which changes to a moth, a seed 'changes' into a tree. Some changes are seasonal: a tree in winter is stripped to bare twigs which bud again the following spring.

Other changes are connected with changes in the environment and are easily changed back: the leaves of a potted avocado pear plant turn yellow as the magnesium in the soil becomes depleted; given a dose of Epsom salts, they are green again within a week.

Other changes are equally due to the environment, but are more permanent. If the grubs of the fruit-fly (Drosophila melanogaster) are subjected briefly to a temperature of 40 °C. instead of their usual 25 °C., the adult flies that eventually emerge are sometimes seen to have one of the tiny cross-veins in the wing missing or broken. And once broken, they are never mended.

There are, however, some changes that most people never see or become aware of. This is not because the degree of change is small, or occurs in only a few plants or a few animals. On the contrary, the changes may be either gross or inconspicuous and all living things are subject to them. Their main properties are that they occur only rarely: one must be very familiar with a particular kind of plant or animal and observe many of them before becoming aware of these changes. Their occurrence is usually completely independent of any change in the environment.

Mutation as an inheritable factor

Their other main property is that they are inherited. If a biologist takes two (a male and a female) of the cross-veinless fruit-flies produced by the temperature shock experiment and allows them to breed, all their offspring are perfect, with not a broken or missing vein among them.

However, one can sometimes – very, very rarely – find cross-veinless flies among stocks kept at a normal temperature all their lives.

Two such spontaneously changed *mutant* flies together produce a brood which are all alike and like their parents – cross-veinless. Cross-veinlessness in these flies is due to *mutation*. *Mutation* is a change in the form, colour, physiology, habits or any other characteristic of a living organism which is inherited.

Mutations are inherited because they are the consequence of changes in the genetic material. This material is a chemical found in every living thing which determines its form, colour, physiology, habits – every characteristic – and also

1

2

1 Wings on these fruit-flies are stunted. Their parents were dosed with radioactive phosphorus. Occurrence of the defect in the second generation shows this is a true mutation.

2 Radiation can be used to produce mutations in wheat. Most of these forms are useless to agriculture, but occasional forms are obtained which lead to new usable strains.

determines whether they are inherited. The chemical is deoxyribonucleic acid (DNA) which consists of a spirally twisted stack of pairs of molecules called *bases*. There are four kinds of bases: *adenine, guanine, cytosine* and *thymine*. Each is attached to a deoxyribose-phosphate molecule. There are only two kinds of pairs: adenine-thymine (AT) or guanine-cytosine (GC), but each can be turned through 180° or substituted for the other without affecting the shape of the spiral. As a

result, four arrangements are possible: AT, TA, GC, and CG. The stacked base pairs are linked through phosphate groups which connect the deoxyribose molecules along the spiral outside edges of the molecule.

The molecule can be of indefinite length, but the phosphate backbones must twist round each other at exactly the right distance apart. Nevertheless, this distance can be achieved regardless of which of the four base pairs is present at any level in the stack. Thus the order of the four kinds of base pairs along the molecule can be unrestrictedly varied. The result is that the number of possible DNA molecules differing in their orders of bases is extremely high. If a molecule only three base pairs long is made, there are 64 different orders possible. A molecule ten base pairs long could have one million different arrangements. The DNA of one of the simplest of living organisms, a virus, contains 200,000 base pairs. A bacterium has 50 times as many, and a man has 100 times as many again.

It is also clear that the molecule is *self-determining*: that is, it could be split down the middle through the stacked base pairs so that adenine separates from thymine and guanine splits from cytosine. But, provided the splitting did not break the phosphate-sugar-phosphate backbone, two new molecules could be reconstructed from the halves. Both would be like the original, as each base can take only one of the four possible bases as its partner – the same one that it was paired with before.

Mechanism of mutation

This process of splitting DNA and reconstructing two daughter molecules identical with each other and with the original occurs in every dividing cell in the living world. It ensures that every daughter cell contains the same amount of DNA as its parent, and that the order of bases in each molecule is the same. Every nucleus in a dividing amoeba, paramecium, or cork-making cell in the bark of a tree contains the same DNA, quality and quantity, as the sister nucleus

1 Mutations in the garden geranium (Pelargonium) may be caused by changes in DNA in the chloroplasts rather than in the cell. This process is rather uncommon.
2 This Malayan five-legged bull is a mutation produced by a natural agent, probably radiation. Such oddities are badly adapted to survival, so that they normally disappear in a generation.

3 Changes in the colour of chrysanthemums are caused by loss of a complete chromosome. Duplication of chromosomes can also cause quite striking changes in physical appearance.
4 A strain of hybrid corn is produced by interbreeding over two generations. This method is used to produce new varieties with special desirable characteristics.

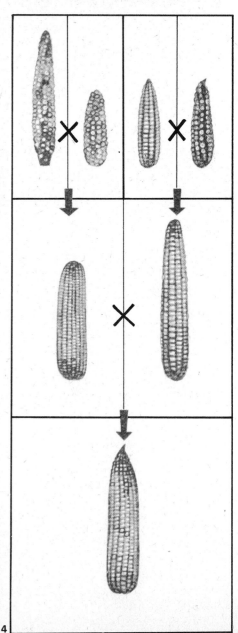

Another sort of mutation is when the total number of chromosomes changes. The change can happen in multiples of the characteristic (basic) number for that cell. Thus, a bean plant has two sets of seven chromosomes. Its pollen cells have one set, and plants (polyploids) can occur with three, four, five or six sets of the basic seven chromosomes. Alternatively the change may be to have only one extra or one too few chromosomes. Such abnormal cells are said to be aneuploid: cells with multiples of complete sets are euploid.

Different numbers

Chromosomal mutations are of two kinds. There are those in which the balance of genetic material has been altered. In duplications, deletions, and aneuploids, genes are lost or gained, while the others remain intact. Such changes in balance usually have very bad effects on the organism. An example is Down's syndrome (mongoloid idiocy) in Man, which is due to the presence of one extra copy of one of the smallest chromosomes in the human set of 46.

In the other kind of mutation, no change in balance occurs. In the polyploid series, the number of genes is increased without changing their proportions. Translocations and inversions only rearrange what is there, without necessarily damaging any of it. Balanced chromosome changes seldom have a serious or even noticeable effect on the appearance or character of an organism, although polyploids are sometimes found to be larger than their diploid relatives. They often, however, have a large effect on the cell divisions that lead to gamete formation. Many gametes (sperm or eggs) die as a result of the mechanical difficulties caused by pairing and crossing-over in chromosomes which have suffered inversions or translocations.

No one knows what causes mutations. Their occurrence appears to be spontaneous and unconnected to any physical or chemical happening in the life of the cell. However, a lot is known about what can cause mutations. High-energy electromagnetic radiations such as X-rays and gamma-rays were the first mutagenic agents to be discovered and ever since they have been used in laboratories to induce mutations. The increase in mutation rate is proportional to the dose of radiation received. The particles emitted in the decay of radioactive substances such as radium (which emits alpha-particles) or radioactive phosphorus (beta-particles) also cause mutations.

The exact chemistry of mutation by these agents is not known, but they do have one property in common – they can cause atoms to lose electrons and become ionized, thus becoming chemically reactive. Ultraviolet light also causes mutation. This is the kind of light most strongly absorbed by DNA.

The second class of mutagenic agents is a mixed bag of chemicals. The first to be discovered was mustard gas, which reacts with various components of the cell, including DNA. It is not certain how mustard gas causes mutations, but it is

from which it divided.

The precision and speed of this process are remarkable. The ten million base pairs of a single bacterial cell are reproduced in exactly the same sequence once every 20 minutes, or 1,000 million times in ten hours. Exactly, that is, except for the mistakes. Now it is unlikely that more than one mistake is made in every ten replications. However, all mistakes once made are faithfully reproduced as such: they are inherited. Because DNA also determines all the characteristics of the cell, some of the mistakes may be detectable as changes in observable characteristics. They can then be described as mutations.

In organisms more complex than bacteria, the exact division of the genetic material is assisted by having it organized into blocks which appear, during cell division, as the chromosomes. The division of the chromosomes, naturally enough, reflects the precise replication of the DNA they contain, so during cell division each chromosome splits into two identical halves. The process is repeated accurately time after time, through countless generations, except for the rare mistakes.

Mistakes can be of any size. A working DNA molecule, like that of a bacterial cell, is functionally subdivided. Every length of 1,000 or so base pairs has a job to do. It determines the structure of one of the tens of thousands of different proteins which perform the cell's chemistry and form its membranes and fibres. Such a length of base pairs is called a gene.

It is easy to see that if one such length is

Huia birds show adaptation producing distinctions between the sexes. The male has a short, strong beak for making holes in tree-trunks, while the female's is long and curved for extracting grubs.

lost, then the protein it determines will disappear from the cell: the cell has no information about how to make it. If a gene is changed, the protein it makes may also be made in a changed form. Sometimes, if the biochemists' techniques are good enough, such an altered protein can be detected, or its absence noted. More often, we can only tell that the mutation has occurred because the missing protein affects the characteristics of the cell in some obvious and dramatic way.

The sequence of base pairs in a gene can be changed in a number of ways: in any position, one base pair can be substituted for another; a base pair may be added to the sequence or deleted from it; or whole sections of the DNA chain may be deleted.

Mutants which affect only one base pair, and therefore only one gene, are known as 'point mutations'. But some mutations are large enough to affect the visible structures of chromosomes. There may be deletions, when a block of DNA containing several genes is lost; duplications, when one or more bits of a chromosome are duplicated; inversions, when a block of chromosomes is turned through 180° relative to the other parts of the chromosome; and translocations, when a part of one chromosome is moved to another part of the same chromosome or to a different chromosome altogether.

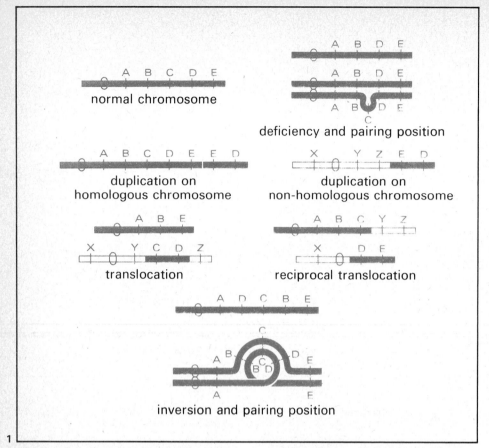

causing mispairings. For example, the substance *2-aminopurine* is very like adenine, but it can pair with either thymine or cytosine. So if 2-aminopurine is given to a cell, it may become incorporated into the DNA instead of either guanine or adenine. Once in, pairing with either thymine or cytosine during DNA replication will cause base-pair changes at the point where it occurs. As a result, mutations can arise.

As far as one can tell, all mutagens except base analogues cause the same range and kind of mutations as those which occur spontaneously. To produce mutations, all mutagenic agents have to be administered to cells in much higher doses than any cell normally encounters. So it is uncertain whether the mutations that occur spontaneously are genuine accidents or are caused by very low chance doses of mutagens, some of which (for example ionizing radiations) are always with us.

The logic of survival

Charles Darwin, when he described his theory of organic evolution, showed that it depends on two things. One is a struggle for existence. The other is the occurrence of variation. Because some individuals of a species are different from others in colour, or size, or habits, or physiology, some are bound to get on better in the struggle than are others. The fittest – those better at 'getting on' – survive. Thus the characteristics which make them better and fitter are passed on to their progeny. In other words, evolution occurs because inheritable variations occur. As we have seen, the variations which arise as mutations are inherited: and mutation is their only source. Mutation is the basis of evolution.

Chromosomal mutations also affect evolution, but often in a rather subtle way. Clearly, if they have effects on the characteristics of an organism, these effects are subject to selection. But as we have seen they may not have such effects on cells, only effects on cell division. This is sometimes an advantage. If two groups of plants are growing in different environments, they will come, by evolution, to have different sets of genes. If the two groups of plants are close enough together to pollinate each other, they will constantly be getting genes in their progeny which are of advantage in the other environment, not in their own. If this could be prevented, both plants communities might benefit. The rhododendrons of Tibet and China are an example of plants in which interbreeding is prevented by chromosomal mutation. But there are many others in which chromosomal mutations which have arisen by chance like other mutations have evolved as internal controllers of the variation passing from one generation to another. As a result, they are controllers of the process of evolution itself.

Within a framework laid down by environment and other evolutionary forces, genes and chromosomes provide blueprints, changes in which caused by external factors, will determine the future shape and cha. acter of animals and plants.

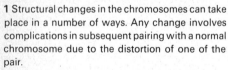

1 Structural changes in the chromosomes can take place in a number of ways. Any change involves complications in subsequent pairing with a normal chromosome due to the distortion of one of the pair.

2 Industrial melanism is an example of current evolutionary change. Its environment determines the colour of each moth.
3 Its colour makes the black moth an easy prey in rural conditions.

able to unite chemically with both strands of a DNA molecule at once. This prevents the DNA strands from separating during replication, and can lead to the formation of gaps or breaks. Breaks can be seen in the chromosomes of cells treated with mustard gas.

The action of other chemicals is better understood. For example, nitrous acid reacts with cytosine, converting it to *uracil,* a base which pairs only with adenine. Thus it can change GC base pairs to AU base pairs, which are subsequently replicated as AT base pairs. Nitrous acid can also react with adenine to convert it to *hypoxanthine*. This then pairs with cytosine, so nitrous acid can also cause AT to change to GC.

Other chemicals, the *base analogues,* act by behaving temporarily as bases, but

Adapting in adversity

Many living species have to contend with extreme or abnormal environmental conditions. They have evolved special ways of dealing with the problems posed by these circumstances.

OF THE MILLIONS of different species of plants and animals on Earth, many face special problems in the struggle for existence. Each animal and plant is adapted to carry out certain functions in a particular way. For example, bacteria which are specially able to resist heat are found in the hot springs that exist in volcanic regions. In other bacteria, the cell chemistry is subtly changed so that the bacterium can extract food from petrol. These tiny animals are found in the petrol tanks of motor cars. Such species as these are intensely specialized to live in the unusual conditions they have chosen. Other species are able to live and thrive in severe cold, in the parched deserts, and in other bizarre and extreme environments. What sort of adaptations are necessary for animals and plants to survive in such environments?

The regions around the Poles are extremely inhospitable to life. The animals and plants face intense cold combined with a shortage of sunlight for long periods of the year. Only a few land mammals are able to live near the Poles. The best-known is the Polar bear, which is to be found within the Arctic Circle. The Arctic bears and foxes develop white fur so that they become inconspicuous when hunting in the snow. This has an obvious advantage for animals that have to hunt under snow conditions. The marine mammals, seals and walruses, require no camouflage, for they have few predators apart from Man. They have developed, as a protection against the cold, a heavy

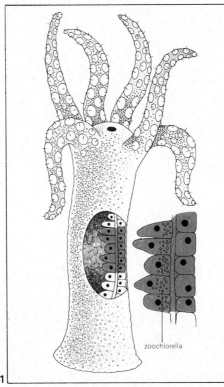

1 Hydra, a freshwater animal, contains a plant, zoochlorella. Each supplies the other's chemical requirements. This is symbiosis.
2 These knots, gathering for their winter migration, avoid the cold Arctic winter by flying south to Africa in vast flocks.
3 The caribou of northern Canada is very well adapted for life north of the Arctic Circle. It lives on moss and can find food beneath the snow.

layer of fat or blubber around their bodies and are hardly affected by the intense cold.

The long Polar night poses special problems for both plants and animals. Plants cannot survive long periods of frost, though some of them are remarkably hardy. For this reason, there are no trees above a certain latitude. The plants almost all lie dormant in the ground until roused to frenzied growth by the rays of the summer sun. Arctic species of plants are able to take the maximum advantage of the limited time at their disposal for reproduction and growth.

Many of the bird species of the Polar regions have solved the problem of the Arctic winter by a complicated migratory cycle which brings them to the far north during the summer and far south during the winter. They have evolved a very sophisticated navigational method to enable them to undertake these long journeys.

Land animals

The land animals have solved the same problem rather differently. Many, like the Polar bear, undergo long hibernations during the worst part of the year. The Polar bear digs out a cave for itself and its family and sleeps through the winter. The animal must accumulate sufficient food in the form of fat deposits during the summer and autumn to last it through hibernation. In addition, it has the ability to slow down its metabolism so that it does not burn up energy at anything like the normal rate. Hibernation is, in fact, typical behaviour

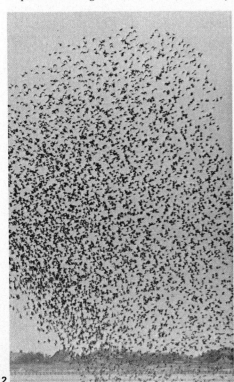

for Polar mammals and even the Eskimos of the far north are far less active during the winter than during the summer. The Eskimos are physically adapted for life in the far north: they are short and stocky in build, a body form which presents the least surface for radiation of heat. Their faces tend to be flattened, with snub noses, again presenting less area to the cold. The physique of the Eskimos is in marked contrast to that of races that live in hot areas. The Dinkas of the Nile, for example, who live in an extremely hot environment, tend to be very tall, thus giving the maximum area for radiation of heat.

. An environment that presents very different problems of adaptation for animals and plants is the desert. The main problem is finding and conserving water. There are two types of desert. In one, water is not available in sufficient quantity – the Sahara and the Kalahari deserts of Africa. The second type of desert is one in which the conditions are so cold that the water is in an unobtainable form. Such deserts are found in high plateaux and in the far north. Various plant and animal forms have evolved in a specialized way to live under these conditions. A familiar example is the camel. It can go for long periods without water and it is able to store fat in its 'hump'. The camel is also well adapted to prevent excessive loss of water. It is able to excrete a highly concentrated urine so that very little of its body water is required to rid it of waste materials.

Special relationships

This ability is shared by a remarkable desert rodent called the kangaroo rat. Its kidney is specially adapted and it can conserve its limited water supply very much longer under waterless conditions than other mammals. Many of the animals that live in the desert have evolved specialized senses – particularly the sense of smell – in such a way as to enable them to find water under adverse conditions. Other animals have become adept at finding food in the sparsely vegetated desert. The Lapland reindeer lives where vegetation is sparse because the ground is frozen for much of the year. It is able to survive on a diet of 'reindeer moss'. This lichen is itself a remarkable adaptation. It is not a moss at all but really consists of two plants, an alga and a fungus, which live together in an extremely close association. This remarkably resilient combination, found in the most exposed sites and spots on mountains and within the Arctic Circle, is an example of a type of adaptation known as *symbiosis*.

Symbiosis is one of the most remarkable adaptations found in Nature. In the case of lichens, the two species cannot live apart because each provides the other with substances necessary for life. Another example of a similar process is provided by the common hydra, a small freshwater plant related to the sea-anemones. Hydra contains inside its body a small freshwater plant called zoochlorella, which produces oxygen and sugar. These substances are necessary to the hydra's development, while the hydra itself produces nitrogen, which is required by zoochlorella. All these

adaptations take advantage of the increased resources that two plants have over one.

A similar type of symbiosis is found between human beings and certain bacteria, which live in the intestines and form a necessary part of the process of digestion. But these are not truly in a symbiotic relationship. Man can live without bacteria and the bacteria can, in some cases, live without the man. But they do provide

1 The sponge crab is host to a commensal sponge which lives on its back and feeds from the scraps of food left after the crab has eaten. The crab is not inconvenienced by the sponge.
2 The prickly pear is physiologically adapted to withstand both snow and frost and temperatures above 100 °F. Succulent to survive drought, its spines discourage animals.

for each other's welfare. This type of relationship is known as *commensalism*. There is a third type of adaptation in which animals and plants of different species live together. This, of course, is *parasitism*, in which one partner derives benefits at the expense of the other. Many parasites are extremely highly adapted for their special mode of life. Many of them are so specialized that they cannot exist unless they find their way into one

3 A hermit crab just about to enter the shell of a periwinkle. The crab has no shell itself, but makes use of empty shells to provide the protection it needs.
4 A dwarf mimulus or monkey flower growing in chips of lava in a volcanic crater in Oregon. The dwarf stature of the plant is an adaptation to the poor environment.

1

2

3

particular species of host. A successful parasite does not kill the host, although it may weaken it. Host and parasite may grow together so that they become mutually tolerant.

A very good example of this type of adaptation is found in parts of Africa and Asia where the disease called tertiary malaria, caused by a form of the malarial parasite or *Plasmodium*, is rife. In the areas where this type of disease is common,

5 The guanaco of the Andes is an animal similar to the camel. It is well adapted to life in the high, dry environment of the mountainous deserts.

6 An Arctic fox in its winter coat. During the summer, the Arctic fox has a reddish coat, but in winter this is replaced by a white protective coat which acts as camouflage.

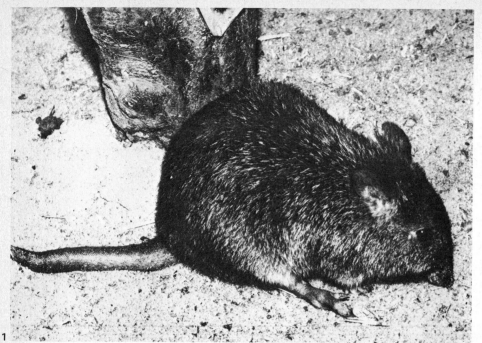

a way that the centre of gravity is brought over the feet.

The advantages of upright posture are numerous. Man is freed from having to walk around on all fours, and can thus use his hands to the full. Standing upright enables Man to increase his range of vision. The most important disadvantage, however, is that the bone structure is not fully adapted to the upright posture, and so tends to become deformed as the man grows older. Back trouble, slipped discs and the like, are the penalty we pay for being able to walk on our hind legs.

Some animals have been able to develop highly specific adaptations for their particular mode of life. Bats provide us with an example. In these highly specialized mammals the vision sense is very poor – they live much of their lives in the dark. But bats are able to 'see' at night because of their ability to sense high-frequency vibrations. In fact, the bats have developed a form of radar.

Protective adaptation

A remarkable example of protective adaptation has been observed in moths. Certain white moths found in Britain used to produce black offspring sometimes as 'sports' or mutants. Where these moths live in industrial areas, however, the species are now almost entirely black. The moths have adapted to the dark background created by the smoke of the towns and are able to survive fundamental changes in their environment. Those remaining white have stood out against a black background and become easy prey for birds and other predators. A similar but more ancient type of adaptation is found in certain insects which mimic more ferocious or inedible insects in order that their predators will pass them by. The harmless grass snake feigns death to fool its enemies.

The hermit crab is born without the customary hard carapace, or shell, and would undoubtedly offer a juicy morsel to a passing fish or to another crab. However, the hermit crab has found a neat solution to its problem. It finds a winkle shell and pushes its soft body inside it for protection.

One is constantly amazed by the very exact way in which natural selection fits an animal for its environment. This is achieved by a long process of survival of the fittest in which those members of the species which fail to adapt to their environment, which are born less fitted for their particular mode of life, are eliminated by predators or are unable to compete with their fellows for the available living space. This process, which lies at the basis of all adaptation in plants and animals, constantly refines the species so that it is better able to live in the existing conditions.

Adaptation of species to fit them for special ways of life is part of this process of constant refinement. In this way it becomes possible for animals originally fitted for life in one type of environment to change gradually and become able to cope with the extreme conditions encountered, for example, in the Arctic, in hot deserts and on high mountains. This ensures that life extends over the entire planet.

1 The kangaroo rat, so called because it moves by leaping with its strong hind-legs, is well adapted to life in the desert. Its kidneys produce a highly concentrated urine.
2 Mistletoe lodges in the cracked bark of trees and becomes parasitic on its host. This property puzzled the early Britons, who worshipped mistletoe as a sacred plant.

it has been found that many of the people have a particular form of hereditary anaemia called sickle-cell anaemia. This disorder is caused by a gene which is lethal when both chromosomes contain it. However, where a person carries only one gene for the disease, that person is normal except that his blood cells under certain conditions become deformed. He is also highly resistant to tertiary anaemia. The advantage conferred by this adaptation in the human population is an example of the successful ability of the parasite's host to develop ways of neutralizing the parasite. Where tertiary malaria has been eliminated, the gene for sickle-cell anaemia, which now carries only disadvantages for its bearer, is fairly rapidly eliminated from the population.

Degeneration of parasites

Another example of adaptation in the host-parasite relationship is found in the mite *Demodex folliculorum*. This remarkable little parasite lives in the hair follicles of dogs, where it gives rise to the disease called follicular mange. The rear part of the mite's body is elongated so that it can fit into the follicle.

Some parasites are almost completely degenerate and their mode of life as parasites has left them permanently altered. Such are the pentastomid parasites, like the tongueworms of dogs. Despite their wormlike appearance, these parasites are in fact closely related to the spiders. Their mode of existence makes it easy for them to get food from the tissues of the host, and they do not have to work hard for a living. The parasite *Sacculina* is a parasite of crabs. This animal is, in fact, closely related to the barnacles, but has

become so well adapted to its mode of life that it is now little more than a sac containing the sexual organs and feeding on the crab's tissues by means of tubes which spread through the body of the host.

In a sense, of course, these animals are not degenerate at all. They are in many cases extremely well adapted to their way of life. But biologists are not immune to the fallacious reasoning that uses human values to judge the worth of animal species, and parasites are often regarded as rather inferior forms of life.

In human beings there are many adaptations that have fitted us for our unique mode of life. One of the most important of these is the ability of human beings, as opposed to the apes, to bring together their thumb and forefingers to grasp objects. This ability is called 'opposing the thumb'. The upright posture of human beings is not so well developed in any other animal species. The change to bipedal movement involved considerable anatomical changes, particularly in the position of the pelvis. This bone, in human beings, is tilted back, and the spine is curved in such

Forming the new generations

The ultimate goal of living things is to produce more living things in their own image, but evolution demands continual variations. The processes of reproduction accommodate both needs.

ONE OF THE CHARACTERISTICS of living things separating them from non-living things is that they reproduce themselves. The legacy of the old to the new is the genetic information or 'blueprint' which will enable the new organisms to develop and function in much the same way as the organism which gave rise to them. Since this 'blueprint' is contained in the genes inside a cell's nucleus, most of the essential mechanisms of reproduction are concerned with securing the passage of this information from the parent to the progeny.

The simplest way of reproducing is to split in two by a process called *replication,* producing an exact copy of the parents. As this involves duplicating everything so that one of everything passes to the new individual, it includes the formation of a duplicate set of genetic information. Bacteria can divide once every 30 or so minutes; as replication continues at this rate, the population arising from one bacterium may reach many millions in a day. Amoeba, too, is an organism which reproduces by splitting.

Pairing for procreation

The nucleus divides first by *mitosis,* the process by which the *chromosomes* (strings of genes) are replicated so that the second nucleus contains exactly the same number. Each new chromosome under normal conditions, is an exact replica of the original. When a cell in an animal or plant's body divides to form new tissues – when a wound is being healed, for example – they divide in this way.

The single-cell individual can reproduce in this way without the need of a second member of its species. In much the same way, spores of fungi or ferns can grow into a new individual without further change. So the process of budding off a new

individual, whether it is from some part of a plant or from the base of a sea-anemone, is similar in nature. No other plant or anemone is necessary. Reproduction of this sort is called *asexual* because only one organism is involved.

Reproduction in most plants and animals, however, involves two individuals each contributing a set of chromosomes to the offspring. The ciliate protozoan, *Paramecium,* for example, undergoes exchange of genetic material. These ciliates each

have two nuclei, a macronucleus (controlling the feeding activities and so forth) and a micronucleus (smaller and concerned with reproduction). Two individuals swim alongside each other to come to lie with the sides on which their mouths are together. The macronuclei in both disintegrate; the micronuclei divide (mitotically) until there are four of them, three of which also disintegrate. The remaining one then divides to form two; one nucleus of each pair passes over into the body of

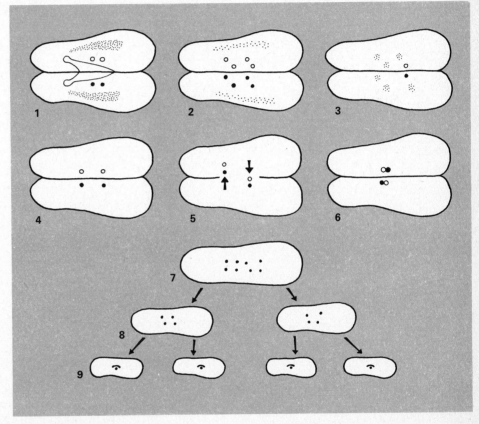

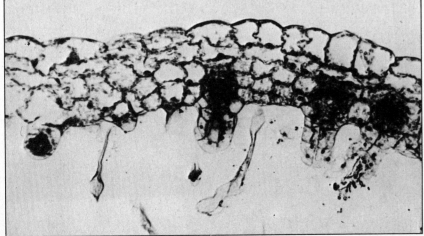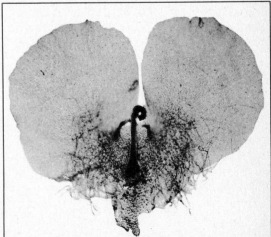

Top, reproduction in *Paramecia* proceeds in two distinct phases. First, two *Paramecia* 'conjugate', exchanging nuclear material (1–6). After the conjugates separate, they individually begin to divide. In this way, each conjugate is capable of producing four daughter cells which swim away as new individuals. *Above left,* a section through a fern prothallus shows a (male) antheridium and three (female) archegonia. In reproduction, sperms swim through a water film on the prothallus to reach an archegonia. *Above right,* a complete fern prothallus with embryo.

the other partner, and fuses with the nucleus which has been formed in it in the same way.

The conjugants then part and swim off. Thus there has been an exchange in nuclear material but no actual reproduction, for no new individuals have been formed. This comes later when each conjugant divides to form four new protozoa in each of which a macronucleus is reformed to give the normal complement of nuclei. This example underlines the fact that the exchange of nuclear material is not all there is to reproduction, for new individuals must also be produced.

There are no obvious differences between the two partners in *Paramecium*; each one receives the same from the other. Yet there must be some difference between the partners, probably ones of a biochemical nature, for a *Paramecium* will not mate with just any other *Paramecium*, its partner must be of a different 'mating type'. *Paramecium aurelia,* for example, has at least 16 varieties, each with two mating types. Effectively this means that the *Paramecium aurelia* has 32 different sexes'.

Settling for two sexes

'Sexual' differences are also found in *Spirogyra*. Strains of this green filamentous alga are simply labelled + and −. Only if a + strain filament comes close to a − strain filament will the gamete formed in the cell of one filament emerge along a conjugation tube to fuse with a gamete from a cell in the other. The result is a hard-covered zygote from which a new filament will grow.

The more familiar gametes, such as those in Man, are unequal in size and plainly different. Often the male sperm can propel itself by a long whiplike tail. The head of the sperm contains little else than the nucleus. But the female egg is a larger cell, with its cytoplasm packed with reserve food. It usually moves very little, and has to be located by the active sperm for fertilization to take place. It seems as if early in evolution all manner of different combinations of 'sexes' were tried, but finally this arrangement of having only two sexes, male and female, proved the best, and so is the rule in higher species.

Among some invertebrates which live in the sea, it is common for both eggs and sperms to be set free into the water. In the clouds of gametes liberated by numbers of sea urchins, for example, fertilization of the eggs will take place by sperms from another individual. Although chemical signals ensure that numbers of the urchins release their gametes together, many gametes are wasted. In other organisms some of this wastage is reduced, because eggs are retained on their parent. Then the sperms must be able to locate the egg and this they usually do by chemical cues.

One of the disadvantages of the fertilization process is that it has to take place in a fluid to allow for the sperms to swim to the egg. Additionally both are unprotected and therefore could dry out were they not in fluid. The egg, at least, can be protected to a large extent if it is retained in the parent organism. But whereas a male frog

Top, the *Pellia* is a very common liverwort which grows on damp soil in wooded areas and other shady spots. *Above,* sporangia grow like stalks from the *Pellia*. The capsule at the top contains spores which will be released when the capsule bursts. *Right,* the capsule has burst, releasing spores. Reproduction by spores is inefficient. Thousands of spores are released, but only a handful ever grow to adult plants.

can fertilize a female's eggs merely by spraying them with sperms as they leave her body, an organism which lives entirely on land cannot simply release the sperms in this way, for the sperms need fluid in which to swim and they would dry up in the air. Therefore many means of transferring sperms to the female have appeared in evolution.

The pollen grain of a flower is one method. The courtship behaviour of a mammal is another. By this procedure, physical mating becomes possible and the male can introduce his sperms into the female's body. Some animals, the scorpion is one of them, deposit their sperms in a small mucus packet, the spermatophore,

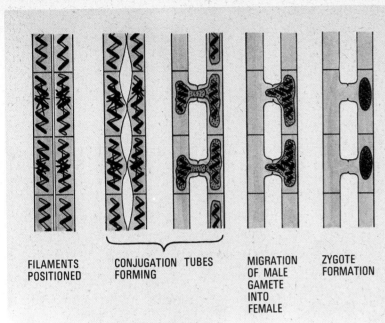

| FILAMENTS POSITIONED | CONJUGATION TUBES FORMING | MIGRATION OF MALE GAMETE INTO FEMALE | ZYGOTE FORMATION | ZYGOSPORES FORMED |

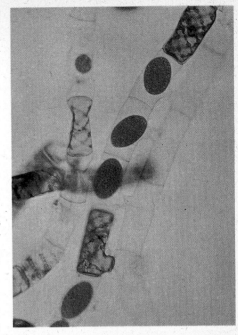

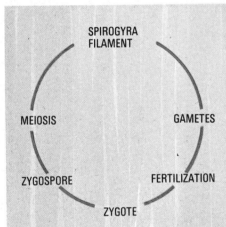

SPIROGYRA FILAMENT

GAMETES

MEIOSIS

FERTILIZATION

ZYGOSPORE

ZYGOTE

Top left, a type of sexual reproduction in plants is demonstrated by the filament-like *Spirogyra.* Two of these algae align themselves side by side and form conjugation tubes through which gametes from one plant pass to the other. Almost immediately after fertilization, the zygote begins to contract into a zygospore. The final stage of reproduction takes place later when the parent plant decays and releases the zygospores, which then develop into new *Spirogyra.* *Top right,* two *Spirogyra* in the act of conjugation. *Above,* a summary of the *Spirogyra*'s reproductive cycle. *Right,* even some more advanced plants, such as moss, sexually reproduce by spore formation. *Below,* plant or animal, the goal of reproduction is the same — new life.

leaving it on the ground for the female to pick up. The next stage in evolution is for the male to put the spermatophore directly on to the genital appendages of the female – this is what a male grasshopper does. Then, finally, the spermatophore is abandoned altogether and the male uses some copulatory appendage (penis) to convey the sperms directly on to the genital system of the female where the egg is protected by the mother's body.

All these methods reduce the wastage of sperms and help to ensure that the eggs are fertilized. In addition, the fact that the eggs themselves are kept in the body of a female means that they can be particularly well supplied with food reserves such as

MITOSIS
6 CHROMOSOMES   12 CHROMOSOMES   6 CHROMOSOMES

REPLICATION   6 CHROMOSOMES

MEIOSIS
6 CHROMOSOMES   6 CHROMOSOMES   3 CHROMOSOMES

NO REPLICATION   3 CHROMOSOMES

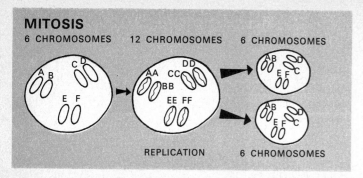

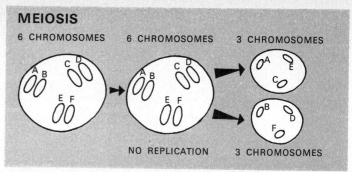

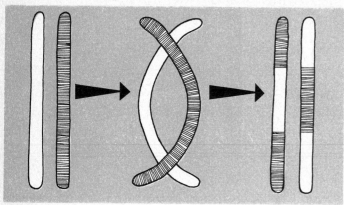

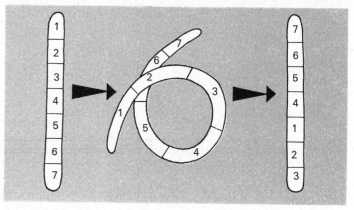

Top, it is convenient to think of meiosis as mitosis with a step missing. In mitosis, each chromosome replicates (creates a duplicate of itself) before the cell divides, so each new cell has exactly the same content as the parent cell. In the final phase of meiosis, no replication takes place. Thus, each of the two new cells has only half the number of chromosomes of the parent cell. Mitosis is ordinary cell division, meiosis produces gametes for sexual reproduction. *Above left,* chromosomes sometimes 'cross-over' one another, interchanging parts. *Above right,* it is also possible for a chromosome to interchange parts with itself. Such mutations help explain the process of evolution.

the *yolk* in animals and *endosperm* in flowering plants.

Also special protective layers can be put round the fertilized egg. The egg membranes, the albuminous 'white' of the egg and, around everything, the shell, are added to a bird's egg by the various parts of the oviduct of the female bird. The fertilized egg cell is the whole of the yolk – one very large cell swollen with the yolky reserve food.

Occasionally an egg will develop without being fertilized. A frog's egg will commence the cell divisions which herald the beginning of development after being pricked with a needle. The mechanical stimulus replaces the natural one of the penetration of the egg by the sperm. Development without fertilization is *parthenogenesis* and happens to the eggs of a number of invertebrate animals. The unfertilized eggs of a honeybee queen develop into males, (drones) while fertilized eggs give rise to females, workers and queens. There is no evidence for parthenogenesis among higher animals such as mammals.

Variety and consistency

But, nevertheless, there is more to fertilization than a mere mechanical stimulus, for in this way genetic information is brought from two sources – the two parents. In this way greater variation can result. However, if we examine the way in which the mature egg and sperm are produced we shall see that they themselves contain the possibility, almost the certainty, of a further increase in variation.

Unlike ordinary cells, which divide so that each new cell has the same number of chromosomes as the original, gametes (sperms and eggs) are formed after a cell

division in which the number of chromosomes is reduced to one-half. This type of reduction division is termed *meiosis.* So if a normal cell has 32 chromosomes (in 16 pairs), the gametes will have only 16 chromosomes.

In the meiotic cell division, chromosomes pair off, so that in Man, for instance, 23 pairs of chromosomes are formed. But before meiotic division is complete, the two partners of each pair become intertwined round each other, and frequently sections are exchanged in this *crossing-over.* On the whole, one of each pair comes from the set of chromosomes derived from the mother and the other from the father of that particular organism. So the exchanges are taking place between chromosomes which are slightly unlike.

The material which passes from one chromosome to the other will contain genes, and therefore the changes will bring about a re-sorting of the genes on those chromosomes. Later in the division, one of the two changed chromosomes goes into each new sex cell. As a result the gametes are themselves different from each other. It is a matter of chance which a sperm happens to fertilize or if either is fertilized at all. Thus, the distribution of the chromosomes is quite random.

One important result of the altering of pieces of chromosomes is that the genes on parts of the chromosomes will now have different ones on either side of them, in other words, their genic background will be changed. This often alters the way in which the genes express themselves in the organism's make-up when it is born. Again, this produces more possibilities of variation from individual to individual.

By doing this they form new organisms

which may be like the original ones or may differ from the old in various degrees. These variations are the essential material from which the evolution of new forms can proceed. If everything were an exact replica of what had gone before, there could never have been the evolution of the huge variety of living organisms which exist in the world today, or in the ages long past. The introduction of variation is one of the main, if not the main, advantages of sexual reproduction involving two partners.

A kind of immortality

In a number of organisms, a cell which will give rise later to the sex cells is set aside very early in development. The remainder of the body of the organism which acts as a carrier and a nurse for the reproductive cells is called the *soma.* The somatic part is mortal, for it dies while the sex cells pass on to the next generation. An amoeba which divides its whole body is potentially immortal, for two new individuals are made and nothing is left behind. Who is to say which is the parent cell? It has been distributed between the two new cells.

But the somatic part of an organism protects the sex cells against the direct influence of the environment. This may be of major importance in preserving the integrity of the genetic information needed for determining the next generation. To a very large extent they are also isolated from the influence of the remainder of the organism's body. Thus, changes which the organism acquires do not change the genetic information which is being preserved for posterity. For fertilization is only the beginning; development of new individuals must follow, if reproduction is really to be attained.

Inside the egg

Eggs are involved somewhere in the reproduction of all higher animals, from insects to human beings. Paradoxically, the human egg is one of the smallest eggs found in nature.

EGGS ARE very simple yet at the same time potentially extremely complex. A hen's egg looks perfectly straightforward but it contains within its simple-looking shell all that is necessary for the growth of a bird. The case of human beings is even more striking. The 'egg' is many times smaller than the hen's, but the final product is decidedly more complicated. This paradox is one of the most interesting of all biological phenomena. The discovery of the genetic code, which shows how the cell nucleus can contain enormous amounts of information in an extremely condensed form, has gone a long way towards outlining how this age-old problem can be explained.

The egg, whether of the hen or of the human being, consists of a fusion between a cell contributed by the female and a cell contributed by the male.

The contribution of the male is the *spermatozoon*, while the female contributes the *ovum*. Some of the genetic material from each cell goes to form the genetic material of the new cell. In this way, the egg contains some of the characteristics of the male parent and some of the characteristics of the female parent.

A unique series of changes takes place in the germ cells before fusion to reduce the amount of genetic material in each germ cell. The aim of this is to make sure that the genetic make-up of the egg contains the same amount of information as is in the cells of the parent. Too much or too little genetic information would be disastrous to the developing egg – either way it would not be able to develop properly and would give rise to monstrous forms of life.

The male cells are formed in the *germinal epithelium*. In Man and other higher animals, this tissue is found in the testes, but in some of the lower animals, the tissue giving rise to the spermatozoa is less specialized. In any event, the creation of a mature sperm is a process known as *gametogenesis*.

All the cells of the germinal epithelium can potentially become spermatozoa, but only some do so. A germ cell destined to become a sperm first divides several times in the usual way giving a number of *spermatogonia,* each of which contains a full complement of genetic material. Later, the spermatogonia come to lie near the outside of the germinal tissue and then undergo a remarkable and unique type of cell division called *meiosis*. In this process, instead of giving rise to two cells each containing two of each chromosome, the cells produced have only half the number of

chromosomes in the normal cell. Each of the two cells thus produced then gives rise to two other cells, also with half the usual number of chromosomes, and these cells then set about taking on the characteristic features of sperms. The exact form of the sperm depends on the species of animal involved, but all sperms have in common the ability to move rapidly and to respond to chemical stimuli which attract them towards the female germ cells. In many cases, the sperms are provided with long tails, which lash about in fluid to provide the sperm with motive power.

In the female, the process of production of the germ cell, in this case an ovum, is similar to that in the male, with the important exception that each of the primary cells produces only one and not four ova. The other three cells produced with only half the normal complement of chromosomes degenerate and form the polar bodies, which are pushed to one end of the ovum and play no further part in reproduction.

The ova vary very considerably in size from species to species but they are always larger than the sperms. The reason for this is that the ova always contain a large amount of protein and nutritive material

1 A Rhode Island bantam hen with her chick. The chick is only a few hours old, but has many built-in reflex actions, such as pecking for food, which enable it to survive.
2 The carpenter ant builds complex warrens inside trees and fallen wood to house its eggs. The eggs are carefully looked after by the whole community.
3 Worker bees on a brood comb. The queen bee lays her eggs in the prepared comb, and the eggs and grubs are fed and cared for by the workers.

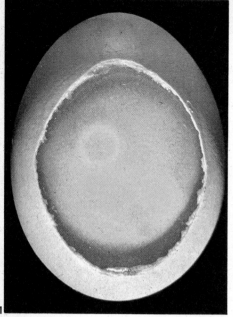

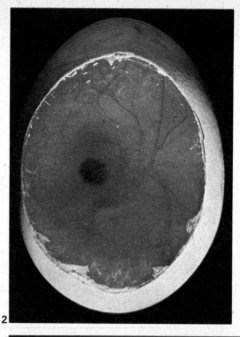

human embryo, at least in its early stages, is very like that of a chicken.

The fusion of the male and female cells depends on the species involved. In different species it is brought about in different ways. In many lower animals, such as amphibia, fertilization takes place outside the body of the female and the male frog injects his sperms over the eggs as they are produced by the female. The fertilized eggs are then left to function as independent cells and receive no protection from the adult frogs. In insects fertilization generally takes place inside the female's body, which means that the eggs are protected from the worst rigours of the external environment until they are nearer maturity. Many insects make complicated provision to ensure that their eggs are well catered for during their development. The female ichneumon fly injects her fertilized eggs into the body of a caterpillar, in such a way that the eggs are provided with the ideal conditions to

1 Twelve hours after the beginning of incubation of the chicken within the egg, the tiny germinative disc can be seen on the surface of the yolk, marking the site of the embryo.
2 Six days later: blood vessels now extend across the yolk, and the embryo, with its large eyes, heart and gut, is now clearly recognizable and digesting the yolk.
3 The 13-day embryo has almost all the organs of the adult. At this stage, the muscles and cartilage are formed, and the feathers and lungs begin to develop.

for the development of the embryo. In birds like the chicken, this provision is greatly exaggerated, and bird ova are in fact the largest animal cells known. The yolk tends to lie at one end of the cell, called the vegetative pole, while the nucleus of the egg lies at the other end of the cell, called the animal pole, in a region more or less free from yolk. In the eggs of birds, reptiles and fish the yolk present is so great that the non-yolky portion is restricted to a small cap at the animal end of the cell. The eggs of the advanced mammals are an exception to this. They do not require large amounts of yolk because the embryo is nourished mainly from the maternal blood-stream, so that a large yolk is unnecessary.

Fertilization takes place by the fusion of the sperm and the ovum to form a single cell. In this process, the sets of chromosomes provided from each partner in the union are brought together. Since each partner has provided only half the full cellular complement of chromosomes, the resulting fertilized egg cell has the same number of chromosomes after fusion as are contained in the normal cell. Once fertilization has taken place, the cells immediately begin to divide and shortly thereafter start to form the rudiments of the different tissues of the body. This process of differentiation of the cellular elements, the growth of the different tissues, and the overall development of the animal, take place in the egg according to a schedule which is similar even in such widely dissimilar species as birds and mammals. Thus, the development of a

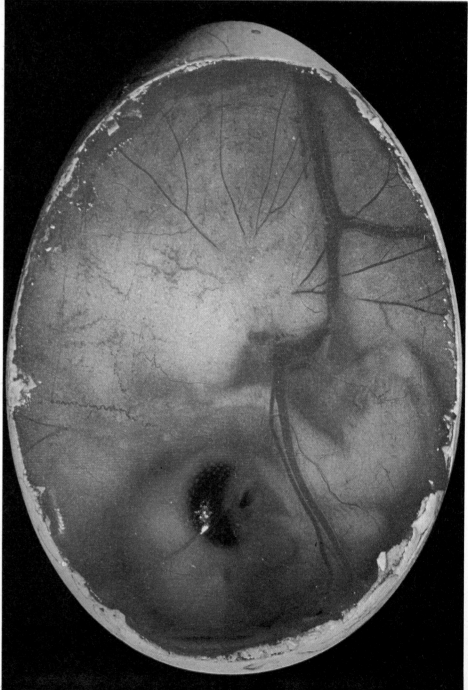

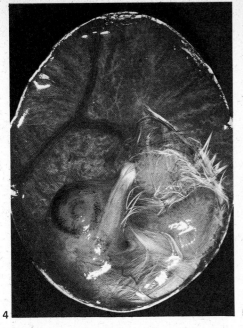

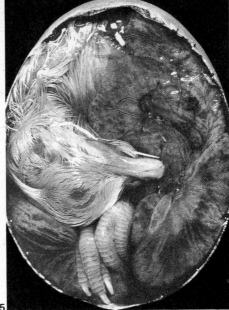

4 At 15 days, the eyelid and the eye with its pigmented iris are visible. The horny beak is able to open and shut, and grows a small bump, with which the chick will break the shell.

5 The 17-day-old embryo is cramped tightly into the shell. By now almost all the yolk has gone. The bird can be heard to 'cheep' at this age when it opens its beak for air.

6 Twenty-one days old: using the bump on its beak, the chick breaks the shell and starts to peck out a circular opening to free itself. It can take between an hour and two days.

7 The shell is cut neatly and cleanly in two and the chicken freed. Still damp from the egg, it fluffs its downy feathers and peers around at the world outside.

hatch out in a protected environment – inside the caterpillar. The larvae are able to feed on the flesh of the caterpillar during their development. Eventually, of course, the larvae eat so much of the caterpillar that it dies.

In other cases, insects go to considerable trouble to build nests for their eggs, to keep them out of the way of predators while they are developing. The logical conclusion of this process takes place among the social insects, the bees and ants, in which the whole colony centres around the nest, and eggs are provided with almost ideal conditions for their development, the right temperature being carefully maintained by the efforts of the entire hive. In these insects there is specialization of tasks so that in many cases only one member of the insect community, the 'queen', is able to produce eggs. In the flying ants, fertilization takes place only once a season, although the queen goes on producing eggs for a long period; she is able to store sperms until required to fertilize her eggs.

Most insects produce very large numbers of eggs. Instead of producing one egg which is carefully looked after, as is the case in the higher species of animals, the female produces many thousands of eggs after mating, although the rate of loss of eggs through death and predation is very high.

Many species make efforts to protect

7

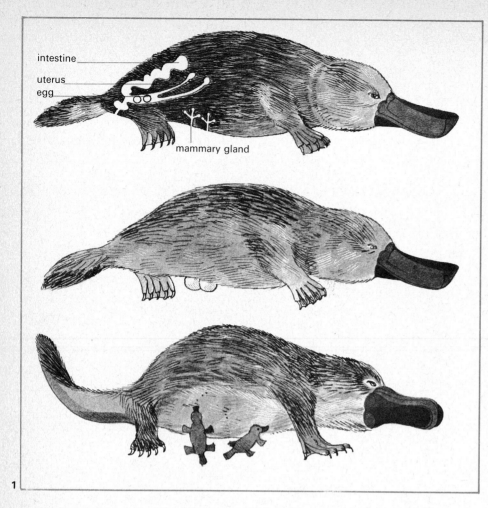

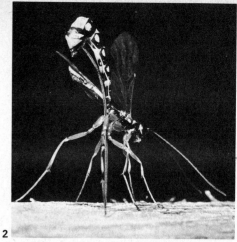

their eggs while they are developing. The eggs may be enclosed in some sort of protective shell as is the case with most birds, or hidden under the ground as in the turtles of the Indian Ocean. Where the egg has to develop in a warm environment, egg-laying may take place at a favourable time of the year, so that the eggs will be exposed to the sun's warmth. In the more developed species, however, particularly in the mammals and the birds, the predominant part is played by maternal care. In birds, a typical example is provided by the hen. In this bird, the egg is large and well provided with nutriments essential to the development of the chick. The embryo at the beginning is no more than a small dot at one end of the yolk. The yolk and the white (albumen) are rich in protein essential to the chick's development. In addition the egg is protected by a hard shell which keeps the chick away from harmful environmental influences.

Hatching the eggs

Many birds camouflage their eggs to keep them from harm; they are usually laid in sheltered or protected places, and nests are built to protect the eggs and later the chicks when they hatch out. Most birds lay relatively few eggs in each clutch, but in birds maternal and paternal concern for their young is frequently highly advanced, so that the few eggs are cared for before, during and after hatching.

In order to develop, eggs must be kept at a certain minimum temperature. This temperature is relatively easy to maintain for those species that lay their eggs in water or underground. Otherwise, among birds, this is achieved by 'sitting' on the eggs from the time they are laid until the time they hatch. This job often falls to the lot of the male bird, although in many bird species the parents take it in turns. Their body heat keeps the eggs warm and provides ideal conditions for them to hatch. If the eggs are left too long without heat they will die. The instincts of the birds provide the motive for continuing this procedure, which is carried on with great dedication by many species.

Reptiles also lay eggs but they are usually left to fend for themselves once they are laid. Many reptiles go to great lengths to lay their eggs in some favoured spot. Turtles, for example, come thousands of miles to lay their eggs at traditional nesting sites in the Indian Ocean. They come out of the water and drag themselves painfully over the sand to lay the eggs at a place above the high-tide mark. In order to provide for the eggs, the female turtles dig holes in the ground, a process involving an enormous expenditure of energy, for these animals are ill equipped for digging on land, although well able to cope with conditions in the sea. Once the eggs are laid, they are covered over by sand, and the turtle leaves them to the heat of the sun. Other reptiles watch over their eggs and build nests for them. This sort of nesting behaviour is common, for example, among snakes.

The only mammals which lay eggs are the extremely primitive Australian monotremes, the duck-billed platypus and the echidna. These animals are midway between the form of reproduction found in advanced mammals and that found in

1 The Australian platypus, a primitive mammal, lays eggs and suckles its young. The fertilized eggs from the uterus are laid and hatched by maternal heat.
2 The ichneumon fly has a long ovipositor or egg-tube. It probes through tree-bark to find insect grubs and then lays its eggs inside the living grubs, which serve the larvae as food.
3 The chain king snake (*Lampropeltis*) lays its eggs in a hollow in the sand, and coils itself around them. Only some of the eggs (those in the background of this photograph) are fertile.

reptiles. They are considered mammals because despite the fact that they lay eggs, they also suckle their young.

In the true mammals the eggs develop inside the body of the mother. They become attached to the wall of the uterus and develop in communication with the bloodstream of the mother. This form of reproduction, known as placental reproduction, carries to its logical conclusion the process of maternal care for eggs found in birds and reptiles. Instead of providing a single cell to accommodate and provide nutrition for the developing embryo, and instead of the parents having to carry out a complicated set of instinctive procedures in order to keep the embryo warm, the egg is fed directly from the mother while it is developing, and thus is given the best chance of 'a good start in life'. In mammals the development of the egg is similar to that in other forms of life, with the exception of the formation of the placenta, but mammals tend to produce only a limited number of young which are not born until after a period of development in the womb.

The platypus diagram labels: intestine, uterus, egg, mammary gland

Why the egg becomes a chicken

What determines the fate of the tiny egg cell? Why is it that hens' eggs always turn into chickens? Modern biology has many of the answers to this long-standing mystery.

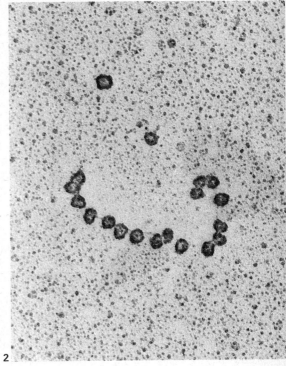

ANIMALS AND PLANTS are made up of countless tiny units called cells. The number of cells in an organism such as Man runs into many millions, yet all these cells have come from a common ancestor. If in the life of the organism we go back far enough in time to the moment of its conception we find that all its cells have stemmed from the conjugation of just two cells – the female gamete, or *ovum,* and the male gamete, or *spermatozoon.* It is remarkable to think that all the many different kinds

1 The structure of the typical animal cell. Outside the central nucleus is the cytoplasm, containing the ribosomes. The whole is surrounded by a cell membrane.

of cells in an animal such as Man – with his heart cells, liver cells, nerve cells, kidney cells, gland cells, gut cells, blood cells, cells for making skin, teeth and bone – should have originated from just one common predecessor; and that this single fertilized cell should therefore contain all

2 A chain of ribosomes from a tobacco leaf cell, magnified 400,000 times. The individual ribosomes are strung out along a 'thread' of messenger RNA.

the information necessary for bringing about the growth and maturity of a mighty oak, a myriad-legged centipede, an elephant in Africa, or Man.

What happens in the development of an organism from one single cell? The fertilized egg of the bird, for instance, is relatively enormous with its great sphere of yolk, and we find that this mass of highly nutritive food does affect what happens to the cell when it starts to develop. The fertilized egg cell, at one pole of the yolk, is minute by comparison with it. This tiny cell first divides into two identical daughter cells by a process known as *mitosis,* but it cannot divide the yolk, which remains as a single mass. The two cells thus come to lie directly on the surface of the yolk, which they begin to tap for food. Shortly, these two cells themselves divide into a total of four cells, and then these into eight cells, until in time a small mass of cells is formed – still overlying the yolk which, at that point, because it is being digested, begins to liquefy.

Now, an event occurs in the minute embryo which is the first indication that the cells, that have resulted from the con-

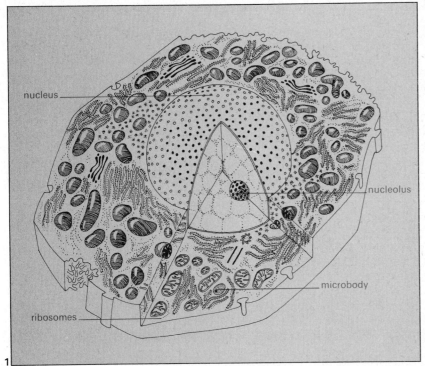

3 The discoverers of the genetic code. Nobel prizewinners James Watson (left) and Francis Crick. Behind them is a model of the structure of DNA, which they discovered.

221

tinuing division, are no longer all exactly the same. This event is the formation of a *primitive streak* by which the cells begin to separate into three layers: an outer layer, known as *epiblast*; a middle layer as *mesoderm*; and a layer closest to the yolk, known as *endoderm*. These layers are destined to become particular parts of the adult bird. The epiblast will give rise to the nervous system, to the skin. to the lining of the mouth, to certain glands and to sense organs like the ear and eye; the mesoderm to the muscles, to the bones and connective tissue, the blood and parts of the kidney; and the endoderm to the intestines, the liver, glands and other organs associated with the animal's nutrition. The primitive streak first shows as a small furrow on the surface of the epiblast, but in time it sinks deeper until, as the top layers of the epiblast close over it, it has formed a tube. This tube is the cavity of the brain and spinal cord.

At the same time the gut is forming. Where the head is developing, the endoderm cells start migrating inwards to what will become the belly of the bird. Migration is going on simultaneously, and soon, rather like squeezing off a balloon with one's finger, the endoderm has met in the belly region, and has closed off a space inside the developing embryo that is the primitive gut. A small space or opening is left in the midline which connects up with the yolk; for the embryo needs more and more nourishment. The other organs are now forming and it is very evident that each region has a particular task of development to enact and seems to know what it is doing.

The cell's fixed fate

Birds are just one particular example of development, and every species of animal and plant has its own variation. Mammals develop in the uterus of their mothers, and nourishment is carried by the bloodstream. Part of the embryo's development is therefore to form a mass of cells, known as the *trophoblast*, which burrows into the lining wall of the uterus and develops blood vessels that make contact with the blood vessels of the mother. The blood vessels passing from the trophoblast into the young embryo are contained within the umbilical cord, which in many ways is similar to the opening through which, in the chick, yolk can pass from the yolk sac into its gut.

Whatever the animal, or plant, and its type of development, there comes a moment when the cells, which have all arisen from the one cell, begin to differ substantially from each other. Depending upon where it finds itself in the developing embryo, the cell appears to have its fate fixed and cannot normally be changed. If we take a small piece of primitive streak from a chick and graft it under the *ectoderm* – the outer skin layer – of a rabbit embryo at a similar stage of development, we see that the graft, as it would have done in the chick, develops into nervous tissue, and even affects the cells of the rabbit embryo in its close vicinity, so that they, too, form nervous tissue. This property of a cell to become fixed on a particular

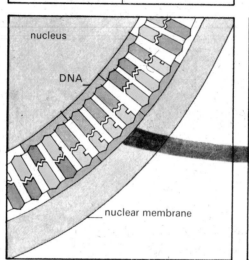

DNA nucleotide	RNA translation
adenine	uracil
thymine	adenine
guanine	cytosine
cytosine	guanine

Diagrams showing the mechanism by which proteins are produced from DNA in the nucleus. A mirror image of the pattern of the DNA in the nucleus is generated on a strand of RNA. The bases on the DNA fit the RNA bases as shown. The messenger molecule then proceeds to the ribosomes, where it becomes attached. Amino acids, which form the 'building blocks' for proteins, are brought to the ribosomes by molecules of transfer RNA. The transfer RNA molecules fit along the ribosome by attaching themselves to the molecules of messenger RNA. The order in which the transfer RNA molecules fit together along the ribosome thus corresponds to the order of bases in the original molecule of DNA on the nucleus. Thus, the corresponding amino acids are brought together and linked up by enzymes (not shown) to form chains according to specifications carried permanently in the nucleus. Messenger and transfer RNA molecules move between nucleus and ribosomes, bringing together amino acids to build proteins.

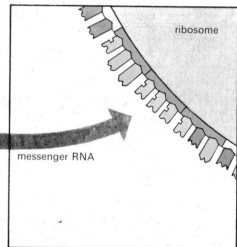
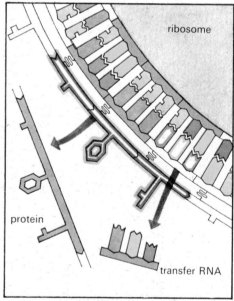
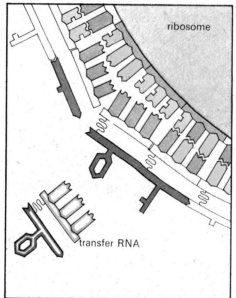

destiny is known as the *determination* of a cell.

But what controls this determination? Does it result from changes within the cell in question, or from outside? The answer, as is so often the case in biology, is neither one nor the other, but both. To understand what goes on inside the cell we must take a look at its basic structure and functioning. Each organism inherits certain characteristics from its parents, and the genes which determine these character-

istics are carried on microscopic threads, known as the chromosomes, which are found in the nucleus of each cell. The nucleus is a membrane-bounded sac that resides more or less in the centre of the cell. After fertilization the ovum, which is about to embark on the long, tortuous course of development into the adult organism, has a double complement of chromosomes; one set coming from the mother's side, and the other from the father's. As the ovum divides by mitosis, the chromosomes replicate into their exact equivalents, and each daughter cell finishes up with its full complement of chromosomes. Thus, each cell, although it may be many divisions removed from the fertilized ovum, has precisely the same genetic material.

But if, as we know, it is the genetic material of the cell which determines the shape of the organism to come, and each cell has precisely the same genetic content as the ovum, why cannot each cell, independently of the others, develop into a complete organism? Given the chance and the right environment, it has sometimes been possible to make a mature cell of a fully fledged organism revert to its embryonic state and grow and develop into a new organism equivalent to the one from which the cell was first taken. In one experiment carrot cells from a mature plant were extracted and allowed to live isolated from each other in coconut milk. Coconut milk provides all the right conditions to make the carrot cell believe that it has now become an embryo, and with no cells about it to affect its own growth, it soon reverts, as we have just said, into an ovum-like cell, and is then able to develop into a mature plant. But this experiment was only successful under very special conditions. Normally, in the embryo, each

cell must adapt to its situation and its neighbours. Otherwise it would be like turning up on a football pitch with a tennis racket; the place and the football players would make it impossible to play a normal game of tennis.

Thus, we have the paradox that every cell has all the genetic material necessary for bringing about complete development from scratch, yet, as the embryo develops, each cell becomes more and more specialized, or *differentiated* as it is called in embryology, so that it is incapable of turning into anything but a highly specific cell type. To understand how this differentiation can come about, we must understand what the genes do in the cell. Their function is to instruct the cell how to make proteins. These are very special proteins; they are enzymes – biological catalysts – which govern the chemistry of the cell, and therefore the cell's function. For example, every cell has to be nourished and one of the main nutrients is glucose to provide energy. But before the glucose can provide energy, it has to be broken down by a series of chemical reactions to carbon dioxide and water. In a fire, glucose would burn up in a moment and give off its energy in the form of heat. In the animal and plant this energy must be used in a controlled way, and this is done by break-

ing down the glucose in stages with a whole series of enzymes.

Every one of these enzymes has to be constructed on the basis of instructions received from the genes. How do these instructions get passed? The genetic material of the cell is deoxyribonucleic acid (DNA), and this DNA consists essentially of four different chemical structures, called bases, sticking out at regular intervals from a continuous backbone of a sugar (ribose)-phosphate combination. The bases are complementary to each other in that two of them, adenine and thymine, will attract each other and fit together, and the other two, guanine and cytosine, will also attract each other and fit together. Now, a single molecule, or chain as it is called, of DNA, which has a series of bases running down its length, has the particular property of being able to propagate itself (replicate) by attracting the complementary bases to it, whereupon these bases themselves get attached to a backbone of ribose sugar and phosphate. By this system of propagation parents pass on genetic material to their offspring, and each cell passes on exactly equivalent genetic material to its daughter cells at the time of division.

The messenger molecule

DNA can also propagate a closely related species of molecule – ribonucleic acid (RNA) – which only differs from DNA by having uracil as one of its bases instead of thymine. This RNA is the messenger molecule of the cell, and it carries the instructions from the genetic DNA, and ensures that they are transcribed in the manufacture of the enzymes. The major synthesis of the enzymes takes place outside the nucleus in special particles called ribosomes, which are also composed of RNA, combined with a protein. Thus, a small portion of DNA carries the code, or blueprint, for making a particular protein – an important enzyme for example. RNA is replicated on this portion of DNA and comes off carrying the code by virtue of having a precise set, in order and in the right sequence, of complementary bases to the DNA. In the cytoplasm of the cell, outside the nucleus, this messenger molecule of RNA encounters the ribosomes, as well as special RNA called transfer RNA. This latter RNA consists of small molecules carrying the building blocks of the proteins, the amino acids.

There are some 20 amino acids in all, and a combination of three of the bases of the messenger RNA in sequence will code for one particular amino acid by attracting a particular complementary trio of bases on the transfer RNA. Thus, in all there must be as many different transfer RNA molecules as there are amino acids. The ribosomes provide the structural machinery which allows this combination of molecules to occur – the meeting of messenger and transfer RNA and the joining together in sequence of the amino acids to form a complete molecule of protein. These proteins, as enzymes, can only carry out very particular functions, and therefore, for every new process a different enzyme is needed and has to be synthesized.

The fertilized egg of the sea-urchin provides a good example of the typical stages found in the development of almost all eggs. The fertilized single cell first divides into two (**1**), and after a short period the two cells again divide along a plane at right angles to the first plane of cleavage (**2**). The cells produced in this way continue to divide and form a compact aggre-

gation of cells. After about the sixth division, when the cluster of cells contains about 64 members (**3**), the cluster begins to form a *morula* (**4**) so-called because the structure resembles a mulberry. Soon after this stage in their development is reached, the different cells in the cluster, now properly termed an embryo, begin to carry out specialized functions.

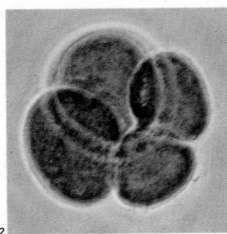

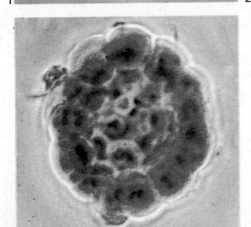

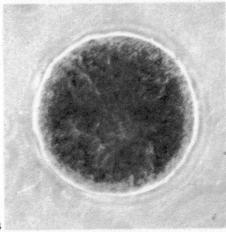

1

2

3

4

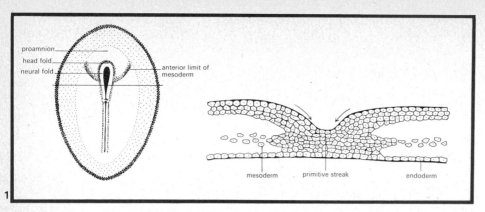

1

number of genes. These latter are the genes which carry the code of instructions for making all the many enzymes that are necessary for acting chemically on one food substance. When a particular sugar, say beta-galactoside, is not present, the genes for making enzymes to break it down are repressed and so inactivated. If now we put the bacterium in a solution containing this sugar, the sugar combines with the repressor substance and stops it from repressing the operator gene. The operator gene now activates the genes under its control, the *structural genes*, and the enzymes for breaking down the sugar can be produced. There is also a control system that works the other way round; in this the repressor substance only acts and is effective in repressing when the substrate substance (the sugar) is present.

We can imagine such systems getting very complicated if a regulator gene should control more than one operator gene, and if these in turn should regulate the activities of other operators. We therefore get a *cascade system* of gene control where by triggering off one gene we control the activities of many others. This is the kind of system we must look for in our developing animal.

Insect metamorphoses

The insect – which can develop from an egg to a caterpillar, then after several moultings to a chrysalis, and the chrysalis (pupa) to a beautiful moth or butterfly – is a superb example of development and gene control. Insects do not have a skeleton and their shape is maintained by a hard outer skin, the cuticle. This cuticle is produced by a layer of cells – the epidermal cells – and as the cuticle gives the insect its shape as we see it, the epidermal cells essentially govern the insect. But the same cells produce all these very different forms of development – the caterpillar, chrysalis and the mature winged butterfly or moth. Therefore these epidermal cells must have a method of switching on and off genes that control at the right time the different stages. The epidermal cells are very sensitive to two hormones that are produced during the development of the insect just before it moults into the next stage. One hormone is known as the *growth and moulting hormone,* and the other as the *juvenile hormone.* The first hormone stimulates the epidermal cells to divide and get ready to moult, and the second hormone governs what form the moulting should take – whether the insect should develop into another caterpillar, or into the adult.

Hormones in animals and plants do in fact change the whole course of development of a group of cells. We know for example that hormones control our sex and our growth, including the shape of our bodies. During embryonic growth and development substances like hormones may, in fact, govern what a cell is going to become. By acting with the regulator genes of the cell a simple substance may induce or repress the activity of a group of genes, and, as in the case of the insect, change the whole course of development into an entirely new form.

2

1 The later development of the embryo showing the differentiation of the various folds and the primitive streak, and (right) the formation of mesoderm and endoderm.

2 The long filament criss-crossing this electron microscope picture is a molecule of DNA obtained from a virus (*B. subtilis* bacteriophage). Magnification: 22,000 times.

As we have seen, only a portion of the DNA operates at any one time, and the remainder is somehow repressed. This repression of particular sequences of the DNA governs what a cell's activity is going to be and how it is going to differ from that of other cells. The DNA is not just on its own. In all many-celled organisms it is covered by a set of proteins called *histones,* and it now seems clear that when a portion of the DNA is uncovered from its coating of histones it is able to attract to it all the components for making a messenger molecule of RNA.

Bacteria are single cells, and therefore do not have to face the problems of development that confront animals and plants with many different types of cell. Nevertheless, by looking at how genes are controlled in bacteria we can get some inkling of gene control in multi-celled

animals and plants. A bacterium's life is always changing; it may suddenly find itself in a situation where the type of food it was living on has run out, and instead it has to make do with another type of food. Each type of food – which in a bacterium's life is often a type of sugar – needs special enzymes to bring it inside the cell, and then to digest it, so that the energy locked up in it can be used.

But it would be a waste of the bacterium's resources if it had made all the enzymes for every type of food when only one or two types of food were available. Thus, when a particular sugar is not available a gene on the DNA chromosome produces a special repressor substance. This gene is a *regulator gene* and the repressor it makes attaches itself to another gene, the *operator gene* and prevents it from functioning. The operator gene has under its control a

After the egg

All growth depends on simple cell division; but variations on this basic theme, from microscopic egg to mature adult, are almost endless. Some common animals never reach adulthood at all.

'MY, HOW he has grown!' This exclamation is probably heard a thousand times every day in a thousand languages all over the world, usually in response to the sight of an infant after a few days' absence. But one would hardly say the same thing about Aunt Agatha who has obviously 'put on a bit round the middle'. The reason for not saying it about Aunt Agatha is more than just good manners. To the biologist and non-biologist alike, the word 'growth' implies a *permanent* change in size and/or weight. If Aunt Agatha puts on a few pounds between visits, she 'grows' in size. But this is not true growth, because it is temporary. However, if the new baby puts on a few pounds in weight (or grows a few inches in height), this is true growth, because the change will last.

Growth results from the metabolic activities of the body. These are of two types: the building up (*anabolic*) processes, and the breaking down (*catabolic*) processes. Even when adult size has been reached, these reactions continue at a steady rate. The breakdown and renewal of tissues occurs all over the body. It affects the gut, the skin, the other organs, the blood cells and the skeletal material. In a growing young animal, the anabolic rate is greater than the catabolic rate, resulting in a general increase in size. Equilibrium is reached in an adult animal (anabolic equals catabolic), and the process is reversed during old age, resulting in very slight decrease in size.

The 'bricks' of life

The structural and functional materials of an animal's body – apart from water and bone – consists mainly of different kinds of *proteins*. So proteins are an essential requirement for growth. Large quantities of protein are taken into the animal's body when it eats, but the proteins in the food generally are not the same kinds needed by the growing cells. So the cells remedy this defect by building their own.

Proteins are very large molecules built out of simpler units called *amino acids*. To create the proteins needed by the cells, the animal's digestive system first breaks up the proteins taken in by eating into amino acids and then the cells put them back together again in the desired arrangement, rather like building a new house from the secondhand bricks of another one. For this reason, good food plays an important part in growth. If there is insufficient food, or the food eaten is not nutritious, the animal will not grow properly.

A generalized increase in an animal's size can be achieved by cell division. The processes in which the nucleus of a cell divides, separates, and the halves draw

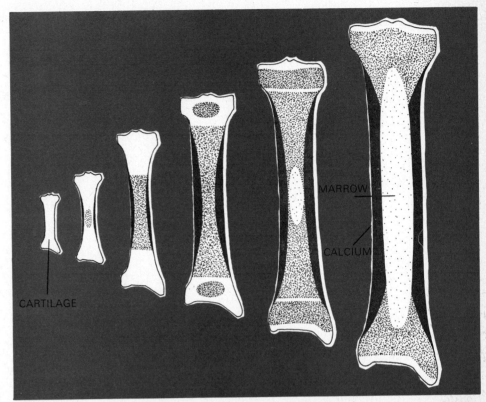

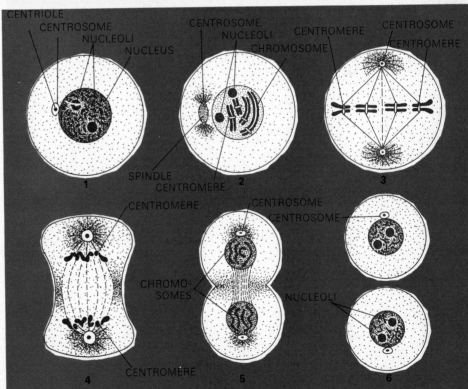

Bones develop from infancy to maturity just like any other organ of the body, starting from soft cartilage and ending with a hard calcium cover over a soft cavity of marrow, *top*. Muscles are fastened on to the lumps at the ends, allowing for movement in vertebrates. *Above*, the onset of mitosis, the splitting of one cell into two, is heralded by the centriole, **1**. Next spindles begin to grow and the chromosomes in the nucleus become visible, **2**. The chromosomes line up along the spindles and reproduce themselves in exact copies, **3**. **4** The chromosomes migrate to the ends of the cell, which then begins to divide, **5**. When the two parts have separated, **6**, the process is complete. Mitosis underlies all growth, in simple and complex animals alike.

1 The axolotl is something of a Peter Pan of the animal kingdom, because it refuses to become an adult. 2 The salamander, a newt-like amphibian, is the fully developed adult form of the axolotl. They were not known to be larva and adult until some biologists showed that stimulation of the thyroid gland of the axolotl can cause it to mature into a salamander. Despite its juvenile form, the axolotl is sexually mature and capable of reproduction. 3 The normal process of larval development is illustrated by the tadpole. Initially aquatic, the tadpole absorbs its tail, enlarges its mouth, grows legs and becomes a frog capable of life on land.

cytoplasm with them to form two new cells is called *mitosis*. Little is known about what prompts cells to divide, although the size of the nucleus (relative to the cytoplasm) may have an effect on initiating the process. The first sign of activity comes from a cylindrical structure in the nucleus known as the *centriole*. The area of protoplasm surrounding the centriole (called the *centrosome*) is relatively liquid. The whole is enclosed by a more solid body, the *aster*.

At the beginning of cell division, the centriole divides and each half migrates to opposite poles of the nucleus. Chromosomes (threads of DNA and protein) become visible and a *spindle* connects the poles of the nucleus. The nuclear membrane then breaks down, completing the first stage, which is called the *prophase*.

During the second stage (*metaphase*), the chromosomes collect on the spindle. The third stage (*anaphase*) is characterized by the reproduction of the chromosomes and the separation of the pair, each exactly like the other, along the spindle towards the two centrioles. The final phase (*telophase*) sees the re-formation of nuclear membranes to produce two separate nuclei. Division of the cytoplasm generally occurs soon after the chromosomes have reached the poles or during formation of the new nuclei. Biologists still do not understand how all these various stages take place.

We have considered growth of protein

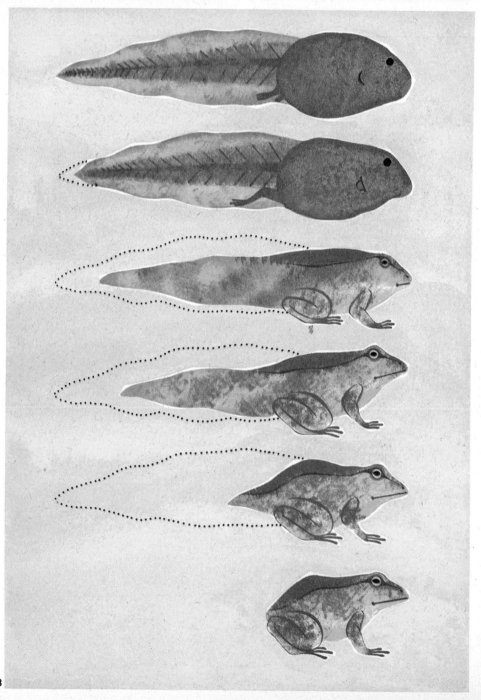

3

6

Some growth processes reveal themselves in seasonal changes. **4** Snakes and lizards periodically slough their skins and then grow new ones **5–6** Other animals, such as the 'snowshoe rabbit', alter their physical appearance in order to blend with the summer and winter environments as protection against hungry predators. **7** Male deer seasonally grow antlers used in fighting for mates. At the end of the mating season, the antlers are no longer of use and drop off.

These are caused by variations in climate, light intensity, and the abundance of food. We do not need to use a tape measure or a microscope to observe such changes. For example, seasonal spurts leave visible concentric 'growth rings' in the shells of molluscs and in fish scales (rather like the growth rings in the wood of a tree). These rings may be used to estimate the age of an animal, and the spacing between them may even show when the animal survived a hard winter or a winter in which food was particularly abundant.

Growth usually slows or stops during hibernation as an economy measure, to conserve the body's food reserves. The *diapause* period in insects is a time of arrested growth, geared to the season. Some reptiles, birds and mammals show seasonal cycles in their moulting and growth processes. Snakes and lizards slough their skins. Birds moult regularly or change from winter to summer plumage. Cattle thicken their coats in winter by growing special long hairs which fall out in the spring. In many arctic animals, there are two seasonal moults; the arctic hare and the ermine grow a white coat in autumn to provide camouflage among the winter snows, and replace it with a brown coat in early spring. These moults are stimulated by varying lengths of daylight, and hormones control the actual process.

Preparing for reproduction

In a similar way, antlers of stags are grown in the spring during the spring mating season when they are used in courtship and fighting. During growth, the antlers must be provided with blood vessels and nerves and may grow as much as two inches a day. At the end of the season, the nerves and blood supply are cut off by a constriction of bone; the antlers eventually die and drop off.

In most animals, growth and development of the reproductive system coincide with warm weather so that the young are born and reared in favourable conditions. This is shown most markedly in arctic regions when spring and summer are short and relatively warm and food is abundant. For example, the insect population leaps to an extremely high level during the days of the midnight sun, and declines during autumn ready to 'overwinter' during the months of total darkness and very low temperatures.

During the spring, the *gonads* (reproductive organs) of all the animals of a given species reach maturity simultaneously so that all the animals are sexually mature and aroused at the same time. This is particularly noticeable in birds, for which the amount of daylight has a marked effect on the nervous and the hormone

molecules and of cells; now let us consider how complete organs grow. If one of the two kidneys is removed from a rat, the cells of the remaining one begin to multiply rapidly, reaching a maximum rate in about 48 hours. If instead part of the liver is removed, the remainder begins to grow. These facts seem to suggest that an organ itself produces a substance that limits its further growth, otherwise it would keep on growing at maturity. If a part of the organ is removed, so are some of these inhibiting substances and it then tends to grow to make up for the part removed. For example, it is thought that some of the globulin proteins produced in the liver may also inhibit its growth.

Different organs do not necessarily grow at the same rate as each other or at the same rate as the whole body. When two parts of the body grow at different rates, growth is said to be *allometric*; when at the same rate, growth is *isometric*. For example, in the gut of most vertebrate animals growth is allometric. The walls of the gut grow faster than the whole and so they become wrinkled into folds called *caecae*. The human thymus gland shows such a marked decrease in growth rate at the end of childhood that the process can then be regarded as 'de-growth'.

Seasonal variations throughout the year markedly influence the growth of individual animals and populations of animals.

The change between the summer and the winter 'coats' of some animals is sometimes so complete that it is difficult to recognize them as being the same creature. *Left,* an Alaskan rock ptarmigan takes on winter white; *right,* another ptarmigan shows off its summer plumage.

systems – mating takes place, eggs are laid, and the young are hatched at almost exactly the same times among birds of a given species. In mammals, the womb of the female becomes much smaller after the birth of the young and the mammary glands become functional to supply milk.

Most of these growth processes are controlled by hormones, chemical 'messengers' which oversee the body's functions. These substances are carried in the blood-stream to all the body tissues. Almost all hormones in vertebrate animals affect growth in some way. The glands that secrete them form the *endocrine system.* The most important hormone for growth is the *anterior pituitary growth hormone* (APGH or *somatropin*). For example, in Man a deficiency of this hormone during childhood leads to dwarfs, and an excess produces giants. An excess of APGH in adults causes the condition called *acromegaly* in which growth of bone (particularly the lower jaw) continues after maturity. It is thought that dinosaurs probably had large pituitary glands, so accounting for their vast sizes.

Constructing the skeleton

APGH appears to promote either the growth of the cell nucleus or to increase cell division. It also appears to affect protein synthesis by increasing the uptake of amino acids by the digestive system. Its most important function is to stimulate the growth of bone.

Many people think of a mature animal's skeleton as an inert system. But it is extremely important functionally. It protects the softer organs, gives the body shape and support, and acts as a system of levers by which the contraction of muscles is transformed into body movements.

Bone formation is called *ossification.* Two types are found in young vertebrates: the formation of thin membrane or dermal bone and, more important, the formation of *endochondral* bone in which embryonic

cartilage is replaced by adult bone. In this second process, the cartilage begins to degenerate within its central region. The cells of cartilage swell and become arranged in columns. Blood vessels and osteoblasts break in from the surface and bone formation takes place from the middle outwards and towards the ends. At the same time, cartilage at the ends of the 'bone' continues to grow until it, too, is caught up by the ossification process. This is timed to take place at maturity and so bone growth virtually ceases.

In higher vertebrates, *accessory* ossifications take place at the ends of bones (the *epiphyses*). These produce 'lumps' of bone for the attachment of muscles and give long bones their characteristic hourglass shape. The central filament of bone is strengthened externally by the formation of surface (*periosteal*) bone.

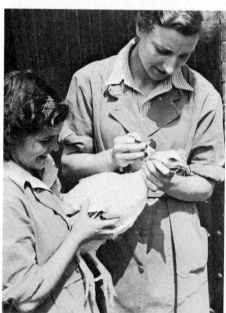

Knowledge of fundamental growth processes has important applications in the food industry. Here, a fowl is being caponized or 'de-sexed', which results in an increase of weight and size.

Another pituitary hormone, *thyrotropic hormone,* controls the growth and output of the thyroid gland. *Thyroxin,* a hormone from this gland, is important in the development of young animals. For example, many amphibians begin active life as small, aquatic larvae – such as the tadpoles of frogs. Tadpoles undergo various changes before young frogs finally leave the water for land. Over a period of about three months, these changes include the formation of external gills, their replacement by internal gills, and finally the formation of lungs. First the back and then the front legs grow, and the tail is ultimately absorbed.

The reluctant larva

A change in diet from plant-eating to meat-eating also occurs and must be accompanied by changes in the feeding mechanism: the fish-like mouth becomes wide and gaping and the long tongue develops. The gut becomes simpler and less spiralled, since meat is easier to digest than plants.

This complete change in form is called *metamorphosis.* In amphibians, it can be greatly accelerated by giving extra thyroid hormone or by stimulating the appropriate gland by adding iodine to the diet. In some amphibians, metamorphosis may never reach completion and the juvenile form persists throughout adult life. Such an animal is the *axolotl,* which is the larval form of a newt-like amphibian called a *salamander.* For many years, people thought that axolotls and salamanders were entirely different animals. But stimulation of the thyroid gland causes the larva (axolotl) to change into the adult (salamander). If this stimulation is not provided, axolotls reach sexual maturity and can reproduce without ever changing into the adult form.

This process, by which larval forms become sexually mature, is called *neoteny* and is thought to have been an important factor in the evolution of many groups of animals. The early chordates (animals with rod-like skeletons), ancestors of vertebrates, are thought to have arisen in this way from invertebrate stock. Insects may have evolved from a millipede-like ancestor. Millipedes develop through several larval stages and are unusual in that segments are added each time the larvae moult. The primitive insect had 21 segments, and it is possible that an ancient millipede larva 'stuck' at this stage, became sexually mature (rather like the axolotl now does), and produced the insect ancestor. This method of evolutionary development is called *paedomorphosis.*

Despite the Peter Pan-like refusal of the axolotl and other neotenic animals to become adults, adulthood is generally the end result of growth. Perhaps it is not really fair to accuse the axolotl of being forever a child, for the chief biological function of adulthood is procreation. And although it may not look like its 'adult' form, the axolotl is certainly capable of reproducing itself. Otherwise, there would never have been any axolotls around for people to argue about.

Life-histories

Growth from egg to adult in animals is not a simple process of getting bigger. The rate of growth of different parts of the body changes to maintain function, and other complex changes occur.

SOME YOUNG ANIMALS are more or less miniature versions of the adult. Crocodiles are a good example. The young crocodiles have a similar environment to the adults, they have a similar way of life, and the only thing that changes throughout their lives is that at some stage they become sexually mature, and that – given the right amount of food and warmth – they get bigger.

But in most animal species the young creature is a very different animal from the adult. It is not only smaller, it is different proportionally, different physiologically, different psychologically and sometimes different anatomically. Part of the difference between young and adult results because different tissues and organs develop at different rates – but at all stages of the animal's life it must, obviously, be capable of survival. Thus a mammal's brain grows more slowly than, say, the bones or muscles of its limbs. The adult mammal generally has a proportionally smaller head than does the young mammal. Again, in the vertebrate, the bones must increase in size while at all times forming a functional, articulate skeleton. Yet it is clear that as, say, the thigh bone and shin bone increase in length and bulk the stresses and strains on the knee joint change.

Joint development

In many vertebrates joint development tends to lag behind long-bone development, so that the young animal has weaker joints than the adult. In mammals, however, this problem is solved by the fact that joint development proceeds separately from the development of the rest of the long bone. Characteristically, in young mammals, each bone develops in three parts – the two ends, which form part of joints, are known as the *epiphyses*, and the central shaft of bone between the epiphyses is the *diaphysis*. In the young mammal the epiphyses are clearly demarcated from the diaphysis, though in the adult they are fused. The point is that the epiphyses in the young animal are proportionally larger than in the adult animal – which is why young puppies or foals appear to have such knobbly knees – and they grow, relatively, more slowly than do the diaphyses. Because the epiphyses grow more slowly the stresses and strains on the growing joint do not change so rapidly throughout life as they do, say, in the growing reptile. Hence the joints of the young mammal are always functionally very strong.

Such adaptations are imposed on the young animal because it must remain viable at all stages of its life-history, while at the same time increasing in size. The interesting point is that differences, other

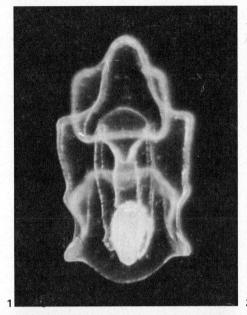

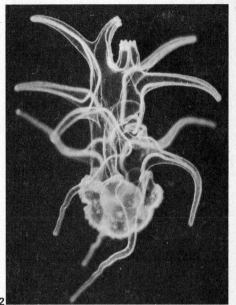

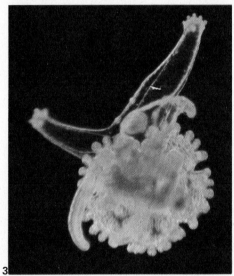

The common starfish (*Asterias rubens*) reproduces both sexually and by fission. Shown here are stages in the development of a starfish produced as a result of sexual reproduction. The egg develops into a tiny free-swimming larva or bipinnaria (1), which grows for about three weeks.

The final stage of the larva is shown in (2). After three weeks or so, the larva settles down on some solid object, such as a rock, and undergoes metamorphosis (3). It assumes the characteristic starfish shape, and finally grows until it reaches the size of the adult (4).

than differences in size, between a young and a mature animal are possible at all. Both the young animal and the adult into which it develops have derived from a single fertilized egg cell, and the genetic content of the egg cell must be exactly the same as that of the young animal, and of the adult. A single cell can give rise to many cells with an identical genetic complement to its own, though each daughter cell may be very different from the parent cell; the daughter cells might develop into liver cells, nerve cells or muscle cells, etc. This is the phenomenon of differentiation. The difference between the young and the

adult animal is the same kind of phenomenon: how can two animals – the baby and adult – be so different, when each has exactly the same genetic structure?

The answer is that at any one time, in fact, an enormous proportion of the animal's total gene complement is dormant. This dormancy has been explained in two ways, and which is the right one has not yet been determined. One school says that each individual gene is naturally dormant unless aroused into activity by some 'switching-on' substance; the other school, the 'depressor' theorists, hold that genes are naturally active, unless actively

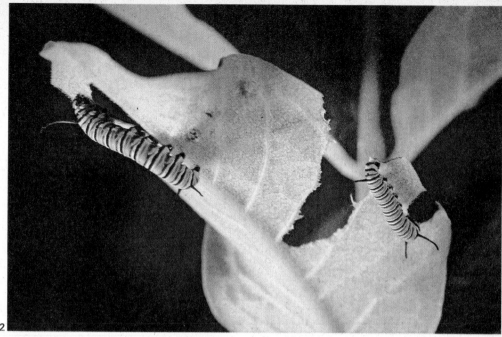

suppressed by some depressor substance. That many genes are dormant can be realized by considering the human embryo. At an early stage of its development it develops gill slits – a hangover from the days when all vertebrates lived in the sea. Later the gill slits are lost. Yet the older embryo, without gill slits, must still possess the genes necessary to produce gill slits, unless we suppose that these genes are physically lost from the baby (a very unlikely proposition). And indeed, not only the older embryo, but the baby that develops from it, and the adult that develops from the baby, must still harbour genes which, given the right conditions, could produce gill slits. In other words, every human being walking around contains within himself the potential to become something like the fish-like creature that was his ancestor.

Thus we see that the 'genetic complement' of an animal is not an economical, static quantity that can produce only one single manifestation of that animal. The development of the animal can, in fact, be thought of as a series of different genetic patterns following one after the other. Thus, in the embryo, one set of genes are operative. In the infant, some or all of these genes are suppressed, and another set takes their place. In the child, another set; in the adolescent, another set, and so on throughout life.

So far we have been talking about animals whose immature forms live much the same sort of life as the adults. But each animal could theoretically carry around with it a set of (suppressed) genes that could make up a very different sort of animal, given the right circumstances. In practice it is possible to have a young form that is *totally* different from the adult – not only physiologically and anatomically, but also in its way of life. And, in fact, more animals than not do have an 'immature' form that is very different from the adult, and the immature forms (that is, the sexually immature forms) make a very different contribution to the survival of the animal than do the adult forms.

The most familiar example of this extreme schism between immature and adult forms is seen in the insects. In the more primitive insects – cockroaches, for example – it is true that the young is more or less like the adult, the chief difference being that it cannot fly. But in more sophisticated insects – butterflies and moths, beetles, bees, wasps and ants – the young animal is totally different in form from the adult. In the bees, the totally different young form – or *larva* – contributes little to the survival of the species. The young larvae are, in fact, spivs, who are waited on hand and foot by the adult worker bees. But in the butterflies and moths, the larva – or caterpillar – is the most important feeding and growing phase. Though many adult butterflies and moths can feed through their long tubular probosci, the tissue that makes up their bodies has been accrued by the voracious caterpillars – well equipped with efficient

230

Growth and metamorphosis in the monarch butterfly. The egg (**1**), laid on a milkweed leaf, hatches out to give small, striped caterpillars (**2**). The caterpillars devour the milkweed leaves voraciously. When they have reached a certain size, and when other conditions are right, the caterpillars hang down from the underside of the leaf (**3**) and shed their skins (**4**). They then become chrysalises, apparently inert, immobile and completely different from the caterpillars (**5**). But inside the chrysalis a remarkable change is taking place. The caterpillar develops wings and becomes a butterfly. The butterfly develops inside the protective chrysalis until it is ready to emerge, a step that is largely determined by the temperature of the surrounding air. The butterfly has to fight its way out of the chrysalis head-down (**6**), and then hangs for some time from the underside of the leaf so that it can unfurl and dry its wings (**7**). Finally, the insect, its beautiful wings fully unfurled, is ready to fly away and find a mate (**8**). This type of life-cycle, characterized by sharp breaks and changes of form and function, is found in many insects. The monarch butterfly provides a beautiful example.

3

7

8

mandibles and an enormous gut – that they once were. The role of the adult is, in fact, only to reproduce. And many adult butterflies and moths – the clothes moth, for example – simply do not feed. They emerge from the pupa, they use their acute sense of smell to detect others of the opposite sex, they use their newly acquired wings to fly to the potential mate, then they reproduce and die. Thus in these animals, the various functions of living things that are essential to survival – feeding and reproducing – are designated to different phases of the life-cycle, and each phase is highly specialized for its particular role, and totally different from the other phases.

The totally different forms and functions that animals like insects adopt at different phases of their life-cycle is a special form of the phenomenon known as 'polymorphism'. The term 'polymorphism' – which means, literally, 'many forms' was originally used only to denote the fact that any one species of animal can appear in several different forms, each form having a different function. The most obvious example of this is the difference in form and function of male and female animals – known as 'sexual dimorphism'. A more sophisticated example is the many different forms of individual – some adapted for feeding, some for defence, some for reproduction – that go to make up the colonial jellyfish, such as *Physalia*, the Portuguese-man-o'-war. It took the genius of Cambridge entomologist V. B. Wigglesworth to see that the very different phases seen in the *single* life-cycle of an insect were, in fact, comparable with the different (though genetically similar) individuals seen in many animal populations, and to use the term 'polymorphism' to describe those different phases.

In fact, as we said, polymorphism exhibited throughout an animal's life is more common than the sort of straight-through development seen in mammals. Most animals, in fact, have a larval phase which makes a distinct and specialized contribution to the animal's life-history. This is particularly important in that enormous and highly heterogeneous mass of animals that live a sedentary life on the floor of the sea. The acorn barnacle, for example, is firmly attached by sticky glands on its head to a rock, or a shell, or a ship's bottom. It is surrounded by rigid calcareous plates that protect it from predators and from the pounding waves. It feeds by sweeping floating material out of the water by means of its brush-like legs, poking up between the plates. The distribution of acorn barnacles is world-wide, from the poles to the tropical seas. Yet the adult barnacles are quite unable to move. They can only become widely distributed because they have a larval form that floats in the plankton, where it can be carried for miles, before settling to change – *metamorphose* – into the sedentary adult form. Thus in this case the function of reproduction, which is the adult's prerogative, is separated from that of distribution – the domain of the larva.

Parasites and polymorphism

Another group of animals to whom polymorphic changes throughout the life-cycle are a vital part of existence are the parasites. Parasites, generally speaking, have an easy time. The point is that the extremely complex biochemical reactions that characterize living things can take place only under very rigidly controlled conditions. Thus, for example, nerve cells are very susceptible to lack of oxygen, and only animals which can keep their nerves well oxygenated – that is, only animals with a good blood supply – can develop a complex nervous system. And, in fact, all animal evolution can be thought of in terms of an 'endeavour' to create a stable 'internal environment' so that more and more complex biochemistry, leading to more and more subtle behaviour, can take place. Many parasitic animals have solved the problem of finding a stable environment not by developing complex mechanisms to distribute oxygen, as all vertebrates have, or mechanisms to maintain constant temperature, as mammals and birds have, but simply by living inside

animals that have already created such conditions. Thus, for example, the blood fluke, *Schistosoma*, gains all the benefits of man's marvellous blood and excretory systems and behaviour simply by living inside human veins.

But there are snags in this way of life. A horse that wants to get from one field to another can simply walk there – its feeding ground is, in fact, continuous. But an adult blood fluke cannot simply stroll from one man to another – it is not adapted to life in the outside world, through which it must pass in order to reach a new host. It solves the problem by polymorphism.

The adult worm lives generally in the veins of the bladder, and its eggs pass to the outside world in the host's urine. The eggs hatch into tiny mobile larvae clothed in cilia, which are known as *miracidia*. The miracidium does not feed, and its life is short; its sole function is to find and enter a *secondary host* – a

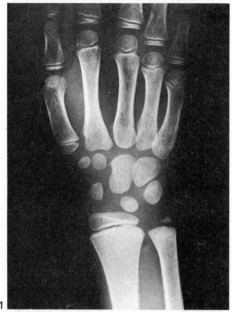

water snail – in which to develop further, and if it doesn't find a suitable snail within a few hours, it dies. Inside the snail the miracidia change into sporocyst larvae, a strange form that, by a sort of 'budding' can give rise to many more sporocysts. This is another reproductive phase, though, unlike the adult reproductive phase, reproduction is here asexual. Eventually the daughter sporocysts, instead of giving rise to more sporocysts, give rise to yet another larval form. This form, like the miracidium, is mobile, but, unlike the miracidium, it propels itself by means of a forked tail. It is known as a *cercarium*. The sole function of the cercarium is to leave the snail and attach itself to a human being and to penetrate the human's skin. Once inside the human it is carried by the blood-stream to the veins of the liver, where it develops into the adult worm, and from thence it is carried by the blood to the veins of the bladder. Then the cycle can begin again – the cycle which was only made possible through the several distinct polymorphic larval forms, each with its highly specialized structure, physiology and 'instinct'.

The different forms through which animals pass in their life-history have provided a tremendously important source of new animal forms. Though some larvae lack the ability to feed, and many are easy prey to predators, many are complete and highly viable animals. The only thing they lack is the ability to reproduce sexually, the prerogative of the adult. If the larva can acquire the ability to reproduce sexually – if, in fact, the genes that give rise to sex organs can be caused to operate during the larval phase instead of being repressed until the adult phase – then the so-called 'adult' phase can be lost altogether, and the young need not achieve metamorphosis.

Neoteny in Man

Perhaps the best example of this phenomenon, *neoteny*, is man himself. The young gorilla has a very man-like face – high forehead, flat face, small jaw. In adolescence it acquires the massive jutting jaw, and the skull crest that goes with it, which characterize the adult male gorilla. But what would happen if the development of the massive jaw were postponed beyond adolescence – were postponed, in fact, so long that the animal had become senile and died before it ever developed? Then the ape would stay looking man-like throughout its adult life.

We are not descended from gorillas, but we are descended from ape-like ancestors who, apparently, did have jutting ape-like jaws. It seems very likely that we have lost those jutting jaws just as our hypothetical gorilla might lose his – the genes that give rise to the big jaw have simply been postponed, that the juvenile stage of skull development lasts throughout life. We are descended not from apes, but from young apes.

Thus each animal's life-cycle, which makes it uniquely different from other animals, is the result of different permutations of its genes being switched on and switched off throughout its life.

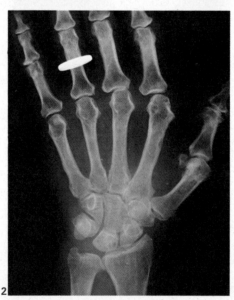

In an X-ray photograph, the fingers and hand of a child (**1**) appear different from those of an adult (**2**). The epiphyses at the ends of the long bones are not yet fused with the bone, thus allowing the bones to grow further without interfering with the efficiency of the joints.

Animals and sexual reproduction

Highly complex reproduction processes in animals involves sexual co-operation between mating partners. This is nature's way of ensuring variations necessary to evolutionary development.

1 Mating is a hazardous business for the male praying mantis, who is often devoured by the female as her bridal dinner.
2 Eggs are laid on twigs and enclosed in a protective egg-case.

FOR ANY SPECIES of animal to persist it obviously must reproduce. Indeed, reproduction may be considered to be the ultimate biological function of an animal and the natural culmination of development to maturity. In the simple animals, *asexual* reproduction is the rule. The cells of the adult animal merely split into two, each producing two identical 'daughter' cells, which then separate to live as two new individuals.

A second type of reproduction, which predominates in higher animals, is *sexual* reproduction. This involves the fusion of two special 'half-cells' called *gametes,* one from the male (the sperm) and one from the female (the ovum, or egg), to form a new cell called a *zygote.*

A study of sexual processes throughout the animal kingdom reveals a trend of increasing complexity and efficiency. For instance, most aquatic creatures shed their gametes into the water. The male and female have to be close together; the female drops thousands of eggs and the male millions of sperm.

Outside and inside

Fertilization is *external,* and a great number of gametes are needed to ensure that this inefficient and rather haphazard process results in a sufficient number of young – and that enough survive their early days, when they are very vulnerable to predators.

On land, however, things have to be very different. Eggs must be protected against drying up and injury, and are retained longer in the body of the female. *Internal* fertilization is necessary, after which several alternatives are possible. In birds and some reptiles, a hard protective shell develops round the egg and the female lays fertilized eggs which, if kept warm, continue to develop away from the mother. Such animals are called *oviparous.*

Another slightly more complex possibility is for the fertilized egg to be retained in the female's body, but for all development to proceed inside the egg before hatching. This is the case with many

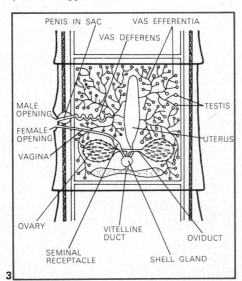

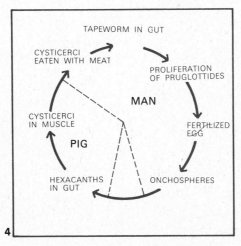

3 The cross-section of the reproductive system of the pork tapeworm reveals both female ovaries and male testis, indicating its bi-sexual nature.
4 The tapeworm is a parasite whose life cycle depends on two different hosts, one of which is Man, who carries the worm in his intestines.

insects, snails, fish, lizards and snakes, which are said to be *ovoviviparous.* The young embryo is surrounded for most of its development by shell-like membranes (there is no need for a hard protective shell) which separate the new animal from the tissues of the mother. It may derive some nutrient from the mother, and is hatched from the egg before it is laid.

The final and most complex case is when the developing embryo spends all its time embedded in maternal tissue and is known as the *viviparous* condition. (Meaning 'born alive', the term viviparous is somewhat confusing because all fertilized eggs are biologically 'alive' on leaving the mother.) The embryo develops in the mother's uterus (womb) and gains all nutriment from it, and may make close contact separated only by a thin *placenta* with no egg membranes. Viviparity is commonest among mammals, although it does occur in other groups of animals.

One group of animals, the coelenterates, makes use of both methods of reproduction, asexual and sexual. This group includes hydra and jellyfish, which take advantage of both methods by alternating between them. During the asexual phase, hydra reproduce by growing 'buds' which develop into young animals and eventually drop off.

Dual sexes

During the sexual phase, ripe ova are shed into the water by the splitting of the gonads (gamete-producing organs) in the body wall. Sperm are released from the same animal in a similar way and external fertilization takes place.

Animals that have both male and female gonads are called *hermaphrodite.* Although this condition presents an opportunity for self-fertilization, this is generally prevented by the gametes of one sex (the male) maturing before those of the other (the female); biologists call this difference in the time of maturity *protandry.* Several invertebrate animals are hermaphrodite, including flatworms and some molluscs. One type of flatworm, called *dendrocoelum,*

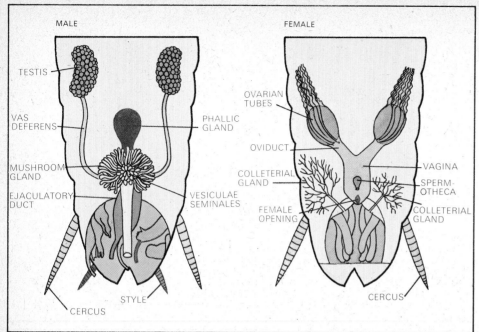

MALE

TESTIS

VAS DEFERENS

MUSHROOM GLAND

EJACULATORY DUCT

PHALLIC GLAND

VESICULAE SEMINALES

STYLE

CERCUS

FEMALE

OVARIAN TUBES

OVIDUCT

COLLETERIAL GLAND

FEMALE OPENING

VAGINA

SPERM-OTHECA

COLLETERIAL GLAND

CERCUS

The reproductive systems in the cockroach show a definite division between the sexes. The male system produces sperms, while the female system receives them and allows for fertilization.

has both male and female genital organs located in a single opening. During copulation, sperm is exchanged by both animals. The complicated shape of the genitalia prevents self-fertilization and ensures that only cross-fertilization takes place.

The tapeworm, a parasitic flatworm, attaches itself by its head to the wall of the stomach or intestines in Man and other mammals. It consists of a series of segments which grow from the head end of the worm. Each segment bears male and female sex organs and comprises a complete reproductive unit.

Hermaphrodites

After fertilization of the ova, the ovaries and testes disappear leaving only the uterus to house the numerous fertilized eggs. The eggs are passed out of the host animal in the faeces and remain dormant in a protective sheath. Eventually some of them are eaten by animals such as pigs and cattle. Digestive juices in the animal's stomach dissolve away the egg-cases and the young tapeworm emerges. It bores through the wall of the intestine into the blood vessels. It finally reaches the muscles where it forms a cyst. The cycle is completed when a man eats infected meat which is raw or under-cooked; the cyst breaks and an adult tapeworm emerges and attaches itself to the man's intestine wall.

The earthworm is also hermaphrodite. It has separate genital openings for its male and female reproductive systems and so self-fertilization is impossible. The sex organs are at the worm's head end. There are two pairs of testes, in segments 10 and 11. Maturing sperm pass out of the testes into a sperm sac, and when mature pass back again to the testes and along a duct to a pore on the lower surface of the fifteenth segment. There are also two sperm receptacles with openings on segments 9 and 10.

During copulation, the two earthworms lie nose to tail with their lower surfaces touching. A swollen ring called a *clittellum,* situated behind the front segments, lies opposite segments 9 and 10. Each worm sheds sperm from segment 15 which pass

back along a tube of mucus to segments 9 and 10 of the partner. There they enter the sperm receptacles.

After the worms have separated, the clittellum secretes mucus and passes forward along the body. As it passes segment 14, a few ripe eggs enter it from the oviducts. When it passes segments 9 and 10, the sperm received from the other worm enter the clittellum and fertilize the eggs. The clittellum is then shed completely and forms a bag to protect the *zygotes* – the fertilized eggs.

This highly specialized reproductive system is an adaptation to life on land which provides the eggs with a very good chance of fertilization and survival. It is instructive to compare it with that in a marine annelid worm called *nereis*. Here the sex cells bud off from the lining of the body cavity in most of the segments. During the reproductive season, the females attract the males and the gametes are discharged into the sea by rupture of the body wall. The adult worms die, and the externally fertilized eggs develop into larvae.

The garden snail, like the earthworm, has a complex hermaphrodite reproductive system and cross-fertilization is again the rule. To ensure that self-fertilization cannot take place, these animals have evolved a remarkable method of copulation. Two snails approach each other and expose the male and female apertures by 'turning inside out' the chamber containing them. Each snail then uses its muscles to fire a naturally formed chalky dart at the other. (The darts travel with such force that they penetrate the body wall and may even become embedded in the internal organs.) This drastic stimulation is followed by normal copulation with a mutual exchange of sperm.

To a zoologist, a snail is a gastropod (meaning 'stomach foot', because it 'walks' on its belly). Marine gastropods, the

snail's salt-water cousins, include the limpet, the periwinkle (sometimes called plain winkle) and the whelk. In these animals, the sexes are separate. The extraordinary gastropod called *crepidula* forms a colony of individual animals arranged in a column. The sexes alternate – stacked male, female, male, and so on – as each new animal is added to the column.

In nearly all insects the sexes are separate. They are primarily land animals and so fertilization is internal. A grasshopper is a typical example.

Courtship behaviour

The male's testes discharge into a sperm duct. Glandular secretions join the sperm before it reaches the genital aperture near the tip of the abdomen. The female grasshopper has a special sac or sperm receptacle into which the male introduces his sperm. The sperm is stored in the female until egg-laying time. Eggs from the ovaries pass down twin oviducts and converge into a vagina.

The egg shell is formed round the yolk before fertilization, contrary to normal procedure. A small hole is left in the shell to permit the entry of sperm which are ejected from the sperm receptacle of the female as the eggs are laid. Strong abdominal appendages dig a hole in the soil so that the eggs are laid and fertilized virtually underground.

Mating can be a hazardous business, particularly for some male spiders and praying mantis who may find themselves finishing up as the bridal supper. A male mantis is considerably smaller than the female and he must arouse her sexual behaviour or she will eat him. Should he

Mating in insects is often preceded by the female exuding a scent to attract the male for copulation. In the case of these moths, the scent is effective at ranges of over a mile.

lose his head over her, his decapitated body can still perform its duty.

As we might expect, courtship behaviour becomes even more involved with vertebrate animals. Among the fish, the stickleback is a good example. The male is attracted to the female by the sight of her swollen abdomen which is full of ripe eggs. He begins a zigzag dance designed to show off his red colouration. The female responds and they dance together for a while, the male eventually leading her to a nest he has built among some weeds. He points at the entrance, she enters and sheds her eggs, and the male then enters and fertilizes them in the water. The female is chased from the nest and from then on the eggs are cared for by the father.

In between an aquatic and a terrestrial animal, an amphibian such as the frog is still very much dependent on water, to which it must return to breed. The croaking of the males attracts the females. The male climbs on the female's back and sheds his sperm over the eggs as the female lays them in the water.

Perhaps the most colourful courtship displays of all are those of birds. Many males have beautiful plumage which, as in the peacock and birds of paradise, they may display to attract the females. The male Australian bower bird makes up for his rather nondescript plumage by building for the female a wonderful shelter from twigs, flowers and even the bright feathers of other birds.

1 Generally speaking, the larger and more advanced an animal, the smaller the number of young produced at a time. An elephant normally produces only one baby a season.
2 Rodents, such as the brown rat, produce large litters. The young rats here are two days old.
3 The blood lip snail, a native of St Vincent Island, violates the generality 'small animal, big litter' by laying only one egg at a time.

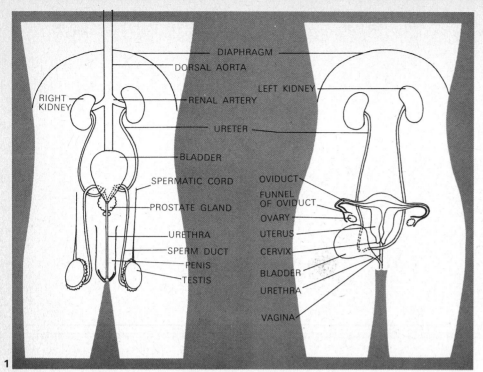

1 DIAPHRAGM
DORSAL AORTA
RIGHT KIDNEY
LEFT KIDNEY
RENAL ARTERY
URETER
BLADDER
SPERMATIC CORD
PROSTATE GLAND
URETHRA
SPERM DUCT
PENIS
TESTIS
OVIDUCT
FUNNEL OF OVIDUCT
OVARY
UTERUS
CERVIX
BLADDER
URETHRA
VAGINA

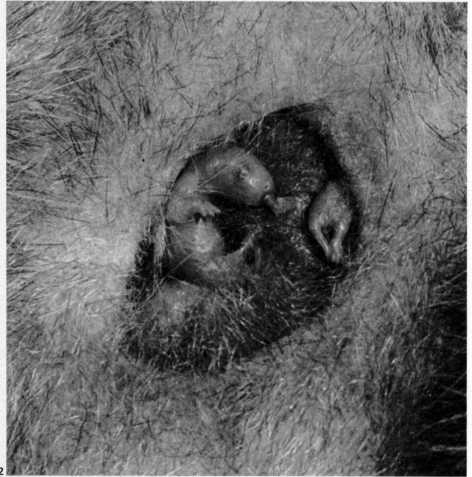

1 The reproductive systems in Man are typical of most mammals. The male injects sperm into the female system, where the egg is fertilized and develops until it is ready for birth.

2 After a gestation period of 12 to 17 days, the opossum gives birth to young only partially formed and about a half-inch long. They must then climb to the pouch to complete development.

The time that elapses between fertilization and birth is called the *gestation period*. In marsupials, this is relatively short, about 40 days in the case of the great grey kangaroo and as short as eight days in the marsupial cat. The pregnancy period in most other mammals is much longer – and of course the young are much more fully developed when they are born. In placental mammals, a long period of development within the womb becomes possible. The gestation period in placental mammals varies from a few weeks in small rodents to nine months in a woman and 20 months in the elephant.

The number of young born at one time also varies. In large mammals it rarely exceeds one, whereas in mice it may be more than a dozen. In general, smaller litters are associated with the more highly evolved animals – quality rather than quantity. The time it takes a young mammal to develop sufficiently to be able to fend for itself also tends to be longer in advanced forms, especially in the primates. However, many herbivores (plant-eaters), such as deer, antelope and cattle, contradict this rule and give birth to young which are able within minutes to join the herd and gain protection from predators.

In most mammals, the female is receptive only during a definite season when she is said to be 'on heat' or *oestrous*. This condition may be communicated to the male by scent, as in dogs, or by colouration, as in some monkeys in which the female's buttocks become red.

Why have sexes?

Sexual reproduction may appear to be unnecessarily complicated because it requires two separate individuals to produce a new individual. However, there are reasons for this. Since gametes contain only half the genetic material (chromosomes) found in ordinary cells in sexual reproduction, each parent contributes half the genetic material inherited by the offspring, so the offspring has characteristics of both. The recombination of genes from each parent during zygote formation leads to the possibility of variation and subtle changes in the individual. For this reason, over aeons of time, sexual reproduction allows evolution to operate through natural selection, so that only those creatures best adapted to their environment by genetic inheritance survive and perpetuate the species.

Evolution has progressed a long way from primitive almost random shedding of gametes into the sea to the long periods of gestation and post-natal parental care in higher mammals. But that is the price we must pay for our advanced development. A young stickleback, externally fertilized and deserted by its mother, can fend for itself almost the instant it is born. But a child, after nine months in his mother's womb, still has to grow for a further 12 to 15 years before he is able to survive completely on his own in his environment. But while lower animals have an initial advantage, the fact that mammals, and Man in particular, rule the land, shows that in the long run, the extra time needed for higher development pays off.

Still in Australia, we find marsupial mammals such as the kangaroo and koala bear, although there are about 300 different species altogether. On the other side of the world in North America lives the opossum, which is also a marsupial. The young of these animals are very immature at birth. For instance, a new-born kangaroo is only an inch long. It is blind and naked, with only its fore limbs slightly developed. It crawls from the mother's genital opening into the pouch, the mother smoothing the way by licking the fur in its path. The baby becomes attached to its mother's nipple and continues its development in the pouch.

Born alive

The most advanced animals, the mammals, and some other species, bear their young alive instead of as eggs. What are the biological advantages of this form of reproduction and how did it arise?

ANIMALS THAT PRODUCE 'live' young instead of eggs – that is animals that are viviparous – would seem to be at a great disadvantage. After all, many successful animals – like the cod, for example – are content merely to produce a whole mass of relatively tiny eggs and then 'forget' about them: reproduction seems to carry few fears or dangers for the parents. The female mammal, on the other hand, faces weeks – sometimes years – of pregnancy, and for at least part of this time is extremely vulnerable to predators or obstetric mishap. Then, during birth, the mother is a sitting target for opportunist predators (as witness the carnage among African antelope herds wrought by hyenas), while for the human female, childbirth is probably the most traumatic and dangerous event of her whole life. Yet viviparity is the hallmark of the mammals, the most influential animal group ever to walk the Earth. Why, despite the obvious drawbacks and dangers of viviparity, has evolution favoured this most complex and difficult form of reproduction?

The simplest animals – like the famous amoeba – can reproduce only by splitting in half. This is a fine method of reproducing under certain circumstances, and many animals much higher on the evolutionary scale than the one-celled protozoa may go through a frenetic phase of splitting or budding when a quick boost to the population is called for. Thus, for example, one of the larval stages of the human blood fluke *Schistosoma* lives inside water snails, and, when in the snail, it buds rapidly to produce many more larvae like itself. The point here is that after leaving the snail the larvae have only a few hours in which to find a new human host – otherwise they die. And a whole crowd of larvae has a much better chance of stumbling across a human being than a

1 The female water bug lays her eggs in a close-packed pattern on the male's back. She then goes on her way, leaving the male to carry and defend the eggs.
2 A male marine stickleback building a nest. He has torn some finely branched seaweed from a rock and is now about to place it into the partly completed nest.
3 Sea-horses produce live young. The female deposits her eggs in a pouch under the male's tail, where they are fertilized and fed from the father's blood supply.

single larva has.

But animals that rely solely on asexual reproduction are doomed to evolutionary failure. Evolution implies change – change of a kind which human beings can generally interpret as improvement. Thus modern horses run faster than prehistoric horses; modern monkeys climb better than their shrew-like ancestors; and modern men think faster than ape-men did. These improvements depend on changes – refinements – in the genetic make-up of the

animal. And fundamental genetic change can occur only if a gene changes its character – that is, if it mutates. So evolution depends on mutation. The trouble is that most mutations are harmful – they are, after all, random changes in a very subtle and complex coding system.

This is the paradox of evolution: an animal stock can improve only by accumulating random mutations–mutations which, *taken in isolation*, are generally harmful.

Sexual reproduction

The answer to this paradox is sexual reproduction. For sexual reproduction means that a selection of genes form one individual. The point is that the 'classical' concept of genetics – that one gene is responsible for one characteristic – is only partly true. Genes operate in combinations – their effect can be radically modified not simply by changing individual genes, but also by re-arranging gene combinations. A mutation that is harmful in one gene combination may not be harmful – or even functional – in another combination. A mutation that is harmful – though not lethal – to a parent animal may be passed on to the offspring. But if in the offspring the mutant gene is combined in a gene combination that is different from that of the parent, the mutant gene may have no effect on the offspring. Thus animals produced by sexual reproduction can 'store' apparently harmful mutant genes that have arisen in their ancestors.

This type of reproduction means that the genetic information in all the individuals of a population can be shared. A beneficial mutation in any individual can be passed on to others, and harmful mutations can be re-arranged in different combinations in daughter animals and 'stored' without detriment to the animal. Later, these apparently harmful mutations might come in useful. (Hence the mutant black form of the pepper moth came into its own after the Industrial Revolution, when the previously lichen-covered trees of the industrial north became blackened with soot. The aberrant black moths, that had been such easy prey when resting on the greyish-white lichen-covered trees, suddenly found themselves very well camouflaged.) In fact, apparently harmful mutant genes are stored to such an extent in present-day animal populations that these populations could probably undergo enormous evolutionary change even if no more mutations occurred – simply by re-arranging and bringing to the fore latent genes that have mutated in the past. But only if all the genes in a population are 'pooled' and constantly re-arranged through the device of sexual reproduction can an animal population come to terms with the essential mutations which would otherwise destroy it. So only animals that reproduce sexually can evolve to a significant degree.

Dramatic events

But sexual reproduction raises enormous problems. When an amoeba splits into two, each of the daughter amoebae is a perfectly good animal – capable of feeding, reproducing and responding to its environment just as did the parent organism. But in sexual reproduction the gene complement of an animal must be split in two and then recombined with half the gene complement of another individual. Such dramatic events cannot happen on the grand scale. Special cells – the gametes – must be developed in which the parent's gene complement is split (by the process known as meiosis). The gametes from two individuals then combine to form a single cell – the fertilized egg – from which the offspring develops. But the egg, unlike the daughter amoeba, is a feeble organism. It has none of the attributes of the adult animal into which it will develop. As a single, motionless cell it is completely vulnerable to temperature and chemical

The young of the green aphis, a common insect pest, are produced alive after gestation inside the mother's body. Here the female aphis is giving birth to a tiny young aphid.

The leathery turtle, a sea reptile, comes ashore to deposit her eggs on the beach. She digs a hole laboriously with her flippers and buries the eggs under the sand.

changes which it can do nothing to avoid, and is a sitting target for predators. Yet, if the species is to continue, the egg must survive and develop into an organism that can forage and fend for itself.

Like most other basic animal functions, sexual reproduction evolved in the sea. There, the problems are comparatively easy. The first problem – causing gametes from two different individuals to come into contact – is solved very simply by animals as distantly related as sea-anemones, starfish, polychaete worms and barnacles by the simplest conceivable method: the animal simply releases gametes into the sea. The sea has a constant temperature, is wet, has a convivial chemical composition, and obligingly carries the gametes around until they come into contact with gametes from individuals of opposite sex. Then fusion can take place. The only

difficulty is that different individuals of the same species must release their gametes at the same time. In general, each species reacts to some change in the environment that affects all members of the population simultaneously. The palolo worm, *Leodice,* for example, sheds its eggs or sperms as the day of the last quarter of the October–November moon dawns over the reefs of the Pacific.

Then, when gamete has met gamete to produce a fertilized egg, the egg may float to the surface to form part of the plankton or sink to the sea bottom. These eggs are defenceless, but because the sea provides a constant environment the eggs have only to consume the food reserves – yolk – with which they have been supplied, until they are sufficiently developed to feed. The outstanding difficulty is predators, and most eggs casually tossed into

A pipestrelle bat cleaning its young. The young bats are born alive like the young of other mammals, and are fed through the placenta while they are in the womb.

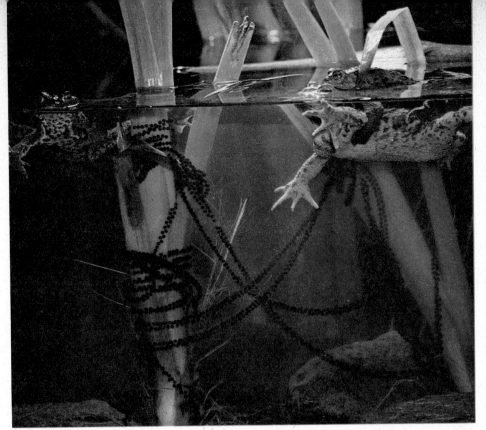

the plankton are destroyed – the only limitation on destruction being that if all the eggs were eaten there would be nothing for the predators to feed on the following year. But the simple device of abandoning gametes and eggs to the tide and to chance is obviously very wasteful and it could only operate in the sea which supplies an easy environment for defence-less creatures.

Thus, though there have been a great many recidivists who have retained the profligate spawning habits of more primitive animals – cod produce 7 million eggs, turbot 10 million – the evolutionary tendency in almost all animal groups has been to make sexual reproduction less wasteful, more sure-fire. In practice, this has meant that animals have developed means firstly of protecting the gametes, and of making sure that each egg produced is

The female woodmouse builds a nest for the young and suckles the tiny mice during the first weeks of their life. Protection of the young is common among mammals.

The eggs of the common toad *(Bufo bufo)* are fertilized by the male during copulation (amplexus) as they emerge in long 'ropes' from the body of the female: upper right.

fertilized; secondly of protecting the eggs, so that they stand a reasonable chance of developing into more-or-less viable organisms; and finally of protecting the young animals until they are mature enough to look after themselves.

To a very large extent the evolution of vertebrates has been a matter of developing these three stages of protection – and they have been acquired in the order outlined above. Thus, though the eggs of bony fish are generally fertilized outside the body, mechanisms have evolved to ensure that few gametes are wasted. Thus the male stickleback is attracted to the female by her swollen pregnant belly, and the female is attracted to the male by the red skin he develops in the breeding season. The female is excited by the male's movements to lay her eggs on the bottom of the pond, and the male is excited by the

female's egg-laying activity into depositing his sperms on top of the eggs. This is a major advance over the method of fertilization practised by the palolo worm – female and male stickleback must respond to specific characteristics in each other, and they must co-operate. This co-operation produces much more sure-fire fertilization than would be achieved if the gametes were simply ejected when the moon was in a particular quarter.

As vertebrates left the water for the land the need to protect the gametes became not a refinement but a necessity; gametes shed into the open air would simply dry up and die. Several marine animals have independently developed means of conserving gametes by evolving means of copulation – the sperms are not shed over the already laid eggs, but are deposited inside the female's reproductive tract so that neither unfertilized egg nor sperm need ever sally into the outside world. But marine animals that copulate – notably the sharks and rays, and the squids, octopi and nautiloids – are rare. On land, copulation leading to internal fertilization is the rule.

Internal fertilization

The beginnings of internal fertilization are seen in the vertebrates that have made the first tentative steps towards the land – the amphibia. For example, during the breeding season the male frog grasps the female around the neck – the position known as plexus – and is carried round piggy-back style for some days. In fact, in frogs, fertilization is external – the female lays her eggs in the water and the male covers them with sperm as they are released. But the action of the frogs is very nearly copulation – with very little modification the male frog could deposit his sperms inside the female reproductive tract. The most essential requirements of copulation – the extreme degree of co-operation and physical contact between animals that are not at other times sociable – are already present.

Reptiles are land breeders and fertilization is always internal. Though most

The Mozambique mouthbrooder male protects the tiny young fish hatched from the eggs by keeping them in its mouth whenever danger threatens the brood.

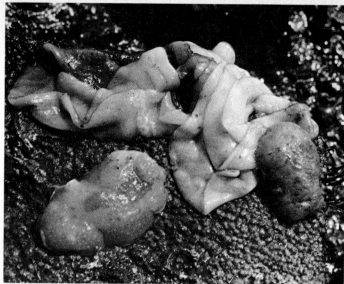

The offspring of many herbivores, like this young zebra, are born with the ability to run. This calf has just been born, but it is ready to take flight if threatened.

The two round jelly-like 'blobs' in the foreground of this photograph are sea slugs. Behind them is a long ribbon of spawn containing thousands of eggs.

reptiles copulate simply by placing their reproductive openings in contact (as most birds do), some – like the snakes – have developed a penis so that the sperms can be deposited deep in the female reproductive tract. Internal fertilization has one outstanding advantage over even the efficient external fertilization practised by amphibia and some fish. After the female gamete is fertilized in the reptilian reproductive tract, protective membranes and even a shell can be added to the fertile egg cell. Thus, because of internal fertilization the reptile (or bird – the same argument applies) can produce *protected* eggs that can withstand drought and can therefore be laid on land.

With most fish, amphibia and reptiles care of the young stops at the egg stage. Once the egg is laid – whether it be the protected egg of the reptile or the naked egg of the frog – it is abandoned. But a few fish, amphibia and reptiles take protection one step further. This they do in one or both of two ways – one way behavioural, the other structural 'physiological'. Thus we saw how in order to make fertilization efficient male and female animals had to evolve behaviour that made them respond to each other. Similarly in some instances one or both parents have 'learned' to respond to the eggs. While the male cod simply eats any cod eggs it finds floating in the plankton (cod are their own worst enemies), the male stickleback is so moved by the sight of its eggs that it stays near them fending off attackers, and actually fans the eggs with its tail – thus increasing their oxygen supply.

The next logical step in egg protection is not to stand guard over the eggs but to carry them around until they are developed into infants that can fend for themselves. For this, structural and physiological adaptations are needed.

The most usual place to carry around fertile eggs is in the female reproductive tract. Thus female guppies carry around the eggs until they hatch and then give birth to 'live' young. This is known as

Grass snakes copulating. The eggs are fertilized inside the female body during the spring, and laid in August, when they immediately hatch to give tiny young.

viviparity. But several amphibia and fish have developed other means of carrying around the eggs. In some catfishes the young develop within the mouths of one or other of the parents. In the seahorse and the related pipefish the male (not the female) is equipped with a kangaroo-like pouch in which he carries round the developing young. Similarly, in the so-called marsupial frog, *Gastrotheca,* the female has a large pouch on her back which opens just above the reproductive opening.

Protection of the young

As the eggs are laid, the male – which, in true frog fashion is carried piggy-back style during mating – holds open this pouch with his hind legs, at the same time covering the eggs with sperm. The fertilized eggs pass into the pouch and are kept there until they develop into tadpoles. In such instances the structural and physiological adaptations evolved to protect eggs and very young animals are combined with behavioural adaptations.

The birds and mammals are by far the most successful land vertebrates – and

indeed, the mammalian seals, sea-lions and whales dominate many marine environments. The success of birds and mammals depends very largely on protection of the young – yet this protection is produced in very different ways in the two groups. Both groups have means of protecting the gametes – fertilization is invariably internal. But whereas the bird, after supplying the fertilized egg with enormous quantities of yolk, and covering it with protective membranes, lays the egg in a nest, the mammal keeps the egg within its uterus (womb) often until it is quite well developed, and so breeds viviparously.

But viviparity in mammals is a much more refined adaptation than in lower animals. In the guppy, for example, the egg is supplied with large quantities of yolk. The egg develops in the mother more or less as it would if it were laid in the water. It gains the benefit of the very stable environment inside the mother, and it is protected from predators, but it is more or less a self-sufficient lodger.

The degree of dependence in mammals has profound implications. Firstly, the mother must develop means of retaining the young egg – after all, there is no theoretical reason why the egg, which is being propelled down the genital tract from the ovary, should not continue on its way after fertilization and be removed from the body. This is prevented through a hormone, progesterone, which acts upon the surface layers of the womb – the endometrium – and makes it capable of ensnaring the fertilized egg so that it can develop in the womb.

Thus, though some fish and reptiles are viviparous, and a few amphibia make a pass at viviparity, only the mammals have developed viviparity into a fine art. Mammalian viviparity has required enormous structural, physiological and behavioural advances – but it is largely because mammals have made those advances that they are now the most influential animal group.

Index

Figures in *italics* indicate an illustration of that subject. The letters a, b and c indicate the first, second and third columns of the page respectively.

Acorn barnacles, living conditions of 232a
Actinophrys sol (common Heliozoan) *9*
Adaptation
  in animals and man 209a–212a
  protective 212c
  to environmental conditions 209c–210a
ADP (adenosine diphosphate) in respiration 72a–72c
Agama (lizard) *47*
Age of Reptiles *see* Mesozoic era
Agnaths (ancient class of true fish) 29c
Albatross *56c*
Alcyonaria (Dead Men's fingers) 12c
Algae 54
Amoeba, (protozoan animal) 110b
  defined 9b–10a
  feeding habits of 10a, 124a
  growth of 204a
  hearing of 85a
  movement of 9b–c
  response to light stimuli 72a
Amino acids 223c
Ammonites 175b, 176a
Amphibians 176c
  aquatic forbears of 32a–c
  as first animals to leave the aquatic environment 37a–40c
  breathing mechanism of 41a–b
    development of 37a–38a, *38*
  circulation of 76a
  conserving water on dry land 38a
  Eryops permian, reconstruction from fossils *38*
  evolutionary changes in 181a
  fertilization of eggs of 218c
  fossilized evidence of 38a–39c
  labyrinthoderths 174c
  lungs of 41a
  of early Carboniferous period 174c, 175b
  respiration of *37*
Anabolism (building up of body tissues from food) 204c
Anaemia
  sickle-cell 192a–b, 212a
Ant-eater 106a, *105*
  spiny (echnida) 220 b–c, *59*
Ants *200, 168*
  behaviour of *197*
  building colonies *149*
  carpenter *217*
  communication between by scent 160a–c
  migration of American army food during 138a
    navigation of 137a–138a
    trails left by 138a
  orientating responses of *122*
  queen *150*
  secretion of pheromone 152c
Anurans (frogs and toads) 38a
APGH or somatopin (anterior pituitary growth hormone) 228
Aphids 142b, *127, 134*
  young of the green *238*
Archaeopteryx (first known bird) 176a

Armadillo 136c, *135*
Arthropod 22a–24c
  chitin of 21b
  defined 21a–c
  importance of 23a
  instinctual organisation of 24c
  reproductive system of 22b
  segments of 22a
  shell of 21b
  thorax of 22a
Asexual reproduction 233, a,c, 237b, 213b
  see also Reproduction
Atmosphere 173a,b
ATP (adenosine triphosphate) 72a–c
Autotrophs 114a
Autonomic nervous system 79c
Axolotl *226*
  metamorphosis of 228c
  Mexican *37*

Baboon, social lives of *153*
Bar (gene) 198a
Bark-beetle 142b
Barnacle *21, 102, 109*
  acorn 232a
  clusters of *23*
  colonies of 141c
  chemical communication of *158*
Barracuda 32a
Bat 106c ; *88*
  blood-sucking 106b–c
  cleaning young *238*
  hibernation of *82*
  migration of *140*c
Bates, H.W. 195b
Batesian mimicry 195b–196a
Bear
  American black *62*
  Arctic 209a
Beaver *64*
  behaviour of *119*
Bed-bug 128a–c
Bee 199a–c
  communication between 159c
  detection of polarized light 139b–c
  development of fertilized and unfertilized eggs 216a
  drinking *125*
  foraging behaviour of 151a–c
  guard *157*
  honey 171c
    aggression of 154b
    removal of dead amongst *149*
    task of in hive 150–*151*b
  queen *90*
    secreting pheromone 152a
  round dance of *152*a
  society of halictine *150*a
  swarming of *144*c
  tongue of 126a–8b
  waggle dance of 120c, 152a, 159c ; *138*
  worker *150*
    on brood comb *217*
Beetle
  Colorado *23*a
  Rhinoceros *24*
Bergmann, Karl 203a
Bergmann's Rule 203a–b, *203*
Bilharzia (disease) 16a
Biological Time Scale 175
Biochemistry, of mammals 57a–b
Birds
  adaption for flight 53a–54a
  adaption for life on or in water 56a
  archaeopteryx 176a

as game 56c
beak of 100a ; *99*
behavioural adaptation of insect eating 56c
behaviour patterns of 148c
  aggressive 153a–c
  change in 153a–154b
  in flocks 154 a–b
  innate 117c
  territorial 117c–118a
bone and muscular structure of 51b–c
brain of 51c
breeding areas 148b
breeding-time 147b–c
circulation of 51c, 76a
control of body heat of 50a
courtship of 153a–c, 200c, 235c ; *199*
diagram of the internal structure of *53*
egg of 51c
  hatching of 52a–b, 153c, 220a–b
flightless 52b–c
  evolution of 183a
flight of 109a–10b, 132b–c, 147c–8a
  technique of 53b–4a
function of hormones in 147c–148a
geographical distribution of species of 54b–55c
honey-eating 56b
migrations of 54a–b, 133a–134a 148a ; *133, 139*
mimicry by 195c
  in eggs 196b
moulting of 49c–50a
navigation by 54b, 137b–c
number of species of 54b
of prey
  beak of *99*
  day-hunting 56b ; *107*
  night-hunting 56b
omnivorous 56b–c
origins of 49a–b
respiration of 51c, 70c ; *70*
skeleton of *49*
societies of 155c–156c
song and voice box of 51c, 117c, 147
speeds reached by 54a
stereotyped songs of *197*
wing-structure of 50, 53b–4a
Birds of Asia (Gould) *55*
Birds of Paradise 158 ; *158*
Bison *65*
Bivalves 176c, *18*
  development of shell of 18b–19a
  foot of 19a
Black widow spider, eggs of *188*
Blood
  as transporter of oxygen 70a–b 71a–b
  fluids carried by 73a–74a
  in respiration 70a–2c
  pigments of 71a–c, 74c–75a
Blood fluke (schistosoma) 110c–111a
  asexual reproduction of 232c, 237a
  human *16*
  life cycle of 16a
  polymorphism of 232b–c
Blood system
  animal 71a–c, 73a
  closed 74a
  of worm 73a–74a
  open 74a–c
  protozoan 73a
  see also Circulation
Blue-bottle *128*
Blue-tit, stealing milk *119*
Boa (snake) *48*
  manner of killing prey 48a
Boll weevil 23a
Bone

development of *225*
  in vertebrates 229a–232a
  endochondral 225a–b
  formation of 225a–b
  pelvic girdle
    evolution of 181c–182c
    in reptiles 43a–b
  structure in reptiles 43a–b
Bony fish *see* Fish
Book-lung 71a
Boot-lace worm (Lineus longissimus) *13*
  Nemerline 16
Braille (language of the blind) 92c
Brain
  bypassing the 77a–79c
  compatability with eye 82a
  evolution of 188c
  of bird 51c
  of reptiles 44
Brill, colour-change of *196*
Brittle star (Ophiuroidea) 27a–b ; *27*
Brontosaurus 45a–b, 65c
Buffalo *65, 137*
Bull, Malayan five-legged *206*
Bumble-bee 150b–152a ; *191*
  establishment of hive of 150a–c
  see also Bee
Butterfly 22
  camouflage of *194*
  collecting nectar *127*
  courtship of 166a
  eyespot of *194*a
  growth and metamorphosis of *231*
  mimicry of 195c–196a
  survival and selection theories on 191c–192c

Caecilian (worm-like burrowing animal) 38a, 40a-b
Calcium Carbonate, in stromatolites 173b-c
Cambrian period, animal fossils of 173c–174b
Camel, adaptation for desert life 210a
Campbell, Bernard 117a
Carbohydrates, as energy sources 113b
  in respiration 72a
Carboniferous period 174c, *174*
  earth movements 175a
Caribou *209*
  two-way migration of 134b
Carp *32*
Carnivores 61b–64c, 105a–108c
  deep-sea *99*
  teeth and jaws of 106a–108c
Cartilage 228a-b
Cat
  canines of *100*
  with litter *57*
Catabolism (breakdown of food for energy) 204c
Caterpillars *118, 192*
  camouflage of *194*
  unpleasant-tasting *195*
Cenozoic era, (the time of recent life) 176b-c
Centipede
  lithobius forticus *24*
Central nervous system 77a–79c
  diagram of *79*
  electric pulses in 77a–79c
  transmission of impulses 78a-79c
Cell
  animal *221*
  blood

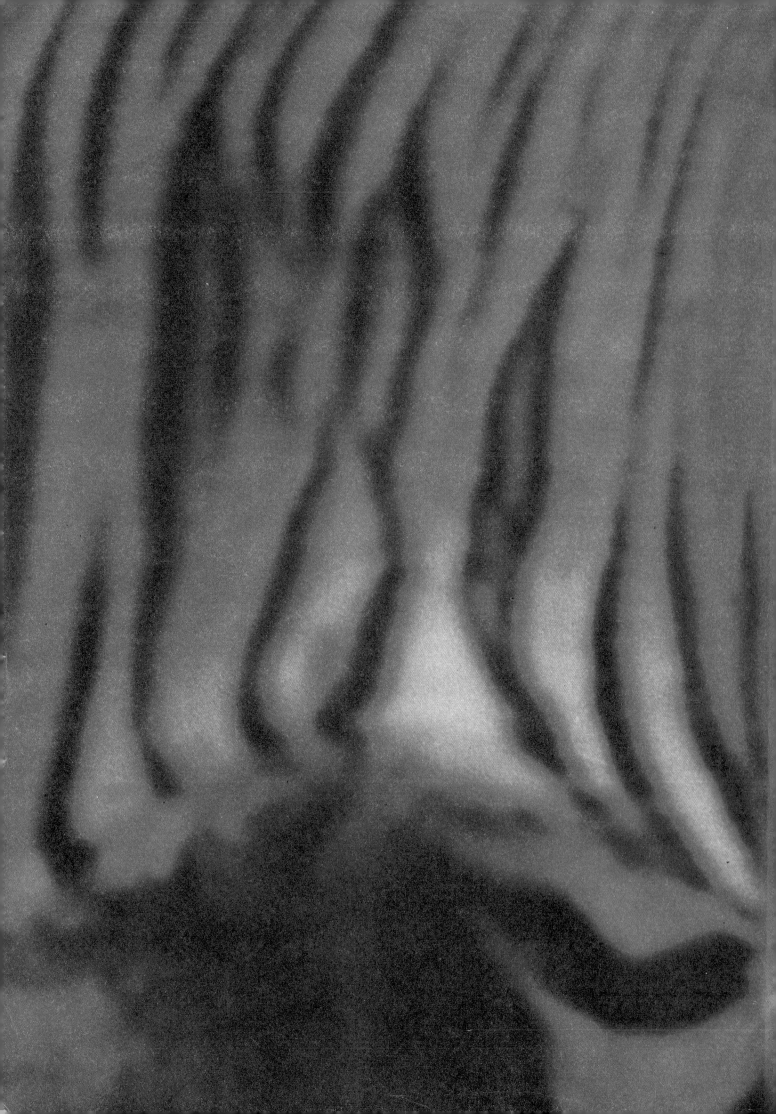